Nicolette Jones is a journalist and broadcaster, and was the author, with Raymond Briggs, of *Blooming Books*. She was educated at Oxford and Yale, and lives with her family in Plimsoll Road. Like Samuel Plimsoll, she has never crewed a merchant ship. *The Plimsoll Sensation* was a Radio 4 Book of the Week. It was also awarded the 2006 Mountbatten Maritime Prize for the literary work that has made the most significant contribution to the UK's maritime heritage during the year, and was praised by the judges as 'superbly researched and written'.

'A story of ambition, treachery, libel, political intrigue and cold-blooded murder on a mass scale. . . told in engaging, witty and racy style'
Hugh MacDonald, *Herald*

'Excellent . . . Jones charts [Plimsoll's] course with skill, insight and elegance'
Piers Brendon, *Sunday Telegraph*

'Nicolette Jones clearly loves her subject . . . Her set-pieces mix sensitivity and narrative gusto. Dickens . . . would have delighted in this story's cocktail of cut-throat capitalism, bleeding-heart politics, evangelical piety and simple common sense'
Jonathan Keates, Critic's Choice, *The First Post* online magazine

'Jones's account is entirely worthy of its deserving subject . . . Plimsoll emerges as a great reformer'
Sarah Burton, *Independent*

'Plimsoll's own level of near-fatal submergence is expertly tracked by Jones'
Simon Garfield, *Observer*

'Plimsoll's campaign as an MP still is a shining glory in the history of a tarnished political establishment. He deserves this excellent, circumstantial biography that alerts us to how much still remains to be done in the cause of safety at sea'
Iain Finlayson, *The Times*

THE
PLIMSOLL SENSATION

The Great Campaign to
Save Lives at Sea

NICOLETTE JONES

ABACUS

First published in Great Britain in 2006 by Little, Brown
This paperback edition published in 2007 by Abacus

A CIP catalogue record for this book
is available from the British Library.

ISBN 978-0-349-11720-1

Papers used by Abacus are natural, recyclable products made
from wood grown in sustainable forests and certified in accordance
with the rules of the Forest Stewardship Council

Typeset in Bembo by M Rules
Printed and bound in Great Britain by
Clays Ltd, St Ives plc
Paper supplied by Hellefoss AS, Norway

Abacus
An imprint of
Little, Brown Book Group
Brettenham House
Lancaster Place
London WC2E 7EN

A Member of the Hachette Livre Group of Companies

www.littlebrown.co.uk

For my father
John Jones

CONTENTS

'In well-known lays we sing the praise of men renowned in war
How heroes brave on land and wave have fought for us of yore;
But I will sing of one who fought, though not in deadly strife,
The noble object that he sought was saving human life.'

First verse of 'A Cheer for Plimsoll', music-hall song
written, composed and sung by Fred Albert, 1876

PREFACE

Once there was a cause that stirred a nation, nearly dislodged a prime minister and has since saved hundreds of thousands of lives. It was taken up by parliamentarians, journalists, businessmen, trade unionists, novelists, playwrights, clergymen, caricaturists and music-hall performers. Its supporters flocked to meetings, where they cheered its advocates, and demonstrated in the streets, condemning its opponents as friends of villainy. It involved all classes, and men and women alike. Florence Nightingale contributed money, Queen Victoria expressed sympathy and the mother-in-law of one of the monarch's daughters lent her time and the cachet of her title. It gave the poor a platform to speak out in their own defence. It is still commemorated in English idiom, in names of streets and ships, in statues and plaques, in the logo of London Transport and in the gym shoes of British schoolchildren. And yet we hardly remember what it was all about.

This is how I came to find out.

In 1995 I moved to a street of Victorian terraced houses, Plimsoll Road, in Finsbury Park, north London, a few doors down from a pub called The Plimsoll. Pasted over the middle of the pub sign was a large picture of what looked like a red baseball boot. Around the edges of the sticker it was possible to make out a patch of grey sea, and its horizon. It made you want to see what lay underneath.

I was interested in how the sign demonstrated the way language changes, with the new meaning pasted over the old. I knew that the street and consequently the pub were so named because of the Plimsoll line, which dictated the limit to which merchant ships could be loaded. But the line, and the man it was called after, had faded from public consciousness over a century or so, and his name conjured, for most people, only a gym shoe. Few even knew that the shoe was named in his honour, so called because it was rubber below and canvas above, and should be immersed in water only up to a certain point, like a cargo ship. The commonest misspelling of plimsoll is now 'plimsole', as though 'plim' qualifies a part of the shoe. People have even started to forget what the shoe looked like: the red trainer in the pub sign had very little to do with a plimsoll as we 1960s English schoolchildren knew it.

Living in a street named after an unfashionable item of footwear with comic associations, I was sorry that the nobler connotations of the word had lost their hold. Plimsoll was a name for silly or sinister characters in fiction and drama: P. G. Wodehouse's American visitor to Blandings, Tipton Plimsoll; Nurse Plimsoll in *Witness for the Prosecution*.* I acquired a pedantic habit of drawing attention to the original meaning. 'Plimsoll, as in the line,' I would say, when I dictated my address, instead of 'Plimsoll, as in the shoe.' I warmed to the people who knew what I was talking about. Then one day the pub changed hands. And name. The sign disappeared.

I woke in the small hours of the morning a few days later seized with the thought that the sign might still be around. It took three conversations during the next week – with surprised but not completely obstructive bar staff – before I was shown into the pub's backyard. There the sign stood, with the baseball boot stripped off. Revealed was an undistinguished bit of artwork: a picture of a ship (circa 1960, as I later discovered) and the Plimsoll mark with its then obscure initials. They stood, as I went on to learn, for the different conditions in which the loading levels applied: Tropical Fresh, Fresh, Summer, Winter and, most treacherous of all, Winter North Atlantic. Beneath them was a name, Samuel Plimsoll, and his dates, 1824–1898.

---

* Tipton Plimsoll appears in *Full Moon* and *Galahad at Blandings*. *Witness for the Prosecution* was an Agatha Christie stage play that became a Billy Wilder film in 1957. More recently the misspelt Oliver Plimsoles of the theatre group Legz Akimbo has been both silly and sinister in the television comedy series *The League of Gentlemen*.

I asked to buy the sign, and after a brief haggle it was mine for £20, though I suspect the proprietor was secretly amazed that anyone wanted it at all. A wiry barfly obligingly loaded it horizontally on to his head and escorted me down the road with my treasure. It now hangs in my back garden, and not everyone is as excited about it as I am. One relation remarked: 'What do you want *that* for?'

I wanted it because it illustrated the significance of the name of my street, but also, I think, because I knew it contained a story. I didn't know then how gripping and dramatic that story would turn out to be. Buying an ugly nautical pub sign launched me into research that revealed a tale of villainy and courage, of humour and surprises, of international consequences and contemporary resonance. It led me to a man who became my hero.

Marking a line on the side of a ship to indicate the lowest level at which it might safely sit in the water is an obvious and sensible measure. If you knew no more, you might expect the idea to have been drafted in some dusty office by a grey bureaucrat working through a pile of health-and-safety paperwork, and swiftly passed into law by yawning politicians one quiet evening in a half-empty House of Commons, since there would be no one to oppose its dull practicality. At subsequent meetings of administrative bodies of foreign shipping you might imagine it being waved through without a murmur until it became an international standard. And there would have been nothing more to say, except that it was a good thing that undoubtedly saved a lot of lives, like having brakes on bicycles, and no more likely to create controversy.

And yet the line has quite another kind of history. It is the fact that it was opposed at all, and the motives for that opposition, that turned its implementation from a bureaucratic procedure into a stirring crusade, and makes the line a monument to victory in an epic battle for justice and right, against an iniquity it is now hard for us to credit.

It was not unusual for Victorian merchants and shipowners to overload cargo ships dangerously in order to make as much profit as possible. But there was alleged to be a worse malpractice than this:

a murderous insurance scam perpetrated by the unscrupulous in pursuit of profit. Some ruthless shipowners were believed deliberately to overinsure their ships, and send them to sea in such a poor state of repair that they were hardly seaworthy. If the ships sank, the insurance paid out as much as several times their value. These became known as 'coffin-ships', and merchant sailors lived in fear of having to crew them. The Earl of Shaftesbury, the celebrated philanthropist, described the use of coffin-ships as 'one of the most terrible, the most diabolical systems that ever desolated mankind'.

Samuel Plimsoll blew the whistle on this practice and proposed a simple remedy for the 'diabolical system': a package of straightforward safety measures, of which the load line was one, and the inspection of ships by an independent body another. He believed that entering Parliament was the means to effect his remedy, but encountered more antagonism in the Commons, where some of the sitting MPs were shipowners with vested interests, than anywhere else. So he stirred up the populace to put pressure on Parliament to introduce his safeguards, which met prolonged resistance. In all, it took more than twenty years from the first proposals for a load line to the time when it was fixed by law. And during this period there was nearly a decade of intense nationwide activism.

Plimsoll enjoyed feverish popularity, but also made enemies. Like many a later whistleblower, he suffered defamation and insult. His own integrity and even sanity were questioned; relentless, impassioned single-mindedness will always be dismissed by some as boring and by others as madness. Meanwhile libel suits brought against him threatened to bankrupt him and forced him to sell his stately home to pay his legal costs. His health was affected by the strain.

Many justifications were used for resisting the introduction of Plimsoll's line: foremost among them was the need to keep up with commercial competition, especially from abroad, an argument that to this day has never lost its currency in circumstances where profit is set against danger or discomfort to those who work to produce it. Some complained that legislation hampered trade by entangling it in red tape. There was anxiety about a standardised measure for different ships – although history has proved this was not insuperable.

And there was the nebulous and self-serving contention that laws took responsibility for care of ships and crews away from the shipowners. Not legislating, it was argued, encouraged them to be responsible.

The Plimsoll Line is a landmark in the history of the ascendancy of people power, and a testament to the might of public opinion in politics even at a time when less than 10 per cent of the population had the vote. Now it is impossible to imagine a politics which is not constantly aware of public reaction, but Plimsoll was a pioneer of the effectiveness of extra-parliamentary pressure. He became a national hero and made the people take his cause to heart in an age when personal appearances and the printed word were the only means to disseminate ideas, and when celebrities could not be beamed into every living room. This story demonstrates how attitudes were shaped in a pre-technological age, and how public feeling could be harnessed and manipulated. It is an instance of a mass movement taking the side of the angels.

The existence of the Plimsoll Line is a philanthropic gesture, a symptom of the fact that in the middle of the nineteenth century the Industrial Revolution found its conscience. Its implementation is an episode in what has been called the 'slow revolution' that transformed Victorian society in Britain, in contrast to the actual revolutions that achieved social reform in other European countries. It is there because Plimsoll was one of those who made Parliament realise it had a legislative responsibility for the poor. We owe our political conscience to the likes of him.

One instance alone of sufferings that might have been avoided if a ship was properly loaded ought to have been enough to bring a load line immediately into being. But there were many such instances, and they were not enough. Take the case of the *London* . . .

INTRODUCTION

On 11 January 1866, Henry John Dennis, expecting to die, wrote his last letter. A widower with a young daughter, Edith, he was known as a brave and decent man: during the American Civil War he was the first, defiant Englishman to employ only free labourers to grow cotton amid the slave plantations of the Mississippi. From a storm-tossed British steamer in the Bay of Biscay, as the sea filled the ship, he pencilled his goodbye to his family in the pretty village of Great Shelford, near Cambridge. The letter said: 'Farewell, father, brother, sisters and my Edith. Ship London, Bay of Biscay, Thursday 12 o'c. noon. Reason – Ship over-weighted with cargo, and too slight a house over engine-room all washed away from deck. Bad poop windows. Water broken in. – God bless my little orphan . . . Storm, but not too violent for a well-ordered ship.'

Around Mr Dennis, other passengers were also writing desperate messages. Mr F. C. McMillan, travelling home first-class to Launceston, Tasmania, wrote to his 'dear wife and dear children. May God bless you all! Farewell for this world. Lost in the steamship London, bound for Melbourne.' Mr D. W. Lemon, an ironmonger from Melbourne, wrote: 'The ship is sinking – no hope of being saved. Dear parents – may God bless you, as also me, with the hope of eternal salvation.' These three messages and three other scraps of writing, one of them inscribed with a plaintive 'May we get home!' were found a month later in bottles that washed up on the Brittany coast, near Quiberon. Their authors were never found alive.

Two hundred and seventy people died in the wreck of the *London*. It was an emigrant ship sailing for Australia with 220 passengers and 69 crew members, but, typically, it also carried cargo. A great deal of cargo: twelve hundred tons of iron, by one account, and five hundred tons of coal, including fifty tons on deck. Another account said there were only 347 tons of 'dead weight' – iron and stone and lead – plus fourteen tons of machinery and a thousand tons of merchandise. The Senior Surveyor, who bore the distinguished name of Gladstone, afterwards declared that the deck was only three feet six inches above the surface of calm water. When the *London* sailed out of the Thames, one seaman who watched it pass near Purfleet later remarked to his friend: 'It'll be her last voyage.' 'Why?' asked the other. 'Because,' said the person from Purfleet, 'she is too low down in the water; she'll never rise to a stiff sea.' A group of pilots in a room near Gravesend, the pier-man at Woolwich, witnesses at Spithead, Portsmouth and Cowes and a number of passengers expressed similar opinions. One of the *London*'s own chief officers was worried. He wrote to his father from Gravesend saying he did not like his ship and feared she would be his coffin. She was.

The *London,* which was masted, like most Victorian steamships, in case of engine failure and for extra power in favourable winds, left the East India Docks on Thursday 28 December. It sailed downriver to Gravesend, where it took on passengers, leaving in a festive atmosphere on 30 December. Watched from the landing steps by two fathers whose young sons were aboard, it 'gradually disappeared in the glorious golden mist of a most lovely winter sunset'. The good weather did not last. It deteriorated enough to justify two separate stops to lie at anchor overnight before the ship even reached the Channel. By 4 January, at Plymouth, a gale was blowing and the ship encountered its first misfortune: a small boat bringing the *London* inside the breakwater overturned and its pilot was drowned.

Fifty-five passengers boarded at Plymouth and fairer weather followed for a few days, but by the 9th, in the open sea, the wind had risen and the sea was mountainous. Disasters rapidly ensued. Parts of masts were lost, a broken jib boom thrashed unrestrained on deck and a lifeboat was washed overboard. (In those days no ship carried enough lifeboats for all the passengers even when there was a full complement.) In the early hours of the 10th, the respected and experienced Australian captain, John Bohun Martin, a kindly, fair, blue-eyed bachelor of forty-seven, now captaining his thirteenth voyage to Melbourne, ordered that the ship turn round and put back to Plymouth. Within hours the second lifeboat was lost and another small boat, a cutter, destroyed. Loose coal broke out of the bags on deck and blocked the 'scupper holes', through which water washed from the deck. That evening the sea demolished the hatch over the engine room and the water that rushed in extinguished the furnaces. Frantic and unsuccessful attempts were made to block the opening with mattresses, blankets and sails. With the steam lost, the topsail was set. It was instantly ripped to shreds, but for a corner that kept the ship before the wind. A boiler on deck provided steam for a donkey engine that worked the pumps, manned all night by the passengers themselves. Many baled with buckets. The sea still got the better of their efforts, the ship grew lower in the water, and at 4 a.m. four portholes were washed away, admitting another flood.

In the morning Captain Martin addressed assembled passengers and crew to tell them that there was no further hope of saving the ship and that they must prepare for the worst. It was reported that 'a remarkable and unanimous spirit of resignation came over them at once' and that there was

> no screaming or shrieking . . . no rushing on deck or frantic cries. The Rev. Mr Daniel Draper [one of three clergymen on board] prayed aloud. Mothers were weeping over the little ones about with them to be engulfed, and the children, ignorant of their coming death, were pitifully enquiring as to the cause of so much woe. Friends were taking leave of friends, as if preparing for a long journey; others were crouched down with Bibles in their hands, endeavouring to snatch consolation . . .

One Australian clergyman, the Reverend Wollaston of Melbourne, later reported excitedly that the wreck had been described to him as a 'beautiful shipwreck' – a reasonable description, he thought, because it was a 'shipwreck which has broken many hearts, but a shipwreck which has saved many souls!'. He was quite indignant about a letter to *The Times* from a survivor who suggested that 'if the passengers had exerted themselves more for their own safety and attended less to the pious exhortations of the good clergymen, more would have been saved. The praying paralyzed them.'

'Consolation in the hour of peril': artist's impression of the Reverend Daniel Draper leading prayers on the doomed *London*.

Given that there were still boats on board, the cynical correspondent had a point. But it was not only prayer that deterred passengers from entrusting themselves to smaller vessels. At 10 a.m. there had been an attempt to launch one of the remaining pinnaces carrying five sailors. It capsized immediately. Two struggling men were thrown ropes and snatched from the sea and the other three managed to scramble back up the sides. This, and the difficulty of getting the boat away from the ship, discouraged passengers and crew from launching the boats that were left, although desperation prompted another attempt at 1 p.m. The captain had little hope for the twelve-man pinnace in the violent sea but told his chief engineer, John Greenhill, to take command of it. Martin declined to do so himself, declaring that his duty was to stay with the ship. Most passengers preferred to stay on board, although not all were given a choice. A Mrs Owen, who had determined to enter the boat with her young son, was dissuaded by the captain, who wept as he spoke to her. He believed that she would be choosing only a more lingering death, but also argued, with Victorian punctiliousness, against the impropriety and risk of entering a boat that contained sailors and a supply of brandy.

Small boats, with their danger of capsizing, were all the less appealing because it was uncommon for Victorians to learn how to swim. Perhaps one in ten might have had any hope of staying afloat for any time at all. Even sailors tended not to learn, believing that if they ended up in the sea, being able to swim would only prolong their agony. Of all the passengers on the *London*, only three second-class ticket-holders got into the getaway craft. One of them, James Wilson, tried to persuade his friend John Hickman to come with him, but Hickman had a wife, Jane, and four children, Elizabeth, Harry, Alfred and Emily. He only asked that his friend help him carry his two sons and two daughters to the higher part of the sinking ship before he left; Wilson did.

Sixteen crew members – one a boy of fifteen, Walter Edwards – crowded into the boat too, eight men jumping in at the last minute. A midshipman and a girl, too afraid of the drop, both missed their chance. As the cutter pulled away, a despairing young woman cried over the noise of the storm, 'A thousand guineas if you take me.' The little boat was already too laden, already a few yards away, and in imminent danger of being sucked down. She was left behind, as were all the other women and children. The bodies of some already washed over the deck.

In a poignantly spirited gesture, some fifty passengers standing on deck waved and cheered the little boat as it drew away, although its prospects seemed as bleak as their own. But the boat was only eighty yards away when its occupants saw the *London* tip upwards and sink completely beneath the sea, taking the wavers with it. Any cries were inaudible over the storm. The last sound the escapees heard from the ship as they rowed away was hymn-singing. A young officer named Angell, who was in charge of the donkey engine that worked the pumps, went down with his hand still on the engine. A final, scrabbling attempt had been made to launch another boat, but it was too late.

In the next twenty-four hours two ships were sighted by the escapees, who failed to attract the attention of the first. The second could not come close enough for rescue, lost sight of the pinnace and abandoned the attempt. A third ship was chased for five hours – much thanks to the tireless efforts of quartermaster William Daniel and able seaman John King – before the Italian captain of the *Marianople* spotted his pursuers, took the men aboard and had them stripped, rubbed and warmly clothed and fed with soup and tea and a specially killed turkey. These eighteen men and one boy were the witnesses to the fate of the *London*. No one else survived.

Among the dead was a four-month-old baby, child of Carlisle tailor William Graham and his wife Ellen. The baby was lost with both parents, two siblings aged three and ten, and two uncles, one a week married; the bride was drowned too. One of the other children on board, of whom there were at least a score, was nine-year-old William D. Burrell, who was to travel with this father to Melbourne. At the last minute, business detained Alexander Burrell, a solicitor from Glasgow, and he gave his boy into the care of his partner, twenty-five-year-old John Patrick. Both perished. A few months earlier young William had been booked to make the journey from Liverpool in other company, but he was so distressed about leaving without his father that plans were changed.

A Mr and Mrs Debenham, on their way home to Sydney, were drowned: hers was one of the few bodies found. It washed up a month later on an island off the coast of Brittany, and her brother-in-law identified it from marks on the linen and from her rings.

There was also a celebrity on board, a popular tragedian, compared by a few to Edmund Kean and known for his Othello, which he played in three separate productions in London: Gustavus V. Brooke. He was reported, despite ill-health, to have helped valiantly to bale out water and operate the pumps, 'barefoot and bareheaded, working only in a Crimean shirt and trousers', and his exit lines were overheard. He said to the steward, 'If you succeed in saving yourself, give my farewell to the people of Melbourne.' Several ballads of meagre literary merit commemorated the wreck of the *London*, one of them fund-raising for a lifeboat to be called the *G. V. Brooke*, another composed in his memory, in which Edwin Tomlin wrote, with a grim play on words: 'Twas in "The Tempest" on the "London Boards"/Thou bad'st thy "Last Farewell".' A song, by W. C. Bennett, lionised Captain Martin:

'. . . when the *London*'s awful end is told in years to be;
One form amid those fearful hours men's swimming eyes shall see,
You, Martin, amid storm and wreck, and hope, dead to despair,
Still grimly wrestling with the seas for those beneath your care;
Still calm, with firm, unfaltering voice, while aught remained to
    do,
Battling with death, still at your post, to God and duty true.'

The newspapers told stories of the vagaries of malign chance. A Miss Batchelor had found all cabins taken when she applied for a passage; when another passenger withdrew, Captain Martin remembered her anxiety to travel and gallantly enabled her to take the place. Four of the passengers of the *London* were survivors of a different ship recently destroyed at sea, the *Duncan Dunbar*. The only one who escaped this time was the brave sailor John King. Among the lost was a businessman, twenty-one-year-old Archibald Sandilands, who had been transferred from the *Duncan Dunbar* to another ship but disembarked at Plymouth, anticipating bad weather. He took the *London* as a safer option. A genial elderly couple, popular with other passengers, survived both the loss of the *Duncan Dunbar* and a previous wreck, only to be swept overboard from the *London*.

Others had narrow escapes: a family of twelve from Penzance whose travelling papers arrived too late; a young man running away from home, detected in the crowd by a local shipbroker and returned to his family; six sailors who deserted at Gravesend (and were replaced by four ill-fated recruits at Plymouth, minus a lucky fifth who was too drunk to go aboard).

And yet there were many who felt chance was not the principal culprit in this case. The ship was owned by Messrs Money Wigram and Sons, who claimed that this was the first of the vessels under their authority to whom any serious casualty had occurred. The *London* was only two years old, and classed A1 at Lloyd's. It was known for its speed. Uncharacteristically, however, the company had taken out insurance for this voyage.

Correspondence in *The Times* began to suggest that the ship was too deeply laden. 'It cannot be denied,' wrote one correspondent, 'that ships have been despatched on distant voyages so weighted with cargo that their arrival at their point of destination has been accomplished almost against expectation. With this knowledge, it is surprising that some Legislative measure has not been taken to prevent any ship carrying passengers leaving port at a draught of water exceeding a certified load-line.'

It was considered damning, too, that the ship went down in a gale through which other vessels passed safely – including her own small cutter.

An inquiry into the loss of the *London* began at Greenwich in February, conducted by the Board of Trade, the body responsible for implementing legislation in industry, shipping, agriculture and transport. It was attended by, among others, the father of Mary Cutting, who drowned, Alexander Burrell, the solicitor who had lost his son, William, and Clifford Wigram, representing the owners. Burrell believed that no blame should fall on the shipowners, who had made, he thought, every effort to protect the passengers and crew. Evidence was conflicting. Some said the hatch over the engine room leaked from the start, and that the deck was wet; others that the hatch was well sealed and the deck dry. The weight of cargo, argued one witness, was no greater than on previous voyages. Ultimately the inquiry found no fault with Messrs Wigram or with the loading, yet it saw fit to repeat a recommendation made regarding another ship that had foundered in the same gale, the *Amalia* (whose crew were all rescued by the passing *Laconia*), that 'the deep load line should be permanently marked on all vessels carrying passengers and merchandise'.

Henry Dennis, he whose last accusatory message survived, had a brother-in-law who was a barrister, Gilbert Highton, and he would not let the matter rest. He wrote a series of letters to *The Times* claiming that there was evidence that was not heard at the inquiry because the families of the dead were not permitted to cross-examine the witnesses. Highton's correspondents had told him that the *London* had taken on two hundred tons of pig iron as ballast when it was already loaded with as much iron, coal and merchandise as such a long, narrow ship could safely carry. A survivor said that a barrel containing letters and papers was thrown overboard which, if it ever turned up, would be 'found to contain revelations somewhat unpleasant to the ears of the owners'. It never did turn up. Highton believed his witnesses more reliable than 'surveyors and inspectors paid and employed by the Board of Trade, who too often . . . drink their glass of sherry . . . and then declare all to be right'. He appealed to the public to petition for further investigation, but whatever public feeling was stirred, the bereaved had to be satisfied with what they had already been told.

The *Sydney Morning Herald* of 17 March 1866, reporting from the homeland of many of the victims of the *London*, was in no doubt that overloading with railway iron was the significant cause of the disaster. Nor was the *London* the only recent case of its kind. It was time, clamoured the paper, to deal with the subject of over-freight.

In the British House of Commons on 7 March 1866 there had been an attempt to do just that. Load lines then fell under the jurisdiction of the Board of Trade, whose President, Thomas Milner Gibson, was asked by Montague Corry MP whether, in reference to the opinion expressed in the official report of the investigation into the loss of the *London,* that a load line might avert a great annual loss of life, 'he would bring in a Bill requiring the deep load line to be permanently marked on all vessels carrying passengers and merchandise.'

All the suffering already recounted, and the knowledge that this was one case among many, was not enough to persuade the Board of Trade or the Government that a load line was a good idea. (Board of Trade reports later attributed as many as 500 of the 1000 wrecks a year in the 1860s to overloading and unseaworthiness.) Milner Gibson replied that the question had often been considered before, but that 'the difficulty would be insuperable of adopting any general rule applicable to all ships by which Government officers should determine the deep load line of a vessel or how deep she may lawfully be immersed in water. The Government have therefore no intention of bringing in a Bill . . .'

The loss of the *London* was the subject of an inquiry because it carried passengers. This was the law. Technically, a merchant ship was any ship that was not a warship and therefore often also carried passengers, but generally the lives of passengers counted more than the lives of sailors. The wreck of a vessel that carried only cargo and crew was not even necessarily investigated.

Such was the state of affairs when this story begins.

Safety had already been established as paramount for transatlantic passenger steamers when Samuel Cunard had won the contract for the passage in 1840 with the motto 'safety first, profit second', a maxim justified by the foundering of two American passenger steamers that had boasted that they made the crossing faster than Cunard's ships. They were the *Humboldt*, which went down off Halifax, and the *Franklin,* lost near Long Island, both owned by the New York and Havre Line. It promptly folded. Speed was seen to be at the expense of safety. (There were suspicions that this was an issue with the *London*, too, which had vaunted its short journey times.)

Passenger ships were, as the century proceeded, increasingly protected against accidents, as the training of ships' officers and adequate provision of lifts and lifeboats were regulated. But the Board of Trade was much more reluctant to intervene when it came to the ships in which most British seamen served: the cargo vessels. It seemed that cargo ships might as well have had the motto 'profit first, safety second' as the number of merchantmen wrecks was rising, in circumstances about which questions needed to be asked.

In 1871, five years after the tragedy of the *London,* the Board of Trade's Annual Report recorded that an astonishing 856 British merchant ships were lost within ten miles of the British coast in conditions that were no worse than a strong breeze. Another 149 ships went down in moderate gales that ought not to have troubled a sound vessel, properly loaded. Some sailors were close enough to shore to be rescued from foundering vessels, but about five hundred

men were drowned, and almost as many had been lost in similar circumstances every year of the previous decade. Between 1861 and
1870, 5826 shipwrecks took place close to the coasts of the British
Isles, and 8105 people died. If ships that sailed further from the coast
are included, about half of the 17,086 wrecks and casualties between
1862 and 1871 occurred in 'very fine weather', and about one in
twelve resulted in loss of life. Ships that could come so easily to grief
were not fit to sail in the first place, and even the Board of Trade
acknowledged that, scandalously, these deaths were preventable. It
identified two avoidable causes of such casualties: ships were either
ill-repaired or they were overloaded. Either way, they had little chance
of reaching their destination in a storm.

In the mid-1800s the commercial life of Britain, and of the world,
relied on merchant ships. (It still does today: 95 per cent of goods are
transported around the globe by sea.) Then Britain's position as an
imperial power was based on its sea trade, and its tonnage exceeded
all other nations'. The US merchant navy, for instance, had only
about two-thirds the capacity of the ships of the British Empire, and
France's trade was a quarter of Britain's. In 1850 the British mercantile marine employed around 240,000 sailors, with another seventy
thousand in the navy, which would draw upon the merchant marine
for men in times of war. That year some thirty-four thousand British
ships carried £75 million worth of goods. Those who made their
living from commerce would scan the list of losses at sea that
appeared daily in *The Times* just below the weather report, rather as
businessmen now peruse the share-price index. Or they would visit
the offices of Lloyd's to see the latest postings of wrecks, collated
from reports sent by more than four hundred agents worldwide.
The phrase 'when my ship comes home' became the title of a
music-hall song.* Men who had made or inherited wealth from

---

* 'When My Ship Comes Home', was a comic song of 1873 with words by Frank W. Green and
music by Alfred Lee: 'I recollect in childhood's days when pretty toys I sought,/They told me I
must wait until my ship came in to port . . . The higher that one's hopes are rais'd the greater is
the fall,/It will be hard indeed if she does not come home at all,/If friendly winds should waft
her here to me with wealth galore/My heart will still be found as true as in the days of yore/No
willing man shall want for work, none penniless shall roam/You see, I'm only waiting till my ship
comes home.'

other sources often invested it in ships, just as they also often patronised the arts. It was not uncommon for a prosperous man, such as Whistler's patron the shipowner F. R. Leyland, to have money under canvas and in canvases.*

At the same time the nation was powered and heated by coal that was transported either by rail from the northern collieries or by ships that brought Newcastle coals down the coast from Tynemouth. As early as 1836, 11,226 ships carried coal from the Tyne; in 1837, 3845 ships carried coal from the Tyne to London alone. But, between 1830 and 1900, 70 per cent of all the sailing ships of the Tyne were lost at sea.

During those same years one out of every five mariners who embarked on a life at sea also died at sea. Despite greater numbers of lighthouses and buoys, intended to make shipping safer, and improvements to navigation, the number of deaths at sea was rising in the decades after 1850. Mortality was higher than in any other occupation, including mining, and areas of the country which specialised in shipping were profoundly affected, Tyneside among them.

Something was clearly wrong. Evidently avarice was creating a rising spiral of competition and the pressure to overload was escalating. Some shipowners were apparently growing more careless of maintaining their ships and profiting from insurance.

The *Sydney Morning Herald*, writing about the loss of the *London*, had considered the issue of insurance. It speculated about 'the millionaire, warm from his wine, who reads in his telegram that he has one risk less in his merchandise, and one large item in his favour at Lloyd's', with whom the ship was insured. It wondered 'if the consciences of men who do such things ever dream at night? Do they see the victims of their covetousness . . . turn upon them their reproachful gaze? Do they, when in their purple and fine linen they fare sumptuously every day, find their feast disturbed by the thought

* Frederick Richards Leyland, shipowner and art collector, one of the 'Liverpool Medici', was a partner of shipping firm John Bibby Sons and Co, and founder of the Leyland shipping line in 1873. John Bibby himself was also a patron of painters, as were shipbuilders William Alexander, William Imrie and Thomas Eustace Smith MP.

that the stroke that destroyed the husband beggared the widow and the child?'

The law afforded no protection from this danger. In fact several ill-advised pieces of legislation played into the hands of wrongdoers. By the 1870 Merchant Shipping Act sailors could be imprisoned for three months for breach of contract if they refused to board an unseaworthy ship once they had signed up for a voyage. Men were often recruited without seeing a ship, and even if the vessel turned out to be obviously in bad repair they were not allowed to change their minds. Between 1870 and 1872, 1628 sailors were sent to jail in Great Britain for refusing to go to sea in ships they thought were unseaworthy. In one case several sailors who refused on sight to board a ship were jailed: the ship set sail, went down in the Bay of Biscay and lives were lost. In another terrible instance two successive crews chose prison rather than go aboard a ship that was eventually crewed by boys no older than seventeen. They were all drowned when the ship foundered.

Under the Act, police could be enlisted to keep reluctant sailors on board, and sometimes police boats would escort a ship out of harbour until it was too far away for anyone to swim ashore. On one ship the lone man who slipped past the police and swam for it was the only member of the crew who was ever heard of again.

The age and condition of ships were furthermore sometimes disguised by name changes, so that sailors were signed up for dangerous ships under false pretences. This was why the measures Plimsoll advocated included a law against changing a ship's name once it was built.

Sometimes dangerous economies were not apparent from the look of a ship. One wooden sailing vessel, the *Kingsport*, built in the 1870s on the Bay of Fundy in Nova Scotia, prompted this admiration from the boatswain Mick Mulligan: 'She was as fine a looking craft as ever I set eyes on.' But the *Kingsport* had a hidden flaw. As Mulligan reported, telling the yarn years afterwards to a young shipmate, the builders had run out of bolts to hold the hull together, and the owners refused to wait for more. 'They said she was good enough and decided to have her sent under sail to England to be finished.' Avarice led to twofold folly. The haste was compounded by squeezing cargo into every last inch. The unfinished ship was loaded with frost-filled timber that had been stacked on shore for months, 'packed so tight there wasn't room for a matchstick in the hold'. The wood swelled as it thawed in the Gulf Stream, eight days out, and exerted a pressure on the hull that opened the seams. As Mulligan put it, 'She begun to leak like a basket.' The crew found the pumps ineffective and spent nine hours lashing the ship together in three places with the anchor chains, by which time the *Kingsport* was 'both rails under and wallowing like a turtle'. The vessel limped along at two knots and took thirty-two days to reach Holyhead, sixty miles short of Liverpool, the port it had been heading for. By then the crew was 'living on dog-biscuits . . . Every man had salt-water boils and we were as weak as kittens.' In this case the resourceful crew was lucky: the carelessness of the owners did not cost lives.

Another practice asked for trouble. Plimsoll insisted there was no provision anywhere in Britain for the break-up of old merchant ships. Worn-out vessels were sold at auction, intended only for salvage. While some became hulks for coal or prisoners or naval ratings, they could also be bought for paltry sums, repainted and sent offshore just far enough to qualify for an insurance claim: they could be sailed until they sank.

Profiteering rogues were also aided by the particular nature of marine insurance. The amount of compensation payable for a ship is not set by an independent valuation, as is the case with, say, house insurance. A shipowner only has to declare the value of the vessel and pay the appropriate premiums. This rule made it possible for near-wrecks to be excessively insured, perilously overloaded with cargoes less valuable than they were purported to be, and sent to their lucrative doom. Plimsoll argued that insurance companies were not likely to question payouts, because losses were borne by a large number of underwriters, each of whom was responsible only for small sums; it was not worth the legal costs of contesting a claim.

Besides, the case against a coffin-ship went down with the ship: evidence of its condition and loading was lost, and dead men tell no tales. Surviving sailors, whose poverty made them powerless, could do little themselves against the might of prosperous ship-owners. Sailors' opinions were as dispensable as their lives. They did not have the vote. Officially, even ships' captains were 'second-class citizens'. As one account later put it: 'The appearance of a sea-man in a court of law as a plaintiff was as rare as giraffes in drawing rooms.'

The issue of sailors' lives sacrificed for profit, and the shipowner's safety net of insurance, had been around for a long time. As far back as 1837 the *Nautical Magazine* had declared: 'If the ship-owner and merchant be so amply protected by the underwriter, and the under-writer by his premium, surely honest Jack – to say nothing of casual passengers – honest Jack who ventures his all, that is, his life – and how precious is that all to the nation! – should by the nation be protected.'

A note of anti-Semitism then crept into the argument: 'Do not let the poor fellow be drowned like a rat, in order to save a few pounds to Aaron, Isaacson, Abraham, and Co.' Shipowning was not a business practised by Jews in particular; but the journal (such was the prejudice of the time) expected its readers to associate the name of its fictitious company with avarice. The recognition that one party enjoyed the profits while the other endured the perils was not new.

There was, from the 1840s, a significant development in shipping: the rise of steam. Steam engines were not immediately suitable for merchant ships. Their huge consumption of coal made them uneconomical by comparison with sail. They were used at first only for passenger ships, and for cargoes with a high profit or, like the mails, a government subsidy. But the invention of the triple expansion engine, which effectively recycled the steam, led to the slow eclipse of sail. It meant that a ton of cargo could be carried a mile on the energy equivalent to that produced by burning a sheet of paper. The dangers of overloading and of neglected repairs applied to both sailing and steam ships. In wooden ships after a time the wood rotted; iron ships rusted and suffered from corrosion of the bolts.

When in the 1860s the Board of Trade was inspired to investigate certain losses at sea, some shipowners protested strongly against 'legislative interference' and 'restrictive practices which favour our foreign rivals'. This last argument was reiterated by opponents of the load line all through the next decade. The then Prime Minister, the Conservative Lord Palmerston, was sufficiently intimidated to make a foolish concession: in 1862 he repealed the law against 'deckloading' – storing cargo not in the hold but on the deck of the ship, which made it top-heavy and less stable. The consequences were fatal. There were cases of ships so overloaded that the crew had to walk over the top of the cargo in order to work the ship. Grain and coal would be poured on to decks in loose piles that would shift if a ship rolled, seriously affecting the ability of a vessel to right itself.

Years later, in 1890, Samuel Plimsoll claimed that the prohibition of deckloading had never in fact been properly repealed by Parliament, but was removed from the statute books by stealth. He said that two Members of Parliament, William Hutt and Thomas Milner Gibson, the same President of the Board of Trade who in 1866 declared a load line an impossibility, had secretly added an extra number – the number of the deckloading clause – into a document listing the clauses to be repealed. Their motive, he said, was a misguided attempt to promote the cause of free trade. Whatever the truth, whether by conspiracy or bad government, deckloads were reintroduced and made merchant ships terribly precarious in bad weather.

In Victorian England everyone was aware of the perils of the sea, with stories of shipwrecks relayed in penny ballads and news reports. Increasingly, the nineteenth century's burgeoning sense of social responsibility gave rise to a series of public bodies who turned their attention to the plight of sailors and their families: in 1818 the British and Foreign Sailors' Society was formed; in 1824 the Royal National Institute for the Preservation of Life from Shipwreck and the Royal National Lifeboat Institution were founded; in 1827 the Destitute Sailors' Asylum opened in Well Street, east London, and three years later the London Sailors' Home next door; in 1839 the Shipwrecked Fishermen's and Mariners' Royal Benevolent Society was among the new voluntary organisations dedicated to sailors, along with the Thames Church Mission launched in 1844 and the Missions to

Seamen in 1856. Charitable appeals were common to raise money for shipwrecked sailors when they survived, and for their families when they didn't. Relief associations were organised in all the large ports. Most people with the means dipped into their pockets at some time to help. Among those who contributed after the loss of the crew of the Whitby lifeboat in February 1861 was one Charles L. Dodgson of Christ Church, Oxford, otherwise known as Lewis Carroll.

The conditions of merchant seamen had become, in some circles, a hot topic in the 1860s. A flurry of papers read or published on the subject in Manchester and London, and correspondence in *The Times,* prompted the formation of the Society for Improving the Condition of Merchant Seamen. It was set up only to establish real grievances, to consider whether these 'were susceptible of remedy' and to dissolve itself once a report had been published and the results of the investigation communicated to the President of the Board of Trade. Its thirty-strong committee consisted of MPs, doctors, merchants, shipowners, masters of merchant ships and a couple of clergymen from sailors' missions, and its report, published in 1867, revealed the general opposition to a load line. It contained scores of 'Suggestions for Amending the Merchant Shipping Act, and Practical Recommendations to Shipowners, Masters and Seamen', but dismissed the idea of load lines in this short paragraph: 'It has been suggested that a deep load-line should be distinctly marked on every ship, to prevent her being overladen and made unsafe, but so much depends upon the nature and specific gravity of the cargo, which may vary every voyage, that this is not recommended here.'

The report reveals that sailors' lives and health were in danger from more than the voracity of the sea and of greedy merchants or unscrupulous shipowners. Life expectancy was very low. The report's gloomy finding was that: 'The majority of merchant seamen who form the crews of our foreign-going ships are broken down in health soon after the early age of 35 years, and the expectation of life of seamen . . . does not extend beyond the 45th or perhaps even the 40th year.'

It added that by 1867 aggravated cases of scurvy were becoming 'very common' in British merchant ships, 'more so than among the merchant ships of any other nation'. Sailors were supplied not with rum, as legend supposes, but with lime juice, as a substitute for vegetables, sometimes spiked with spirits to encourage consumption. But it seems that citrus fruits had been nowhere near some of the liquids presented as lime. Besides, the drink was not always meted out in regular daily measures, which, since the body does not store vitamin C, was crucial. Drink a week's ration at one go after ten days of salt pork and you get only a day's worth of the vitamin.

The 1867 report's recommendations suggest that sailors had a great deal to endure. It was felt necessary to propose the following remedies for current deficiencies. There should be a penalty for failing to provide provisions fit for human food. Salt meat should not be of so poor a quality that it shrivelled in the cooking. Rainwater caught on board should be used only for washing. Biscuits kept a long time should be in airtight cases. Soap should be provided. Medical chests, often forgotten, should be supplied, and someone in the crew should know what to do with their contents. Lime juice should be kept in closed containers. Sailors who refused their lime juice (perhaps deterred by the state of it after being stored in open barrels) should be punished. Deaths should be subject to an inquiry, though 'the unavoidable absence of the body . . . might prevent the charge of murder from being brought in'.

There was damning evidence too of poor accommodation for crews. 'Even in some large vessels the seamen's quarters are inexcusably bad, deficient in light, ventilation, space and every sort of comfort.' Sometimes the bulkhead that divided sleeping quarters from the hold was removed to make room for cargo, which meant that when, for instance, sugar or guano was carried 'free entrance is given to most pestilential and foul-smelling vapours'. The forecastle was meant to be for sailors, but sometimes space was stolen there by cargo and stores. The accommodation was therefore 'often too crowded, and from leakage and general filth frequently quite unfit for habitation'.

And there was another feature of seaboard life that made for discomfort and ill-health. 'Considerable risk and indecency arise from the absence of privy accommodation,' said the report. 'It is, therefore, recommended that every sea-going ship should have at least one weatherproof privy, for the use of the seamen; it is also recommended that there be in addition at least one urinal for their use.'

Sailors were each allotted six pints of water a day, but this included water for cooking and washing. In hot weather the water allowance, dished out at 4 p.m. daily, could be consumed at once. It meant the sailors did not wash from week to week. Havelock Wilson, later the founder of the National Union of Seamen, had been at sea from the age of eleven. He wrote in his memoir *My Stormy Voyage Through Life* (1925) that on his first voyage in about 1860 the only washing was done on Saturday afternoons, when an extra bucket of water was provided – between sixteen men. 'Those who felt inclined to wash the salt from their faces would wash in the bucket, but by the time nine or ten had performed this operation, the water was somewhat thick. Being fresh water, it was too precious to throw away so some of them would wash cotton shirts, jackets or trousers in it, and rinse them out in salt water.' Tropical storms provided an opportunity to block the scuppers and turn the deck into a laundry where all the clothes were washed in some five inches of collected rainwater.

The recommended diet for merchant sailors was principally bread, beef, pork, preserved meat and potatoes, suet, raisins and pickles. In port, watercress, oranges and shaddocks (an oriental citrus fruit) were advised to protect against scurvy, but at sea the main sources of Vitamin C were condensed soup and potatoes – preserved, if necessary, and in imitation of foreign shipowners, in molasses. Molasses was known by sailors as 'black jack' and said to have been taken out of the bilges of ships that carried cargoes of sugar. But then sailors were full of stories of the origins of their provisions: preserved beef, a Sunday treat, was, after 1875, called Harriet, said to be after one Harriet Lane, the mistress and victim in 1875 of an East End murderer, Henry Wainwright, who chopped up her body and was arrested after he tried to transport her remains in a cab. Other accounts say the name appeared on tins of mutton and was perhaps a tribute another Harriet Lane, who had acted as hostess, or ambassador's wife, to her bachelor uncle, US President James Buchanan and had been admired as a beauty at the Court of

St James's in London in the 1850s. Or perhaps it was an address in Melbourne, where the canned meat came from. But this gave rise to another story: that Harriet Lane was a lady who had visited the canning factory and fallen into a vat of boiling mutton, which the canners chose not to waste.

Supplies might not have been bad enough to contain unfortunate women, but they were known to fall short of the ideal proportions. Havelock Wilson recalled a menu that consisted in cold weather of 'a pound of hard ship's biscuits daily. In hot weather we could have as much as we wanted of "hard tack" – that was because it was known we could not eat all of it.' Tack could be dipped in tea to soften it, but the taste might not improve much. The tea was sometimes put on to stew two or three hours before it was drunk.

Still, the tea was not as old as the tack: there are records of it being supplied forty years after it was baked. The baking, whenever it had happened, produced biscuits which had holes on one side and were smooth on the other. Legend had it that sometimes tack walked across the deck on its own, propelled by the weevils that occupied the holes: the usual procedure was to tap it hard to shake them out, although there were sailors who ate it without tapping, on the principle that the weevils were at least fresh meat. By the 1890s, when jam and fat were more often provided, pounding the tack to powder with a belaying pin, mixing it with these and with water and then giving it to the cook to bake became a popular recipe to make it edible, and the result was known as 'dandy funk'. Bashing tack to bits and mixing it with pork fat and left-over pea soup was another option: this concoction was called 'cracker hash'.

Salt junk or beef was also tough to eat. If left to dry in the sun it would go as hard as mahogany. Skilled whittlers used it to carve small models. A sample of this was once presented in Poplar Town Hall, east London, to Samuel Plimsoll in his old age by a grateful sailor: he said he wanted to give Mr Plimsoll the dinner he had had off Cape Horn about three months earlier. As the ladies present pulled out pocket handkerchiefs, expecting something smelly, the sailor produced a finely wrought ship whose hull and half-sails were carved entirely out of salt junk.

If both the biscuit and the salt beef were too hard to eat they could be minced into small pieces, boiled up together with seasoning and consumed as 'scouse'; with a bit of potato and onion added, this was 'lob-scouse'. While the ordinary crew members enjoyed such treats, some choicer provisions were reserved for the captain's cabin. Havelock Wilson remembers a ship on which butter, for instance, was not for the consumption of the rest of the crew.

The ordinary seamen had most to endure, working by turns four-hour watches, from midnight to midnight, with the exception of two two-hour 'dog watches' between four and eight in the afternoon. The better-paid bosun, carpenter, sailmaker and cook, with their specific duties, were known as the 'idlers', while master mariners and officers had relatively comfortable accommodation, and even sometimes the privilege of taking their wives and children to sea. The painful separations of Jack and Polly were inescapable for able and ordinary seamen.

It was not just accommodation and diet and work and danger that made a sailor's life hard. It was also crimps. Crimps were swindlers who would take advantage of the system by which sailors were paid in advance, and would swarm aboard ships as they came into port, collecting sailors' bags together and taking them off to their lodging houses, where the men had no choice but to follow. By various inducements they would part them from their money and then pass them on, as drunk as it was possible to make them, to any old ship in need of men, in exchange for their advance pay on the grounds that it covered their debts. Admiral W. H. Smyth, author of the *Sailor's Word-Book* of 1867, defined crimps thus: 'Detested agents who trepan seamen, by treating, advancing money &c, by which the dupes become indebted, and when well plied with liquor are induced to sign articles, and are shipped off, only discovering their mistake on finding themselves at sea robbed of all they possessed.'

Sometimes this theft included clothes. Sailors were responsible for their own clothing, so the jaunty uniform of beribboned hat, bell bottoms, blue jacket, striped shirt and sailor's collar was an ideal, based on the contents of naval 'slop-chests', which sold clothes to sailors who possessed none or had worn out their own. Merchant sailors tended to be a still more motley crew. Some came aboard with no shirt, and it was common for them to work a ship barefoot, both in climates where the deck was so hot it burnt their feet, and where it froze. Baggy trousers and short blue jackets were standard where possible, but those who owned the tight jacket and decorative hat usually saved them for impressing the ladies on shore. Other than that 'their dress varied according to their taste and pocket'.

To be a boy on a ship in the 1860s was to be particularly at risk, not just because the innocents were the most likely to be robbed by conmen and scroungers. By some accounts the lives of the youngest members of the crew were the least valued. Boys were assigned the most dangerous tasks, on which men's lives would not be risked. They were responsible for the topmost sails: the royals and skysails, which were as high as the fourteenth storey of a building and were reached, in any wind, by walking along a loose wire rope slung beneath the yardarm while holding on to an iron bar, the jackstay, that ran above it. Furling the sail, though, required both hands. If a youngster went overboard, he might evoke no stronger reaction than the one reported of a certain captain unwilling to risk the unthinkable loss of precious spars, which were endangered by quick, emergency manoeuvres:* 'What, only a boy? Keep her as she goes.'

A sailor's chances were lessened by the tendency to scorn life-saving equipment. Representatives of the Royal Lifeboat Association would go aboard and try to persuade captains to buy more than the two lifebuoys merchant ships usually carried. The prevailing attitude was that safety devices made sailors cowardly. One account of 1874 records this response from a captain with a crew of twenty-two men: 'I've got seamen aboard my ship . . . we don't want life-buoys here, nor any nightcaps, nor no smelling salts, nor warming-pans; and I wish you a very good morning.' Another captain said: 'I like my fellows to understand that they've got to

---

* If a square-rigged ship had to make a quick, emergency manoeuvre, it increased the risk of breaking a spar (any wooden part of a ship's rig), most likely one that carried a topsail or other upper sail. If not carried out properly, the manoeuvre could even bring down some part of the mast. To replace a broken spar the only option was to make one with unseasoned, and therefore weaker, wood from the nearest island. Ships' captains tended to guard their spars with the utmost caution.

keep my craft afloat, or sink with her. Men will work like devils to save their own lives, but how much respect would they have for my property if, a few miles off shore, we were in danger of foundering, and every fellow could dance over the side with one of these nuisances made fast to him!'

Given the number of sailors who drowned, it may have eased congestion in the hereafter that sailors had a heaven of their own. In a pessimistic mood they spoke of Davy Jones's Locker – a reference to the sea in general but in particular to a sea you spent eternity in. Davy Jones was an evil spirit – a corruption perhaps of 'duppy', a West Indian word for a malevolent ghost, and 'Jonah', also a person believed to bring bad luck. The bottom of the sea was a locker because nothing was lost there: you knew where it was. But sailors preferred to think not of Davy Jones's Locker but of a paradise called Fiddler's Green, a place that lay 'seven miles to loo'ard* [downwind] of Hell, where the drinks and smokes are logged but never paid', where there was eternal fiddling for tireless dancing, and good-looking women to spare, offering for free 'those amenities for which Wapping, Castle Rag and the back of Portsmouth Point were once noted'. When a sailor died he was said to turn into a gull or albatross (hence the superstition that doomed the Ancient Mariner) and to fly to the South Pole and await his moment to slip into the ever-spinning entrance to Fiddler's Green, which moved with the motion of the earth.

This happy, and complicated, notion was very far from the hardships of the seafaring life, and from the suffering faced by the family left behind by the breadwinning mariner. For most sailors' widows, orphans and elderly dependants the only choice was destitution or the workhouse if Jack never came home – and two-thirds of the thirty thousand sailors who died in service between 1860 and 1870 left widows and orphans. (At least a quarter of the lost sailors drowned, and as many again died from accident or privation.) Sometimes widows remarried to save themselves. What they could not count on was any kind of pension.

* 'Loo'ard' is 'leeward', written as it is pronounced.

There had been some pension provision for widows and orphans of merchant seamen from 1834 until 1850 from the Merchant Seamen's Fund, to which seamen were obliged to pay one shilling a month and masters of vessels two shillings. In 1850 the Fund had given close to £20,000 to seamen pensioners and over £41,000 to seamen's widows and orphans, although the amount it paid out to any individual varied according to the whim of Trustees who had charge of it in different ports: some paid £7 a year in pension, others less than £1 and some nothing at all.

This great inequality was most felt in the ports on the north-east coast, and those which were principally engaged in the home trade. At these ports a very much greater proportion of the men were married and the loss of life among them from shipwreck far exceeded those employed in the foreign trade. While the Fund existed, 10s per head was paid to the Shipwrecked Mariners' Society for every shipwrecked seaman relieved and forwarded to his home by it or its agents on the coast.

Once the Act was passed in 1851 that wound up the Fund, as a consequence of mismanagement and insolvency, the Board of Trade refused to provide any pension at all, 'and thus the Merchant Seamen of the country were left to suffer from the blunders of the Government, and England, unlike any other maritime country in the world, left without any public provision for her Merchant Seamen'.

The life expectancy of sailors' widows was also short. Some of the estimated seventy thousand sailors' children who were left fatherless in the 1860s went to specialist orphanages if they also lost their mothers or their widowed mothers could not keep them. One such was the Sailors' Orphan Girls' School and Home at Hampstead in London, which, in 1870, housed and educated seventy girls. Another was the Merchant Seamen's Orphan Asylum, at Snaresbrook in Essex, which cared for 270 children in 1875. These children were the lucky ones. The Asylum was a large, airy building with a cricket pitch, a chapel and a playground, and the children were taught music and French, and played fifes and drums in their marching band on the parade ground. The institution was maintained by charitable donations mainly from 'gentlemen and ladies connected with the shipping interest in London', because, as one promoter put it, 'in this island, whose rightness and tightness are so dependent on the exertions of the sailor, the sailor's orphan becomes everybody's care, and . . . of all destitute British babies, the water-baby has, perhaps, the most urgent claim.'

Whatever the urgency of their claim, for some sailors' orphans wretched poverty was still their fate. The time was ripe for a reformer to challenge the shipping industry's 'widow-and-orphan-manufacturing system'.

I

A LOVING SPIRIT

At the age of thirty-two Samuel Plimsoll was arrested for assault on Waterloo Bridge. In 1856 there was a toll on the bridge, operated by a private company, with a turnstile that recorded the numbers who passed, and it cost a halfpenny to cross. One September evening, around 8 p.m., Samuel Plimsoll, coal merchant, just returned from an International Free Trade Congress in Brussels, arrived at the north side of the bridge with a friend, who paid a penny for them both. Plimsoll stepped into the road and walked past the turnstile. The tollkeeper called him back, insisting that he had to go through it. Plimsoll refused, the tollkeeper tried to stop him and Plimsoll committed the unspecified assault. A crowd gathered, the tollgate was closed and Plimsoll was taken into custody. Later that night, released on bail, he called again at the bridge, put down a halfpenny, and asked to see the Act of Parliament that said he could not walk in the carriageway. The tollkeeper, predictably, did not have it about him. After an interlude of three days (how swiftly the wheels of justice turned then), Plimsoll was charged at Bow Street.

He argued in his own defence that there was no law obliging him to pass through the turnstile. His halfpenny 'purchased the freedom of the bridge'. He was provoked further, he said, by the tollkeeper's insolence. The magistrate, a Mr Jardine, told him that he was quite in the wrong: the company had complete control over the bridge and could stop anyone from crossing who didn't comply with its regulations. He fined Plimsoll £3.

This incident, years before Samuel Plimsoll's name was associated with the safety of sailors, illuminates the character of a man who became celebrated as an agitator. It tells us that he was relentless when he thought he was right. That he could be contrary, questioned authority, reacted emotionally, could lose his temper and liked to take a stand. That he acted on points of principle and perhaps even enjoyed confrontation. Also that he trusted in his own capacity to argue a case and expected the rest of the world to give in to his reason. All these traits characterised his subsequent career.

There may also have been something other than self-interest in his behaviour. The judge said that 'there had been hundreds of similar cases' in his court. Perhaps Plimsoll knew of the petty tyranny of the jobsworth on the bridge and set out to provoke him. At any rate his attempt to vindicate himself escalated for a moment into a crusade to win back the right of the road for all the pedestrians who crossed the Thames. He treated a trivial inconvenience as an infringement of liberty, and turned the argument into a battle for justice.

The one uncharacteristic aspect of Plimsoll's conduct in this incident is his resort to force. He always deplored violence in a mob, and, while he stirred up national outrage, never incited damage to property or people. Violence was ever afterwards confined to his language – the pen being mightier – and even this was directed only at those whose actions were dangerous to others. Injustice made him furious, but it was never known on any other occasion to make him throw a punch.

So where did this defiant individual come from, and what were the circumstances that disposed him to become 'the sailor's friend'? Samuel Plimsoll had never worked in shipping. When he took up the sailors' cause he had made his fortune as a coal merchant, having followed his brother Thomas, manager of the Sunderland and Hartlepool Coal Company, to London in 1853. By the time he got into Parliament he was the member for landlocked Derby. When he became famous his detractors did not hesitate to make fun of his lack of nautical experience. A spoof of Plimsoll's writing in *Punch* magazine had him refer to 'the Cinque Port of Newport-Pagnell'.

Plimsoll did have a little salt water in his blood. His paternal grandfather was a chandler, his maternal grandfather a shipwright. He was the son of Thomas Plimsoll, an excise man, and Priscilla (née Willing), and was born in a port, in Colston Parade in Bristol – round the corner, prophetically, from Ship Lane, and, also aptly, just along the road from a charitable institution, an almshouse for widows, Fry's House of Mercy.* His birthplace overlooked the Gothic church of St Mary Redcliffe (then lacking the original spire for which it is now famous and which was restored decades later).

The family did not attend this church, although they could have stepped out of the front door and taken four paces into the churchyard. But when the seventh child of Priscilla Plimsoll died at a few days old, the baby boy was buried here, close enough for the mother to watch over her child's grave from her own windows. Almost exactly a year later Samuel was born, on 10 February 1824, the eighth birth of thirteen.

The Plimsolls worshipped at a nearby Congregational church where Samuel was baptised (his name and his father's were spelt 'Plimsall' in the church records).† Congregationalism was a dissenting Church characterised as 'the Liberal Party at prayer' that left all rule and discipline to the discretion of each congregation, emphasising the individual's relationship with God, and playing down the intermediate role of the clergyman. The Plimsolls preferred this egalitarian form of Christianity. The heritage that influenced Samuel was not a seafaring tradition but one of practical faith and social responsibility. In the Plimsoll family philosophy, to believe was to be obliged to act; his grandparents had been known to invite the hungry in off the street to dine. At thirteen, Samuel,

---

* Plimsoll's birthplace is No. 9 Colston Parade, formerly No. 3. The house was rebuilt after a railway line to the docks ran through the churchyard and the Parade. The new house nevertheless had a plaque, installed with ceremony in 1935, which has recently gone missing.

† Bridge Street Congregational Church, now demolished, where Plimsoll was baptised on 30 January 1825. His father worked at the Excise office in nearby Queen Street. In 1827 the Plimsoll family moved to Sion Place, Bristol, now just by Clifton Suspension Bridge, which was begun in 1831.

who believed fervently all his life, told the local clergyman that he 'wanted to do a great work for the Lord'.

Plimsoll's six elder siblings would have had a memory of the comings and goings of the port of Bristol, but Samuel was only three when his family moved to the Lake District town of Penrith in Cumberland. There William and Dorothy Wordsworth had gone to school; there Plimsoll received his basic education from a staymaker's wife.* A favourite childhood memory was the view from Penrith Beacon, looking towards the hills of Lakeland: 'a glorious panorama . . . the wide plain . . . closed by the dark hills of Ullswater on the west, and by the dim ridges of Scotland to the north.' When he revisited in his thirties Plimsoll was dismayed to find that fir trees now obscured his beloved vista of the Eden Valley. He persuaded the landowner, the Earl of Lonsdale, to have the trees cut down to restore a sight that is still vaunted as one of the attractions of Penrith.

It was typical of Plimsoll that he could not bear this universally accessible source of pleasure to be lost simply because of the negligence of a man already more privileged than his neighbours. Benefits that belonged to the people had to be preserved for the people. Views and public spaces mattered to him. He once raised a question in the House about 'lofty and ponderous' railings for London's Regent's Park, which would interfere with the view for passers-by. He campaigned successfully with a petition to save, for the public, gardens on the Thames Embankment that belonged to the Duke of Buccleuch. A monument to Plimsoll now stands beside these gardens, which are still public. Public access was a lifetime's preoccupation: in his sixties he was concerned enough to attend a meeting at Leamside, near Shields on Tyneside, to protest against the closing of public footpaths.

When Samuel was almost fourteen the family settled in Sheffield.† That year *Oliver Twist* was published, and Samuel was inspired to write a pamphlet called 'A Plan to Have Fatherless and Motherless Children Cared For Instead of Being Consigned to the Work-

* Mrs Jenny Dalton's infant school at Great Dockray.
† On 22 January 1838 the Plimsoll family moved to 50 Regent Street, Sheffield, and Thomas Plimsoll went to work at the Sheffield 1st District Collection.

house'. At a young age he showed empathy for the poor. But in his later speeches and writings Plimsoll claimed that his solidarity with them grew out of his own experience. His background was not the most deprived, but when his father died he found himself, at sixteen, the eldest child still living at home, responsible for his mother and five younger siblings, who all lived together in four small rooms in Sheffield. He knew then the price of bread, and what it was to struggle to make ends meet: 'Left with five younger than myself dependent on me, I know what twenty, then thirty shillings a week can and cannot do; I have paid as much as 4s 6d for a stone of flour, before the dreadful Corn Laws were abolished.' (Four shillings and sixpence was a fortnight's income for a sailor's widow in a generous part of the country before pensions were abolished altogether.)

Plimsoll showed traits of character in his youth that the public man was to be known for. The boy Samuel had an entrepreneurial spirit: he would save up five shillings to buy a bundle of hareskins and ship it south from Sheffield to his furrier brother Thomas in London, who would buy the skins from him at a profit. As an adult the same spirit took him from bankruptcy to ownership of a mansion in only nine years.

He was ambitious and determined to make good. He supplemented his abbreviated formal schooling – he left the irascible Dr Samuel Eadon's school at fifteen – by the diligent acquisition, from the age of seventeen, of a classical education at the People's College, attending classes at 6.30 a.m. and in the evening after work.* Plimsoll's first jobs were (for two years) as a lawyer's clerk, for Henry Waterfall, a Sheffield solicitor, and then, for ten years, as a clerk in the brewery of Thomas Rawson and Co. He took positions of responsibility when he could, and made sure his ideas and innovations came to the attention of those who could help to fulfil them. Early in his working life Plimsoll showed potential as a public man. He wrote speeches for the Mayor of Sheffield, Thomas Birks, a managing partner of the brewery where he worked, and he was popular and engaging.

In 1845, at twenty-one, Sam and his friend Joe (Joseph Ridge

---

* The People's College was founded in Sheffield in 1842 by Robert Bayley, a Congregational minister and ardent social reformer.

Simpson) had their pictures taken, and each bought a pair of daguerreotypes – at the time, the equivalent of cramming into a photo booth with your mate. Joe's set, of himself and his friend, passed on to his grandson, C. Ridge Simpson, who wrote about them in a Sheffield newspaper in 1928. The surviving daguerreotype of Samuel Plimsoll as a young man, clean-shaven, shows that he was good-looking despite a certain snubness of nose, with curly dark hair, sideburns, deep-set eyes, dark brows and a well-shaped mouth – which was hidden, from middle age onwards, by his moustache. He had an earnest expression that nevertheless suggested underlying good humour. About this time he enjoyed some celebrity as a stalwart of the local Liberal Club and in his immediate circle he was thought charismatic.

In 1851, as secretary of Sheffield's Great Exhibition Committee, Plimsoll organised the exhibits for the Sheffield Court in London's Hyde Park. This pavilion, thanks to his tireless efficiency, was the largest hosted by any single town, with an array of iron and steel artefacts from several hundred companies and individuals, and was a notable success, the excellence of its cutting instruments singled out

Daguerreotype of Plimsoll at twenty-one, taken in Sheffield.
(*Sheffield Telegraph*)

in a handbook to the exhibition. The Sheffield pavilion even inspired 'A Visitor' to pay lengthy metrical tribute with a 'Poetical Rhapsody in six parts'. Quantity and skill may have been the pavilion's strong points; the architect Pugin's judgement at the time was that Sheffield was 'a mine of bad taste'. Tasteful or otherwise (and Plimsoll had no pretensions as an aesthete), the Sheffield Court included scores of stoves, fenders, ranges, ovens and grates, and hundreds of samples of cutlery, knives, tools, machinery and gadgets ranging from 'coromandel-wood cases of ladies' and gentlemen's toilet cutlery' to 'ladies' steel busks, made by registered apparatus'.

Throughout his career Plimsoll demonstrated that he was also at heart an inventor, as was his brother Henry, who eventually held a dozen patents for pieces of industrial machinery. Samuel specialised in simple, logical solutions that someone else should have thought of before. While Plimsoll worked at the brewery he patented a system of suspended porous bags for straining impurities out of beer. He looked at the way things were done and came up with ways of improving them that were gloriously straightforward. The Sheffield pavilion at the Great Exhibition displayed three inventions by Plimsoll himself. One of these was 'an improved warming and ventilating apparatus' whose special feature seems to have been a coat of white enamel to keep the heat in. Another was a pocket umbrella 'with improved runner, wheel, cap, rib and stretcher', distinctive because it didn't have a handle and was made to be attached to a walking stick. The third contribution was a selection of handles for files which were adapted to the shape of the surface that was to be filed; there is no graphic record, but this too sounds commonsensically simple.

Long before he qualified for the enduring accolade 'the sailor's friend', Plimsoll was known as a benefactor of the miners, and called 'the miner's friend'. In January 1852 he raised subscriptions for the relief of twenty-four widows and fifty-three orphans after an explosion which killed fifty men and maimed others at the Warren Vale Colliery at Rawmarsh in Yorkshire. In February 1857 he orchestrated another relief effort, this time after one of the worst mining disasters, at the Lund Hill pit, where a fire in a mine cost 189 lives. Over £10,000 was raised, £200 of it from Queen Victoria, and more than £2000 from Sheffield; many families were thereby saved from the dreaded workhouse. In this Plimsoll acted from the same motive that governed him in the crusade that would make him famous: compassion for the anguish of those left behind. He also learned in these years how much more effective an appeal could be if it were made personal. In 1867 he witnessed the impact on a huge public meeting of the appearance of the widows and relatives of seventy-three men who died at the Oaks colliery in 1846. He went on to borrow this strategy. When he opened his campaign against overloaded and unseaworthy ships, the widows of the men lost on the *Sea Queen* sat with him on a platform in Manchester; when he was moved to write a book about the malpractices of shipowners, he told stories of the tribulations of real people; by 1890 he used the names and photographs of widows and orphans in his denunciation of the horrors of cattle ships.

After the Lund Hill disaster Plimsoll put forward possible safety measures: he had noticed that sheets of paper covered with acetate of lead blackened in the presence of gas, as did the flannel of a miner's shirt. He suggested that miners should have specially treated sheets of paper to serve as a warning. He also proposed the use of a balloon full of hydrogen installed in a glass tube the height of a seam; since hydrogen, which caused the explosions, was lighter than air, the balloon would rise to the level at which the gas was present. His only motive in this, he said, was to stem 'the great loss of life' in the mines. Although to the wider public it was to seem that Plimsoll came out of the blue as a friend to sailors, it was entirely consistent with his history that he saw the prevention of needless deaths as a 'vital matter'.

Plimsoll made much of the fact that he lived for a while as a young man in a charity lodging house in Hatton Garden in London, when a business venture sabotaged by vested interest bankrupted him. When, on 8 August 1850, the Great Northern Railway had opened between Leeds and King's Cross, Plimsoll had had the idea of transporting coal to London from the South Yorkshire pits by train instead of by sea, breaking the monopoly of supply from the North Yorkshire pits. In 1853 Plimsoll announced to the GNR that colliery owners in Barnsley, Rotherham, Doncaster and Sheffield were willing to ship their coal via this line, and in 1854 he opened a London office in readiness. No one told him the important fact that the General Manager of the GNR, Seymour Clarke, had a brother, Herbert, who was a London coal merchant. Seymour, wanting to protect his brother's business, told Plimsoll that in order to use the railway he had to buy his own coal trucks. Plimsoll was obliged to buy ten at £800 each. Clarke then forced the trucks to stand unprofitably idle by delaying the necessary certification. He also then claimed there were no coal-unloading facilities at the other end of the line. These self-interested machinations froze Plimsoll's business, and three days before his thirty-first birthday, on 7 February 1855, he was driven to declare himself bankrupt. Plimsoll had a tendency ever afterwards to believe that those in authority had a secret agenda; this episode must have encouraged the suspicion.

Years later he spoke of the way his experience of living in charity accommodation among the unemployed and the hungry impressed upon him their noble character – how they supported one another and shared their meagre food. Plimsoll lived there, he said, 'for months and months' and went 'of stern necessity . . . with strong shrinking, with a sense of suffering great humiliation, regarding my being there as a thing to be carefully kept secret from all my old friends. In a word, I considered it only less degrading than sponging upon friends, or borrowing what I saw no chance of ever being able to pay.' He wrote of men who trudged miles, day after day, in pursuit of rumoured jobs, returning unsuccessful and weary, and how they would be 'accosted by another, scarcely less poor than himself, with 'Here, mate, get this into thee,' handing him at the same time a piece of bread and some cold meat, and afterwards some coffee. And adding, 'Better luck to-morrow, keep up your pecker.' And all this', wrote Plimsoll, 'without any idea that they were practising the most splendid patience, fortitude, courage, and generosity I had ever seen.' Such behaviour, and the bravery and selflessness of miners that he had witnessed, also cited in his book *Our Seamen*, confirmed his commitment to helping those who could not help themselves.

Many of the episodes of Plimsoll's early life prefigure the great campaign that dominated it. Plimsoll, typically, did not accept his bankruptcy meekly. As his resources had dwindled, he had sold his shares in the railway in which he had also invested such high hopes, but this did not stop him from crashing a shareholders' meeting afterwards to expose those who had thwarted him.* The meeting was sympathetic to Plimsoll, insisting nonetheless that he should put his own financial affairs in order before he did business with the company. His protest ultimately put an end to Seymour Clarke's scheming, although both Seymour and his brother Herbert held positions with the Great Northern Railway for at least another four years.

In August Plimsoll was suspended from his membership of the Nether Congregational Church in Sheffield, as a gesture of censure of his bankruptcy and his failure to express 'moral regret' at his 'hazardous employment of borrowed capital'. Debt was a disgrace, in conflict with Christian values; his conduct 'inflicted injury on his friends, on his creditors and on the Gospel and Church of God'. Suitable penitence led to his reinstatement by the church on 2 April 1856. (By 1872 this same church appreciated him enough to form a special committee to support his campaign for sailors.)

In time Plimsoll broke the monopoly of coal transport that held back his business, and changed the pattern of the British coal industry. A matter of months after his bankruptcy certificate was issued he was able to pay dividends to the shareholders in his coal business.

The period of Plimsoll's life in which he opened the way for the South Yorkshire pits to send their coal to London by rail taught him the value of the press. He would never, he said, have achieved all he did without its help. He understood how useful a tool it was for influencing opinion, and for the rest of his life did all he could to ensure coverage of the issues that concerned him. He was an indefatigable publicist. He wrote regularly to the editor of *The Times*, sending, where it was expedient, copies of his speeches and even of his private letters. His name would be mentioned in a thousand articles in *The Times* alone during his career. He wrote, published and circulated pamphlets, and penned articles himself for such publications as the nonconformist journal *The Nineteenth Century* and the *Westminster Review*.

---

* Plimsoll sold his shares in GNR on 16 March 1854, but attended a shareholders' meeting at the London Tavern, Bishopsgate Street, on 26 August 1854.

In his mid-thirties Samuel Plimsoll met the person who did most to initiate and sustain his campaign for sailors. She was beautiful and good-hearted, and six years younger than Plimsoll, and without her there would surely be no such thing as the Plimsoll Line. She was, when Samuel met her, Eliza Ann Railton, the stepdaughter of John Chambers of the mining company Newton, Chambers, and Co., which owned the Thornecliffe Colliery near Sheffield. Eliza's mother, a draper's widow, was the daughter of the company's original Mr Newton. She married John Chambers, the son of her father's partner, when Eliza and her sister were very young. Chambers treated the girls as his own, setting a pattern for Eliza, whose own daughter Nellie was adopted.

Plimsoll approached John Chambers to enlist him in his scheme to transport coal from the local pits to London. Chambers, who offered Plimsoll a job as a clerk, was impressed with the young man. So too was his stepdaughter; she told him when he proposed that she had loved him from the first moment they met. Their courtship was conducted on Sunday walks to church and over tea at elegant Belmont House, where she lived, and at his mother's home.*

She admired his 'zest for living, his well-stored mind, his compassion for those in distress and his high sense of social duty', as well as the hearty way he sang hymns. As a suitor he was doubtless ardent: his taste was romantic and in all his actions he was demonstrative of his feelings. Part of his charm must have been that, for all his earnestness, bearded and bespectacled Plimsoll had, as his speeches and letters show, a playful and irreverent sense of humour. Children grew up to remember the twinkle in his eye. He was ambitious but unpretentious, and Eliza, cultured and wealthy, brought up a Methodist, seems to have had something of *Middlemarch*'s Dorothea Brooke in her nature: she burned to serve a greater good and was ready to be a helpmeet to a man with high aims. Throughout Plimsoll's campaign for sailors her sacrifices were as great as his, and at every crucial turn of his career it was Eliza who suggested his course of action. Chambers's business cooperation was the first step

---

* Belmont House is now an old people's home, and made the news in recent years because of an allegation of the abuse of an elderly patient. Eliza Plimsoll's ghost would have wept.

on Plimsoll's road to a fortune. Eliza's love for him made possible his life as a philanthropist.

In all his writings Samuel acknowledged Eliza's help. Sailors recognised it too, and made presentations to her in Sheffield and Liverpool. Witnesses spoke of her hard work and her dedication. The Plimsolls' lifelong friend George Howell wrote: 'His good wife was not at all behind her husband in the fervour of her devotion to the cause of "Our Seamen" and in her readiness to sacrifice wealth and position to the sailors . . . [Between them] there was but one unselfish thought – the safety of the sailor, the cost was seldom reckoned. I have never seen devotion more thorough and complete.'

Eliza was, by all accounts, more level-headed than her husband, a moderating influence on his emotional temperament, her 'patience and mature deliberation' contrasting with the 'precipitancy of his impassioned earnestness'. It seems she was gentle, intelligent and well-liked. A note in the Hon. Georgiana Cowper-Temple's diary suggests she was affectionately known to her friends as 'Lizzie'.

And yet, while Samuel's voice rings through history, in the pages of Hansard, in his speeches, his books, his articles, his pamphlets and his letters, public and private, Eliza's voice is silent. Plimsoll spoke for her in public. He told audiences what she thought and felt. He even quoted her verbatim – by which we know that she called her husband 'Sam' and that she cared passionately for him. We know her by her actions and see her pretty face and elaborate braided coiffure in photographs, but we know nothing of her by her own account. She regularly accompanied her husband in his public appearances, but the press failed ever to seek her opinion. Even when the occasion reported was a presentation being made expressly to Eliza, the only comments quoted are from her husband and those who made the presentation (and then the reports are sparing about praise for her, though it was surely uttered). This was a time when even birth announcements never gave the name of a mother: the form was 'To the wife of Mr So-and-So, a son'. Small clues suggest Eliza had an independent mind: when her sister Sarah was married, for instance, Eliza, already a bride of one year, signed the witness book with her maiden name. Her history has to be read, to some extent, between the lines, but she had contemporary admirers enough and appreciation enough from those who knew her for it to be clear that the Plimsoll Line should be regarded as a commemoration of Eliza Plimsoll as much as of Samuel.

Newlyweds Eliza Plimsoll née Railton and Samuel Plimsoll.
(*From Masters,* The Plimsoll Mark)

Eliza and Samuel were married on 1 October 1857 in Ecclesfield church, near Sheffield, known for its grandeur as 'the Minster of the Moors'; here Eliza's mother had married both her father and her stepfather. Eliza's sister Sarah and two of Samuel's sisters, Fanny and Caroline, were bridesmaids. Everyone approved of the match, and the local press, as is the nature of such coverage, commented on his dignity and her beauty. Their life together began in a few rooms above Plimsoll's second office in a row of houses in Hatton Garden, only doors away from the charity lodging house where he had lived when he was bankrupt. It was a considerable step down for Eliza from the home she had grown up in, but from the moment of his marriage Plimsoll's fortunes improved. The patronage of his father-in-law helped. Plimsoll married for love, but he also married well. There is no doubt that this union with the boss's daughter helped him to make good.

Plimsoll's prosperity was also boosted by his discovery, reported in *The Times* a month before his wedding, of how to make best-quality locomotive coke in ovens from the smudge left in the pits as worthless. 'Several of the principal coalmasters are joining in for the purpose of erecting ovens and making coke on a large scale under Mr Plimsoll's superintendence,' said the piece. 'Considering the high price of railway coke and the small cost of the materials, considerable profit will attend its manufacture, which will also cheapen to the railway companies their most costly article of consumption.'

Considerable profit attended both this and the supply of the uncrushed coal made possible by the grate Plimsoll patented in 1859. He invented a sloping grille, a loading chute that prevented coal from being crushed to dust when it was transported. The coal slid, instead of being dumped, into the bags, and at the same time any pulverised detritus was filtered out of every sackful. With no useless crumbs at the bottom, his bags, which were bought by weight, were better value for money than his competitors'. Plimsoll the coal merchant prospered. He was adept at encouraging business. On 6 July 1859, for instance, he invited two hundred London coal merchants and the representatives of gas and water companies (which consumed coal) for a day out with their wives to visit Yorkshire pits. A special train left King's Cross at 7 a.m. and the day culminated in a dinner, with a rousing speech from Plimsoll, at the Barnsley Corn Exchange. A timely property purchase behind King's Cross also obliged the railway to pay rent to him.

Yet his public declarations all suggested he thought more highly of the poor than of the rich. In *Our Seamen* he wrote: 'I absolutely glory in the working men, and aspire no higher than to merit equal respect with them.' And, when he was himself a wealthy man, he had this to say of the rich:

> If the lives of nearly a thousand of our ministers of religion, or of our lawyers, or of our doctors or of our public men were sacrificed every year . . . all England would ring with indignation at the outrage; yet I venture to say . . . that any thousand of what is called the working classes are as worthy of respect and attention as any of these. If hon-

esty, if strong aversion to idleness, if tenderness to one another in adversity and if splendid courage are claims to respect, I am not sure that . . . you can find these moral qualities in equal degree in any other class. I don't wish to disparage the rich, but I think it may be reasonably doubted whether these qualities are so fully developed in them . . . riches seem in so many cases to smother the manliness of their possessors, and their sympathies become not so much narrowed as, so to speak, stratified – they are reserved for the sufferings of their own class, and also the woes of those above them.

Plimsoll's granddaughter talks about her father's affinity, inherited from Samuel, with both the aristocrat and the working man. It was the well-to-do middle classes he found tiresome and self-absorbed.

With an instinct Plimsoll often displayed for issues that now seem ahead of his time, he wrote a paper in 1863 entitled 'Is it desirable to consolidate the existing railways of the United Kingdom into one system under government control?' His business, meanwhile, continued to thrive. It was not long before Plimsoll could afford a pretty house in a north London square.* It was here that Garibaldi came to call.

Plimsoll was among the multitude of Britons who admired General Giuseppe Garibaldi, the dashing, blue-jacketed rebel who had led volunteer forces of Italians to oust the Austrian oppressors from occupation of their country and thereby facilitated the unification of Italy. When Garibaldi visited London in 1864, to the acclamation of the throng, Plimsoll chaired his reception committee. Garibaldi's arch-enemy was the preposterously mustachioed Austrian Baron Haynau, whose Italian campaigns were notorious for their brutality; at the capture of Brescia, for instance, he had earned the name 'The Hyena of Brescia' for flogging women, and for the execution of twelve men in retaliation for the massacre of wounded Austrian soldiers in hospital. He was dismissed as dictator of Hungary in 1850 for excessive violence. That same year Haynau had come to London, where draymen from the Barclay and Perkins brewery in Southwark

* 9 Harrington Square, off Mornington Crescent, in Camden. Only one other side of the square still stands.

had set upon him and flogged him. Fourteen years later Garibaldi wanted to visit this admirable brewery. Plimsoll accompanied him there, and addressed the cheering employees. He was also among the dignitaries on the platform when Garibaldi appeared to a crowd of twenty-five thousand at Crystal Palace; and Plimsoll's six-year-old niece Edith Falding presented him with a bouquet of flowers. Garibaldi, who made a point of visiting Tennyson in the Isle of Wight, also called on Plimsolls' Camden home, where he was kind to little Edith, sitting her on his knee and putting her to bed.

Within seven years of his marriage and nine years of his bankruptcy, Plimsoll was able to buy a sixteenth-century mansion near Sheffield, Whiteley Wood Hall. It was his second home until his denunciations of shipowners unleashed a storm of litigation and Eliza decided it should be sold to cover legal fees in 1873.

There might have been a particular reason, other than her selflessness and practicality, why Eliza could bear to sacrifice this splendid residence. It was the scene of an unhappy memory. On 24 July 1865, attended by a midwife at Whiteley Wood Hall, Eliza gave birth to a child, also Eliza. The baby died at four hours old of 'imperfect respiration' and was buried at the nearby Fulwood Chapel. Eliza had waited seven years for a child, and she never bore another. Instead she adopted one. On 9 April 1866 when Plimsoll's twenty-two-year-old nephew, Thomas Joseph Hatch Plimsoll, died of typhus in Kentish Town, north London, he left a two-day-old baby fatherless. The family wisdom of later generations was that the mother died in childbirth, but the records tell a different story. Elizabeth Margaret Plimsoll (née Palmer), who registered the birth on 7 May, was twenty-one. Apparently she gave up her baby to her husband's uncle and aunt, who were better able than she to care for the child. In October, Plimsoll's great-niece Ellen Mary Ann Plimsoll, known as Nellie, was taken into his home as his daughter.

By Victorian standards, the Plimsoll family was small. Having only one child to care for gave Eliza time to further, and direct, her husband's aims. Whatever medical condition prevented her from bearing more children, her loss was others' gain.

By Plimsoll's own account, the epiphany that determined the direction of the rest of his life took place in 1864. In a landmark speech in Exeter Hall in London nine years later, Plimsoll recounted how that year he sailed from London to Redcar, on the Cleveland coast (where there is now a pub called the Plimsoll Line), in a ship that struck bad weather: 'Mrs Plimsoll had waited many hours for the long overdue ship on which I was a passenger. She feared the ship had been lost in the fierce storm and that I had been drowned. I myself was harrowed by the awful sight of four wrecked ships as the vessel struggled against giant waves.'

When Plimsoll arrived his wife flung her arms around him and sobbed: 'Oh Sam! Thank God you have been spared! Thank God! Thank God!' But four ships were lost that night. Eliza stood in a crowd of distraught women on the quayside at Redcar, and, as Plimsoll reported in his speech:

> I mingled my tears with hers, because I was thinking of those other women who had also spent a sleepless night and who would never see their husbands again. I was thinking of good and brave men who would never return home, and I resolved, deep down in my heart, as I stood on the sands of Redcar, to devote myself to this work. What was the difference between me and these poor, drowned sailors? Parliament had cared for my safety by sending me to sea in a ship which had been surveyed, while the sailors went to sea in any ship an owner liked to send them in . . . Since the morning when I stood in the sands at Redcar my wife and I have regarded everything we possess as held in trust for the sailor. If it is necessary, we will spend it for them as freely as our sailors would shed their blood for their country, if we got into trouble.

It helped the cause that the Plimsolls' marriage was a partnership, not a union in which a despotic patriarch held unchallengeable sway. Perhaps Samuel derived his respect for women from growing up with great admiration for his mother. He said when Priscilla Plimsoll died: 'To her indomitable spirit we owed, under God, everything. She was a wise, gracious and witty woman.' He was also close to his sisters, who were clever girls: Ellen and Priscilla set up a Ladies' School in Sheffield, a bold, if short-lived, venture. (It lasted a year.) Ellen, who continued to teach, was a particular friend and support to Samuel. If there is a criticism to be made of Plimsoll's attitude to women it might be that his sympathy bordered on the sentimental. But that might be said of his character in general.

A letter written to his adopted daughter in 1892, when she was twenty-six, offers rare first-hand evidence of his domestic side, and shows him also to have been an affectionate and unstuffy father, for all the impetuosity and zeal that characterised him. It also reveals Plimsoll's humour and his irreverence for Parliament. It is on inappropriate black-bordered House of Commons mourning notepaper and reads:

> My dear Nellie,
> It is quite your turn to have a letter. It will resemble proceedings in Parliament generally, that is to say – it will look to be very important indeed but will not have much in it.
>   Give my dearest love to everybody – All's well – Your loving father,
> Samuel Plimsoll.

Plimsoll's capacity to feel so strongly for families torn asunder by bereavement surely derived from his great fondness for his own. By various accounts, he felt the unhappiness of others with more than usual keenness. Once he had turned his attention to the plight of sailors he would be restless and distressed on stormy nights, imagining the agony of those in peril on the sea. Howell reported that he 'could not refer to some of the incidents of the [seafaring] life and its dangers without a sob in his throat and tears in his eyes'. Other people's pain hurt him. The Hon. Georgiana Cowper-Temple, who became a supporter, once wrote in her diary that 'he is made quite ill by all the terrible cases brought under his notice of cruelty & carelessness in Ship owners & suffering & loss of crews'. Once he left a church in the middle of a sermon on a windy day; asked if he was ill, he replied: 'Do you hear the wind? It is the shrieks of drowning men and their wives are trembling at home.' It was the intensity of Plimsoll's empathy that seems to have fuelled his fight through all obstacles: he could not understand how anyone could know of suffering and be indifferent to it, and he could not detach himself from it any more than we can ignore our own. He even cultivated his empathy: he once related a story of how, hearing that the soldiers of the Crimea had to sleep on the ground, he tried it himself, 'to bring my sympathies into touch with them'. (He found it conducive to early rising.)

Plimsoll's Exeter Hall account insisted that on the terrible night at Redcar he and his wife pledged themselves to the welfare of the seaman, but in fact there was no mention of the plight of sailors in his personal manifesto in 1865, when he first stood for Parliament. The ticket he then stood on was: the wide extension of the franchise; the secret ballot (which became law in 1872, helped through by Plimsoll's parliamentary vote); unrestricted free trade; non-intervention in foreign affairs – notably national conflicts in Europe; the repeal of the game laws (with their penalties for poachers); the emancipation of labour; financial reform; the abolition of church rates 'and all invidious religious tests' (which countered freedom of conscience); and the 'steady reform of the many abuses in most departments of the state' – in other words, the elimination of corruption and nepotism.

Eighteen sixty-five was a tough year to stand for election as a Liberal in Derby, judging by the experience of Plimsoll's fellow candidate Michael Bass. Bass was to speak in the town's lecture hall, but the crowd that waited for him there was a 'rough mob' including poachers determined to take revenge on Mr Bass for voting for the Night Poaching Act that banned the practice of their nocturnal livelihood. The troublemakers attacked Bass when he entered the room, and invaded his platform, pelting him with dead creatures: 'dead dogs, cats, rabbits etc were thrown in all directions'. The beleaguered candidate had to escape by the back entrance and was escorted to the Old King's Head Hotel by a 'strong body' of police, where he addressed his friendlier constituents.

Plimsoll was spared the bombardment with carcasses but his candidacy was still a rough ride. He was unpopular with the local satirical paper, the *Derby Ram*, which supported the Conservatives. The *Ram* lampooned Plimsoll mercilessly. 'Plumpsoul', it called him, and then 'Pumpswill'. It was offended that he did not live in Derby, although his country seat near Sheffield, Whiteley Wood Hall, was not far away.* The house was renamed 'White-lie Wood' in the *Ram*'s pages.

Plimsoll was mocked for using a Shakespearean quotation in a speech – which suggests that he had not yet learned the man-of-the-people manner he exercised so successfully in his heyday. The *Ram* satirised this with a *Macbeth* spoof in which Plimsoll appeared as Banquo's ghost. And it made fun of the incoherence of his speeches: one parody swiftly turns into gobbledygook. A decade or so later Plimsoll had a real rhetorical flair, and crowded halls would cheer him to the echo, but in 1865 he was not recognised as an orator. He was still learning how to relate to the public.

The *Derby Ram* declared that Plimsoll was a teetotaller, which was not true. He went on to defend sailors who were denigrated for drunkenness, saying that after all the hardships they endured at sea, who could blame them for taking a few drinks when they came ashore? The Derby electorate, despite the fact that Plimsoll's stance on poaching contrasted with Bass's, decided against him (he polled 693 votes of a total of some 3400 cast between four candidates). Perhaps the voters were protective of their tipple, or they shared the hostility of the *Ram* to such radical measures as the secret ballot – a licence, thought the paper, for deviousness and corruption. Whether in 1865 Plimsoll nurtured an as yet unpublicised wish to help the sailor, he was at any rate denied the opportunity to do so in Parliament.

The number of voters in Derby, as elsewhere, was soon to increase significantly. By 1866 agitation for electoral reform and enlargement of the franchise was increasing. One protest took place in London on 22 July, when a large number of banner-carrying demonstrators converged on Hyde Park, which the government, anticipating trouble, had closed pre-emptively. The demonstrators, with legal advice, made the gesture of testing their right to public assembly by asking politely under whose authority they were excluded, and then most of them moved on to hold a meeting in Trafalgar Square. Some stroppier lingerers knocked down half a

---

* Whiteley Wood Hall, near Fulwood, was built around 1570; it was demolished in 1956.

Plimsoll, with sideburns, satirised in the *Derby Ram* bowling to Michael Bass before the 1865 election – against the Tories Cox and Beale. (*British Library*)

mile of Hyde Park railings and there were minor skirmishes with police; the incident was branded the 'Hyde Park riot'. Plimsoll, then president of the Sheffield Reform League, wrote to George Howell, secretary of the National Reform League, offering to contribute to the fines incurred by demonstrators for the damage to the railings, on the principle that public places should not be closed to public gatherings. He paid £10 in fines and found in Howell a friend and ally for life. Shortly afterwards Plimsoll chaired a gathering of twelve thousand people in Sheffield that condemned the conduct of the government – and of the police who were said to have overreacted and injured the innocent – and was vociferous in support of reform.

In 1867 the Electoral Reform Act doubled the size of the franchise (which favoured the Liberals) and, despite the *Derby Ram*'s best efforts to keep him out again, Pumpswill entered Gladstone's House of Commons in 1868 as a Liberal MP with a majority of two thousand.

Ambition and altruism, in fine balance, were at Plimsoll's core. Here was a man who worked hard to become very wealthy, but then

was willing to spend much of his money in the interests of others –
as if riches did not matter to him. His own account was that making
money was a means to an end. In 1873 he told a Sheffield audience:
'I went to London 20 years ago with £18 10s in my pocket. That
was all I had in the world, and I worked hard to get rich, because no
man can do much unless he is rich.' It took independent means to be
a Member of Parliament, which was an unsalaried position until
1911; the average cost per candidate of standing for election in
England in the 1870s was about £3000. Plimsoll campaigned assid-
uously for a seat in government, persisting in a second attempt when
the first failed, but apparently sought his position principally in order
to serve – as if power, too, were not intrinsically gratifying to him.
He transformed himself from a poorly educated son of an excise-
man into a friend of the great, attending a levée of the Duke of
Edinburgh, visiting Gladstone at home and enlisting the cooperation
of lords and ladies, and yet his door was always open to the needy
and he was not afraid to make enemies of powerful men. He sought
the limelight and put himself forward, and yet he did so out of
a conviction that it was the way to help others. He was noisy and
insistent but never pompous or proud.

His detractors believed he sought personal glory; his supporters
praised his selflessness. Both his drive and his selflessness were perhaps products of his Protestantism: his talents were to be used, not
buried, but he was also his brother's keeper. Certainly his was not the
first or last political career in which self-advancement and philanthropy went hand in hand.

When he arrived in Parliament, opinion was harsher than it had
been at the Sheffield Liberal Club. In 1873 *Vanity Fair* described him
as a poor speaker. But Plimsoll had seen and heard men who moved
their audiences when they spoke. The brewery owner Thomas
Rawson had addressed a crowd in Sheffield's Paradise Square soon
after the Battle of Waterloo and demanded the vote for every adult
citizen, and was stirring enough for the local gentry to call him a
dangerous agitator. And the Reverend Robert Bayley, founder of the
People's College, was an eloquent opponent of the Corn Laws and
an idealist campaigning for a fairer society. As a young man Plimsoll
had mentors who were passionate and articulate about social justice.

He also grew up with the rhythms of biblical language and the rhetoric of sermons, which are a fine training for speeches (as Martin Luther King was to show). Later he had the opportunity to learn from hearing such political orators as Gladstone, Disraeli and Joseph Chamberlain.

Nonetheless, Plimsoll's first speech when he entered Parliament was not received as great oratory, nor did it concern sailors. It was a defence of trade unionism, and he spoke as second fiddle to his fellow Liberal newcomer Anthony Mundella, MP for Sheffield, who thought Plimsoll made a bad job of it and 'talked rot'. When *The Times* published brief profiles of 'Our New Members of Parliament' it mentioned Plimsoll's writings on the coal industry, but made no reference to any particular interest in shipping. He went on to vote on the big issues – in favour of the disestablishment of the Irish Church, for instance, and for the 1870 Education Act, which established School Boards to provide primary education for all – but in neither case did he make a noteworthy contribution to the debate. He was slow to make a name for himself in the House. His contributions were inmemorable.

The profile of the House of Commons had changed after the election of 1868, owing to an influx of members who had made money from manufacturing and trade. The extension by stages of the franchise was enabling the wealthy middle class to enter the ruling class. *The Times* called the new intake 'an ugly rush', 'sent up from the lowest depth of democracy', composed as it was of the *nouveaux riches*, whom it called 'the very genteelest, richest, grandest, most exclusive, best-to-do band of robbers we ever saw'. *The Times* did not believe that the increased franchise had done anything to make the government more radical: 'The people have surged, the ground below has heaved, the mountains have laboured, and the result is a Parliament, if anything, more respectable, more staid, and more elderly, as we expect, in its ways than the last.' Making their debut in the House with Samuel Plimsoll were such men as Mundella, the half-Italian Nottingham hosier, the newsagent W(illiam) H(enry) Smith, replacing the economist John Stuart Mill as the representative for Westminster, and Alfred Illingworth, carpet maker, the member for Knaresborough. There were also self-made shipowners joining the men of property who had invested their inherited wealth in shipping. The election of Plimsoll, a coal merchant with no blue blood, was characteristic of this Parliament.

Like a scholarship boy at a public school, Plimsoll was one of the new bugs who didn't quite have the right pedigree. He was from a family, and from a class, that had no track record in government. Perhaps he was looking for a way to command attention and earn respect. He had the disposition of a rebel, but it seemed he had not yet found a cause.

In December 1868 Plimsoll spoke at the Fulwood Chapel in Sheffield, where, two and a half years earlier, his child had been buried. In a place that was sacred to him, he announced: 'I have just been elected to Parliament. This is my opportunity to help those in peril on the sea. I shall do all in my power to put an end to the unseaworthy ships owned by the greedy and the unscrupulous.'

Nevertheless, it took him time to bring up this subject in the House. When a Merchant Shipping Bill was introduced on 9 August 1869, with the aim of giving sailors the right to an automatic survey, it slipped away without being adopted and without a contribution from Plimsoll.

By this time Plimsoll's former role as a defender of miners had become complicated. As relations between owners and men deteriorated in the twelve years after his marriage, it grew increasingly difficult for Plimsoll to take sides, since his father-in-law was a mine-owner. In 1869 things reached a head when eight hundred miners were locked out of the pits at Newton, Chambers and Co. for demanding higher wages, and John Chambers refused to see a deputation from the Miners' Association. Policemen and troops became involved, and the stress of this conflict led to Chambers's death at the age of sixty-four on 8 June of that year. Plimsoll was then in Parliament and his allegiances were divided. All his instincts were on the side of working men, but his relationship with the miners was soured by this death. His sympathies, it seemed, might be better concentrated in another direction. After 1869 he needed other representatives of the deserving poor to defend.

Plimsoll's first cause as an MP, in 1870, was a less than vital matter. He took pity on the plight of second- and third-class railway pas-

sengers, whose carriages were inadequately heated. He proposed, in
the Railway Travelling Bill, the supply of stone hot-water bottles as
foot warmers. The simple cast of mind that had made Plimsoll a millionaire did not go down well in the House. He was mocked for
wasting time on a triviality, and although he tried to strengthen his
case by arguing that his measure could be a significant boost to the
profits of the rail industry, his bill was refused a second reading by a
majority of thirty-two MPs – all of them no doubt accustomed to
travelling first class.

In his old age Plimsoll took up the cause of conditions, for animals and men, on cattle ships, and proposed a way of preserving the
colour of transported meat by coating it with fat, which could
eventually be wiped off, because deterioration in colour was the
strongest argument for shipping live animals instead of carcasses.
This idea didn't catch on, but was typical of his approach: that a
layer of grease was all it would take to circumvent misery. A porous
bag, a grid, a coat of enamel, a hot-water bottle, a gap between the
trees, a sheet of paper, a layer of grease: these were the means by
which Samuel Plimsoll aspired to change the world for the better.
It is not surprising that such a man set out to save lives with a thin
line of paint.

But it was not until 1870, a month after his meeting with a
Newcastle shipowner called James Hall, that Plimsoll entered the
fray as 'the sailor's friend'.

While Samuel Plimsoll was concentrating his attention on the
issue of suffrage, as president of the Sheffield Reform League, there
were others who were considering the rising loss of life at sea. One
documented case in particular triggered a feeling that something
must be done. In March 1867 the Utopia was loaded at the
Brunswick Dock in Liverpool for a voyage to Bombay. In the dock,
the ship ran aground and was damaged. The harbour surveyor
warned that it might be safely immersed only up to twenty feet six
inches, and marked the limit on the side. But the ship was loaded six
inches deeper than the load line indicated. Then in the Wellington
Docks another 120 tons of coke were taken on board. Only five feet
of the sides were above water, and the ship was still taking in cargo.
The captain, by the name of Lean, protested to the cargo owner,

who ignored him. Lean resigned. He was replaced by a Captain Dickie, who also objected and was sent a bullying letter by the shipping agent: 'I am very much surprised to hear that you are making difficulties about going in the Utopia, and I must inform you that if, after I have recommended you to the owner, you do not go in the vessel, I will take care you never get any employment in a ship out of Liverpool, if I have power to prevent you . . .'

On the morning of Sunday 10 March 1867 the *Utopia* was towed out to sea, overloaded, undermanned and leaking. When the tug left there was already more than three feet of water in the hold, and the pumps worked continuously for three days, at which point Captain Dickie and the crew took to the long boat. They were just in time before the ship sank. It was still a very long way from India.

The magazine of the Royal National Lifeboat Institution, *The Lifeboat*, reported indignantly on the case of the *Utopia* in July 1867, and recommended two remedies for the 'discreditable state of things': an independent inspection of ships and a 'thin white line' showing the legally binding level to which they should be loaded. No one did anything about it.

But there were those who felt someone should. Two men who crossed Samuel Plimsoll's path ignited the flame that he carried on. One was the wealthy Newcastle shipowner James Hall, who had spent his life in shipping and knew its technology in a way that Plimsoll never did. He was a carver's son who left school at eleven, but turned himself into a man of refined tastes and a collector of art, after travelling in his youth on the Continent and living and working in Marseille at the time of the 1848 revolution. Hall, who had a patrician look about him with his high forehead and Roman nose, was a respected man, a JP and a prominent figure in the Newcastle Chamber of Commerce. He knew what it was to have influence in his world. He had organised a petition, for instance, that had saved a historic tower in Newcastle from demolition. In his later years he introduced training ships to turn street children into sailors, founded Industrial Dwellings for workers and extended the power of County Courts to cases previously dealt with by the Admiralty. His authority in shipping matters was never questioned.

He may well have hoped to make an impact with an idea he had come up with to improve safety at sea: the idea of a fixed load line.

In November 1867, when he was an established and prosperous shipowner and a director of two marine insurance companies, Hall wrote to the *Shipping Gazette* arguing that legislation was 'urgently required' to remedy 'the unseaworthy condition in which many vessels, frequently overladen besides, are sent on their voyages'. He recommended a Government Inspector of Shipping at each of the major ports, to grant or withhold a certificate of seaworthiness. He also advocated an inquiry by a Local Marine Board into any loss that could not be satisfactorily accounted for. The article was repeated in the *Newcastle Daily Chronicle*, where it met with approval in the leader columns. But the approbation of a local newspaper was not enough to change anything.

Hall wrote again to *The Times* in 1868 to tell the story of a ship nearly thirty years old that had sailed the previous July for Shanghai. On the day before departure, an official of the Lloyd's Salvage Association found the ship was letting in water. Its rigging was also in a bad state. The owner was notified, but on the following morning the ship set sail, with the rigging in the same condition. By the time it reached the open sea it had two feet of water in the hold, although the crew had been at the pumps since the night before. By noon on the third day this had risen to seven and a half feet of water. When another vessel hove into view, the crew forsook the pumps and made their escape from the sinking ship.

On 15 December 1869 Hall wrote once more to *The Times*, saying that although insurance claims were increasing in the north-east for losses 'some of which are directly traceable to the effects of over-loading', he could not find 'any disposition whatever to put a stop to such a state of things'. He went on:

Every practical authority I have consulted admits that a vessel should have a certain 'side' or 'freeboard', and yet we have spar-decked ships [those with another deck built above the main deck] . . . sent to sea immersed some feet above the main deck and foundering on the voyage. Underwriters and marine insurance companies are charging increased premiums to meet the increased risk, and thus the merchant who ships his cargo and the shipowner who does not overload his vessel are paying for those who do . . . The first duty of a Government is to protect the lives of its subjects, and to every other class of workmen, excepting sailors, this duty is discharged.

A load line marking the extreme limit of flotation was the answer, and it was 'in the interest of humanity, not less than the duty of Government' to establish one.

In March 1870 the Associated Chambers of Commerce of fourteen ports petitioned the government for a Merchant Shipping and Navigation Bill,* with James Hall one of its proponents. Plimsoll showed Eliza a copy of the petition and she, the catalyst at every significant point of Plimsoll's campaign, encouraged him to meet the man behind it. Plimsoll attended a meeting at Westminster Hall in London at which Hall proposed resolutions on the inspection of ships: a load line, surveys of unseaworthy ships and the training of seamen. When Plimsoll heard Hall speak he lost no time in arranging to visit him at his office in Newcastle, recognising that the importance of the issue warranted a special train journey.

All the measures later promoted in Plimsoll's campaign for safety at sea were consistent with Hall's recommendations, which Hall articulated clearly and with authority. Plimsoll acknowledged his debt to Hall, quoted him in his publications and invited him to speak at his meetings (and, on at least one occasion, Hall accepted).

Hall's biographer and lifelong friend William Hayward thought Plimsoll a publicity hunter rather than a philanthropist, who stole from Hall the credit for instigating the load line; Plimsoll was, after all, only its promoter. Hayward asserts that Plimsoll declared, when he first discussed the sailors' plight with Hall: 'How will that tell in the House of Commons!' Certainly Plimsoll's approach was more personal than Hall's. Plimsoll used his own experience as a rhetorical device. He told his readers and listeners that, for instance, he had known poverty and therefore understood hardship. He set out to strengthen his case by giving himself sympathetic credentials, and in

* The Merchant Shipping and Navigation Act was passed in 1871 without fulfilling James Hall's hopes.

the process he constructed for himself a popular image. Hall, a man more moderate and less emotional than Plimsoll, was also less of a showman. Whether the showmanship benefited the cause in the long run has ever since been the subject of debate.

Hayward also believed that Plimsoll impeded the legislation he aspired to bring about: that by demonising shipowners and drawing up lines of battle between them and the sailors, by prompting libel actions and by turning the need for shipping reform into a national drama he slowed down a process that would have been speedier without his interference. But in the beginning Hall was delighted that Plimsoll promised to take his arguments, including his proposal for a load line, into the House of Commons. He was glad to find a man offering to use his political influence to precipitate their common ends.

There is a third individual credited with instigating the load line campaign: the editor of the *Sheffield Daily Telegraph*, William Christopher Leng, who was also particularly concerned with the rising loss of life at sea. Eliza Plimsoll read a report he wrote in his newspaper in November 1869, and urged her husband to contact the author. Leng later wrote of this meeting: 'I felt like one who was groping in the dark for the hearts of mankind's humaner souls. No response. My voice had been as the voice of one crying in the wilderness. But at last it fell upon the pained ear of one who united a keen sympathy, a quick intelligence, abundant leisure, a loving spirit, a position of absolute independence and immense moral courage.'

W. C. Leng was already a public figure and a local hero with a history of speaking out in defence of the underdog. In the 1850s he had campaigned for slum clearance, writing anonymously for the *Hull Free Press*. (His disgust at the self-interest of the Liberal MPs of Hull in this matter eventually made him transfer his allegiance to the Tories.) He had been a vociferous supporter of the North in the American Civil War, writing in the pages of the *Dundee Advertiser*, which was owned by William Leng's brother John. When he and Plimsoll met, he had recently shown his mettle by denouncing the practice of 'rattening', or the intimidation of non-union labour by trade unionists, as led in Sheffield by William Broadhead, whose violent methods included paying men to commit murder. Leng's condemnation persuaded the government to appoint a Royal Commission of Inquiry into trade unions; chaired by the Earl of Derby, it upheld Leng's allegations and had an impact on later legislation. Plimsoll, addressing fifteen thousand colliers in Barnsley in September 1867, called Broadhead and his associates 'as cruel a set of cowards as ever cheated the gallows', though he believed the union movement should not be condemned in general for the sins of a few. Trade unions were necessary to the working man, since 'so long as human nature was human nature the weak would be obliged to unite themselves against the strong'.

The Victorians had a tradition of expressing their gratitude to public men by collecting money by subscription and then making a present to the person they admired. For his stand about intimidation by trade unions Leng was in 1868 the recipient of one of these gestures. Grateful men 'of all political opinions' clubbed together to present him with a purse of six hundred guineas and a portrait of himself by H. F. Crighton, an artist who happened to be a fellow member of the Sheffield Town Council. Plimsoll was to receive similar tributes for his activism.

For more than a decade Leng had been writing about the evil of overloaded and unseaworthy ships. As early as 1856 in the *Hull Free Press* he wrote: 'If you have ever stood at the Humber-dock gate and seen a long, low steam boat, narrow as a racing gig, deep as a sand barge and wall-sided as a house, waddle up with rocking stagger on her way out, you will have wondered whether it was possible that that cranky, rolling, deck-piled, half-handed vessel could possibly be expected to go to sea in that condition.' (This echoes descriptions of the *London*, ten years later, which was a long, narrow steamboat built for speed, described by witnesses both as 'cranky' and 'deep as a barge'.)

A week after Eliza read Leng's article about loss of life at sea, a meeting was held in Sheffield Town Hall to relieve the distress of fishermen's widows in the Yorkshire fishing ports of Scarborough and Filey. Plimsoll attended, donated a generous sum and introduced himself afterwards to Leng. Like Hall, Leng needed a champion to bring the wrongs he deplored to the attention of the world.

Plimsoll was, said Leng, 'chafed at heart that such things should be and no man interfere. With all his heart and soul and strength, he flung himself into the tremendous task – the task of securing justice for our sailors. Nothing daunted him. His life, his fortune, his whole being were henceforth dedicated to the material salvation of our sailors.'

Principled Mr Leng was, as it happens, the original of a fictional character expressively called Mr Holdfast, who appeared in *Put Yourself in His Place* (1870), a novel based on William Broadhead's disreputable career and written by the dramatist and novelist Charles Reade, who enjoyed a greater reputation in his time than he does today. (His death warranted a marble plaque in the Crypt of St Paul's.)

Reade, whose brother Bill was a sailor, was another who had a hand in paving the way for Plimsoll's campaign. He wrote a stirring novel of romance and adventure called *Foul Play*, published in 1868, which recognised the dramatic possibilities of insurance fraud. The idea that shipowners might not care who drowned to make them rich was current before Plimsoll promoted preventative measures.

Foul Play appeared in instalments in the literary magazine *Once a Week*, from January to June 1868, with illustrations by George du Maurier, and was the fifth of Reade's fourteen novels. *The Times* singled it out as one of the 'most remarkable' novels of the year, suggesting it might be among the few titles that would be 'permanently remembered'. After its serialisation it also achieved 'a wide popularity in its three-volume form', its success helping Reade to buy a house in Knightsbridge in 1869. Reade belonged to that strain of Victorian novelists, including Dickens and Mrs Gaskell, who took up issues of social injustice in fiction. He had already been in trouble for his espousal of issues. In 1865 at the Princess's Theatre, the drama critic of the *Morning Advertiser*, Frederick Guest Tomlins, had been so dismayed by a stage adaptation of Reade's novel *It's Never Too Late to Mend* (1856), which attacked conditions in prisons, that he rose from the stalls on the first night to protest aloud against its 'brutal realism'. A comment made of Dickens in the *Edinburgh* Review in 1838 could as well have applied to Reade: 'The tendency of his writing is to make us practically benevolent – to excite our sympathy in behalf of the aggrieved and suffering in all classes; and especially in those who are most removed from observation.' George Orwell was a fan, describing Reade as 'a middle class gentleman with a little more conscience than most'. He said, eccentrically, that he would back *Foul Play* and Reade's two other reformist novels 'to outlive the entire works of Meredith and George Eliot'.

Reade described himself as a 'writer of romances founded on facts'. Whether or not his fiction mirrored real events, it promoted an idea of villainy and its victims, and, in *Foul Play*, a picture of avaricious shipowning rogues exposed by resolute heroes which Plimsoll could make use of. Just as newspaper stories about cruelty in workhouses and factories resonated for audiences who knew Mr Bumble and Mr Gradgrind, it helped that when Plimsoll declaimed against shipowners his audiences were already familiar with Reade's types. If the types happened to be exaggerations, it served the political ends of both the fiction and the propaganda.

The villain of *Foul Play*, Arthur Wardlaw, is a young Liverpool merchant and shipowner who deliberately has a ship scuttled and lies about the insurance value of its contents, as a cargo of gold is secretly swapped with a cargo of copper coins, or 'specie'. This altogether despicable individual also lets a friend, a young clergyman called Robert Penfold, take the rap for a forgery of his own and be deported to Australia. The tension increases when the fraudster and his former friend become rivals in love, and Helen, the girl they both adore, unwittingly boards the ship that is destined for scuttling. The good guy, in disguise, follows her. The ship goes down and, after horrors in an open boat, Robert and Helen find themselves the only survivors on an idyllic desert island where there is plenty of scope for a decent chap to prove his worth and a young girl to lose her heart. (As Orwell put it: 'It is only a month or two before this wonderful clergyman has got the desert island running like a West End hotel.') There is a finale of detective work, name-clearing and the exposure of the miscreant, who goes mad when he loses the girl, his fortune and his reputation, and ends up in an asylum forging letters from Napoleon. It is a satisfactory fate for a man who lets others drown as a means of paying his debts. Just as *Oliver Twist* shaped attitudes to workhouses, *Foul Play* stirred a sense of indignation against the real-life Arthur Wardlaws.

Foul Play reached a wider audience still as a result of a stage version, on which Reade collaborated with the celebrated farceur Dion Boucicault. The play, which opened on 28 May 1868 at the Holborn Theatre in London, unfolded the drama in broader strokes than in the novel, with more and lower laughs, and put yet more emphasis on the insurance scam. On stage Arthur Wardlaw declared: 'There's not a day passes that ships are not scuttled on dry land! and they go down with a precious freight and many lives! The authors of the scheme escape, as we have, with the plunder.' Having established that Wardlaw was merely one example of a widespread villainy, the play finished him off completely: he was exposed, went mad and dropped down dead, all within the last few lines.

The dramatisation of *Foul Play* has been described as 'more or less a failure', though the play also toured, to Leeds and Manchester, and the story was sufficiently widely known, and the run sufficiently long, for *Punch* to run a cartoon on 26 September 1868 that referred to the romantic scene in the play, set in a shell-lined cave, in which Robert and Helen declared their love for each other.* Just as the scene in the cave must have caught the romantic imagination of the public, so could its theme of a shipowner's fraud and avarice have stoked a general indignation. *Foul Play* was the subject of a small controversy when a satirical magazine, *The Mask: A Humorous and Fantastic Review of the Month* (February 1868), accused Reade of stealing the plot from a French play, *Le Portefeuille Rouge*, also involving a couple on a lost ship. This Reade indignantly denied in an essay entitled 'The Sham-Sample Swindle' in *Once a Week*. As Reade pointed out, the French play (which he had not read when he wrote his novel) did not contain the 'fundamental incident' of 'the scuttling of a ship to defraud the underwriters', and he threatened to sue for libel. *The Mask* retaliated with a picture of him as 'a hideous gorilla in knickerbockers'.

---

* In the cartoon a young girl and her amorous cousin are sitting in a cave at the seaside with mother close by as sabotaging chaperone. '"Oh I say, Cousin George," says Helen (19), "If it wasn't for 'Ma sitting there, wouldn't this be like that beautiful cave in Charles Reade's Foul Play, where you know—" Cousin George (ditto) was just going to say that the same idea had struck him, &c., when 'Ma rose, and called out it was time to go home to tea!'

The popularity of the stage production also warranted a parody, which Reade thought 'a desecration', called *Fowl Play, or A Story of Chikkin Hazard: An Entirely New and Original Burlesque* by F. C. Burnand, first produced a few weeks after *Foul Play* in a theatre only walking distance away. On 20 June 1868 the spoof was staged at the New Queen's Theatre, Long Acre, with Wardlaw renamed Waddler, rhyming text like a pantomime, music from Offenbach, silly parodies of popular songs and lots of bad puns: 'It was our bullion and you're bullyin' us.' The actors were extravagantly dressed with 'very peculiar hats' and suits for Robert and Helen made of seaweed and shells, though hers, according to the costume notes, was fashionably cut. The burlesque ended with a rhyming acknowledgement of its debt to both the book and the drama. And Waddler got his comeuppance by falling backwards out of a window and crashing into the conservatory.

This happy ending was, for Plimsoll's campaign, a happy beginning.

2

THE POWER GAME

Plimsoll's campaign was to be a milestone in the progress of people power, but he was by no means the first to put extra-parliamentary pressure on government. The history of the nineteenth century is partly the history of a rising tide of popular agitation for reform. The century began with violent demonstrations, violently repressed: with Luddites fighting the advance of industrial technology and, for instance, the execution in 1812 of four people, including a twelve-year-old boy, for setting fire to factories near Bolton. (The boy wept for his mother on the scaffold.) Even peaceful protest was mercilessly subdued. In 1819 a crowd of fifty thousand men, women and children gathered in their Sunday best at St Peter's Fields in Manchester to press for reform and the repeal of the Corn Laws; a mounted militia charged the demonstrators, cutting them down with sabres and trampling them under the hoofs of the horses. Eleven were killed and four hundred injured, one man having the nose sliced off his face. This event, the Peterloo Massacre, inspired Shelley's angry poem *The Mask of Anarchy* ('I met murder on the way/He had a face like Castlereagh'*), which could not be published until after the poet's death, in 1832.

---

* The then Foreign Secretary.

This was, as it happened, the year of the first, grudging Parliamentary Reform Act, which doubled the national franchise to some 800,000 electors, but still left all women and most men, including the entire working class, without a vote. Plimsoll grew up through the demonstrations of the Chartist movement, named after its 'People's Six Point Charter', which called for: universal manhood suffrage, annual parliaments, payment of MPs, vote by ballot, equal electoral districts and the abolition of the £300 property qualification for MPs.

When Plimsoll was fifteen he saw Chartists march through the streets of Sheffield, not only agitating for electoral reform, but protesting against low wages and unemployment. He was shocked to find that his local church did not support them; it disapproved not of their aims but of their belligerent methods. Chartism was rife at a time when there was turbulent revolt on the Continent: in France a republic was established, and King Louis-Philippe was forced to flee. It was feared that Britain teetered on the edge of the civil unrest that shed blood in other European countries, and the Chartist agitation caused profound alarm. When a mass meeting was planned on Kennington Common in London in 1848, 150,000 citizens were recruited as special constables, with Louis Napoleon Bonaparte in command of the military forces, and for a day London was under something like martial law. The movement died after Chartist proposals were turned down by Parliament three times: in 1839, 1842 and in 1848, when a petition to Parliament that was claimed to contain nearly six million signatures proved to contain fewer than two million and include forgeries.

But, by degrees, nineteenth-century legislation began to take account of the existence of people outside the ruling class and include humanitarian measures, so Britain experienced 'a slow revolution' instead of a sudden one. Over the century, for instance, a series of Acts of Parliament progressively limited child labour. One such was the 1833 Factory Act, which appointed factory inspectors and decreed that children between nine and thirteen years old were not to work more than nine hours a day in textile factories. Gradually, the Industrial Revolution was finding its conscience, although some reforms were misguided. The 1834 Poor Act looked like welfare reform, but made the mistake of establishing work-houses instead of offering help to the poor in their own homes, enshrining the terrible philosophy that workhouses should be fearsome places in order to discourage the poor from resorting to them.

Chartism failed partly because its methods were violent, although some of its ends were achieved after its demise. But Plimsoll also grew up seeing instances of peaceful public demands that succeeded. One notable example was the agitation against the Corn Laws. These protectionist measures were designed to safeguard British agriculture, but forced up the price of bread and brought about decades of hunger for the poor. When Prime Minister Sir Robert Peel wished to repeal the laws and open British ports to free trade but met opposition in his own Cabinet (from the Duke of Wellington, Lord Stanley and others), it was pressure 'by petition, by address and by remonstrance' that helped to bring about the desired legislation in January 1846.

There is no doubt that the Anti-Corn Law League, founded in 1839 and orchestrated by Richard Cobden, was a model and an inspiration to Plimsoll. Cobden and his associate John Bright, one of the outstanding orators of the age, toured the country in a national campaign. Bright, imbued by his Quaker upbringing with a passionate belief in equality, attacked the selfishness of privilege and urged the working and middle classes to unite in the cause of free trade and food the poor could afford. Both Cobden and Bright also became Members of Parliament, Cobden for Stockport in 1841, and Bright for Durham in 1843. Their tone of moral righteousness and their strategy – of tireless countrywide speech-making and tenacious persistence in the House – were exactly what Plimsoll emulated. The Anti-Corn Law League was also well funded and centralised; Plimsoll's campaign used his wealth to copy this too. A chest containing Plimsoll's correspondence with Cobden and Bright was destroyed by fire in 1915.

Richard Cobden lost his seat in 1857, was re-elected for Rochdale in 1859, and died of bronchitis in 1865. Plimsoll so admired him that some twenty years later he called his son (by his second marriage)

Samuel Richard Cobden Plimsoll.* Meanwhile it was partly thanks to Bright that Plimsoll entered Parliament at all: Bright was instrumental in securing the 1867 Reform Act. And when Plimsoll became an MP Bright was in the House, where he had represented Birmingham since 1857.

By then social reform had achieved some momentum. The concept of health and safety had been introduced, at least in a rudimentary way, in mines and factories. There was a feeling that the powerful had a duty to the powerless and a recognition that other working men were already protected by law in ways that sailors were not. There was legislative progress in religious freedom, social welfare, primary education. But all the time two currents worked against each other – the tide of philanthropic endeavour and the conservative resistance to it. None of the reforms was easily won.

By 1868 another of Plimsoll's heroes, the Earl of Shaftesbury, had already had bitter experience of the intransigence of both Houses when it came to helping the neediest members of society. He had been the driving force, against opposition, behind several acts that improved conditions in lunatic asylums. He had also fought for twelve years to secure the passing of his amendment to the Ten Hours Bill, limiting the employment of children under eighteen in the mills and the mines to ten hours a day. He, like Plimsoll, was driven to repeat himself. 'I have long been regarded as a monomaniac on these subjects,' he said in a speech about child labour in 1844. Shaftesbury's eventual success owed much to public outrage once the stories of suffering were told, and to having the newspapers on his side – and nothing to coal owners in the House of Lords.

When Plimsoll entered Parliament there was a Bill before the House of Commons which would give the Board of Trade the power to detain any ship it believed to be unseaworthy and offer sailors who refused to sail on the grounds of unseaworthiness the right to a survey at the taxpayer's cost. It would make it a misdemeanour subject to criminal prosecution for owners to send unseaworthy ships to sea. But the Merchant Shipping Code

* Samuel Jr was known all his life as 'Richard', or 'Dick' to his family.

Consolidation Bill had 696 clauses. It was not passed in 1869 when it was first presented on 9 August by George John Shaw-Lefevre,* parliamentary secretary of the Board of Trade (1869-71), because there were continual adjustments to be made. It was overloaded, and so it sank.

James Hall is one of the few who bothered to examine all 696 of this Bill's clauses and to consider its shortcomings – notably its failure to prevent overloaded ships going to sea. On 13 April 1870, honouring the promise he had made to the Derby electorate in the Fulwood Chapel in 1868, and to Hall only weeks before, Plimsoll moved the insertion of three clauses into the Merchant Shipping Bill that would provide for an inspection of all ships, a maximum load line and a prohibition on insuring any ship for more than two-thirds of its value.

At the same time Sir John Pakington, Conservative MP for Droitwich, president of the Institute of Naval Architects and former First Lord of the Admiralty,† moved a motion to appoint a commission of inquiry to look into the loss of life at sea and determine what changes could be made to stowage and overloading 'with a view to the greater safety of property and passengers'.

Prolonged newspaper coverage ensued. W. C. Leng was quick to publicise Plimsoll's proposal and show his support in the pages of the *Sheffield Daily Telegraph*. The press at large began to criticise Parliament's delays, as Plimsoll's measures were deferred and Pakington's call for a commission failed. For months the *Pall Mall Gazette* covered the issues, waxing Darwinian on 5 May, for instance: 'it would seem that in the desperate struggle for life the weaker are sacrificed to the necessities of the stronger, and the seaman, who has to accept terms, dies for the sustenance of the capitalist who imposes them.' There was heated correspondence in papers from the *Shipping and Mercantile Gazette* to the *Suffolk Gazette* and the *Sheffield and Rotherham Independent*. Murmurs of discontent began to spread as a series of disasters at sea in 1870 intensified public pressure for legislation.

---

* Liberal MP for Reading, Postmaster General from 1880 and later Lord Eversley.
† First Lord of the Admiralty 1858-9 and Secretary of State for War 1867-8.

Early in 1870 there were two shipwrecks in particular that aroused comment: of the *City of Boston* and the *Sea Queen*. The *City of Boston* was considered by experts to have been 'dangerously overloaded'. It left port on 28 January 1870 with 177 passengers and crew, and was never heard of again. Some months later Sir John Pakington queried the state of its loading in the House. The question drew from Shaw-Lefevre the avowal that the Board 'did not intend to introduce any legislation in the Merchant Shipping Bill for the repression of the perilous or even criminal practice of overloading, nor to appoint a commission of inquiry'. This was despite the fact that the inquiry into the *London* had been followed by a strong report from the Institute of Naval Architects in favour of some legislation.

Ultimately, an inquiry cleared the owners of the *City of Boston* of the 'imputation of having endangered their vessel, as was unfortunately the case a few years ago with the *London*, by an excess of cargo'* and revealed that the ship was uninsured to the extent of £50,000.

Then *The Times* reported on 15 February 1870: 'During the gale on Sunday night rockets were seen east of the Cockle Lightship, supposed to be fired from a distressed vessel, but no assistance could be rendered. Yesterday morning a quantity of wreck was picked up on Caistor Beach, among which was the sternboard of a boat marked "Sea Queen, London". It is feared a vessel bearing that name and her crew have been lost.'

The *Sea Queen* was a coal-carrying steamer two days out of Newcastle, on its way to Málaga. The ship had been recently lengthened, and it sailed, against the better judgement of several experts, without a mainmast. As it left the Tyne 'some very strong remarks were made by the people on the shore as she proceeded to sea on the impropriety of a vessel so deeply laden as she was venturing into such uncertain weather as then prevailed'. It went down near Yarmouth and the crew of nineteen all died.

A five-day inquiry by the Board of Trade was held in Newcastle

---

* This is an official change of heart about the *London*. Its own inquiry cleared it of the charge of overloading.

in April. Its conclusions are puzzling. Evidence presented included the following assertions. That the freeboard (the side between the waterline and the deck) was some eight to twelve inches. That there were twenty-five tons of coal left over from the *Sea Queen*'s previous voyage, before the next outward journey's loading began. That the bill of lading specified eight hundred tons of coal to be put on board, but other documents variously suggested that in fact 916 or even 952 tons were loaded. That George Hudson, third engineer on the *Sea Queen*'s previous voyage, had said: 'I left the ship because, owing to overloading . . . my situation on board was uncomfortable; I was afraid she would be loaded in the same manner on the next voyage, and left her.' He also said that 'the ship was a crank ship and the water came in, and my berth was always wet . . . on the voyage from Danzig to the Black Sea . . . I did think she was likely to go [by which he seems to mean sink] in consequence of overlading; she did not deliver her grain in perfect order, a great deal of it was wet . . .'

Courageously, three widows and a sister of men from the *Sea Queen* gave evidence to the inquiry. The first of these was Elizabeth Wells, widow of the captain, Joseph Benjamin Wells. She declared that the chief officer (Mr Kitchen) had, in her presence, given the second mate (Mr Nanowmore) instructions to load to a certain mark on the side. But he forgot which mark had been indicated and asked Mrs Wells which it was – Nanowmore knew no more. She replied that 'it was not my business, nor did I remember, but he had better put her down too little rather than too much'. When Mr Kitchen returned, he said the second mate had put more on board than he was instructed to. 'I said,' reported Mrs Wells, 'if anything happened I would blame Nanowmore for that.' She had remarked to the owner, Mr Seymour, how deep the ship was in the water, but he had replied that 'she was not deeper than she was when she left London last time'. When Mrs Wells left the ship she took one step up from the deck to the boat that lay alongside.

(Mr Seymour had occasion to speak to Mrs Wells again; he gave her a package of letters from her husband which had been retrieved from the sea.)

The steward's widow, Ellen Taylor, told how her husband thought it 'shameful' for the ship to go out in this state. 'Why don't you leave her if you think there is danger?' said Ellen, but her husband had replied, 'I daresay we shall be all right.' Jane Ritchie, widow of the cook, reported that 'My husband made a remark about her being so deeply loaded and so long and narrow. When I saw he was so low spirited, I asked him to back out and leave her; he said he would have done so had it not been for my sake and my two children. He said he would get two months' imprisonment. He had been very unwell for two and a half years, and did not wish to leave them without food . . .' Mary Ross, sister of seaman John James McKeddy, tried to urge her brother not to go, 'but he said he had signed articles; that he would not disgrace himself; if he did not go he would get three months' imprisonment, which would forfeit his [second mate's] certificate'.

Other witnesses corroborated the women's testimony: one sailor had told his father that 'he could wash his hands over the gunwale' and a Tyne Dock pilot stepped off the jetty on to the *Sea Queen*'s upper deck.

After these and similar representations, on the fourth and fifth day of the inquiry the officials and owners were heard. London shipbroker William Westcott said, 'I would treat the opinion of persons who called her a coffin as nothing.' Speculative evidence was given, though with plenty of detail of weights and measures, of the strength and capacity of the ship. It caused the chief surveyor of the Board of Trade, Mr Galloway, to doubt the opinions of the bereaved and the sailors and the casual observers, and to conclude that the ship was 'not too deeply laden'. But he did agree that 'considering the dimensions of the vessel, the section through the cargo ports was not of sufficient strength to enable the ship to carry so large a cargo of dead weight in safety . . . As she was, such a weight was decidedly a source of danger.' Bizarrely, Mr Galloway argued that this proved 'the absurdity' of government interference with loading – because everything depended on the particular construction, material and workmanship of each ship.

It was against this backdrop that Plimsoll took up the case again in the House in July 1870, arguing that, since five hundred lives were lost unnecessarily at sea every winter, his Bill for a load line and a survey should be swiftly passed. If Parliament refused, 'then these men must die'. It was then that the opposition revealed itself, and it became clear that Plimsoll was not to have an easy time. Some disguised their delaying tactics as support, by proposing alternative measures that did not have any structure for implementation. Others claimed that Plimsoll had 'greatly exaggerated the situation'. The following men may go down in history as would-be saboteurs of a simple life-saving measure: the naval architect and shipowner Joseph D. A. Samuda (who later came round to supporting Plimsoll) and other shipowning MPs (who did not), Thomas Eustace Smith and Charles Morgan Norwood, representing Tynemouth and Hull respectively, as well as Shaw-Lefevre, who regretted that he was unable to proceed with the Merchant Shipping Bill and urged the House to 'questions of greater magnitude'.

Thus began a stalling game in Parliament that was to go on for years. On 4 August Plimsoll pleaded again for immediate legislation. The shipowning MPs Thomas Eustace Smith, Edward Temperley Gourley, MP for Sunderland, and Samuel Graves of Liverpool contended again that Plimsoll had 'taken an exaggerated view of the facts'. Shaw-Lefevre reminded the House that the consolidating Mercantile Marine Bill, so long in preparation, would make sending an unseaworthy ship to sea a misdemeanour. Plimsoll was persuaded to withdraw his motion by Shaw-Lefevre's promise that this Bill would be implemented in the next session. It was not. Leng's newspaper condemned the government's prevarications, and it was not alone.

After an autumn session in which nothing was done, Plimsoll researched his case and planned more legislation. In January 1871 he held three public meetings on consecutive days in the Free Trade Hall in Manchester, built on St Peter's Fields, where the Peterloo Massacre had taken place half a century before. In their black weeds the tearful widows of men lost in the *Sea Queen* sat with Plimsoll on the platform. They did not address the audience, but shook their heads mournfully when Plimsoll asked: 'Would your husbands have gone in the ship, if they knew the state she was in?' (In fact the women's evidence to the inquiry suggested the men did know, but had no choice.)

The *Sheffield Daily Telegraph* issued a special edition which reported every word of the Manchester proceedings. Plimsoll quoted a Liverpool insurer, Mr Marshall of Preston, addressing a recent meeting of the shareholders of the Maritime Insurance Company. He deplored a 'very large class' of accounts in which loss and disaster occurred because of 'positive design and interference on the part of the insurers'. 'I know there are men,' said Marshall, 'who think of underwriters as a jolly fat morsel out of which they are eager to get a slice.' Such men, he thought should be 'spurned and condemned'.

By the time the Sheffield newspaper's special edition was published on 14 February, a momentous event had occurred that stirred public opinion and stoked Plimsoll's campaign.

In the corner of a churchyard in Bridlington, a small port and sea-side resort on the Yorkshire coast, stands a monument. It is an obelisk of pale stone, taller than a man, and it has inscriptions on four sides. One reads: 'In lasting memory of a great company of seamen who perished in the fearful gale which swept over Bridlington Bay on February 10th 1871. The waves of the sea are mighty and rage horribly, but the Lord who dwelleth on high is mightier.' Another says: 'Forty-three bodies of those who that day lost their lives lie in this churchyard near this monument.'

The monument, at the Priory Church in the centre of the old town, is not neglected. It stands in a neat square of weeded pebbles, and is cleaned by volunteers, and once a year, on the Sunday morning nearest to 10 February, it is the focus of a service of remembrance attended by local dignitaries, sailors and lifeboatmen. Recently snow-drop bulbs have been planted all around the obelisk, so that in February there is a sea of flowers, intended to resemble the white-tipped waves, by way of commemoration. More than 130 years after it happened, the people of Bridlington still tell tales of what they call 'the Great Gale'. It is easy to see why. Six well-known and respected local men died a heroic death: they crewed a lifeboat that overturned in a rescue attempt. And the scale of the tragedy was exceptional. In all, seventy sailors are thought to have died in less than twenty-four hours, although only forty-three bodies were recovered; the others were identified only from enquiries after the missing. Twenty-three known ships were wrecked and others were believed to have gone down with no trace but signals of distress on the horizon. And on top of all this, the horrors unfolded within sight and sound of helpless witnesses on the shore.

It happens, by a grim coincidence, that 10 February was Samuel Plimsoll's birthday. He turned forty-seven on the day of the gale. Although he was not present, the Bridlington commemorations now conjure his name as the events of that day gave impetus to his campaign. The lost ships were carrying coal from Tyneside destined for the south, and eventually for Paris, and many were loaded to deck level. There were those, Plimsoll among them, who believed that the death toll would have been lower if the ships had not been so deeply laden, and had been in better condition. And the disaster, on a scale that spread its fame, intensified public concern about the lot of the merchant sailor.

On the afternoon of Thursday 9 February 1871, no one could have anticipated tragedy. It was a balmy, early spring day and a crowd gathered in the sunshine along the front at Bridlington Quay to watch a fleet of some four hundred ships set sail. Such spectacles as this were one of the vaunted attractions of Bridlington in 1871: as many as five hundred vessels at a time would take shelter in a bay that was known to merchant sailors all along the coast as a refuge from north-east winds, and together the ships would make their way out to the open sea at the first favourable breeze. Their departure, in the words of one commentator in 1868, 'presented an animated scene which can be equalled in few parts of the coasts of England'. Onlookers had a fine view of the sails and the sea from the elegant new esplanade, and from the two piers that enclosed the harbour, on each side of which the curving sands of the bay stretched away to distant headlands. On this occasion an auspicious north-west wind carried the ships away from the waving spectators.

But the benign wind did not last. By 4 a.m. on Friday the wind had turned and a storm blew up, building to a hurricane and catching the fleet in the lee of a harbour – the most dangerous of circumstances for sailing ships in a gale. By daybreak, crowds that had watched the ships in the afternoon sunshine were back, this time trembling in a blizzard near the beach and harbour. A lifeboat, the *Robert Whitworth*, was prepared for emergencies. So too was the rocket apparatus that sent a rope to ships near shore, so that sailors could secure and climb along it, if they were not too weak or frozen, using it as a lifeline to reach land.

The crews of six ships in distress were brought to safety by the lifeboat, after harrowing scenes in which life and death hung in the balance.* The men came ashore in a 'perishing condition'. Some had bags of clothes, soaked through with saltwater. The townsfolk came to meet the sailors and helped them to shelter, and even noble-women carried their bags up the beach. The crew of a brig (a two-masted ship) whose bottom was smashed and cargo lost took to their own boat and were only saved by coastguards who waded into the sea up to their armpits and grasped the drowning men on the boat and dragged them to shore.

The lifeboat crew worked until they were exhausted and had to be lifted from their seats, their hands bleeding. As the wrecks piled up, it was decided to launch a smaller boat, the *Harbinger*, built locally and donated to the port by a refugee Hungarian count by the name of Batthyany who lived nearby. It saved seven crews before exhaustion overcame some of these men too. The man who built the *Harbinger*, thirty-eight-year-old David Purdon, and his assistant John Clappison volunteered to make up the numbers, and with seven others set out for a brig stranded on the south beach, from which they rescued five men and 'managed to land their shivering brethren amidst the applause of the hundreds of spectators'.

But the jubilation was premature. A brig from Whitby, the *Delta*, was in danger to the south of the harbour. Four of its crew, includ-ing two teenagers – apprentice Richard Lindup and Simon Butterwick, who was on his first voyage – launched their own boat to try to reach the shore. It was swamped by a 'terrific billow', and all four went under and were never seen alive again. The *Delta*'s captain, William Calvert, was spotted still clinging to the vessel, and

---

* They included four men from the barge *Friends Increase* of London, six from the brigantine *Echo* of London and six from the brig *Windsor* of Lynn.

A lifeboat goes out to colliers making for harbour during the
Great Gale, Bridlington, 1871. (*Bridlington Library*)

the *Harbinger* set out to save him. It reached the stern of the ship,
where Calvert was hanging on to its chains. The lifeboat's coxswain,
James Robinson, told him to drop into the lifeboat as soon as
the next wave had passed. But the next wave was fateful. It hit the
lifeboat with terrific force and plunged it down, prow foremost,
tipping all nine of the crew into the water.

When the boat righted itself, Robinson was clinging to the
ropes on its sides. His colleague Robert Hopper was hauled in to
the ropes with Robinson's scarf. The next wave washed the two
men back into the boat, with a third, Richard Bedlington, who
had been underneath it. But the other six, including Purdon,
drowned 'in sight of their relatives and friends and within view of
their homes'. Among them were two single men, Clappison and
young William Cobb, who had just finished his apprenticeship at
sea and was visiting his parents in Bridlington. Purdon, Richard
Atkin, Robert Pickering (thirty-four) and James Watson (forty-
three) were husbands and fathers. Watson had already been out
three or four times in the lifeboat, and had taken a break only to go

home for dry clothes. As soon as he was changed he was back in the lifeboat. His death deprived his wife Eliza of her wits: she never recovered from the shock. It turned her, reports said, into 'a raving lunatic' and she was taken to the nearby asylum at York, where she died, aged thirty-two, on 1 March. She is buried beside her husband, whose body was washed ashore, in the Priory churchyard.

The monument lists the names of the six men who died 'while nobly endeavouring to save those whose bodies rest here'. It transpired that although the lifeboats had lifejackets, they were not in a fit state, and that the rescuers knew they were unusable when they set out.

William Calvert, the *Delta*'s captain, was washed away too. The lifeboat, drifting uncontrollably without oars, came ashore a mile south of the harbour with only Robinson, Hopper and Bedlington in it. The dismayed crowd on the pier and the sea wall worked on to save what lives they could. The empty places in the lifeboat were filled by other volunteers, who rescued that afternoon the crew of a ship from Scarborough, the *Vivid*, which had run ashore; its captain, Vary, said that this gale was the worst he had known in his thirty-year career.

But there were more horrors to come as the colliers made for shelter. Also in the afternoon, a brig from Folkestone, the *Produce*, struck within thirty yards of the north side of the pier. Two sailors were pitched into the sea from its lifeboat, before this had even left the side of the ship. One of them disappeared, but the other surfaced, at the outer end of the pier, where witnesses were standing. He was almost within arm's reach but it was too far for him to be helped. The frantic onlookers watched as he braved the waves but a large piece of timber fell from the ship and crushed his legs. The crowd was still watching as he went under. His name was never discovered. His corpse was later identified only as 'a coloured man belonging to the *Produce*'.

Meanwhile on the *Produce* the other four crew members had climbed the rigging. They too were near enough to see but not near enough to save. 'For three terrible hours they called for help, and stretched out their benumbed hands to those standing in safety within a few trifling yards of them.' Around 4 p.m., with the rising tide, the ship 'began to reel violently to and fro, until, with one terrible lurch towards the shore, she turned over'. The *Produce* lost all hands.*

There were other casualties painfully close to onlookers, and the cries of the drowning could be heard over the howling of the storm. As darkness fell, a man was seen signalling with a light from the fore-yard of a schooner, and attempts were made to reach him with the rocket-launched rope. As each attempt failed, the bystanders, including women, helped to haul the rope back, in order to try again, which they did without success. Another sailor was illuminated by gaslight, floating on a piece of wreck. He too couldn't be reached, and drowned towards 7.30 p.m.

Tyrrell, the chief coastguard, boarded a ship to rescue a sailor who had climbed to the foretop, and found him there, frozen to death. When Tyrrell climbed down, the deck had caved in, and he fell into the hold and was himself badly injured.

By one account four sailors from a schooner, the *Margaret* of Ipswich, were saved by the lifeboat, but the captain and owner of the ship, William Howard, and a sailor, William Mills, made for the ship's boat and were drowned. Of the *William Maitland* from Whitby only the captain, Newton, was saved. He tried to persuade the rest of the crew to take to the water, using anything that would float. They preferred to stay on board. Captain Newton jumped overboard with a lifebelt and reached the shore. The rest of the crew were still in the rigging when a wave took the mast and swept them to their deaths. Of the crew of the *Caroline* of Yarmouth only the captain and mate were rescued. From the *Arrow* of Sunderland three sailors were saved by a group of fishermen who found a coble (a small fishing boat) and carried it on their shoulders over slippery rocks to launch it near the ship. One of the fishermen, Leonard Mainprize, climbed aboard the brig and found a seaman tangled in ropes and almost unconscious, freed him and hauled him into the coble. But two of the ship's crew were killed by the mast falling when the ship struck ground, and the mate, who made it to the shore, died on land. Two ships from Seaham, the *Lavinia* and the *Endeavour*, went down with all hands.

---

* Including the captain, by the name of Fisher, and the mate, Court, whose brother came in vain to find him among the recovered bodies.

Soon after 9 p.m. a brig carrying coal from Hartlepool to London, the *IMOD*, managed to make its way through the narrow entrance to the harbour, with all hands at the pumps. It was afloat, but, when it struck ground between the two piers, its cookhouse and galley were gone, along with its boats, and its deck was swept clean. It was hardly more than a shell.

There were those who never left the piers or the beach all through Friday night. Some left to carry six bodies which came ashore one by one among the wreckage, to be laid out and 'carefully and delicately washed' in local inns. Other townsfolk were tending to the sailors who survived. Many were given shelter in nearby hotels but already groups of sailors who had lost everything were making their way through the empty streets of Bridlington Quay to the railway station, their journey home paid for by the representatives of the Shipwrecked Mariners' Society. Some of the dead were identified by the numbered medals of this society, which sailors wore for this very purpose. Eighty-eight seamen in all came through the storm and lived to go home safely. They were the complete crews of fifteen wrecked ships, and ten sailors who outlived lost crewmates on another four vessels.

Wreckage piled up on the sea front the morning after the gale, painted by an eyewitness. (*Bridlington Library*)

When dawn rose on Saturday the grey light illuminated a beach covered with debris, swept up in piles against the sea walls. Among the spars and sails, chains, ropes and anchors, were more poignant remains: a sou'wester, a boot, a solitary oar, a child's blue dress. Since most of the wrecked vessels were colliers, there was also an immense quantity of coal dumped by the sea. Scavengers got busy making sure it did not go to waste.

By Sunday evening the bodies of nineteen men and youths had been found. By Monday night there were twenty-two, including those of three of the lifeboatmen. Inquests were held, and on Tuesday all but two of the corpses were laid out in the back of the Albion Inn. Most were muscular and young. In the yard behind the inn, the seamen's clothes were hung on a line of rails, tattered and stiff with salt. Telegrams had been sent bearing the news to all parts of the coast, and throughout Saturday, Sunday and Monday strangers arrived in town, many of them relatives of the drowned, from Whitby, Sunderland, Seaham, Yarmouth, Lowestoft and Hartlepool, to identify the bodies. One mother recognised her nineteen-year-old son (a crewman on the *Delta*, presumably either Simon Butterwick or Richard Lindup). She was so distressed, and wailed so desperately for her 'darling boy', that she had to be taken gently but forcibly away. Her son had left home on the Wednesday and died on the Friday.

A mass funeral took place on Tuesday 14 February. Coffin-makers had worked ceaselessly to provide twenty-two plain black coffins, photographs had been taken of the corpses of the strangers for the purposes of identification,[*] schools were given a half-day and the mayor had − unnecessarily − distributed handbills asking tradesmen to shut up shop during the service. Long before the hour of the ceremony, which was to take place at 2 p.m., all the blinds were drawn on the businesses of the town.

The permanent population of Bridlington and Bridlington Quay in 1871 was some six thousand people. Four thousand took part in the funeral, joining the cortège as it made its way half a mile inland from the top of King Street to the Priory Church, until the crowd

[*] By John Waite Shores of 2 Marlborough Terrace, Bridlington Quay, who also photographed the funeral procession.

After the Gale, February 1871: the flag-draped coffins of drowned sailors
in the funeral procession, King Street, Bridlington.

seemed to be 'an endless living stream'. In Prospect Street the procession halted briefly for a photograph to be taken of the coffins on
six 'rolleys' – flat horse-drawn carts.

At the head of the procession were officials and dignitaries, followed by James Watson's coffin, covered with the Union Jack and
carried by his fellow lifeboatmen. And then came the six rolleys,
bearing the flag-draped coffins of twenty-two seamen, with, behind
them, cabs carrying relatives and friends. All along the route solemn
faces appeared at the windows and in the crowd 'many a weather-
beaten cheek was wet with tears'.

The crowd became so dense as the procession approached the
church that it came almost to a halt. It proceeded slowly through the
archway of Bridlington's ancient stone Bayle Gate, and reached the
gates of the Gothic parish church, where the crowd stood aside to let
the rolleys enter. Many helped to carry the coffins inside and arrange
them on forms inside the entrance. The organ played a death march
and the service was conducted by the vicar, the Reverend Fred
Banes, and his curates.

The interment took place in a piece of ground in the north-east corner of the churchyard, donated by a Captain Beauvais. Nineteen coffins were buried in one grave, in the spot now marked by the monument. The three captains were buried in a second grave.

The scenes at the graves were reported as 'truly appalling and beyond description'. Unless accounts were exaggerated, the Victorians were noisy in their grief: fathers, mothers and brothers of the dead wailed and wept. The mother who showed such distress in the Albion Inn again 'created a painful scene' as her son's body was put into the grave, crying 'My darling boy, my darling boy' again and again. One commentator observed: 'It is said that some present would have faced death itself, if by so doing they could have given her back her darling boy.' Many people lingered by the graves until night fell.

In a row not far from the monument are three gravestones of men from the lifeboat. One is for James Watson and his wife Eliza, whose body was brought back from the lunatic asylum to share his grave. In the middle is David Purdon's; buried soon afterwards with him was his twenty-nine-year-old wife, Harriet, who was eight months pregnant when her husband was lost, and died in childbirth twenty-eight days later. Robert Pickering's body was not found immediately: he was not interred at the mass funeral, but buried in the third grave on 3 March. The stones record the fact of their sacrifice. 'So early numbered with the dead,' says part of the verse on Pickering's grave, 'Who perish'd midst the waves.'

In the days that followed, the effects of the drowned were returned to relatives who could not be present. The widow of a sailor called Jameson, another victim from the *Delta*, received his Mariners' Society medal in a bag, a knife, a tobacco pouch, a six-pence, an account of the funeral and £1 11s 6d (now worth just under £100) from a public subscription set up to reward lifeboat crews and help widows and orphans. She wrote to say thank you. In the aftermath of the tragedy a new lifeboat was swiftly donated to the town by the Reverend Graeme of Sewerby House, and before long a reversible lifeboat was invented and patented that would float either side up.

Although Bridlington Bay suffered most that day, the hurricane caused wrecks elsewhere along the north-east coast: including at

Filey and, with great loss of life, at Hartlepool. At Tynemouth rocket apparatus reached sailors in distress, who were not trained in the use of safety equipment, and did not understand that the rope had been sent to them for securing to the vessel and climbing along to shore. They used it to lash themselves to the ship, and went down with it.

Public shock at the scale of the disaster, both locally and nationally, should not be underestimated. Contributions to the charity fund came in from all over the country. The weather conditions of 10 February 1871 were exceptional, but both the loading and the condition of the lost ships were called into question. The fact that colliers broke up when they touched land was considered damning. A coastguard quoted in the *Leeds Mercury* of 14 February said the ships were 'nothing but graves for the seamen, and we shall always have wrecked coastal colliers so long as such vessels are allowed to leave port'. The newspaper itself drew the conclusion:

> There is one lesson to be learnt from the storm which swept with such disastrous results over the northeastern coast on Friday that we hope will not be forgotten. The utter worthlessness of a large portion of the fleet by which the northern coasting trade is carried on has long been notorious, and if this storm should lead us . . . to secure the country in future from such disasters . . . there will be some compensation for the loss of life which attended it . . . Mr Plimsoll will find his hands strengthened in a way which cannot well be resisted . . .

The paper pointed out that there were no rocks at all in this stretch of Bridlington harbour and that the beach was pure sand, sloping in a gentle shelf into the sea.

> Those who know the force of an easterly gale on this coast know it is terrific but a good ship well beached on a sandy bottom ought not to go to pieces like a pack of cards. And yet this was very much the case in this instance. Several of the ships sank before reaching the beach at all – went down bodily like blocks of stone; and of the fifteen or sixteen which went on shore, scarcely a wreck remained,

with one exception, the next day. They were simply fair weather ships. At the first strain of the sea, or at the first shock on the beach, they swamped like old tubs, or tumbled to pieces like rotten timber . . . Surely it is time that something was done to bring about a better state of things.

The *Newcastle Daily Chronicle* of 11 February was angry too: 'We can scarcely believe it possible that another session of Parliament will be allowed to pass without such stringent legislation as shall have the effect of sweeping these lumps of painted touchwood from the sea without previously freighting them with precious human lives.'

The *Penny Illustrated Paper* of 18 February, commenting on the 'lamentably disastrous' gale, remarked: 'High time for Mr Plimsoll's bill providing for the survey of presumably unseaworthy ships, and for the prevention of over-lading to become law!'

Malpractice mattered because human life was precious, and because merchant shipping was central to the economic life of the nation, but the losses at Bridlington also played a part in an international drama. From 19 September 1870 to 28 January 1871 Paris had been under siege in the Franco-Prussian War, triggered in August 1870 by a dispute over the Spanish throne. Less than a fortnight before the Great Gale, after a last desperate attempt to break out (the Battle of Buzenval), the starving Parisian forces had surrendered to Prussia. The coal that was collected up by the poor on Bridlington beach was intended for the surviving allies in Paris. There was a patriotic dimension to the intensity of public feeling.

The memory of these events has endured. For at least sixty years after the Great Gale there was not only the special remembrance service at the Priory Church on one Sunday in February; there was even a procession, for which the crowds turned out, from the quayside to the parish church, following the route of the funeral in 1871. Lifeboats were paraded where once rolleys had carried coffins. And still it is possible once a year to join a congregation that walks out of the Priory Church along a stone-flagged path through the grassy churchyard to the obelisk. Around this the company assembles, while a lifeboatman reads a report of rescues that have taken place during the year, and prayers are said, interrupted only by the cries of gulls.

And if you visit any day of the year you will see that inside the Priory Church the walls are adorned with an embroidered tapestry recording the history of Bridlington, which includes a panel that represents the Great Gale. Looking down from a stained-glass window, as it looked down upon the funeral, is an image of the church's patron saint, the fifteenth-century St John of Bridlington. The miracle attributed to him is that he walked on water to save the lives of drowning men.

3

THE INSANE FARRAGO

Armed with the horrors of the Bridlington Gale, and the general indignation against unseaworthy ships that it had provoked, Plimsoll presented Parliament with his new Merchant Shipping Survey Bill on 22 February 1871. Again it aimed to provide a load line and to have all ships surveyed before they set sail. Again Eustace Smith and Norwood were obstructive. During the attendant debate Oxfordshire MP Joseph Henley suggested that Plimsoll, whose business was transporting coal by rail to London from the north, was acting only out of self-interest; he alleged that 'all this fuss about losses at sea is nothing more than a "humanity dodge" to set up a monopoly for inland coal at the expense of sea-borne coal'. Plimsoll's second reading failed.

Plimsoll's Manchester meetings, with their copious coverage, had not been enough to influence government. Nor had a heart-rending maritime tragedy, blamed by the press and public as much on unseaworthy ships as on the weather. Three times Plimsoll's Bills or amendments had now been rejected. Disillusioned with Parliament, he turned for support to the nation, knowing from such examples as Shaftesbury's and Bright's that real power might lie there. His cause needed a properly orchestrated campaign.

He began with an appeal to the working man. Plimsoll's friend the trade unionist George Howell recorded how, in March 1871,

Plimsoll 'was desirous of enlisting the Trades Union Congress in what he had then vaguely in his mind, a campaign on behalf of the sailors'. Plimsoll consulted Howell and his fellow officials, including Alexander Macdonald and George Odger, and Karl Marx's associate Randal Cremer, about how to 'bring the question before the delegates'. He invited them all to dine, and then 'spoke at some length on the subject and enlisted the hearty sympathies of the delegates on behalf of those for whom he so feelingly and eloquently pleaded. The resolutions subsequently proposed were carried by acclamation and the Congress as such was fully committed to some remedial measures for the safety and comfort of those who go down to the sea in ships.'

Afterwards Plimsoll retreated to the peace of picturesque Grange-over-Sands in Cumberland, close to his childhood haunts, to work on a book that would put his case to the rest of the world.

Our Seamen: An Appeal took a year to write. 'Few books', one commentator has since remarked, 'have ever moved a generation of British people so widely and deeply.' By the time *Our Seamen* was finished the Trades Union Congress had reiterated its support for Plimsoll in Nottingham in January 1872, and there had been a spate of maritime tragedies: 1872 was notorious for gales and the suffering of sailors was rarely out of the news. Then in January 1873 600,000 copies of Plimsoll's book were printed and distributed at his own expense, in both fine and cheap editions, with a smaller pamphlet distilling its main points circulated through the trade unions.* (His friends talked him out of the extravagance of printing a round million.) Copies were sent to the newspapers, with a bound-in note encouraging editors to use as much of the text as they pleased. Lengthy extracts appeared in, among others, *The Times*, the *Penny Illustrated Paper* and, thanks again to W. C. Leng, the *Sheffield Telegraph*. *Vanity Fair* called *Our Seamen* 'a book jumbled together in the fashion of an insane farrago, written without method and without art, but powerful and eloquent beyond any work that has

---

* The quarto edition with more than sixty illustrations officially cost 14s; the cheap edition, with only a frontispiece showing the Wreck Chart for 1871, was 2s 6d; but before very long copies of *Our Seamen* were available from the offices of the Plimsoll and Seamen's Defence Fund at 4 Victoria Street, London SW for only 6d.

appeared for years because it is the simple honest cry of a simple honest man'.

Between its covers was all the evidence and all the outrage Plimsoll had mustered in support of his case against overloading and unseaworthy ships, and its aim was to urge the public to exert pressure for a Royal Commission of Inquiry to investigate the shipping industry. Plimsoll was convinced that the evidence presented to a Commission would persuade it to recommend his measures: a maximum load line, to be above the water as a ship left port, as recorded in a photograph; and an annual inspection of all ships by surveyors appointed by the Board of Trade.

The book was dedicated to 'The Lady, Gracious and Kind, who, seeing a labourer working in the rain, sent him her rug to wrap about his shoulders'. The lady was Queen Victoria, who was said to have made this gesture in Scotland, and whose authorisation Plimsoll needed for a Royal Commission.

The opening words of *Our Seamen* were:

> I have no idea of writing a book. I don't know how to do it, and fear I could not succeed if I tried; the idea therefore is very formidable to me. I will suppose myself to be writing to an individual, and to be saying all I could think of to induce him to lend his utmost aid in remedying the great evil which we all deplore; and I will write, so far as I can, just as I would speak to him if he were now sitting by my side.

Plimsoll did not purport to be a stylist, but this simple, direct, confiding approach was persuasive. He was not in fact so inexperienced a writer as he made himself sound, but already a prolific author of speeches, pamphlets and articles. (He would use a comparable 'unaccustomed-as-I-am-to-public-speaking' approach when he addressed the House, eliciting sympathy before he spoke, which he did competently, although sometimes, at first, rather too fast.) Nevertheless, *Our Seamen* was his first full-length book, it was eccentric in both tone and organisation, and Plimsoll did have an ill-educated habit of triple underlining and using multiple exclamation marks. The book's combination of plain-speaking naivety and furious invective prompted some cynical sneering. But it was also a work of absolute passion and conviction, and it made Plimsoll and his cause famous. He was not only sincere; he was superlative at sounding sincere, and he made the nation feel as he felt.

The book made much use of the details of James Hall's petition for a load line, acknowledging loud and clear that this was a shipowner's initiative. It praised those shipowning companies whose good care ensured that they had never lost a life. It was a fact later much overlooked that Plimsoll did not denounce shipowners collectively. He wrote: 'Shipowners, as a class, are really careful of their men's lives, and neglect no means of safety known to them, and that they are so, considering that the law leaves them entirely free to neglect these means if they pleased, is a fact very much to their credit.'

But Plimsoll went on to say: 'There are in every class of men some who need the law's restraint, who without it have no hesitation in exposing others to risk, if by doing so they can augment their own profits.' And about those few careless profiteers Plimsoll was damning: 'I have heard one ship-owner say that if a small number of well-known ship-owners were put aboard one of their own vessels when she was ready for sea, we should, in the event of bad weather, see that with them had disappeared from our annals nine-tenths of the losses we all deplore.'

Plimsoll asserted that: 'there are gentlemen of high character in Cardiff, Newcastle, Greenock, Port Glasgow, London, Sunderland, Hull, Liverpool and other places who are longing for the opportunity of telling a Royal Commission what they know but whose lips are sealed by the terrible Law of Libel.' He wanted the libel law to be suspended for evidence before the Commission, so that witnesses could speak without intimidation. There might have been in this list something of a threat. Five of these towns had shipowning MPs: Samuda, Gourley, Norwood, Bates and William Graham of Glasgow, while James Johnston Grieve, MP for Greenock, was a merchant importing cod from Newfoundland.

The arguments of *Our Seamen* ran, in a nutshell, as follows. Plimsoll believed that the fear that once prompted shipowners to take every care – the fear of their own financial loss – had been eroded by the existence of insurance. Pressure on margins seduced the needy and the reckless into wrongdoing, and the boundaries of safe practice were pushed back little by little. If the expenses of transporting a proper volume of freight were nine-tenths of the income from it, only another tenth added to the cargo would double the profit, which presented a great temptation. Meanwhile every overloaded or unrepaired ship that came safely home – as some did, by luck – set a precedent, suggesting that the risk was worth taking. So carelessness augmented like a slowly rising tide.

Plimsoll insisted that neither underwriters, because they were too numerous, nor sailors, because they were powerless, were likely ever to prosecute a case against those responsible for the avoidable loss of a ship. He urged that protection for sailors should catch up with the protection given to workers in other industries, and (citing a demolition order on a property of his own) that it should be no more acceptable to own unsafe ships than to own unsafe buildings. He considered the dangers of undermanning, bad stowage and deck-loading of cargoes. He quoted Board of Trade reports and statistics of wrecks that demonstrated that lives were lost unnecessarily. He railed against the negligent and the avaricious, and all but named and listed miscreants and their ships, the omission of letters not being enough to disguise the identities of the accused from those in the know. He gave instances of shipowning MPs self-interestedly thwarting legislation in the Commons that would curtail their malpractices, including one story of a member who hastily retracted his opposition to Plimsoll from the order paper when threatened with exposure.

He digressed upon the virtues of the working class, presenting himself, in his down-and-out days in Shaftesbury's charity lodging house, as comrade in their sufferings and witness to their nobility. He cited the bravery and altruism of miners, common soldiers and sailors he had known, heroic in the face of catastrophe. He conjured pictures of the piety of seamen, singing hymns at Sunday services on deck and yet 'abandoned to the tender mercies of unchecked irresponsibility – of competition run mad'. He drew poignant vignettes of desolated families he had visited in the back streets of Shields in Tynemouth, whose good-hearted menfolk had taken their cheerful dispositions and the hopes and health of their dependants to salty graves. And the men went to those graves recognising the danger posed by the loading and condition of the ships they boarded, but were coerced into sailing by need or threats, by fear of jail or of the taint of cowardice.

Drowned sailors and their families were identified in *Our Seamen* by names and addresses with letters omitted. One passage, ran thus:

> I also saw Mrs W - - - ks, of 78 B - - - d Street, who had lost her son Henry W-ks aged twenty-two. She too cried bitterly as she spoke with *such* love and pride of her son, and of the grief of his father, who was sixty years of age. Her son was taken on as a stoker, and worked in the ship some days before she was ready for sea. He didn't want to go then, when he saw how she was loaded, but they refused to pay him the money he had earned unless he went; and he was lost with all the others.

The 1871 census identifies mariner William Wilks and his wife Elizabeth, living at 78 Bedford Street in North Shields with their children, son-in-law (also a mariner) and two grandchildren. None of the three living children (aged eleven to twenty-four) was Henry Wilks, born to them, as his birth certificate shows, on 24 June 1848. He was twenty-two in 1870 and so would have died before the census. Plimsoll was not inventing these people. He did, however, overestimate William's age by eight years, misled perhaps by the effects on his face of grief and a life at sea.

Plimsoll included in his book photographs of ships' bolts eaten away by rust, and elegant if gratuitous views and cross-sections of wooden ships, expertly drawn by Harry J. Cornish, later an esteemed chief surveyor at Lloyd's Register and a prize-winning marine draughtsman. The images were intended to lend authority to Plimsoll's descriptions of overdue repairs, improper lengthening and structural faults.

He concluded with as fierce a condemnation of inaction and indifference as ever thundered from any ranter's pulpit:

> I tell you, you who read these lines, if you are a man, you deserve to perish suddenly, lacking sympathy and succour in your hour of utmost need, and leaving your nearest and dearest only the cold charity of the world to depend upon – for this is how sailors die – if you don't help.

If you are a wife, you deserve that your husband should be taken from you without warning, and that to the anguish of bereavement should be added the material miseries of hunger and destitution – for this is how sailors' wives suffer – if you do not help. If you are a father, descending it may be in to the vale of years, with sons strong and brave, the pride and support of your age, you deserve that they should suddenly perish with no hand to help them, leaving your remaining years uncheered by one filial greeting – for so the fathers of sailors are bereaved – if you do not help; if you are a mother, you deserve that your son should be taken from you in the pride of his young manhood, if you don't help to stop this homicidal, this manslaughtering, this widow-and-orphan-manufacturing system.

The imaginary auditor, sitting by Plimsoll's side, would surely by now be in some distress.

Our Seamen may have been written as if for one listener, but it was always intended for the widest possible audience, and Plimsoll began by launching it among his friends the trade unionists, who had twice reiterated support for his remedial legislation. It was to the next annual Congress in Leeds in January 1873 (held at the Assembly Rooms in Cookridge Street) that Plimsoll took the first finished copies of his Appeal.

The Leeds papers that week were preoccupied with the belated news, which had taken five months to reach its audience, that the African explorer Dr Livingstone had been visiting the cave-dwellers of Ironda and Mayemba.* Pages were devoted too to the death of the Emperor Napoleon III in London, and his funeral at Chislehurst. Other snippets give a flavour of the time: the notice of a women's suffrage meeting to be held at nearby Bradford on 15 January; the news from Washington that President Grant had forbidden members of the US army to hold state office; the death of a man from the 'imbecile ward' who fell down the stairs of the Leeds Workhouse.

But in spite of this competition for the attention of the press, on Tuesday 14 January 1873, during the Congress, at which Plimsoll

---

* As told in letters brought, presumably on foot, to the coast by 'a few slaves' and received by the Foreign Office.

had addressed the 130 delegates, a leader in the *Leeds Mercury* commented on his cause:

> Mr Plimsoll has undertaken the thankless but very important task of directing public attention to the condition of large numbers of the ships engaged in the coasting and foreign service of England, and forcing upon Parliament, by the pressure of public opinion, the necessity of legislation, with a view to the abatement . . . of the evils which have grown up under the system of modern marine assurance . . . If these old tubs are caught in a storm, they either go to the bottom without a moment's notice; or, if they go ashore, they fall to pieces with the first shock like a house of cards. Every storm brings us a record of the wreck of these ships, and of the loss of their crews. Mr Plimsoll . . . has worked hard for the cause for some years, and he tells us that he intends next Session to appeal to the Government to grant a Royal Commission to inquire into the matter, with a view to legislation. The question is not free from difficulty . . . but there is a real grievance and a *bona fide* attempt ought to be made to redress it.

On the sixth and last day of the Congress, copies of *Our Seamen* were given to every union delegate at a banquet in the neo-Gothic Queen's Hotel beside the station. All pledged their support, while an enthusiastic vote of thanks was carried by acclamation. As George Howell recorded in his handwritten history of the Plimsoll Movement: 'The unique character of [*Our Seamen*], the illustrations, the curious and delicate matters discussed, the facts and the persons dealt with, the "libellous" nature of some of the statements and references were calculated to produce a great sensation and a great sensation was produced.'

The cause snowballed. *The Times* lamented the fact that the government recognised no responsibility for preventing merchant vessels leaving port in an unseaworthy state, and that 'a trader may leave port in midwinter with her main deck sunk below the water with railway iron, with her plates rusted through, her timbers rotten or parting, or her machinery out of order, without violating one jot or tittle of the law. Such an anomaly is wicked and ridiculous and must not be allowed to exist any longer.'

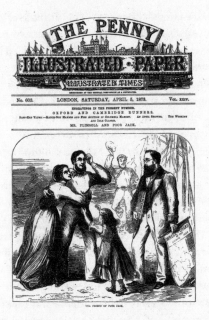

The *Penny Illustrated Paper* pays tribute to the friend of Poor Jack,
5 April 1873. (*Illustrated London News*)

The newspaper cited, in support of the contention that unseaworthy ships were indeed sent to sea, two cases inquired into by the
Board of Trade in 1869. One was a forty-three-year-old collier, the
Elizabeth, whose loss was attributed to 'her great age, apparently
inefficient repairs, and stress of weather when deeply coal laden'.
The Court of Inquiry was able to conclude only that 'while deprecating the custom of deploying old vessels of this description in the
coasting trade to the manifest danger of life . . . in the absence of any
enactments to the contrary the Court [can] do no more than call
attention to the practice'. The second case, 'still more scandalous',
from the same report, was that of the *Nelly*, a collier that sailed
between Belfast and Ayr and sank in a 'moderate gale' – not dangerous enough to harm a well-found, properly laden ship. The *Nelly*
was a hundred years old. 'Two of the crew and four of her passengers
lost their lives, and no inquiry whatever was held. Such a state of things

is simply licensed murder,' thundered 'The Thunderer', adding: 'It is a foolish and wicked distinction which has been drawn between passenger and trading vessels; it is a law not worthy to be called law at all which minutely inspects an emigrant or store ship, but lets a mere merchant-man go to sea and founder at the sweet will of weather and its owners.'

The newspapers had accepted the principles of Plimsoll's case, and none of them now, as the House had once done, questioned his motives. He was well on his way to becoming a national hero. Plimsoll's audience became so wide that the author in 1880 of a study of London was able to write confidently: 'Everyone – for surely everyone has read Mr Plimsoll's appeal on behalf of the poor sailors – must remember his experiences in a lodging house of the better sort.'

As enthusiasm for the cause and the man escalated with the public meetings and the pronouncements of the press, there was also a growing opposition. As *The Times* put it: 'Mr Plimsoll's "Appeal" has excited a storm of indignation throughout the mercantile community.' Every owner of merchant ships wanted to dissociate himself from the accusations as soon as *Our Seamen* was published.

The 'simple honest cry' prompted several to libel actions. One of these was Charles Morgan Norwood, MP for Hull. From the first days of Plimsoll's espousal of this issue in 1870, Norwood, who was always a vehement opponent of government intervention in the shipping industry, insisted that Plimsoll exaggerated his case. Norwood's lifelong attitude was once expressed in this remark: 'I can assure you that we require on board our large ships a barrister even more than we require a doctor. There are so many acts under which we conduct our business that it is impossible for a ship's captain to know how to act to keep within the four corners of the law.'

Objecting to legislative interference is not the same as being guilty of the crimes the legislation would have aimed to discourage, but Plimsoll seemed to regard all opposition as suspicious. And perhaps objecting to the inconvenience of government regulations was indeed suspect when the price of non-interference was human lives. Just as Plimsoll tended to think the best of sailors, he tended to think the worst of any shipowning Member of Parliament who would not support protective measures for sailors. Norwood was a Liberal MP, but not a radical. Sixteen years later he earned himself notoriety as he led the employers in the 1889 Dock Strike, who held out for five weeks against a desperate resistance from dockers and their families that was prompted by terrible hardship. Then Norwood was described by the *Star* as 'in appearance and manners, the very embodiment of the insolence of capitalism. He is stout, well-fed, and arrogant.' He and Plimsoll would spend decades at odds with each other. (In 1889 Plimsoll was one of the many who gave money to help the striking dockers.)

Norwood had been stung by *Our Seamen,* which had cited the case of a ship, unnamed but identifiable as the *Livonia*, which set out with a cargo of railway iron from Jarrow Dock on the River Tyne for the east of the Baltic. As Plimsoll reported the circumstances, James Hall had been offered in mid-September the generous sum of thirty shillings a ton to take this cargo, but when he consulted the captain of one of his own ships, the man said: 'For God's sake don't send us into the Baltic at this time of the year, sir. You might as well send us all to the bottom of the sea at once.' Hall declined the offer, but five weeks later – and five weeks further into the season of bad weather – Norwood accepted the cargo for the *Livonia*. Plimsoll argued that the ship was then loaded five feet lower in the water than it should have been. 'Of course she was lost,' wrote Plimsoll. She went down eighteen miles from the English coast, though fortunately her crew was saved by a fishing boat. 'She was insured, of course,' added Plimsoll, 'and this ship-owner had the hardihood to say to me, "The underwriters have paid, and is not that proof that all was right?"' Plimsoll went on to suggest the shipowner lied about the weather and the loss of a logbook from the ship.

Norwood, recognising himself, was having none of it. Immediately he sued for libel. And a letter to *The Times* countered with a number of assertions. That the ship was commissioned not five weeks on from mid-September, but on 23 September. That the tonnage and construction of the boat were not as Plimsoll described. That the ship foundered because of an accident to its machinery, sixty miles offshore, not eighteen. That the ship was, at its lowest point, two feet higher above the water than Plimsoll reported (though the letter failed to admit this was still lower than the recommended depth). And that the ship was uninsured (which implied that Plimsoll had fabricated the shipowner's remark to him).

Plimsoll's friends were worried. Shaftesbury wrote in his diary, on 23 April 1873: 'Plimsoll, worthy man, is growing wiser – but it is too late. The explanation that would have satisfied Norwood . . . before the matter went into Court, must now be a public retraction, and probably with payments of costs. This is very sad.'

The case occupied a Liverpool court until June. Prosecuting the case against Plimsoll, the Attorney General said, in a good summary of the suspicions of many of his enemies,

> Mr Plimsoll's reasoning seemed to be that so long as he had a laudable object in view he was entitled to say anything he pleased, and to make any accusation against whomsoever he chose . . . Mr Plimsoll believed his bill to be a good one, and perhaps it was, but . . . when members who were conversant with the subject got up and pointed out the discrepancies he was unable to substantiate them, and, in consequence he launched these libels at their heads in order to discredit their explanations, to shut their mouths and to put an end to their opposition to what he considered his good ends.

However, experts, including James Hall, agreed that the *Livonia* had sunk, as alleged, as a result of overloading. The ship was so deep in the water that, as it left the harbour, coal and iron had to be unloaded to get the ship over the sand bar. One of the two stevedores who had loaded the ship declared: 'In our opinion, for the time of year, the ship was very much and dangerously overloaded, and I would not have sailed three miles in that ship if I had to receive the whole ship and cargo at the end of that distance.'

Norwood lost his case, but Plimsoll's wrist was slapped for his hyperbole. The court decided that he should not have inferred from the instance of the *Livonia* that Norwood was 'one of the greatest sinners in the Trade', and consequently ordered Plimsoll to pay costs. Plimsoll had, it must be admitted, chosen his target carelessly. The *Livonia* was the only ship that Norwood had lost, and it was not in fact insured. Norwood did not have a history of using coffin-ships – but he did have a history of opposing the load line in Parliament, and this apparently clouded Plimsoll's judgement.

★

Edward Temperley Gourley, the MP for Sunderland, was also implicitly accused in *Our Seamen*, though not named, and was characterised
thus: 'There was one ship-owner whose name was often mentioned
to me in the course of the years 1869 and 1870. During my inquiries
in the north and east, I heard his name wherever I went as that of a
ship-owner who was notorious for the practice of overloading, and
for a reckless disregard of human life.'

Plimsoll went on to say: 'it is really awful to contemplate the
loss of precious human life from the operations of this one man
alone'. His book included a disguised list, below, of Gourley's
lost ships. The actual names of the ships he referred to, as revealed
in the libel case Gourley brought against Plimsoll, are added on
the right.

Date.	Ships lost.	Lives lost.	
1867.	S.S. C..... th.	–	Christian IX (9th)
1868.	A...........s.	–	Admiral Kabris
"	V........e.	29	Venice
"	F........e.	10	Florence
"	V...........r.	–	Volunteer
1869.	L........e.	28	Lucerne
"	P........n.	–	Parthenon
"	C......a.	22	Cambria
"	H...........r.	16	Harbinger
"	M..............y.	–	Missionary
"	A..............r.	Not known.	Ancient Mariner
"	L...........s.	"	Libertas

There were, suggested Plimsoll's book, more of Gourley's losses
that could be cited, but this 'melancholy list of 105 lives lost' was, he
argued, condemnation enough. It was a shocking allegation. Gourley
had been an alderman and three times mayor of Sunderland, was a
magistrate and a pillar of the local community and the Baptist
Church, and a much respected bachelor (although, according to the
evidence of one of his relations, he had a secret mistress in London).
Plimsoll's accusations made many in Sunderland angry on Gourley's
behalf. Gourley had, however, opposed Plimsoll's 1871 Bill. And he

had recently got into trouble with his constituents and in the Commons in a way that may have persuaded Plimsoll that he was capable of duplicity and not a good friend to seamen. In 1872 there was a Bill before the House proposing to extend the vote to sailors. Gourley had opposed it, to the annoyance of the seafaring inhabitants of Sunderland. Their objections made him change tack and propose the measure himself in May 1872, but the House was not persuaded that his motives were noble. The response to his contribution in the Commons was scathingly reported thus:

> Mr Gourley is a thin spare man with a weak little piping voice, and no sooner had he sat down than Mr Collins,* in tones like those of the cracking of a great whip, fell upon him, and in Parliamentary language called him a humbug, because he had not voted for a clause of precisely similar import, which had been suggested previously by Mr Graves.† Mr Collins went so far as to say that the only reason Mr Gourley now had for proposing this clause was that he had got a message from his Sunderland constituents reprimanding him for his former opposition, and directing him to make amends. Poor Mr Gourley was completely doubled up, and looked very much distressed. His clause was promptly negatived without a division.

Weeks after publication of *Our Seamen*, Gourley's lawyers wrote to *The Times* on 15 February 1873 informing readers that libel proceedings against Mr Plimsoll had been commenced.

When Norwood failed to ruin his accuser, other litigants, including Gourley, were persuaded to withdraw their actions. The judges clearly had sympathy for the cause, and it had become apparent by then that public opinion was against men who opposed Plimsoll. His enemies only blackened their own names by taking him to court.

Adding to the sense of injury perceived by Norwood and Gourley, Plimsoll sent a copy of *Our Seamen* to hundreds of mem-

---

* Thomas Collins, 'Liberal Tory' MP for Boston in Lincolnshire, known as the 'arch-interrupter of the House'. 'He has a command of appalling sounds, articulate and otherwise, which well suffice to earn him the . . . name of Noisy Tom.'
† Samuel R. Graves, Conservative MP for Liverpool and Chairman of the Liverpool Shipowners' Association.

bers of the House of Commons – although not to the shipowning MPs. Three hundred wrote back, of whom ninety-seven offered to support a Bill to end overloading and to call for a Royal Commission to inquire into untoward practices in the commercial marine. Late one Monday night in the House of Commons, on a date chosen perhaps for its auspiciousness because it was his birthday, 10 February,* Plimsoll read for the first time yet another 'Bill to provide for the Survey of Certain Shipping and to Prevent Overloading'. The names of the first ten of the ninety-seven MPs were cited as seconders.† After so much stalling, Plimsoll's book had, it seemed, turned a tide. The reading met no opposition at all, not even from Norwood, though (months before the outcome of the court case) he did express a hope that the 'Hon. Members who had received the book referred to would suspend their judgement on the ground that it was an *ex parte* statement capable of being satisfactorily answered'. Norwood also sent a letter to *The Times* reiterating this point.

In the following days coverage and correspondence in *The Times* revealed the strength of feeling for and against Plimsoll. A leader wondered why

> Over the seaworthiness of vessels carrying passengers, or even Government stores, a most careful supervision is exercised, but over that of private merchantmen not at all . . . Any enactment touching the question of a load line would require to be carefully considered, but so do most things which have to be done and are worth doing. From what we know of the feeling of the different Chambers of Commerce, we have not the slightest doubt that with just a little thought some measure could be framed which would be cordially adopted by every respectable shipowner.

---

* The less auspicious fact that this was also the second anniversary of Bridlington's Great Gale was eclipsed by the frequency of maritime losses; there was not a day passed that was not also the anniversary of deaths at sea.
† A Bill to provide for the Survey of Certain Shipping and to Prevent Overloading. Prepared and brought into the House of Commons by Mr Plimsoll, Mr Horsman, Mr Charles Lewis, Mr Staveley Hill, Mr Samuda, Mr Carter, Sir Henry Selwin-Ibbotson, Sir Robert Torrens, Mr Eykyn and Mr Villiers.

However, one Charles Mercier wrote in defence of Gourley asking Plimsoll to send proof of his allegations of overloading and accusing him of 'ill-considered and libellous' assertions 'against persons with whom he happens to be at variance'. By contrast, a Captain James Goodenough of the Royal Navy wrote that Mr Plimsoll's 'noble' appeal 'will gain the approval and gratitude of every seafaring man' and urged a proper investigation into every instance of loss of life at sea.

Shortly afterwards Thomas Eustace Smith, the Liberal MP for Tynemouth, complained that *Our Seamen* was 'a breach of parliamentary privilege'. He spoke, he said, in defence of the 'six or seven' shipowning MPs in the House. (He was referring, presumably, to himself and to the other Liberal MPs: Norwood; Gourley; John Candlish, MP for Sunderland; the naval architect Joseph Samuda, MP for Tower Hamlets; and the Conservative Edward Bates, MP for Plymouth. These were just the men whose principal occupation was shipping; one study has concluded that in 1873 there were twelve Liberals and six Conservatives in the House who owned ships.) Plimsoll had implied in his book that three MPs were guilty men. Two, Norwood and Gourley, had taken steps to defend themselves through the courts. The identity of the third was, said Eustace Smith, a matter for speculation that cast suspicion on all half-dozen, and even (and this was an emotive point) upon the late Conservative member for Liverpool, Samuel Robert Graves, former chairman of the Liverpool Shipowners Association, who had died the previous month.*

Eustace Smith insisted he found no reference to himself in the book, but Plimsoll had written: 'Owing to the fact that two or three of what we call in the North "the greatest sinners in the trade" have got into the House it is there and there only that opposition to reform is to be expected, and there and there only can it be found.' As a Northerner, Eustace Smith was likely to have been under suspicion. Plimsoll had implied a threat of exposure if these men continued to oppose him in the House, which Eustace Smith argued

---

* Graves had died on 18 January; Eustace Smith was addressing the House on 20 February.

was a challenge to the freedom of parliamentary debate. He proposed the motion: 'That to accuse in a printed book members of the House of grievous offences and threaten them with further exposure if they take part in its debates is conduct highly reprehensible and injurious to the honour and dignity of this House.'

Plimsoll was obliged to apologise to the House of Commons (not for the last time) for casting aspersions on its members. He expressed 'sincere regret' for committing 'inadvertent offence against the House' and blamed 'the earnestness with which I sought help for the helpless' and his own parliamentary inexperience, insisting that 'for the House I entertain and ever have entertained feelings of the very highest respect. For my most unintentional fault I offer to you and to the House the most ample apology it is in my power to make, and I assure the House that to have become one of its members I esteem, and ever shall esteem, to be the greatest honour and the highest distinction of my life.'

He was received with cheers. His expression of pride at being an MP apparently diverted attention from the fact that he did not apologise to Norwood, Eustace Smith or Gourley. Thin little piping Gourley said he had been recommended by his legal advisers not to allude to any of Plimsoll's allegations, and submitted to the House's opinion that he should remain silent. Gladstone backed up Edward Horsman, MP for Liskeard in Cornwall, who argued that Eustace Smith's motion of censure should be withdrawn. The House agreed that it need not interfere in any personal disputes between members which could be settled, as they were to be, in court. Plimsoll learned the power of an effusive apology in the Commons, a procedure which was to rescue him again.

Yet another shipping disaster, which took place on 22 January 1873, had fuelled feeling. In this case there was no implication of either unseaworthiness or overloading, but it rekindled an awareness of the murderous potential of the sea. The *Northfleet*, bound for Tasmania with pig iron and passengers, was lying at anchor overnight off Dungeness, and was struck amidships by a hit-and-run Spanish steamer, the *Murillo*, which sailed away into the darkness. The captain failed to realise the gravity of the damage, not raising the alarm until fifteen minutes after the collision. Then three local ships rescued fifty-nine passengers from the sinking ship, the captain waving his revolver to protect the women and children, but other nearby ships were unaware of the crisis.* On one, three hundred yards away, the nightwatchman slept while 320 people drowned, including the captain.

As the newspapers continued into March to report instances of bodies washed up from the *Northfleet*, including those of teenage sailors, the spark lit by *Our Seamen* swiftly became a blaze. In the early months of 1873 support for Plimsoll came from sources as disparate as the earnest pages of the *Christian World* and a motley gathering of seamen in a hall in North Shields. Plimsoll's Derby constituents were noisy in their encouragement at a meeting on 28 February and he was lauded in Liverpool Town Hall. There was even a meeting in Sunderland, Gourley's constituency, of sea captains who thought the charges against their representative 'absurd, libellous and totally unjustifiable' and insisted that the corrosive action of sugar on iron was more to blame for unseaworthy ships than greed or neglect. (This points a finger at Tate & Lyle, the sugar company, rather than at any other shipowning firm, an accusation corroborated by the fact that the corroded bolts illustrated in *Our Seamen* were from sugar ships.) Nevertheless, the meeting approved of a load line and a Royal Commission.

Plimsoll proposed in full his motion calling for a Royal Commission on 4 March in the House of Commons. He spoke in language that was 'not that in common use in modern parliaments, but rather that of seventeenth-century Puritanic sessions' and his stern rhetoric was supported by the MPs Roebuck and Samuda. Within days of this motion there was an unrelated parliamentary crisis when Gladstone, defeated over his Bill to extend university education in Ireland, resigned. This was the kind of news that could squeeze out issues of little moment and yet the papers continued to fan the flames of Plimsoll's agitation. In fact the issue of rotten ships was so much in the air that *The Times* used it as a metaphor when Disraeli declined to form a minority Conservative government, and Gladstone withdrew his resignation: 'It is enough to say that Mr

---

* 'The Wreck of the Northfleet', a folk ballad that commemorated this disaster, related that the captain shot a passenger who tried to escape before the women and children.

Gladstone will probably take the command of a demoralized, not to say mutinous crew. They have been taken into port to refit and are ordered out again; but they are by no means sure that they are not sent afloat in a "rotten ship".'

As these events unfolded, *The Times* concurrently reported the case of the *Peru*, whose crew refused to sail in her because they thought her unseaworthy. Fifteen sailors were imprisoned in Dorchester Castle for twelve weeks. When the ship did set sail, it went down in the Bay of Biscay and three men drowned. The Home Secretary, Henry Bruce, trying to make light of the case in the House, put the loss of life this way: 'All the crew were saved, except three.'

Plimsoll's crusade, his name and face were becoming familiar to every man and woman in the country. But, like many a whistle-blower before and since, he found that the more his popularity grew, the more personal attacks upon him became. Detractors put it about that he was insane.

There was a letter from one J. W. Mitchell in the *Shipping Gazette*, declaring that 'Plimsollism is another word for terrorism'. In Whitby shipowners and marine insurance agents crammed into the Talbot Hotel to complain (without having read his book) that 'Mr Plimsoll was dealing with the subject without due knowledge of it' and that his statements 'were those of a mere fanatic'. One shipowner, Robert Harrowing, opined that there should be no legislation until after 'the present unnatural and feverish excitement which has been created on the subject shall have abated'. The following resolution, proposed by Mr Bedlington, shipowner and maritime insurance agent, was carried unanimously:

That any legislation should be preceded by the most careful investigation and the best scientific and practical evidence, in order that
no injustice may be done by adopting a hard and fast load-line,
applicable to vessels of every description, and other objectionable
penal provisions such as are contained in Mr Plimsoll's Bill, and
which, if they become law, will bring absolute and immediate ruin
on a very large number of British shipowners, and will prevent a
considerable proportion of the remainder from working their ships
to any advantage whatever.

John Glover, shipowner, published a pamphlet entitled *The Plimsoll Sensation: A Reply*, refuting the arguments of *Our Seamen*. He wrote:

> Out of bad weather, the bad storms, and the *Northfleet* excitement, there has emerged a live British hero, whose name is Samuel Plimsoll Esq. . . . with his strange book, his heliotypes, his Royal Commission, his bill, his grotesque appeals to Divine Majesty, all mixed up with questions of load-line and insurance, quotations of hymns and colliery accidents and texts of Holy Scripture and a threat to his readers that they 'deserve to perish suddenly . . . if [they] don't help . . .'
>
>   As heroes are not very particular about facts, and as sensations are very apt to subside after the first explosion, the best help I could give to Mr Plimsoll was to add to his facts and half-facts . . .

Glover argued that it was already illegal to send unseaworthy ships to sea, and it was just a question of enforcing the law. He complained that Plimsoll's 'zeal exceeds his knowledge . . . if not his discretion'.

In Sunderland shipowners met and passed a resolution deprecating hasty legislation as likely to injure those it sought to protect. It approved a load line but condemned a survey as impracticable. On the same night in South Shields the Chamber of Commerce decided it would be unwise to legislate before a Royal Commission's report. The *Nautical Magazine* was scathing about churchmen coming out in support of Plimsoll. When the Baptist Union Assembly urged churches to petition Parliament and a deputation of leading Baptists went to see Gladstone, the magazine declared that unreason had prevailed: 'If "Little Bethel"* would look after the spiritual and social condition of the seamen and "Mollys" of Wapping Old Stairs . . . and would leave practical men to do the practical work of building and repairing ships, it would be better for all parties. Would it not be better and wiser if "Little Bethel" were to petition Parliament to enact that all women shall be virtuous and all teachers of the people sensible?'

* 'Little Bethel' referred to nonconformist chapels, generally the seamen's church.

Even as the Baptists were passing a supportive resolution, W. F. Moore, the Mayor of Plymouth, was critical of Plimsoll's Bill in a speech to the local Chamber of Commerce.

But the sailors' widows believed in Plimsoll. They wrote to say so. George Howell related that: 'On one occasion I was with him at 11 Victoria Street; he was lying on his couch profoundly disturbed, his head rolling on the cushion.' He read aloud to Howell a letter from a widow whose husband's ship had foundered with all hands. The sailor had feared its fate, but, as he told his wife: 'If I refuse, there is no other berth.' He tried to reassure her that he had weathered storms before. But he 'sent his best clothes, watch and other belongings home on the night he sailed. It was his "Farewell". His wife knew it. She, with her two young children, never saw him again. The widow told this pathetically and simply in her letter and prayed Mr Plimsoll "To go on with his holy work".'

Punch paid tribute to Plimsoll with a caricature drawn by its house cartoonist, John Tenniel (better known as the first published illustrator of *Alice's Adventures in Wonderland*), who projected a happier scenario still a little way into the future, prematurely portraying a grateful Jack blessing the name of Plimsoll as he takes leave of his sweetheart Polly, safe in the knowledge of Plimsoll's protection.

The same issue of *Punch* included stanzas in praise that began: 'Here's more power to Plimsoll, for Derby MP/His pluck and his bottom I like.'* It was a parody of a popular ballad by Charles Dibdin (who died in 1814), which included the refrain: 'There's a sweet little cherub who sits up aloft,/To keep watch for the life of Poor Jack.' (In another verse it is Providence that keeps watch.) *Punch*'s version made Plimsoll into the cherub, concluding: 'More power to Plimsoll, who sits up aloft/To keep watch for the life of Poor Jack.' *Fun* magazine used the same reference in a cartoon, quoted Dibdin, sat Plimsoll among the clouds, and gave him a pair of wings.

* See p. 315 for complete poem.

POOR JACK.

"For, d'ye see, there's a cherub sits smiling aloft
To keep watch for the life of Poor Jack."—DIBDIN.*

* And we hope Mr. PLIMSOLL will keep life-drawing it into the ears of the House.

Plimsoll as the cherub who 'sits up aloft/To keep watch for the life of
Poor Jack', *Fun* magazine, April 1875.

Vanity Fair published a caricature accompanied by a satirical account
of the man that revealed how much his fame had grown. 'If anybody
had asked last year who Mr Plimsoll was, the question could hardly have
been answered off-hand by one person in a hundred,' it said. 'But
Samuel Plimsoll has suddenly placed his name in the mouth even of
Society.' It described him as 'a man bold enough to tell what he believes
to be the truth . . . He has his reward. Any number of actions for libel
have been commenced against him, he has been forced to apologise in
the House of Commons, and were it not that he has found strong and
passionate support among the public, he would be a lost man.'

The magazine, tongue in cheek, made fun of the prejudice of those
who accused him of madness: 'he claims sympathy and admiration for
[the labouring classes] although it is well known that they are ill-
washed, uncouth and rude of speech. Manifestly such a proceeding

John Tenniel's cartoon, 'The Coffin Ships', from *Punch*, which was captioned:
Polly: 'O, Dear Jack! I can't help crying, but I'm so happy
you're not going in one of those dreadful ships.'
Jack: 'No, No, lass, – never more – thanks to our friend
Master Plimsoll, God bless him.'

could only be the offspring of a distempered brain, and so it has gone
forth that the sailors' champion is "mad on this question". Moreover
he is very fond of his wife, and continually mentions her as having
assisted in his work, which is another proof of madness.'

Vanity Fair was, like Plimsoll, on the side of the working man. It
mocked: 'in due course of time we shall learn . . . that there never
was a country where the humble capitalist was so enslaved by the
arrogant labourer as this, nor a trade in which the labourers' arro-
gance was so strongly marked as in that which has to do with ships.'

People began to send Plimsoll money to help, and on 1 March the
banker brothers Walter and Harvie Farquhar offered in a letter to *The
Times* to open a Plimsoll Defence Fund for contributions large and
small, and themselves donated £100 each. Plimsoll resisted financial aid
to begin with, not liking to receive cheques personally, for fear it might
expose him to malicious rumour. But he was persuaded that he had 'no
right to exclude others from taking a share in the work' and made the
condition only that any money left over from immediate expenses
should go to relieve sailors' dependants. By this time Plimsoll perceived

his campaign as a battle: he described it as 'the contest in which I am engaged'.

The Fund, quickly renamed the Plimsoll and Seamen's Defence Fund, was intended firstly to help Plimsoll pay his legal costs and to cover the expenses of his publications, and it led to the formation of an administrative committee, with Walter Farquhar as its treasurer. It had the declared aim of rendering assistance in Plimsoll's efforts to prevent loss of life at sea, promoting in particular his immediate measure, and seconding his call for a Royal Commission.

The original supporters of the Plimsoll and Seamen's Defence Fund were trade unionists, but what began as a working man's movement swiftly embraced the leisured classes. 'Sympathies,' wrote George Howell, 'were soon found in all ranks of society.' The first contributors to the Fund included knights, ladies, captains, honourables, a major-general, as well as 'Four children' who raised six shillings, 'Jack's brother, Newcastle' (two shillings) and 'Poor Nancy'* (one shilling), apparently fulfilling the founding banker Walter Farquhar's hope for both the liberality of the rich and the widow's mite, or 'the small but earnest offerings of dead sailors' wives, who, but for the nefarious practices denounced by Mr Plimsoll, might now, with Jack ashore, instead of fathoms deep, be in happy instead of desolate homes'.

The contribution of Samuel Plimsoll's own family covered, he said, the printing costs of *Our Seamen*: £1000 was given to the Fund in his name, £500 in Mrs Plimsoll's and £50 in the name of their daughter, 'Little Nellie'. A donation of £1066 16s even came from Lloyd's, with the proviso (so as not to alienate shipowning clients) that none of the money should be used towards Plimsoll's legal fees in his libel cases.

Other news kept the cause fresh in the minds of the public. On 19 March, listed in *The Times* among the 'Disasters At Sea', was the story of the brig *Demetrius*, from which three lives were lost. Three days later a report of the statistics of *Maritime Disasters* revealed that roughly half the European sailing ships and steamers that were lost in January and February were English.

* The name Nancy, like Molly and Polly, implied a sailor's wife or sweetheart.

The growing fervour was reflected in the choice of public entertainment. Among the performances advertised in *The Times* in March were a rendition of a heartily patriotic number by J. L. Hatton, 'The British Tar', sung by Mr Charles Santley in a composer's benefit concert ('Our sailors' pluck, all peril scorns,/ The world in arms it braves;/Their spirits but with dangers rise,/As ships rise to the waves'); and Mme Osborne Williams (the married name of Lilian Dundas, later of the D'Oyly Carte), singing 'The Sailor's Story', by Henry Smart, in Shoreditch's new town hall.

Plimsoll continued to address public gatherings whenever he could. Fortunately, since he was to travel the length and breadth of the country to spread the word, he was very fond of trains. George Howell recorded that he liked to walk the platforms of Victoria Station for recreation as other men go for walks in the park. His call for a Royal Commission now looked likely to succeed, but he continued to campaign for the other provisions of his Bill of 10 February to be introduced as interim measures: that all ships should be surveyed; that a maximum load line should be compulsory; and that deckloading should be prohibited. He circulated a pamphlet with a copy of his Bill, with these words in its preface: 'It is certain that unless a very vigorous demand for its enactment this Session be made by the public, the opposition, determined, unceasing and persistent, of a small minority of the ship-owners, and the hostility of the Board of Trade, will prevent its being carried into law.' As the 'contest' proceeded, the Board of Trade increasingly became the enemy.

On 16 March Plimsoll attended a meeting in Leeds and afterwards visited the grave of an old friend, buried, according to Plimsoll, twenty-seven years earlier in Woodhouse Lane Cemetery. The evidence is circumstantial, but it is possible that this visit reveals an interesting association. Buried in the cemetery in 1848 (in fact twenty-five years before Plimsoll's visit) was a circus performer, Susannah Darby. She died at the age of forty-seven during a show, interrupting her twelve-year-old son Lionel's tightrope act, when a circus gallery collapsed. Six hundred people fell with the structure, but she was the only fatality. Her husband, Pablo Fanque (real name William Darby), was a trick equestrian, and the UK's first black circus proprietor. In a letter written in 1934, Pablo Fanque's son Ted Pablo claimed that his father was a 'great friend' of Samuel Plimsoll. Plimsoll and Fanque could have met in Sheffield, with which Fanque had connections and where Plimsoll lived from the age of fourteen. Pablo and Susannah had a home in Lancashire but toured in Yorkshire; months after Susannah's death, Fanque married a Sheffield woman. Plimsoll would have been twenty-four when the accident killed Susannah. Fanque himself died in 1871 and was buried beside Susannah in Leeds (after a splendid funeral parade which included his horse).*

The inscription on Pablo and Susannah's joint grave mentioned the collapse of the circus in Leeds's King Charles Croft. Was Plimsoll moved to look at the site? Later that day Plimsoll attended a lecture-sermon in a music hall (now demolished) in King Charles Croft, having seen posters advertising it under the headline 'Rotten Ships!' The connections between the places and people might be coincidence, but taken together they could corroborate Ted Pablo's report of a friendship. And this friendship offers a shred of proof that Plimsoll disdained social barriers not only of class and wealth but also – as did the circus community of the time – of colour.

The afternoon's lecture-sermon was to be held in the Amphi-theatre music hall, and Plimsoll went along to hear what was said, and if possible to take part. After an address by the Reverend William Thomas Adey, minister of the Burley Road Baptist Church, Plimsoll was invited to speak, and stood on the theatre stage and urged the people of Leeds to help him ensure that Parliament did not disband that year without doing more to save the lives of sailors than merely appointing a Royal Commission. He gave examples of cases that had come to his attention during the previous eight days. One was the story of a Scottish ship that had been sailing

* Pablo Fanque's name is familiar to many from a Beatles song: John Lennon had a poster from one of his circuses and put his name into 'For the Benefit of Mr Kite', from *Sergeant Pepper*.

from a port in the north of Scotland for longer than any of the locals could remember and that they thought should have been 'broken up for firewood' any time in the previous twenty years. It was so notoriously unseaworthy that hardly anybody would sail in it. 'The captain himself stuck to her because he was an old man and had a large family, and the choice for him was that or destitution. He had sailed so many years in her, and had always escaped that he thought he would risk it.' Together he and the owners recruited a crew of young boys, all of them under seventeen. When the ship went down all were drowned. 'Shame,' cried the Leeds crowd.

He told too the story of another ship whose first two crews refused to sail in her and were imprisoned. The third was drowned while the refusers were still in jail. Remembering that this was a Sunday and a lecture-sermon, Plimsoll concluded:

> If the people of Leeds lent a helping hand in the movement, they would never regret it, the recollection would remain with them until their dying day; it would be a solace when flesh and heart failed because of physical prostration and weakness; it would be with them sustaining their sinking spirits even to the confines of an eternal world, and would precede them even into that world, and plead for them with Him who said: 'Inasmuch as ye have done it unto one of the least of these my brethren, ye have done it unto me.'

A leader in the *Leeds Mercury* on 18 March, considering whether it was suitable to use a Sunday sermon as a platform for this cause, remarked:

> there was nothing in the application irreverent either as regarded the day or the occasion. The fresh cases mentioned by the Hon Gentleman were as startling as they were painful, and were as fit subjects for Sunday thought as the more recognised forms of immorality. It has unhappily been so long notorious in seaport towns that owners will run their ships until they sink, or go to pieces like touchwood, with the first shock of a collision, whether at sea or on the beach,

that people have ceased to think of the iniquity of the thing. Familiarity has bred contempt.

Four days later Plimsoll spoke in the Egyptian Hall of London's Mansion House, with the Lord Mayor presiding over the annual general meeting of the National Lifeboat Institution, and

dwelt upon the constant and extreme perils attending deck loading, and said he believed the commission which was about to inquire into those matters would reveal a state of things of which the public were but little aware. He hoped that, in addition, a temporary measure would shortly be passed through Parliament to prohibit the practice of overloading, and he felt sure that it would meet with the approbation of all respectable ship owners.

But it was the next night that his most emotional and celebrated public meeting was held.

4

THE GREAT PLIMSOLL MEETING

A small porticoed doorway squeezed between two buildings on the north side of the Strand was the entrance most visitors used to one of the grandest arenas for protest in Victorian London.* Inside Exeter Hall, built in 1830, were polished marble staircases with 'banisters of cedar, curiously inlaid with gold' and hangings and tapestries, carvings and paintings inspired by early-Victorian enthusiasm for Ancient Egypt and the Orient. This was the headquarters of the evangelical movement, famous for its 'May Meetings', a month of piety attended by the faithful of all denominations. It was also London's main concert hall, in which Mendelssohn conducted his own work, and a great forum for the discussion of social and political ideas. Up the marble stairs was the Great Hall, an auditorium large enough for three thousand people, with a ceiling as high as a three-storey building.

In this chamber, on Tuesday 17 March 1873, the economist, philosopher and former MP John Stuart Mill, 'no orator but merely a reciter of passages in a weak voice and an even tone from his books', spoke on behalf of the Land Tenure Reform Association,

* No. 372, Exeter Hall, was demolished in 1907.

which sought the abolition of primogeniture to prevent the amassing of large-scale landed wealth. Its overall goal was the reduction of poverty, and many of Plimsoll's sympathisers, including Henry Fawcett, Robert Applegarth, W. R. Cremer and Charles Bradlaugh, also allied themselves with Mill.

The *Penny Illustrated Paper*'s prediction of the crowd at the 'Great Plimsoll Meeting', March 1873. (*London Illustrated News*)

Four days later the chamber was the scene of a clamorous assembly which had been advertised in *The Times* for a week in advance. On Saturday night at 7 p.m. Samuel Plimsoll was to speak, with the Earl of Shaftesbury in the chair. The *Penny Illustrated Paper* printed an engraving of a crowd in Exeter Hall before the meeting took place, anticipating that this was what it would look like.

It was an accurate prediction. *The Times* reported that 'all classes of Londoners thronged the Hall from floor to ceiling'. They crammed the gallery that ran along the back and part of the sides of the hall, and filled the seats that rose from the central arena like an amphitheatre. Shaftesbury's form of address, though, indicates that the audience was exclusively male: 'Men of London', he called the crowd. Eliza, as far as we know, was not present at this momentous demonstration, which was later described as 'the Great Plimsoll Meeting'. (She would have her moment on the platform at Exeter Hall, but not for another two years.) Eight Members of Parliament, a couple of lords, half a dozen trade unionists, three clergymen, an actor-poet and a clutch of sympathetic shipowners were among those who joined Plimsoll on the platform, against the splendid backdrop of an organ, half-covered in gold leaf, that was the height and width of a house.

Plimsoll was fortunate in securing the allegiance of Lord Shaftesbury, to support him in what the Earl called in his diary Plimsoll's 'glorious defence of the wretched, oppressed seamen of the Mercantile Marine'. Shaftesbury, then seventy-two, had already distinguished himself as a social reformer and was a role model for Plimsoll. He too had experience of reforms that were resisted in Parliament. At the time of the Exeter Hall meeting Shaftesbury was still working to rescue young boys from employment as chimney sweeps; he had been thwarted in this cause for more than thirty years. (Shaftesbury's frustrations were only part of this story: the first man to agitate for the abolition of climbing boys in chimneys was Jonas Hanway, friend of paupers and inventor of the umbrella, in the 1780s. It took over a century for this cruelty to be stopped.)

Shaftesbury also had a long interest in the welfare of sailors. He was president of the Missions to Seamen and a patron of the Seamen's Hospital Society, and he had inaugurated in 1866 the first training ship, the *Chichester*, to apprentice 'ragged boys' to become sailors and give them a future – if they escaped coffin-ships. (The *Chichester* was, as it happens, fitted up by Messrs Money Wigram & Sons of Blackwall, owners of the lost *London*, perhaps rebuilding their reputation.)

In Exeter Hall, Shaftesbury rose from the chair Prince Albert had occupied on his first appearance at a public assembly.* The Earl was

---

* In June 1840 Prince Albert presided over a meeting of the Society for the Extinction of the Slave Trade.

always eloquent on behalf of the poor, but on this occasion the feel-ing with which he spoke of the loss of loved ones was given resonance by his own bereavement. Only five months earlier his beloved wife Emily (known to him as 'Minny'), the mother of their ten children and, he said, the 'purest, gentlest, kindest, sweetest and most confiding spirit that ever lived', had died after forty-one years of marriage. (He had set up a fund in her name to provide loans to flower girls, paid back in pittances, which saved them from resorting to prostitution outside the season for violets and watercress and fruit; they borrowed money to set up coffee stalls in winter instead.) And two months later his carefully nursed daughter 'Conty', Lady Constance, who had long been sickly with phthisis, also succumbed. 'Never was a death so joyous, so peaceful,' said Shaftesbury of Conty's death, but despite his absolute conviction that wife, daugh-ter and three other deceased children awaited him in Heaven, he was still wrestling with his grief.

The matter at hand, said Shaftesbury, was one his audience must know 'from the newspapers, from the pamphlets and from the con-versation everywhere since Mr Plimsoll had spoken'. They met to denounce and put an end to 'one of the most terrible, the most dia-bolical systems that ever desolated mankind'. He spoke of the need to 'prevent the enormous extension of widowhood and orphanage' and to preserve 'the lives, the limbs and the generous character of those noble fellows who were being submerged beneath the waters of the ocean'.

Shaftesbury's characterisation of sailors as 'noble fellows' is signif-icant. One of the effects of the Plimsoll campaign was that it changed attitudes to sailors. It countered the opinion that they were idle, dissolute wastrels, who no sooner came ashore than they spent their pay in brothels and on drink.

This attitude to sailors persisted, but thanks to the campaign it became harder to express condemnation of seamen without qualifi-cation. Two years later, in the House of Commons, Thomas Eustace Smith MP would say: 'We have heard much about unseaworthy ships but not so fully understood the question of unseaworthy crews. I myself have lately had a large ship going to sea and every man of the crew had to be carried on board and had to be looked after for

twenty-four hours until he had become sufficiently sober to undertake his duty.' But even in telling this anecdote he felt obliged to add,
post-Plimsoll, that: 'There were large numbers of sailors who were
sober and respectable and many of them were as anxious to support
their families as Members of the House could be to support theirs.'

Plimsoll and his friends never spoke of sailors but as brave and big-
hearted, patriots and family men, whose loyalty was all to their
shipmates on board, to their loved ones at home and to their country, which they would serve beyond duty and until death.
Repackaging the poor for middle-class consumers was a prerequisite
of reform. If the needy were not credited with virtue, it gave the
powerful licence to be dismissive. All Victorian writers enamoured
of social justice exploited this fact, and Shaftesbury, a veteran of
mining and factory reform, understood it well. The idealisation was
certainly preferable to the denigration: the important fact was that
these were human beings who, like anyone else, had the capacity for
honourable behaviour and attachment to their families, and whose
lives should not be squandered by the self-interested. All means of
arousing proper sympathy for them were appropriate.

Appeals to national feeling were an effective tactic. Shaftesbury
asked (as reported in *The Times*):

Who were those for whom the ardent sympathy of the English
people was besought? Were they not our seamen? Were they not the
pride, the strength, and the security of Great Britain? Did not our
commercial marine supply the military marine? And should
Englishmen sit and allow ignorance, neglect and covetousness to sacrifice as many fine fellows every year as died in their country's cause
at the Nile and Trafalgar? All Britons loved the British sailor.

And he stressed the sailor's role in contributing to the 'comfort
and civilization' of his native land and in its defence against 'insult
and menace'. Shaftesbury, skilled politician and rhetorician that he
was, set up a sense of debt to seamen, which their countrymen
were morally obliged to repay.

While Shaftesbury 'asked for no restraint of language, and hardly
for restraint of manner' in denouncing the current system, he urged

the audience 'not to declare that all shipowners were of the same character and temperament' for among that body were 'some of the best men and noblest hearts that England could boast'. He quoted a letter from John Burnes, head of the Cunard Steamship Company, approving Shaftesbury's support of Plimsoll and saying that 'there was a great necessity for keel-hauling'.

Shaftesbury drew attention, too, to the fact that protection for sailors lagged behind other philanthropic legislation. The agitation on behalf of the seamen was a catching-up. Parliament should instantly ensure 'that our seamen . . . enjoy the protection . . . extended to miners, colliers and factory children, and to emigrant ships'.

Such was the strength of popular feeling that when Plimsoll advanced to the edge of the platform the whole audience rose en masse, waving their toppers, their bowlers and their handkerchiefs, and cheered for some minutes. Plimsoll, currently assailed by libel suits, said, recalling the Highlanders who in 1857 had famously relieved the Indian Mutiny siege, that this reception gave him 'the same hope and encouragement which the sound of the distant bag-pipes gave the beleaguered garrisons at Lucknow'.

The man who had been described by *Vanity Fair* as a poor speaker held this audience for over an hour while he outlined the Bill he had put before Parliament as an interim measure to save lives until the Royal Commission reached its conclusions. Once ridiculed for quoting Shakespeare, Plimsoll had found his plain-speaking voice. A contemporary described his delivery thus: 'Mr Plimsoll is a popular as well as an excitable speaker. His words do not halt by the way, but usually muster and march with speech, swift to the purpose before him. He has no hesitation in using good, simple, Anglo-Saxon terms.' He came to be known for speaking in the House of 'bur-glarious intentions', which revealed his childhood in Cumberland and Yorkshire, and of complaining, in demotic idiom, that his Bill was 'burked' – or quietly suffocated.*

---

* Burke (v. t.): to murder by suffocation, or so as to produce few marks of violence, for the pur-pose of obtaining a body to be sold for dissection. To dispose of quietly or indirectly; to suppress; to smother; to shelve; as, to burke a parliamentary question. Derived from Burke of the grave-robbing duo Burke and Hare.

Well into his Exeter Hall oration, he apologised to the audience for taking up their time with 'dry business details'. 'No, no,' 'Go on!' cried the crowd. He then rewarded their thirst for drama with the reasons 'why he troubled himself so much on this subject'. He related 'with much graphic power and effect' the tale of his peril at sea and the resolution he and his wife made at Redcar. He went on to call Gladstone 'one of the best men that ever lived' and made fun of shipowners who wanted his survey and load line to apply only to new-built ships.

Plimsoll also revealed that the campaign had had from the beginning ambitious plans for influencing public opinion. He had once hoped, he said, to obtain the aid which he 'felt sure the late Charles Dickens would have given', thus invoking his name for the cause without having to prove his support. Dickens had died in June 1870, months after Plimsoll opened his campaign in Parliament, but at a time when the press was already criticising the government for its prevarication on this issue. So Plimsoll could have considered an approach to a man whose social conscience had helped to awaken his own. Plimsoll also shared with his Exeter Hall audience the curious information that he 'was now proposing to Gustave Doré to paint a harrowing picture of wrecks, and drowning seamen at the bottom of the North Sea, in the two great channels of trade, from the Baltic to Newcastle and Hull'.

Doré, the great French engraver and illustrator of Aesop, Cervantes, Dante and the Bible, had lived in London, in a suite at the Westminster Palace Hotel, in 1871–2, and had produced a series of illustrations to text by the English writer Blanchard Jerrold, published as *London: A Pilgrimage*. This book, which Plimsoll would surely have seen, depicted in loving detail the docks by day and night and the ships that sailed the Thames, and dwelt on the poverty and misery of the back streets of the capital, particularly those East End alleys frequented by sailors. It is not surprising that Plimsoll might have expected to find sympathy from this man, who had been a pictorial chronicler of the Crimean and the Mexican wars and a satirist of the Communards of Paris in 1871 and so had a record of reportage and political engagement. He also had experience of portraying anguished bodies in a raging sea (he depicted the biblical Deluge, Coleridge's Ancient Mariner, the Wandering Jew in a shipwreck). Doré was acquainted with Queen Victoria's daughter Princess Louise and entertained by the Rothschilds, all of whom came to have connections with Plimsoll's cause.

Doré did not take Plimsoll up on his surprisingly specific commission to illustrate the trade route from the Baltic to Hull, despite Plimsoll's confident assertion that 'the talents of the great artist should be exercised for the good of humanity'. But this titbit reveals that Plimsoll believed that artifice could be employed to arouse indignation just as well as fact. He did not require Doré to record real suffering, but only to suggest it in a fictional image.

Besides the speeches, there was also a recitation. Arthur Matthison, actor, librettist and poet, regaled the gathering with 'Coffin Ships' (see p. 307), his ten-minute, tear-jerking, verse narrative of an old mariner, about the wreck of a coffin-ship and the death of a young sailor whose last thoughts are of his sweetheart. It condemned the coffin-shipowners and urged that those who had a voice to speak in

'Prepare to shed them now': in another costume, Arthur Matthison, who performed his recitation, 'Coffin Ships', at the Great Plimsoll Meeting, March 1873. (*Picturehistory.com*)

defence of sailors should use it. Once again fiction was put to the service of political ends. The campaign for the welfare of sailors owed its efficacy to emotion as much as to facts, and sentimental imaginings were interpreted as valid representations of the truth. The blurring of fact and fiction has long played a part in propaganda and in social reform, from *Uncle Tom's Cabin* to *Cathy Come Home*, and has worked before and since to change attitudes. It was not only the Victorians who were affected by it.

The meeting ended with a resolution unanimously carried to form a committee to further Plimsoll's ends. Its first members were named and included six members of the House of Lords, and eleven members of the Commons, some of them titled, as well as a couple of admirals and four sea captains, among them Captain Goodenough, whose support for Plimsoll had been printed in the letters column of *The Times*.[*] After Exeter Hall, there was no class of Victorian society that was not involved in Plimsoll's campaign. The cause had been taken up by the Establishment.

In March 1873 the state of a ship in St Katharine's Dock in London had come to the attention of Samuel Plimsoll. This, here with the original spelling mistakes, was the affidavit of a rigger by the name of J. Harris, resident in Lambeth, about the *Parga*:

> Walking round St Katherine's Dock I saw a shipwright cutting out a piece under a barque's port quarter. Seeing he <u>cut it so easy</u> caused me to look at hir name – I then thought I would have a good look at hir and she was just one of those ships Mr Plimsoll had so often spoke off. I was then determined to state the fact of the ship to Mr Bulten – which he went on board and I went with him – we went down in the forecastle she smelt afull and Mr B was forsed to go on deck. The mate asked him to go in the cabin. I examined the deck's. I found a hole in

* The Members of Parliament on the committee were Lord George Cavendish (North Derbyshire), Viscount Bury (Berwick-upon-Tweed in Northumberland), Lord Elcho (Haddington in Scotland), Sir John Hay (Ripon in Yorkshire), Thomas Hughes QC (Frome in Somerset), William Wells (Peterborough), Lord Claud Hamilton (Tyrone County in Ireland), Henry R. Brand (Hertfordshire), George Bentinck (Whitehaven in Cumberland), James Elphinstone (Portsmouth) and Admiral Erskine (Stirling in Scotland).

the decks with fully 2 lbs of putty in it and aloft it looked enough to frighten you . . . If I had been unfortunate enough to signe articles in the 'Parga' without seeing her one glance would have been enough for me. As soon as I was on board I would have got every thing ready for going on shore at Gravesend and put myself down for 3 months' imprisonment . . . and be very glad to get off so easy.

Plimsoll brought a complaint against the *Parga*. The 1871 Merchant Shipping Act dictated that the Board of Trade could detain a ship suspected of being unseaworthy only if someone complained. (And even then it could not be stopped for being overloaded. Five members of any crew could also detain a ship, but if surveyors found they were mistaken about its unseaworthiness, they were liable for costs. The threat of this expense deterred sailors from making use of the law.) The owner of the *Parga*, William Gardiner, a master mariner and chandler who had bought the ship (built 1840) at a very low price, immediately had his solicitors write to Plimsoll asking for the source of his information and demanding apology and compensation. They sent the letter on the day of the Exeter Hall meeting. In its giddy aftermath, two days after the great assembly room echoed with cheers of support, Plimsoll wrote back with swashbuckling bravado:

> *Sirs,*
> *Yours of the 22nd inst to hand.*
> *I will not give the name of my informant. I will make no apology, and as to compensation, the only compensation due to your clients and all other ship owners who load unseaworthy vessels to sea with men a thousand times better than themselves on board is, in my opinion, a halter apiece and the offices of the hangman.*
> *Do your worst.*
> *Samuel Plimsoll*

The Board of Trade thought there were indeed grounds for considering the ship unseaworthy, and had it unloaded for inspection. Gardiner said he would hold the Board responsible for expenses and damages. One account says that Plimsoll was proved wrong, and cost the state £1200. But Chichester Fortescue (perhaps through

gritted teeth) thanked Plimsoll in the House for drawing his attention to the state of this ship, and eighteen months later it was
condemned at Wapping.

The Board, it seems, was encouraged to be more proactive by the
bad press it received after Exeter Hall. This, for instance, is what the
Penny Illustrated Paper, in the week after that assembly, had to say about
the Board's conduct: 'We only hope . . . that an earnest word from
Mr Gladstone will dissipate the cold-blooded indifference which
(previous to Saturday last) seems to have led to a pooh-poohing
treatment by Board of Trade officials of the hon. Member for Derby.'

The Plimsoll and Seamen's Defence Fund was officially opened, a
few weeks after it was first mooted, by the Lord Mayor of London
on 26 March 1873. Within weeks of the Great Plimsoll Meeting
twenty-five peers of the realm had taken up two-thirds of the places
on the Committee, alongside the Lord Mayor himself. Hereditary
landowners rubbed shoulders with such controversial figures as the
shoemaker George Odger, who volunteered to lend what anonymous help he could to the sailors' cause and to have his name left off
its literature if it might deter those chary of keeping his company.
Odger, former secretary of the London Trades Council and a leader
of working-class radicals, had a reputation as the most extreme of
democratic republicans, and so was something of a favourite object
of ridicule in burlesques of the early 1870s. He made five unsuccessful attempts to get into Parliament, baulked partly by the Liberal
Party itself, which opposed his candidature.

Although Shaftesbury was its president, Plimsoll's right-hand man
on the Defence Fund Committee, and officially its secretary, was the
trade unionist George Howell, who had allied himself with Plimsoll
and his cause from the first. Howell had been secretary of the
Reform League when the two met in 1866, and had since helped
to establish the Trades Union Congress, borne out of the Trades
Councils in 1868. Howell served as the first secretary of the TUC's
Parliamentary Committee.* He was originally, until the mid-1860s,
a bricklayer, and his long, determined and slightly melancholy face,

---

* The Parliamentary Committee was the forerunner of the General Council, established in 1871
to put pressure on Parliament to amend the 1871 Trade Union Act.

even when he was photographed with his white collar and tiepin, would always also have looked at home above a leather apron and a fistful of tools. His ambition was 'to become one of the first working men to secure election to Parliament'. (He would go on to succeed, after three unsuccessful attempts, becoming the member for North East Bethnal Green in 1884, and entering Parliament with ten other working men, most of them miners.)

Howell was not always popular, even with one of his own biographers, who concluded that he was vain and self-promoting, but he was a steadfast friend to Plimsoll, and the Boswell to his Johnson in keeping a record of the workings of the Defence Fund Committee. He wrote of the hours he spent with Mr and Mrs Plimsoll at their home in north London: 'Mr Plimsoll was a man in earnest. He was fearless and enthusiastic in the cause he had espoused, even to the extent of recklessness in so far as he was personally affected by litigation and expenditure ... No one had better means of judging, for I was often with them from early morn to dewy eve, and even far into the night ...'

Howell was keen to demonstrate in his own account how much of a contribution he himself had made to the campaign. He claimed credit for turning what Plimsoll planned as a working men's committee into 'something broader than a mere sectional committee of workers, as represented by the Trades Congress, for the question was of national importance.' Plimsoll enlisted Howell as an organiser. 'My consent being given, Mr Plimsoll left the rest to me.' It was the idea of Thomas Hughes MP to ask Lord Shaftesbury to chair the Committee, but Howell, as he made clear, was the one who approached the Earl. Hughes became vice-chairman.

Thomas Hughes, the author of *Tom Brown's Schooldays* (published in 1856 and based on his own experience at Rugby School), was, with fellow author Charles Kingsley and educationalist Frederick Denison Maurice, a founder of the Christian Socialist movement.* This movement grew out of the belief that Christians were morally obliged to alleviate suffering through reform, and that the Church

---

* Founded after the government's rejection of the Chartist petition in 1848.

should intervene to right real social grievances. It is hardly surprising that Plimsoll and Shaftesbury excited the sympathies of such men. At the time the Plimsoll Committee was formed, Hughes was Liberal MP for Frome in Somerset and principal of a working men's college in London.* Charles Kingsley is not listed among the members of the first Plimsoll Committee, but his brother Henry is.

George Howell, on behalf of the Committee, which met at 27 Villiers Street, a terrace just off the Strand (the building is now a pub), circulated a draft petition for citizens to sign and send to the House of Commons. It urged that a short Act be passed this session to prevent ships in need of repair from going to sea; to prevent deckloading between 1 September and 1 March; and to adopt a maximum load line. All these were measures Plimsoll had proposed three years earlier, and James Hall before him. It was time for the nation to make itself heard.

There was in nineteenth-century Britain an interconnected class of liberal aristocrats, very wealthy families who not only gave money to good causes but were politically involved in the welfare of the less fortunate. The landed gentry bred a good many radical politicians. Just as there were shipowners in both parties, so on both sides of the House there were plenty of men with titles, particularly younger marquises and honourables who would not inherit peerages until their fathers died (and thus give up their seats in the Commons to take up their places in the Lords). Some aristocrats came from families that had been reformers for generations. Others were rebels against a family tradition, such as Lord Shaftesbury, whose cruel and unloving father was a Tory, and not known for his altruism, although Shaftesbury never allied himself to any political party.† Members of such families were quick to stand beside the 'sailor's friend'.

In many aristocratic families there were not only men who were reformers and Liberal MPs, but women who made their mark as activists and innovators, with an impact of their own on social change. No sooner was the original Committee formed, with the

* In Red Lion Square, the Working Men's College was founded by Christian Socialists in 1854. Hughes went on (in 1880) to spend much of his fortune founding a Utopian town in America: Rugby, Tennessee.
† Shaftesbury was a hereditary lord, eventually becoming the 7th Earl, born Anthony Ashley Cooper and inheritor of the title Lord Ashley at the age of ten.

object of raising funds to finance Plimsoll's printing costs and, as accused shipowners began to retaliate, his legal fees, than Elizabeth, the Duchess of Argyll, expressed to Plimsoll her willingness to preside over a Ladies' Committee. Around her soon gathered a group of formidable women. They were the wives and daughters of powerful men, but their achievements and writings commanded respect in their own right.

The Duchess, then forty-nine, gave the cause cachet. She was Mistress of the Robes to Queen Victoria and so the senior lady in the Royal Household. She was also the mother-in-law of a princess. Four of Queen Victoria's children had married members of the German royal family, but the monarch's unconventional artist daughter Louise had broken with tradition and in 1871 married the Duke and Duchess of Argyll's son and heir, John Campbell, the Marquis of Lorne, himself a Liberal MP and Cabinet minister. (The marriage gave pleasure to a nation 'tired of German princes coming to the English courts with their large suites and ridiculous manners' – although ultimately it was a rather unhappy union for Louise and Lorne.) The Duke and Duchess were good friends of the Gladstones; the Duke was a prominent Liberal politician, a scientist, economist and man of letters, and he had been close to the late Prince Albert. The Duchess was the mother of eleven children, and a Roman Catholic who exchanged ideas with her friend Cardinal Newman and corresponded, disapprovingly, with Darwin. She had grand connections, but also a history of concern for the disadvantaged and the victimised, dating from her opposition to slavery in the 1850s.

Two admirals' daughters took up positions under the Duchess's presidency on the Ladies' Committee. One of these was the indomitable Mrs Henrietta Baden-Powell, then a widowed mother of seven, including Robert, later founder of the Boy Scouts; she herself was one of the instigators of the Girls' High School movement. Her father, Admiral W. H. Smyth, was an astronomer and author of *The Sailor's Word-Book* (which is still in print). In it the entry for Load Water-Line read: 'The draught of water exhibited when the ship is properly loaded; in a word, her proper displacement, not always sufficiently considered'; Henrietta had grown up with nautical matters, and had it on her father's authority that ships were sometimes irresponsibly overloaded.

Taking on the role of treasurer to the Ladies' Committee was the Hon. Georgiana Cowper-Temple, daughter of Admiral Tollemache and the childless second wife of William Francis Cowper-Temple, MP for South Hants. His sister was the Earl of Shaftesbury's beloved wife Minny, so Georgiana was sister-in-law to Plimsoll's great ally and the chair of the Men's Committee. Cultured, charitable, pious, Georgiana was known for her tolerance. She had a certain unconventional curiosity about mysticism and was not easily shocked: she went on to offer Oscar Wilde a refuge between and during his two trials. (Another friend, the painter John Ruskin, who never consummated his marriage to Effie, countered accusations of impotence by writing to Georgiana that he could 'prove his virility' to her in a moment, which would have been a memorable demonstration if she had taken him up on it.) She was sensitive to the suffering of others, even of animals, and her many charitable and temperance activities included visits to workhouses. The worst that was said of her was that she revelled in the spectacle of demonstrative faith at deathbeds. She was almost universally adored, except by Archbishop E. W. Benson, who thought she had a smile which 'was the result of always being told it was like something heavenly'.

Alongside the admirals' daughters sat the Countess of Airlie, Henrietta Blanche Stanley, the wife of the High Commissioner to the General Secretary of the Church of Scotland, who had homes on both sides of the border and was a friend of the painter James Whistler. Also a patron of Whistler was the wealthy Mrs Margaret Pennington, Yorkshire-born wife of Frederick Pennington, JP, landowner and later MP for Stockport. She had a grand Hyde Park home with eight servants and made the most flamboyant financial contribution to the campaign, outdone only by Mrs Plimsoll: she donated £100. She was also generous with her time to those less fortunate: in the 1880s she would become the honorary secretary to the Board Schools Free Dinner Fund, an organisation that fed half a million indigent urban schoolchildren.

With these women on the first Ladies' Committee was a Miss Courtenay, probably Caroline, older daughter of the late Rt Hon.

Thomas Peregrine Courtenay; the Hon. Mrs Locke King, wife of the Hon. Peter John Locke King, MP for East Surrey; and Mrs Pennington's friend Mrs Caroline Rylands, mother of five and the wife of Peter Rylands, a wealthy wire manufacturer and the Liberal MP for Warrington in Lancashire (her home town), in which capacity he was supportive of Plimsoll in the House – where he was known as 'Preposterous Peter' – until he lost his seat in 1874. He was a Free Trade reformist, with an interest in ornithology and phrenology. About Caroline we know less; her son, Louis Gordon Rylands, chose not to mention his mother in his 1890 account of his father's life.

Among the Carolines and Henriettas, Eliza Plimsoll was honorary secretary to this committee. The actual secretary, then living in semi-rural Kentish Town in north London, was Sarah, wife of the novelist and newspaperman Henry Kingsley and sister-in-law of Charles Kingsley, author of *The Water Babies* (1863) and therefore the inventor of the good fairy Mrs Doasyouwouldbedoneby. Kingsley's sister-in-law was being a good fairy herself and putting the precept of the name into practice.

This group of intelligent women in their thirties and forties, capable of well-informed discussion of religion and politics, art and science, if not too taken up at their meetings with the immediate matter in hand, were as effective a force in Plimsoll's campaign as the scores of distinguished men who associated themselves with it, although their methods were less vocal. Despite their array of achievements, their catalogue of claims to greatness, there was a pressure on these able, thoughtful, active women to be quiet campaigners operating in a private network.

It was not then generally accepted that women should make their political mark, although there were plenty, from the Garrett sisters to Florence Nightingale, who were doing exactly that, and effecting huge social transformations. All women had to contend with the fact that charitable works were more acceptable than those perceived as reformist. The prevailing opinion, even among some women, was that women should perfect themselves as comforts and helpmeets, preferably inside the home. The Ladies' Committee was part of a protest movement, but it helped to be seen to be benevolent rather than angry. Uniting to raise funds for poor sailors and their families was not dangerously ambitious. The acceptable model for women was not Liberty Leading the People but Ministering Angel (hence the reinvention of the tough, practical and relentless Florence Nightingale as the demure Lady with the Lamp). Nevertheless, even the Ladies' Committee was eventually driven to noisy demonstration: they organised, for instance, a marching band leading a procession along the Strand, with banners and scarves waving, to another Plimsoll meeting at Exeter Hall in April 1875, hosted this time by the women and attended by some three thousand people.

In March 1873 the Ladies' Committee published a matter-of-fact appeal that cited the loss in the previous eleven years of 8694 sailors' lives within ten miles of the English coast. It deplored the terrible practice of vessels being sent to sea overloaded, undermanned, unseaworthy and deckloaded. It opposed the jailing of sailors for refusing to sail in rotten ships, and the deceptive use of renaming. It insisted that during the deliberations of the Royal Commission 'rotten ships will be sent to sea and great loss of life occasioned. It is therefore necessary that a Temporary Bill, which will be brought before the House of Commons by Mr Plimsoll for second reading on the 14th May, should at once be passed.'

It earnestly appealed 'to all Englishwomen to assist them in this important work, either by aiding them in the formation of Local Committees; by promoting the presentation of Petitions to the House of Commons, by collecting subscriptions, or by spreading information on the subject'. The Ladies' Committee prevailed upon a wide circle of other distinguished women to contribute financially to the cause. Among these was Florence Nightingale herself, who gave a generous £5, which was as much as a sailor might earn in a month. Her sympathy with the cause prompted the Plimsolls to invite her in July to accompany them to a temperance fête in the gardens of the Crystal Palace in Sydenham.* She declined

---

* On Tuesday 22 July 1873 Mr and Mrs Plimsoll visited the National Temperance League fête in Sydenham (the site of the Crystal Palace), which was attended by 53,000 people. Plimsoll was to preside at an event but although he was present, he was too ill to do so; at the time illness even prevented his attending to his House of Commons duties.

politely, pleading ill-health, in a letter of 16 July written on her behalf by her sister Parthenope, which was her usual strategy for avoiding unwanted society. This does not suggest any particular aversion to the Plimsolls; at the time she saw hardly anyone but family.

Patronisingly listed in the *Penny Illustrated Paper* under the heading 'The Lass that Loves a Sailor', Nightingale was cited with the following distinguished women who were among the first subscribers to the Fund. The witty and fearless Katherine Russell, Lady Amberley, committed supporter of women's rights and advocate of free love,* and the mother of the philosopher Bertrand Russell, then a year old, gave £5 to the cause. (A year later she died at thirty-two of diphtheria that also carried off her six-year-old daughter Rachel.) The widowed Countess of Aberdeen and her daughter Lady Katherine Gordon, mother and sister of Sir George Hamilton-Gordon, a sailor who had drowned at sea in 1870 at the age of twenty-eight, were moved by their own loss to contribute £15. Louisa, Lady Goldsmid, one of the first members of Girton College, Cambridge, an active supporter of the education and enfranchisement of women and the wife of the first Jewish barrister and MP (himself a Committee member), donated £6 6s. And Juliana Cohen, Baroness Mayer de Rothschild, whose many charitable works included the establishment of lip-reading among the deaf and dumb, and was the wife of the MP for coastal Hythe, gave a handsome £25. (Her obituary called her 'the lady with the masculine mind and the feminine heart'.) Thus it was that men and women, rich and poor, Jews, Catholics, Congregationalists, Scottish Presbyterians, evangelists and atheists united in 1873 for the life of poor Jack.

On 28 March this concerted pressure seemed to bear fruit. Chichester Fortescue, President of the Board of Trade, announced to the House of Commons that a Royal Commission on Unseaworthy Ships would sit until July. The 'Lady Gracious and Kind' had not only sanctioned the Commission but signalled her approval of Plimsoll's cause by giving her son the Duke of Edinburgh charge of the hearings,

---

* Lady Amberley's opinions prompted Queen Victoria to say privately that 'Lady Amberley ought to get a good whipping.'

although his place was taken in the end by the Duke of Somerset. In this moment of triumph the *Penny Illustrated Paper* spoke of the 'glorious task which [Mr Plimsoll] has proposed to himself as the great achievement of his career', and reported the terms of his Bill 'with offences against the act to be punishable by summary procedure'. This was a Bill, said the paper bullishly, 'which the British public expects the British government to pass into law forthwith'.

Yet the battle for Plimsoll's life-saving measures was still a long way from the winning. The expectations of the British public were, for the time being, to be disappointed.

5

ROYAL COMMISSION: CELEBRITY AND SETBACKS

In 1873 there was another interim victory for Plimsoll, apart from the appointment of a Royal Commission: the passing of the 1873 Merchant Shipping Act. It gave the Board of Trade power to survey ships suspected of defects or overloading. The Board's surveyors detained 440 ships in the first year on the grounds of complaints lodged by members of the public. Of these, only sixteen were found to be sufficiently seaworthy to be allowed to sail. Plimsoll, it seemed, had a case. But the 1873 Act did not oblige all ships to be surveyed, and there was still no law enacting a load line.

Plimsoll proposed the second reading of his temporary Shipping Survey Bill (for a survey and load line) as promised on 14 May 1873. He spoke of the support he had been given that week at a meeting of shipowners in Newcastle. But he also referred to shipowners 'who were always on the lookout for some crazy craft to insure . . . who pursued their nefarious calling under an honourable garb, and sometimes under the cloak of religion'. He told a story of one of these men, a 'well-known shipowner of Shields, who had made over £100,000 by these practices, in such a way that when he died the police had to be brought in to protect his remains to the grave, on account of the indignation of the multitude of women and children who followed to pelt the hearse with mud'.

He shamelessly read aloud, too, a letter from a customs officer, O'Dowd, who told Plimsoll: 'You have made a move in the cause of humanity for which you deserve immortal credit,' and went on to relate the case of a ship so loaded with bales of cotton that the crew had to walk on top of them in order to navigate the ship; the shipowner, defending himself, had sworn that 'the higher the bales were piled the more it conduced to safety, as, if the ship went down the crew and the passengers would have a better chance of escaping'.

Plimsoll's speech on that occasion countered a criticism now being levelled against him: namely 'that his head was turned', as Hansard reported his words,

> with the favour which he had received from the public and from that Honourable House. No such thing. In the book which he had published, it would be seen that he had already traced for himself the course which he was now pursuing. He had done nothing hastily, nothing rashly; he had discounted beforehand, and still did discount, all the annoyance that might come upon him, and he was able to bear up against it because he was prepared for it. He had taken up the matter calmly and deliberately, believing that no good would be done until some one should take it up regardless of consequences. His course therefore was a resolute and consistent course, taken up after full deliberation and pursued through good and evil report.

Plimsoll's account of himself is always likeable. That he gave a likeable account of himself is what gave his opponents ammunition. And yet it was always, it seemed, not the noisy adulation of the people that bore him along, but an absolute, resolute conviction. He knew, as no one could dispute, then or now, that ships were safer if they were not loaded too deeply in the water. And that the only motive for loading them deeply was profit. And that any man who resisted legislation against overloading was prepared to expose other men to mortal danger in the hope of making more money. And ultimately that, recognising these indisputable facts, he was under a moral obligation to act as he did.

Meanwhile the speech stoked Plimsoll's conflict with Chichester Fortescue of the Board of Trade. It included these, hardly conciliatory, remarks:

> The compulsory survey of the unclassed ships would be a great advantage to the President of the Board of Trade. He [Plimsoll] often had occasion to make remarks with reference to the Department of the Honourable Gentleman, which were not intended for himself personally, but for certain officials connected with the Board of Trade of whom he had a very bad opinion. It was not his fault when he spoke of the Board of Trade if the President appropriated those remarks to himself; but this he would say, he believed that Board to be one of the worst managed Departments of State.

There was uncharacteristic hostility to the Prime Minister, too, in Plimsoll's oration – which, given his adulation of Gladstone, was evidence indeed of increasing frustration at the government's equivocation. Plimsoll grumbled aloud that he had enjoyed more support from the other side of the House than from his own and he took a dig at Gladstone, implying that the PM did not really care about the sailors: 'When he saw the Prime Minister there that morning, he thought his presence was owing to the fact that the right hon. Gentleman felt some anxiety in the fate of our seamen. Unfortunately, however, the right hon. Gentleman had to go away in order to attend a meeting elsewhere.' Only two months earlier Plimsoll had told the Exeter Hall audience that Gladstone was 'one of the best men that ever lived'.

Plimsoll's speech ended with a plea for support from his fellow MPs, without which 'hundreds of men now living would not be living next year'. He could not protect these people, he said, without 'the co-operation, active and sympathetic', of the government. He 'begged, he implored, he entreated' the House to read his Bill a second time.

On the day before Plimsoll was to speak about this Bill, a clutch of MPs presented petitions from their constituents in support of it.* But the fact that Plimsoll had achieved an investigation by a Royal Commission gave his enemies an excuse to oppose his temporary Shipping Survey Bill. The President of the Board of Trade, Chichester Fortescue, and Thomas Eustace Smith stole Plimsoll's thunder by proposing that same day an amendment of their own to existing Merchant Shipping Acts, which Eustace Smith said he hoped would 'put things on such a footing that further legislation would be unnecessary'. They were devious antagonists.

Eustace Smith had been spoiling Plimsoll's hopes from as far back as 1870. On 14 May, he revealed himself once again as Plimsoll's adversary, while pretending not to be. He couched his opposition, as he always did, in support for Plimsoll. 'Mr T. E. Smith', reported Hansard, 'wished to reassure the House that he was not actuated by any hostility towards the hon. Member for Derby . . . On the contrary, he sympathised with the objects of that hon. Member and if a different course had been pursued by him, he should have been ready to co-operate with him.' Eustace Smith argued that legislation should await the Commission's conclusions, although they would be months or even years away.

This opponent was a man of great wealth and even greater extravagance. After the death of his father and brother, Thomas was sole heir to the £60,000-a-year family empire, which included docks in Newcastle, a fleet of colliers, shipbuilding yards and ocean-going liners. The family seat, Gosforth Park, was rich in art treasures, and Eustace Smith was a patron of the Pre-Raphaelites. He owned pictures by Dante Gabriel Rossetti and Edward Burne-Jones and was himself painted by G. F. Watts, who called him a 'long-bearded little man'. In the 1860s he spent £12,000 on the building of the church of St Mary's in North Gosforth, which has stained-glass windows by Burne-Jones.

Smith's wife, née Mary (or Martha Mary) Dalrymple, known after her marriage in 1855 as Eustacia (thereby escaping the anonymity

* Petitions came from the people of Southampton (represented by Mr Cowper-Temple), Cheltenham (Mr Samuelson), Lynn (Colonel E. Leigh), Nantwich (Major Tollemache) and others.

of 'Mary Smith'), was notoriously unfaithful. She had an affair with a younger man, twenty-five-year-old Charles Dilke MP, in 1868, after bearing Eustace Smith ten children, culminating in twins. (Eustace Smith's neighbour and fellow shipping magnate Frederick Leyland described Eustacia ironically in a letter to Whistler as 'la respectable Smith'.) The affair with Dilke was to flare up again in 1874, after his wife's death.

In 1874 Eustace Smith would commission, under his wife's influence, four painters of the up-to-the-minute Aesthetic Movement, including Frederick Leighton, later president of the Royal Academy, to decorate his new London home at 52 Prince's Gate in a kind of interior-design competition with Leyland, who lived at no. 49 and for whom Whistler decorated the Peacock Room.

After the intervention of the extravagant cuckold Eustace Smith, the debate on Plimsoll's Bill was adjourned 'until the next day'. It was not only the pre-emptive strike by Eustace Smith and Fortescue of a rival Bill that sabotaged Plimsoll; there was another stratagem used against him: 'talking out' his Bill by dwelling excessively on the matters that preceded it. In this case, Plimsoll was stymied by what he called 'a wretched debate on occasional sermons'.

As things turned out discussion of Plimsoll's Bill was not resumed until the end of June. At a private meeting with a group of Northern shipowners, including MPs Eustace Smith, Gourley and Candlish, on the following afternoon at the Westminster Palace Hotel in London, Plimsoll answered their objections to a load line, agreed to exempt ships less than five years old from his compulsory survey and to let the position of his load line be determined either by Lloyd's Register or by a special Commons committee. He also agreed to postpone further discussion for six weeks, in the hope that the Commission might by then have made an interim report. In fact the report was four months away.

On the very day that Plimsoll was 'talked out' of his second reading in the House and his Bill 'dropped but not rejected', he went straight from the Commons to take a train to Birmingham to speak to a 'crowded and enthusiastic' meeting in the Town Hall, organised by Councillor Jesse Collings, Plimsoll's relation and secretary of Birmingham's Plimsoll Committee.* A speaker for the meeting had cancelled, and Plimsoll, who was 'eagerness itself', 'engaged a special train at the very last moment' in order to stand in. When Plimsoll arrived, at a quarter to ten, Collings and Howell had already addressed the gathering, so feeling was running high, and manifested itself in what Plimsoll called a 'magnificent reception'. The Conservatives had supported his Bill, Plimsoll told the crowd, and it was only the 'mean tactics' of his opponents that prevented it from being carried twenty to one. He said then that he would go on putting his Bill down on government nights until the end of the session. (Government nights, distinct from private members' nights, were those on which the government brought on its own Bills in any order it pleased. Putting a Bill down repeatedly on those nights, when government business had precedence and his Bill stood no chance of being debated, was a way of being a persistent nuisance, and reminding the government that he was there.)

Outside the Commons, Plimsoll was consolidating his status as national hero. As George Howell put it: 'A wave of popular feeling swept over the country such as had never before been evoked in the cause of any section of the working class. The Press, the theatre, the music-hall, the pulpit, the platform were all enlisted in the cause of "Our Seamen".'

Since the Great Exeter Hall Meeting, Samuel Plimsoll had been greeted by acclamatory crowds wherever he went. Local committees organised receptions for him. Arriving in Hull in April, for instance, he was met by a band and some two thousand people, mostly sailors, carrying flags and banners, before he addressed a meeting at Hengler's Circus – a circus venue used for public meetings in the off season. The crowd of about three thousand received him with 'long continued cheering'. Well might a man's head be turned.

Speaking with him in Hull was E. J. Reed, MP for Pembroke, who urged Plimsoll's measures as 'necessary' while imputing to him – and equally to the President of the Board of Trade – some capacity to make errors. Nevertheless Reed reported having seen, a year or two

* John Collings's sister's married name was Plimsoll. She (Jane) was the wife of Samuel's cousin John.

Public face: Plimsoll in a photograph he used for a carte de visite.
(*National Portrait Gallery*)

previously, a ship bound for China that not only had no freeboard at
all but had a deck that was actually below the water amidships. He was
'perfectly amazed' that both 'commercial' and 'humanitarian'
Members of Parliament should allow such a thing to be possible. A
resolution was passed by the meeting urging the legislature to pass a
temporary Act for the protection of seamen pending the Commission.

Support sometimes came from unexpected quarters. Shaftesbury
revealed in a speech to a church charity in May:

I was never more astonished than on last Monday morning when, sitting as Chairman of the Plimsoll Committee, I had placed in my
hand a cheque for £1000. From whom did that come? From the
miners of Durham alone. A number of them met, and, at the close of
a short sitting, they voted that each miner in that district should give
a shilling per head towards the Plimsoll Fund. The money was paid;

and on Monday morning . . . I received £1000 to be devoted to the cause, in which these men manifested such great interest. There see what may be done among these people if you do but appeal to them so as to touch their hearts. Appeal to their justice and generosity, and depend upon it you will meet with such a response as you could not have imagined unless you had had experience of what they are capable.

Subscriptions of a shilling a head were similarly levied on the Yorkshire miners and on the members of the Engineers' Union, both of which bodies also gave £1000 to the Fund.

Eliza was with her husband in June, at a meeting in Grimsby on the mouth of the Humber, where the chairman gave her the credit that 'her heart was as thoroughly in the cause as Mr Plimsoll's'. When Plimsoll asked his audience if their own experience did not tell them that many maritime losses were easily preventable only one man among the twelve hundred in the Town Hall shouted 'no'. The rest gave him united acquiescence and the now predictable cheers.

In Grimsby, Plimsoll was critical of the Royal Commission. There had been objections in the House in May to the fact that he had been allowed to attend all their deliberations, while no shipowners were permitted to do so. Now he was banned. He complained that the Commission met, unlike the Royal Commission that had considered the Broadhead case and trade union malpractice, behind closed doors. 'If the Government had wanted to shut out the light on this important subject, they could not have designed a more effective plan,' said Plimsoll, who was clearly beginning to fret that the Commission for which he had called so fervently might not in fact advocate all his ends. He thought, as he told a Sheffield audience in June, that the Commission was working too slowly, too, meeting twice a week and sitting for four hours instead of daily, morning to night. He predicted: 'A report would come out in four or five years in two or three large blue books, which few would see, and none would care to read.' In fact it was just over a year and one very large book, but he was otherwise prescient.

★

In some places, as in Hull, there was, when Plimsoll came to speak, an atmosphere of carnival, and he was met with ceremony to rival the reception of royalty – or, nowadays, cup-winning football teams. Nowhere was this truer than in Bristol, the port where he was born. Stepping off the 2.26 from Paddington at Bristol Temple Meads Station on Saturday 21 June 1873, he and Eliza were greeted by the committee that had organised their visit, and by twenty men from the Naval Reserve. The visitors were to share a carriage with the local MP, Mr Kirkham Daniel Hodgson, himself a merchant and shipowner. The sailors lined up in two rows of ten and pulled the coach the mile or so up the gently sloping roads to the White Lion Hotel in Broad Street (now the Thistle Hotel), in a parade eighteen hundred strong that included four bands, banner-carrying ship-wrights, boilermakers, craftsmen and tradesmen, and a convoy of carriages containing the rest of the committee. Floats bore ships and boats, one a model of a wrecked coffin-ship with the words 'pump or sink' chalked on it. It was escorted by a 'friend of the sailors' carrying an umbrella, which he used to point at Mr Plimsoll and conduct the crowd in cheers. Twenty or thirty thousand people lined the streets to watch and traffic was halted for more than an hour.

In Broad Street, which is in fact quite narrow, the crowd helped to lift the carriage into position close to the entrance of the White Lion. Plimsoll entered the hotel and swiftly reappeared on the balcony, where he uttered these few, but rapturously received, words: 'I was born in Bristol and you have made me feel today as if I had come home.'

Summoned by the crowd, the local MP Mr Hodgson appeared, and added, prompting laughter and more acclamation: 'I had not the luck to be born in Bristol, but I mean to live with you as long as I can.'

During the afternoon Plimsoll was presented with an address by the members of the Bristol Trades Council, who expressed their 'warmest sympathy for his noble and disinterested efforts'. But the highlight of the day was the evening meeting at Bristol's resplendent Colston Hall. The warm-up for Plimsoll was two Bristol bands playing popular tunes, and the audience of three thousand in the packed hall gave him a frenzied welcome when he appeared.

Plimsoll spoke of the case of the *Wimbledon*, brought up in the House the previous week by Charles Gilpin, the member for Southampton. The ship had, in June 1872, been found to have timbers so worm-eaten they were ordered to be replaced. Although some repairs were done, five successive crews had declined to sail out of Cardiff in it in January 1873, and twenty men were jailed for ten weeks. The ship was last heard of in May in Cape Town, leaky and with its crew in a state of mutiny. Before it had sailed it had been found necessary to lighten the ship of 250 tons of excessive cargo, and recaulk it.

The Bristol speech demonstrates that Plimsoll was not afraid to attack even his friends if he thought this might avert deaths that augmented 'the ill-gotten wealth of those who are careless who suffers so that they get rich': 'We will make our government do the work, or we will hurl them from power. (Loud cheers.) If Mr Gladstone will not do it, we must find somebody that will. (Applause.) I put the whole responsibility upon him, because he has the Cabinet obedient to every wish of his.'

The party he was threatening to hurl from power was his own. For Plimsoll, the cause outweighed political allegiances in the Commons. This is extraordinary for a man who went on to stand for election in 1880 with the slogan 'For Gladstone and for Jack'. And who, in that same year, was to try to organise a public celebration of Gladstone's re-election (which Gladstone would resist). But Gladstone had refused to meet a deputation of working men while the Royal Commission was still sitting, and a pro-Plimsoll Conservative MP, J. A. Roebuck, speaking of the Cabinet, had told Plimsoll: 'You are mistaken in supposing that certain men you have a high regard for will be willing to risk losing the votes of the shipowners of the North Eastern ports for so poor a mission as assisting working men to get their rights.'

Plimsoll devoted some of his Bristol speech to refuting a letter printed in that morning's *Western Daily Press*, inaccurately accusing him of having involved the whole class of shipowners in the charge of 'unmitigated scoundrelism'. And of 'rousing the passions of those who are totally ignorant as to any difference that exists between "a bobstay and a mainbrace, or freeboard and topmast trussel-trees".* He declared: 'Are we not able to say, without technical knowledge, that a ship shall not go to sea overloaded . . . [and] that a ship which needs to be repaired ought to be repaired?' These were matters on which 'any man out of Bedlam ought to be able to give a good opinion'.

Plimsoll addressed too the accusation of the aforementioned letter-writer that sailors were a sad lot, in need of 'moral reformation'. 'I do not care to go into that,' said Plimsoll drily. 'But . . . they are a great deal too good to drown.' He went on to say: 'I want to protect the sailor's life before I mend his morals.'

He answered the charge of being 'sensational' thus: 'So I am . . . Is it not a sensational thing for men to choke in the water and to die, and is it not fit that I should speak of that as a sensational matter and in a sensational manner?' And to the charge that he was an 'agitator' he said:

I have been made an agitator by the simple fact that when, for years past, the storms of winter were blowing, I knew that men were being wrecked and dying, and I could not lie in my bed. Then I determined, deep down in my heart, that I would give myself no rest, but that, quiet and timid as I am, I would go the length and breadth of the land and would speak wherever the people will listen to me and say 'Will you have them drowned – good, brave men – drowned, by the dozen and the score to make a few scoundrels rich?' We'll have no more of this; we'll stop it; we'll see that our men, when they go to sea, shall have a tight ship, sound gear to their hands, the ship properly loaded and properly manned, and if that is done they will do the rest, for we have no gale in these latitudes that would destroy such a ship.

---

* A bobstay is a heavy wire or chain cable attaching the bowsprit – a spar that projects forward towards the bow of a ship – to the stem, or foremost timber of a ship; the mainbrace is the rope attached to the main yard; the freeboard, crucial to this story, is the distance from the waterline to the upper deck of a ship (measured at the waist or centre of a ship); trussel-trees, normally tressel-trees (or trestle-trees), are two short pieces of timber on each side of the lower masthead that form part of the support for the topmast – that is, the (sometimes removable) second section of a complete mast.

A collection at the doors raised something over £11, and Mr and Mrs Plimsoll took a train back to London the following night.

Plimsoll's popularity barrelled along. The meetings he addressed between March and June 1873 are too many to record in detail. As George Howell later reported,

> Immense and enthusiastic meetings in support of the general principles laid down by the committee and of the Bill of Mr Plimsoll have been held in Liverpool, Manchester, Leeds, Birmingham, Hull, Grimsby, Bristol, Sheffield, Newcastle, Hartlepool, Shields, Sunderland, Whitby, Derby, Brighton, Southampton, Barnsley and many other towns, and in Scotland large meetings have been held in Edinburgh, Leith, Greenock and Dumbarton, besides which at great gatherings of workingmen not called for this special purpose, resolutions have been unanimously carried to support Mr Plimsoll in his good and humane work.

Howell's list was not even comprehensive. The punishing itinerary of travelling the country to meetings was beginning to take its toll on Plimsoll's health. In July 1875, after illness prevented him from presiding at the event at the National Temperance League fête in Sydenham, he asked Howell to permit him a holiday for a month or so to recuperate.

Conflict did not help his health, and in August there was a bitter correspondence with Chichester Fortescue over an assertion Plimsoll made to the Royal Commission – namely that he believed many officers of the Board of Trade to be corrupt. Fortescue insisted on having names, in order to clear his officers of the calumny. Plimsoll declined to give them, on the grounds that the opinion was pressed from him by the Commission, and that it was a 'collateral issue' that would distract the commissioners from their main purpose. At the same time he alluded to instances of extortion, obstruction and papers that had gone missing that were needed for prosecutions for negligence. Fortescue countered that in the cases Plimsoll apparently referred to, officers had been investigated by the Board, and those guilty of petty bribery dismissed. The alleged missing papers (relating to a ship called the *Druid*, whose boiler blew up) were in the hands of the Home Office. Fortescue had 'no further reason to entertain a suspicion of the honesty of the officers of my department'.

Plimsoll was well enough in August 1873 to address a vast miners' demonstration in Chesterfield, while one Saturday that month the Edinburgh Trades Council mustered a demonstration to protest against laws that were perceived to be punitive to working men.* In a procession of fifteen thousand people, the shipwrights carried a model of a ship, a three-decker, which had been used in two previous demonstrations, one in 1832 and the other in 1866, on each occasion bearing the name of a hero of the hour. In 1832 it had been Earl Grey and in 1866 John Bright, the men responsible for the Electoral Reform Acts of 1832 and 1867. For this demonstration the name was changed to Samuel Plimsoll.

And a real ship was called after him. An Aberdeen shipowner, George Thompson, had been praised in *Our Seamen* for his good care of ships and excellent safety record since in thirty years he had lost only one ship of a fleet of twenty-two. In September Thompson asked if he might name a ship after Mr Plimsoll. The Plimsolls came to Aberdeen for the launch of the three-masted iron passenger clipper whose figurehead was a frock-coated image of its namesake. The vessel was christened not by Eliza but by the wife of the captain, a Mrs Boaden. The *Samuel Plimsoll*, known for her speed from London to Melbourne, went on to carry hundreds of emigrants to Australia, before ending her days as a hulk in Fremantle in 1903.† The figurehead is now in the Maritime Museum of Western Australia, along with the ship's medicine chest.

Some years later there was a suggestion that the same company might rename a ship after Mrs Plimsoll – the *Salamis*, launched in May 1875, and described as 'the dream of an artist and poet. The most beautiful thing afloat. Her lines and proportions were a joy to

---

* The Criminal Law Amendment Act, the Conspiracy Act and the criminal clauses in the Master and Servant Act.
† 'Built in 1873 by W. Hood & Co, Aberdeen for the Aberdeen Line, the *Samuel Plimsoll* was a three-masted full rigged ship of 1,520 gross tons. Length 73,53m x beam 11,88m x depth 7,04m (241.3ft x 39ft x 23.1ft), iron hull and accommodation for 50–1st class passengers carried in the poop. Fitted for the carriage of emigrants in the 'tween decks . . .'

the eye.' But in the end, despite the unusual grace of the ship in question, 'Mrs Plimsoll was thought to be too feminine to have an iron ship named after her.'

In Aberdeen, after the 1873 launch, Plimsoll addressed another impassioned meeting, in the Music Hall, presided over by the Lord Provost, at which, although he described instances of overloading and unseaworthiness, he declared that he would no longer name individuals responsible because 'it was the legislature that was the guilty party'.

In October and November civic receptions were held for Plimsoll in Southern ports. He spoke at banquets in Portsmouth and, while it lay in Plymouth Sound, on the *Samuel Plimsoll*. In November he was entertained on the *Great Western* steamship in Bristol at a dinner for more than a hundred and sixty people, and he said: 'They can call me an agitator or what they please; wherever I can get a crowd of men to hear me, I will tell the story of the sailors' bitter wrongs and how wholesale murder is done, and how it is sending woe and anguish into the humble homes of the poor.'

Plimsoll's face was now familiar from newspaper caricatures and *cartes de visite* that were sold to the public for album collections. (For one photographic session which produced two such cards he was dandyish in a velvet-collared dress coat and a polka-dot waistcoat.) All over the country support was being voiced. The Association of Chambers of Commerce in Cardiff voted unanimously in favour of a load line on 24 September (and, as it turned out, needed to reiterate this every year until 1876). On the same November night that Plimsoll was being fêted in Plymouth, Thomas Brassey, MP for Hastings, argued in a lecture to his constituency that overloading should invalidate insurance. On 2 December the supportive Liverpool steamship owner David MacIver wrote to *The Times* from Liverpool attacking the inadequate 1871 and 1873 Merchant Shipping Acts.

Responding to the current Plimsoll excitement, the novelist Charles Reade revisited his story of a villainous shipowner and an insurance scam, *Foul Play*, and wrote his own stage version, independently of Dion Boucicault. Ellen Terry, lured out of 'retirement' (i.e. motherhood) to tour the provinces with a trio of plays, took the part of Helen, the romantic heroine, and Reade renamed the play

Our Seamen. One biographer wrongly speculates that this was to dissociate it from the theatrical failure of the previous version. It was not; it was Reade's way of participating in the cause, and identifying his villain Arthur Wardlaw with the callousness Plimsoll attacked. Plimsoll had written to Reade in March 1874: 'I am truly glad to hear that you will for cause shown not merely break a lance but fight a good battle for our fellow subjects at sea. 'I shall be delighted to see you and will lay before [you] such things as make me <u>stamp</u> with impotent rage when I get them.'

He went on to tell the story of a ship's carpenter jailed for refusing to sail in a ship he thought was not seaworthy after the owners found witnesses to say it was. It went down with all thirteen hands. Reade annotated Plimsoll's letter: 'Worthy Mr Plimsoll, who deserves a civic crown.'

However, the 1874 tour that included *Our Seamen* was not a financial success, and Ellen Terry could not bear to be paid £25 a week in the circumstances; she thought it might be an economy to find a different actress. Reade, who had devoted much time to engineering the effect of the vessel going down and nightly operated the machinery himself in the company of a 'rough lad', responded: 'Madam! You are a rat! You desert a sinking ship!'

As the campaign reached all corners of society, in 1874 the first of several tribute songs was written, in rather serious voice, by comic lyricist F. W. Green, with music by Alfred Lee, composer of 'The Man on the Flying Trapeze'. 'Our Sailors on the Sea' was 'respectfully dedicated' to Mr Plimsoll, whose face appeared on the front of the sheet music. The music halls rang with pious sentiment. Two verses ran thus:

> The sailor little dreams when he
> Sets out upon the wave
> The worn-out ship in which he sails
> Will bear him to his grave.
> Should storms arise, her rotten planks
> To pieces soon would go,
> Yet ships like this are sent to sea
> That men may richer grow.

Such things we often hear of, and
The wealthy merchant thrives,
But what about the priceless freight
Of precious human lives?
Poor honest Jack from such a fate
Protected ought to be,
So let each do his best to help
Our sailors on the sea.[*]

In the round of meetings that spread the word, it was not always Plimsoll who addressed the crowds. Sometimes the stalwarts of his Committee stood in for him. Some of the glory of the campaign went to proxy speakers. As, for instance, on an occasion in 1874 proudly recorded by George Howell.

He and a fellow supporter, the activist and trade union arbitrator Lloyd Jones, were to hold a meeting in Hartlepool, but discovered when they arrived in the morning on the train from Shields that the local MP, Thomas Richardson, whose son was to have chaired the proceedings, had countermanded the meeting and that there was no hall in which to speak that night. 'We found out,' wrote Howell, 'that the member had addressed a meeting of the Chamber of Commerce on the preceding Saturday when he rather fell foul of Mr Plimsoll, though previously said to be in favour of legislation.' Howell found another venue by offering the lessee of a local theatre more than enough money to cover what would have been his takings at that evening's performance. Persuading him of the worth of the cause, he then enlisted his help to get a band together and find a printer of handbills.

By one o'clock the band was out, playing and distributing notices of the relocated meeting, and the town was abuzz with what Howell called his 'small-scale coup d'état'. Mr Richardson Jr then agreed to take the chair as planned if his father was not attacked in the speeches; and the father expressed a wish to attend. The theatre 'was crammed from pit to ceiling, the stage itself being full'.

[*] See p. 310 for complete lyrics.

Howell, supposing himself to have been 'on good form', spoke for nearly an hour: 'When I sat down there was round after round of applause which was renewed when Mr Richardson sprang to his feet and, taking me by both hands, shook them warmly, declaring that he "agreed with nearly everything I had said."'

Lloyd Jones spoke 'most eloquently' for half an hour and Richardson gave a 'kindly, handsome' vote of thanks and said he would support Plimsoll in the House. Howell urged the crowd to ensure that the theatre lessee had a full house for his usurped show the following night.

Meanwhile the Royal Commission had been at work. Chaired by the Duke of Somerset under the authority of the Duke of Edinburgh, the Commission's ten officials included two MPs – Thomas Brassey of Hastings and the Hon. Henry George Liddell of Northumberland South – and the former President of the Board of Trade, Mr Milner Gibson, who had a history of opposing a load line. They gathered every few days from 22 April to 29 July 1873 for twenty-four days in all. They sat in a room with drawings of different kinds of ships, to ask the experts their opinion on loading them to different depths, and heard evidence from forty-eight witnesses, several of whom returned repeatedly. Samuel Plimsoll addressed the Commission on three separate occasions. In all 11,457 questions were asked and answered. The published record of these interrogations was a two-foot-high tome of 445 closely printed pages in two columns.

In all the to and fro of questioning, facts were hard to establish, and guilt harder still to prove. There was a good deal of strong opinion on both sides of the argument for and against safety measures, and a hint of bias among some of the questioners.

One Plimsoll enthusiast, quoted in *Our Seamen*, was the first witness, a former merchant seaman and naval officer, George Reid, who had been nearly forty years at sea and had surveyed ships, most of which carried guano, for a private company (Gibbs and Co.) in Callao in Peru. The company would not charter a ship without a survey, prompting some ships to tout elsewhere for a charter. Reid had imposed a load line and checked the condition of ships, and it made all the difference to safety. Ships did not sail if they did not pass his survey, and none of the ships he passed was ever lost. 'When owners know that this precaution is taken, they send good ships. After this survey, they used not to send the old coffins, as they were called, to Callao, because they knew they would not be taken up, and therefore A1 ships came there.'

Reid's evidence included the following remarks. 'I am sorry to say that I had the most trouble with English ships. The foreigners did not appear to be so eager to load their ships so deeply.' 'Overloading is very often not the fault of the masters, it is very often the fault of the owners; they urge the masters to overload their ships: they say "If I get £3 a ton, you can get 50 tons more into the vessel, and that will pay for the men's wages."' 'Most of these ships are insured; they not only insure the ship but they insure the freight, and sometimes they insure the stores on board. Therefore, in most cases, if a ship sinks, everything is insured but the men's lives.'

Reid did his apprenticeship, he reported, in a brig called the *Crescent*, 'which loaded in the West Indies . . . so deeply that they painted the [guideline] white mark out of the side'. This was sanctioned by the master, who had a share in the ship. The *Crescent* was bound for Hamburg but before it reached Falmouth 'the pumps were choked and we had to call there to get them up. The men were forced to be lashed to the pumps while pumping, to prevent them being washed away by the sea breaking on board, and the brig lay for nearly three days in a gale of wind like a half-tide rock, with the water going over her.' When masters have an interest in the ship, said Reid, 'the masters are quite as bad as the owners'.

Reid also told the story of a ship that came to Callao from Cardiff in 1862, arriving with four feet of water in the hold after a 'tremendously bad passage out'. 'The ship's company said they would rather go to prison than to sea in her.' Reid recommended a minimal load, which she carried back safely to England. Then 'she took in a heavy cargo to the Baltic, and foundered with all hands on board, only six months after I surveyed her'.

Thomas Farrer, the permanent secretary to the Board of Trade, gave the Commission an overview of the existing legislation in which he argued that the deckloading ban before 1862 was withdrawn because it was too difficult to enforce. Ways were found round it. Ships were cleared first and loaded afterwards. Spar decks were built above the top deck, level with the poop, so that cargo stored under them was technically inside. Rough timber stored in the open was said to be spars for use on deck, which was permitted. Ships were sold to foreign owners and flew foreign flags to evade the law. It was hard to fine a foreign ship, cleared at its point of departure, when it had already arrived safely in a British port. And shipowners complained that a ban on deckloading favoured rivals from the Baltic and North America to whom it did not apply, while merchants in the colonies threatened litigation against the government for the losses they sustained. Attempts to plug loopholes in the law were thwarted by the failure of Lloyd's and the Liverpool underwriters to give records that would help the case: they did not seem to find the issue sufficiently important. Farrer therefore opposed a ban on deckloading, rather as one might make burglary legal because it was hard to prevent it.

Farrer had opened his evidence to the Commission by declaring that he did not wish to express any opinion either for or against Mr Plimsoll, but he had written contemptuously elsewhere of Plimsoll's campaign and load line. Farrer's network of associates was to have a detrimental effect on the cause for years to come: he was the brother-in-law of Stafford Northcote, who would have significant influence as Disraeli's Chancellor of the Exchequer.

Examined by the Commission about a Board of Trade official who knew of fifteen ships that left port overloaded, Farrer said: 'but the fifteen ships all reached their destination'. This, he argued, did not amount to 'wholesale manslaughter'. Plimsoll regarded this as a monstrous indifference to safety and was moved to call the Board of Trade 'the stronghold of the worst men in the shipping interest'.

One of the most culpable interviewees before the Commission seemed to be W. J. Fernie, managing director of the Merchants' Trading Company. His firm had owned seventy-three ships, both wood and iron, in the previous ten years, and in that time had lost eighteen. They included four iron steamers: the *Royal Victoria* was off the north coast of Scotland on its first voyage in 1864, bound for Calcutta with a cargo of coals, when its crew of fourteen drowned;

the *Royal Albert* sank in 1866 off Cornwall, homebound from Calcutta, with no survivors; the *Royal Arthur* went down in 1871 near Waterford, homebound from California, though the sailors were saved; and the *Royal Adelaide* was lost in 1872 near Portland, taking seven lives. An iron sailing ship, the fifteen-year-old *Golden Fleece*, sank off Barry Island in 1869; a Liverpool court found that the ship was unseaworthy, its iron considerably corroded; one man perished. In 1863 three wooden sailing ships were lost: the *John Linn*, built nine years earlier, was abandoned at sea; the *General Simpson*, homebound from Bombay, laden with cotton, went down in a monsoon with eight sailors; and the *Dawn of Hope*, also carrying cotton from Bombay, disappeared without trace and was never heard of again. The *Uncas* collided with a steamer in the Channel in 1866; and in 1868 the coal cargo of both the *Viceroy* and the *Malvern* caught fire between Liverpool and San Francisco, condemning both ships. Sixteen hands from the *Great Northern* died off Bombay in 1869, when the ship went ashore in a fog; the same year the coal cargo of the *Windsor Castle* (formerly the *Emilie St Pierre*) shifted and only one man was saved; twenty-two died. In 1870 the *Woburn Abbey* (formerly the *Bellwood*) was lost off Pernambuco, run ashore, according to Fernie, by a drunken crew.

And then there was the *Denmark* (formerly the *Great Republic*), abandoned, leaking, in a gale in 1871. The ship, bought for £3500 (a measly £1 per ton) in 1868, had been built in 1853. Fernie conceded that the *Denmark* was 'a weak ship' but not, he claimed, rotten. The captain and the crew thought otherwise. Fernie insisted the company had spent £850 to make her good. But his memory of the history of the ship was faulty, and the Commission put him right. In July 1870 the *Denmark* had unloaded a cargo of guano, and was damaged and leaking badly. She was partly remetalled and seams were recaulked, but while this was happening water was still being pumped out. She sailed for Bombay with a cargo of coal, but unloaded instead in Rio. She foundered soon after.

Mr Cohen, of Lloyd's Salvage Association and a member of the Commission, had written a report in 1868 that described the ship thus: 'She was trussed with transverse bars of iron screwed up amidships, like an old barn or church, before she started on this last voyage . . . the fastenings at the beam ends and knees were so rotten that . . . the only way of fastening the ship together was to introduce these enormous amounts of iron.'

Cohen submitted this report and received a letter back from Fernie's firm: 'A large sum of money has been expended on the vessel, and she is now in complete seaworthy order, and in perfect repair.' This was not true. Nothing had been done about the iron trusses between the Lloyd's report and the loss of the ship.

Fernie's answers to the Commission were vague, conflicting and defensive. He conceded that the company's mortality rate among sailors was twelve men per thousand (the thousand apparently being calculated as man/voyages, which is not the same thing as men in total; if each man made ten voyages before being drowned, the figure for loss would in fact be roughly one man in ten).

A poignant piece of evidence to the Commission was presented by B. C. Stephenson, secretary to Lloyd's. It was a letter written from Thomas J. Williams, chief officer of the SS *Huelva*, on 8 February 1871, to his sweetheart, whom he was shortly to marry, and posted in Cardiff just before his ship sailed.

Dear Lizzy,

We sail to-night, and I wish she was going without me, for I don't like the look of her, she is so deep in the water; but I won't show the white feather to any one. If she can carry a captain, she can carry a mate too. But it's a great pity that the Board of Trade doesn't appoint some universal load water-mark, and surveyors to see that ships are not sent to sea to become coffins for their crews. But don't torment yourself about me. I dare say I shall get through it as well as any body else. Write to me on Monday or Tuesday: 'Mr Thomas Williams, care of Mr Carless, Ship Chandler, Grev de Valencia'. I sent you a letter yesterday.

Hoping you may continue well, I remain,

Yours fondly,

Tom

The ship, loaded with coal, went down with all hands. The loss to the owners was covered by the underwriters. There was no compensation for Lizzy.

Despite such persuasive evidence for Plimsoll's cause, not all went well for him with the Commission. Hostile assertions about Plimsoll expressed by witnesses included the following: that he was 'a hare-brained enthusiast', a 'notoriety hunter', a 'man who got all his facts wrong and would not even apologize for doing so', and 'one who sought to prohibit death by Act of Parliament'. Sailors were blamed for the loss of ships because they were 'overloaded with liquor', and the motives of everyone on Plimsoll's side were suspected by conspiracy theorists.

Another exchange with an interlocutor who was very supportive of Plimsoll got him into trouble later when he quoted it elsewhere. Samuel Robins, a shipping agent licensed under the Board of Trade, was interviewed about a coal-laden sailing ship in Cardiff called the *Satellite*, for which he engaged the first crew. Robins, an outspoken chap, said, 'I had heard reports respecting the vessel from shipmasters and . . . considered in some respect that she was a bad class of vessel and not fit for the voyage upon which she was going.' He was asked: 'I thought that you engaged the seamen for her?' and replied, 'I had not then seen the vessel, and after engaging the men it was my duty to see them again aboard, at the time of sailing, and that was when I first saw the vessel.' 'And at that time you considered her not a fit vessel for the voyage?' asked a commissioner. 'I considered her an old trap,' came the answer.

Robins was nonetheless obliged to see that the men sailed in her. If they had objected on the pier, there were police who could have taken them to make a complaint about the ship before magistrates; and he declared he would have supported them. But the sailors left, planning, as Robins believed, to go no further than the nearby stretch of water known as the Cardiff Roads and then desert. This is exactly what they did. Another captain was brought from Liverpool, with a crew who did not know that the former men had deserted. Some of the new crew, as Robins understood matters, were landed at Gibraltar and so escaped, but the new captain was lost with the ship.

Later Robins met a member of the ship's crew: 'He said to me that for the future he should go and look at the ship before he signed for another vessel. I asked him the reason, and he said he would not go in another "old basket".'

The *Satellite* was owned by Messrs Houghton and Smith of Liverpool, a well-known firm of merchants and shipowners. Plimsoll not only circulated a pamphlet with this extract about the *Satellite* from the Royal Commission interview, but referred to the case elsewhere in print, notably in an appendix to a novel called *Ship Ahoy!* which appeared in the December 1873 issue of *Once a Week*. Messrs Houghton and Smith took him to court.

Plimsoll had paid for reprints of the novel, several thousand copies of which were circulated anonymously, sent out free to working men, with his damning appendix. A spoof in *Punch* in 1877 of a novel written by S----l P-----ll, which shared certain details with this book, suggested that the magazine had concluded that Plimsoll was himself its author. In fact a note in George Howell's account of the campaign indicates that the story was written by George Manville Fenn, editor of *Once a Week* and author of a good many sensational seafaring stories for boys.

The villain of *Ship Ahoy!*, Philip Merritt of Rutherby & Co., wittingly and deliberately sends an unseaworthy ship to sea for profit. In the novel an old salt decries the practice thus: 'Heav'ly insured – rotten old hulk – sent out a purpose. Half the men drowned and the owner turns his eyes up like a gull in thunder, wipes the corners, and then rubs his hands and goes to church. There's lots o' them games carried on, and owners make fortunes from it.'

The prosecution in Liverpool in April 1874 argued that the juxtaposition of the novel and the extract from the Royal Commission report implied that Houghton and Smith. did the same. A solicitor's letter gave Plimsoll the chance to deny that he intended any such imputation, but it received a characteristically stroppy response: 'I was not aware that a quotation from [a parliamentary blue book] was liable to an action for libel. Had I been so, however, it would have been just the same, as I do not mean to be silenced or otherwise deterred from laying before the public the infamous wrongs which are daily practised upon our brave seamen, even should the consequences to myself be utter ruin.'

An inquiry triggered by the Commission concluded that the ship was not overloaded, nor even unseaworthy, and that the cause of its loss was that coal got into the pumps, which therefore could not bale out water taken on in a gale; the water was six feet deep in the hold before the ship was abandoned. The crew took to the boats and were picked up by a passing schooner and taken to Gibraltar, but the captain, 'whose mind had given way from exhaustion and fatigue', refused to leave the sinking ship, and so was a victim of his own stubbornness.

Although the prosecution in the court case doubted Mr Robins's first-hand knowledge, argued that Plimsoll's extract 'garbled' his evidence and called the denigration of the *Satellite* 'gossip', the judge advised the jury that public parliamentary papers were legitimately open to comment and interpretation. The court found in Plimsoll's favour because he was 'without malice', although the jury expressed their 'great sympathy' with Messrs Houghton and Smith for having been obliged to bring the action.

A preliminary report was published by the Commission on 22 September 1873. It damned Plimsoll with faint praise, acknowledging that he had 'the merit of having called attention to the loss of life which occurs in the Mercantile Marine from the culpable neglect of shipowners . . . Some allowance must therefore be made for mis-statements and exaggerations which we are obliged occasionally to notice.' But it went on to say 'we cannot recommend any enactment for establishing a fixed load line on the proportion of free-board to the depth of the hold of the vessel'.

Plimsoll's sister Fanny died at the age of forty-three on 23 January 1874. The next day Gladstone resigned as Prime Minister. This was another blow. For all his procrastination, Gladstone was an ally, and Plimsoll had hoped to see a law passed while he was still in office. Now there was the hurdle of a general election to overcome. As it turned out, the campaign had served to make Plimsoll's own future in government more secure. *The Times*, reporting on the forth-coming election, said that in the borough of Derby: 'There is no apparent probability of the present Liberal members being disturbed, Mr Bass being exceedingly popular, owing to his lavishly generous gifts to the town, and Mr Plimsoll having disarmed opposition by his recent espousal of the cause of our seamen.'

In the election in February, in which the Liberals lost crushingly,

Disraeli coming in with a majority of over fifty, Plimsoll increased his share of the vote. Some concluded that Gladstone's failure to do more for sailors was a factor in the Liberals' demise.*

Chichester Fortescue, the President of the Board of Trade, lost his seat at Louth to Plimsoll's friend Alexander Sullivan, the lawyer and journalist, and co-founder of the Home Rule party. That was the good news. The bad news was that Disraeli appointed, in April, Sir Charles Adderley as the new President, a 'dull man' (as John Bright said), who, according to the parliamentary journalist Henry Lucy, 'would have made an admirable country gentleman with an intelligent steward to manage his farms . . . but he is always a day behind the world'. Adderley had no sympathy at all for Plimsoll and his followers. He announced that he had no intention of bringing in a new Shipping Bill, declared that he 'would be sorry to see unseaworthiness defined by act of parliament', deplored the expense that Plimsoll's misinformation had already incurred, and advised 'caution' in dealing with the cases Plimsoll brought to the Board's attention.

In one case Adderley's caution would have terrible consequences. In December 1874 he was notified that a ship sailing from Cardiff, the *Thornaby*, was overloaded. Instead of telegraphing, he sent a written order to stop the ship. His instructions predictably arrived too late. Twenty-nine sailors drowned.

Adderley and Plimsoll were at loggerheads throughout Adderley's tenure (until 1878). When, in June 1874, Adderley insisted that no measure was necessary that session, Plimsoll forced the House to a division. To Disraeli's amazement, Plimsoll only lost this vote by 173 votes to 170. Adderley, on Disraeli's urging, was obliged to draw up a measure after all.

Punch commented on Plimsoll's speech:

To lose the Bill by a majority of three under such circumstances (that is, with some MPs anxious to await the report of the Commission) was to carry it. The House, like the Country, has made up its mind against further toleration of floating coffins. Mr Plimsoll deserves

---

* The votes of trade unions for some Conservatives who were prepared to repeal the Criminal Law Amendment Act, rather than for some Liberals who were not, may also have been a factor.

the credit of having brought England to this mind, and *Mr Punch* hereby awards it him. Of course, Mr Plimsoll has been indiscreet. People who attack great evils and large interests always are – more power to such indiscretion . . . At the same time, in this as in all war upon evil, the less mud flung and the less ill blood stirred the better; and so *Punch* congratulates his friend Plimsoll on the most moderate measure, and the least aggressive speech, yet made on a subject fit to provoke a saint and make an angel aggressive.

Then, on 1 July 1874, the final report of the Royal Commission was published. It concluded that responsibility for both loading and seaworthiness should be left to shipowners. As J. A. Roebuck had predicted, things went on just as they were.

The *Western Daily Press* believed that 'Mr Plimsoll need not be discouraged'. *Punch* thought (in verse) that: 'though [Plimsoll] failed the other night –/He'll gain his object nearly, if not quite./The Government will take his cause in hand . . .' The TUC reiterated support at its Liverpool Congress in January 1875. And Plimsoll did not give up.

Correspondence between the Board of Trade and shipowners in January 1875 revealed the strength of feeling against him that was creeping through the shipping industry. Plimsoll had asked the Board for daily copies (at his own expense) of its Draught of Water records, had gone through them and had drawn attention to the ships that seemed to have left the country overloaded. Plimsoll's communications were referred to the shipowners. Some responded by saying that in future they would keep a closer watch on the loading and condition of their ships. But others replied with these and similar remarks: 'The charge, like much [Mr Plimsoll] has written and said, will not bear inspection'; 'We have yet to learn that the nautical knowledge of Mr Plimsoll is of any value whatsoever'; and 'We do not think it is worth our while to reply to the raving sensations of a political mountebank.' They accused Plimsoll of using 'spies' to obtain inaccurate information. In fact Plimsoll's only information came from the Board of Trade.

In the months that followed there was a battle between a government Bill and one proposed by Plimsoll. In January 1875 Adderley received a deputation of shipowners, including C. H. Wigram (owner of the lost *London*). They were fearful of the plan expressed by trade unions to intervene in shipping, and of the fact that members who had once opposed Plimsoll had come round to voting with him. The shipowners asked for a judicious measure that they could support 'without undue restrictions on trade'. Adderley introduced a Bill dealing with all issues relating to causes of casualties, including overloading and deckloads, and proposing a periodical survey of all ships, although he said he thought this would be a 'mischievous and vexatious proceeding'.

Adderley was not equal to the task of trying to please the shipowners, keep Plimsoll at bay and bring in an adequate measure. He had a bad time over his Bill. This was a newspaper report of the events of 10 February:

> Oh! Sir Charles Adderley, is there no method by which we can turn you into an interesting speaker? . . . [he] was rambling almost to obscurity and when he sat down there was the smallest idea of what he intended to do. He has told us that he did not intend to please Mr Plimsoll and he has succeeded in not pleasing him. What we suffered as a result you may conceive from Mr Plimsoll's opening words. We were already nearly in despair – gloom of the deepest dye was on our countenances, when the member for Derby rose, adjusted his spectacles, looked under them at his notes and proceeded thus: 'I feel like a shipwrecked crew in an open boat. A vessel was bearing down which gave hope. But she has passed away again, abandoning us to our fate with the promise that our loss "shall be inquired into".' It was too heartrending and I nearly fled the dismal scene . . .
>
> It was noticeable in the debate that followed that only Liberal critics spoke, and that generally even shipowners – Mr Gourley of Hull, Mr Wilson of Hull, Mr Brassey of Hastings, himself a certificated seaman – were in favour of Mr Plimsoll's bill rather than Sir Charles's. And it is really significant that Mr Plimsoll's proposal for surveying 'unclassed' vessels was almost universally pressed upon the Government.

In the end Adderley's Bill limped on, with amendments from Plimsoll, presented on 10 March, in the Merchant Shipping Acts Amendment (no. 2) Bill. Plimsoll, dissatisfied as he was with the government Bill, was prepared to allow it to take precedence, in order to ensure some helpful measure. But even this was a struggle. On 8 April the government's own Bill* was read without a division. Long debates got Adderley into a 'hopeless muddle' from which he had to be saved by Disraeli and Sir Stafford Northcote. One left him, after 'struggling for five hours with the ship owners', drooping on the Treasury Bench, 'with downcast head, pulling at his moustache and biting his forefinger'.

The Commons had not been amused by Plimsoll's tactics in February when he circulated a placard to members of the public around Westminster, criticising the Westminster MP Charles Russell for thwarting a Bill against the deckloading of grain cargoes. It was not considered a gentlemanly way to behave, and in the House Russell called it a breach of privilege.

But the House was entertained by the news that Plimsoll had called on the Marine Assistant Secretary at 3 a.m. one morning to warn him about the loading of a ship called the *International*. The story of this episode, as Plimsoll wrote in a letter on 13 March 1875 to Edward Baines, proprietor of the *Leeds Mercury*, was this: 'Every day brings me so many letters about ships and seamen that, with all the help I can get, my life is almost a burden to me. Only last night, for instance, I reached home from the House soon after midnight, and when I went to bed there was a telegram came from a seaman, saying, "For God's sake do your utmost immediately; they are sending us to sea with only three inches of side below the main deck."'

Plimsoll dressed, drove to Whitehall and rang up the porter, who gave him the Secretary's private address, four miles away. But Plimsoll couldn't find the house, woke three sleeping households in turn ('for which I got anything but a kind reception') tried unsuccessfully to rouse the occupants of a local inn and was forced to go back to Whitehall to fetch the porter, who accompanied him, bringing three

* The Merchant Shipping Acts Amendment Bill.

telegrams which had arrived in the interim. All concerned 'cases of gross over-loading'. The Secretary, 'having overcome his natural disgust at being roused out of bed', wrote telegrams to stop all four ships. (The *International*, loaded with telegraph cable, was later lightened after examination by two surveyors; so too was the *Nuphar*. The *Elizabeth* was also stopped, but the *Gazelle* left Shields before it could be detained.)

Plimsoll also reported that the Marine Secretary had told him of a case, just occurred, where 'the owners of a ship, loaded with maize in bulk, had discharged the captain for insisting upon shifting boards to keep the cargo from shifting, and engaged another, and forced the vessel to sea; that the discharged captain's warning had been vindicated by the vessel turning over and drowning the crew – seven men'.

These things, wrote Plimsoll to Baines,

> are happening every night and nobody cares, nobody takes it to heart; and brave and hardy men are going to almost certain death every night while we lie soft and warm . . . It was piercingly cold coming home, for I had forgotten my overcoat, but we had the telegrams which would save four crews from almost certain death, and that made up for all. It was after five o'clock in the morning before I got home and to bed, well satisfied with the result.

When Adderley referred to Plimsoll's nocturnal excursion, he seemed to expect such meddlesomeness to be mocked. But the House cheered. This did not stop Adderley rejecting Plimsoll's suggestion that there should be an officer at Whitehall overnight who could act on telegrams.

Plimsoll thought Adderley's Merchant Shipping Bill feeble, but hoped that with some discussion it would be worth passing. By April there was a feeling that the delays could not possibly go on in the face of the widespread pressure for a remedial law. When the Ladies' Committee led a parade along the Strand to Exeter Hall in the hope of a reprise of the Great Meeting of 1873, Plimsoll, on a platform he shared this time with Eliza (although she did not speak), said that he 'expected a satisfactory measure this session'. Some three thousand mustered again, but many drifted away during the course of the meeting. Plimsoll told his audience that he could 'say on excellent authority that the government had come round and were going to adopt a load line', as specified by his own amendments incorporated into Adderley's Bill. Good news was no news. If they had only known.

Success seemed so close that the Defence Fund Committee, which had raised more than £12,000, decided it was the moment to disband, public opinion being now so emphatically in favour of legislation and so many politicians in agreement. Just in case, the Committee also resolved that 'it held itself prepared to reorganise itself for Mr Plimsoll's assistance, should the just expectations of the country as to legislation be disappointed'.

On 28 May Plimsoll went to witness a curious feat. An American adventurer, Captain Paul Boyton, had invented an inflatable vulcanised rubber suit as a life-saving device, and crossed the Channel wearing it. It allowed him to lie on his back on an oar on the water, using an umbrella as a sail, with a screw propeller on an iron hoop around his waist. Plimsoll was with the journalists who sailed to France to watch the floating captain set off.

About the future of his legislation he felt as buoyant as Boyton.

Boyton and his brolly: the intrepid captain and the
inflatable 'dress' in which he crossed the Channel. (*Mary Evans*)

6

DISRAELI'S ERROR

On the warm evening of Thursday 22 July 1875, a young American who wanted to observe the proceedings of the British Parliament visited the House of Commons at the invitation of William Harcourt MP. He presented his card and was ushered with other spectators into the inner lobby of the House. A door opened from the Chamber itself, and a wildly agitated man, evidently a Member of Parliament, rushed out, throwing his arms about, shaking his fists and exclaiming, 'Cheats!' and, 'I'll expose the villains, all of them!' The man was accompanied by friends, including the blind MP Henry Fawcett, who were trying to calm him.* It was, the American later wrote, 'a strange introduction to the then decorous British House of Commons'. What he had witnessed from the wings was the most notorious incident of Plimsoll's career and his last-straw exasperation at the latest in a series of obstructions. And by a coincidence that would have given both parties pause if they had been aware of it at the time, the visitor was the son of one of Plimsoll's heroes, Richard Henry Dana Jr, the campaigning

---

* Fawcett, a former Cambridge professor of political economy who had been accidentally blinded by his father's shotgun at twenty-five, was Liberal MP for Brighton and a campaigner for women's suffrage, married to the suffragist Millicent Garrett Fawcett. He and Samuel Plimsoll had known each other at least since October 1865, when they both gave papers at the Social Science Congress in Sheffield.

lawyer, friend of sailors and author of the classic 1840 exposé of the conditions of the American merchant seaman, *Two Years Before the Mast*. He had served two years in the merchant service while he was a law student; his book was a record of the experience. He said in its preface: 'If it shall . . . call more attention to the welfare of seamen, or give any information as to their real condition which may serve to raise them in the rank of beings, and to promote in any measure their religious and moral improvement, and diminish the hardships of their daily life, the end of its publication will be answered.' Dana *père* was a man after Plimsoll's own heart, and Plimsoll, said his son, admitted his influence.

When Plimsoll burst into it, the lobby was immediately cleared of strangers, who were not readmitted to the House until Plimsoll and his friends had left. Richard Henry Dana III had missed unprecedented events inside the Chamber.

This Thursday, with Parliament's dissolution for the summer some three weeks away, was the day of the so-called 'Slaughter of the Innocents', when the government abandoned any Bills it would not carry through that session. Among those outstanding was the Merchant Shipping Bill that fell far short of Plimsoll's hopes – since it did not make a fixed load line compulsory or legislate against the dangerous practice of deckloading. Plimsoll himself called it 'an atrocious sham', but all the same he believed that it was a starting point. 'There is enough humanity and knowledge in the House of Commons to change it into a good measure,' he argued. And a good measure was overdue.

But lots of innocent Bills were inevitably going to be slaughtered. Satirical cartoons in *Punch*, leading up to this day, indicate that the volume of business was already an issue. John Tenniel, the *Punch* house cartoonist, drew for the issue of 31 July 1875 a cartoon of Disraeli and Lord Hartington, the Leader of the Opposition, in drag, as two bonneted matrons at a 'baby farm', with Bills crowding round in the guise of orphan children. Baby farms took in illegitimate babies, supposedly for fostering, and had a justified reputation for infanticide and neglect (there had been a committee of inquiry instigated by Shaftesbury in 1870). The caption suggested that Disraeli was feigning compassion and had been keeping all the potential Bills in play longer

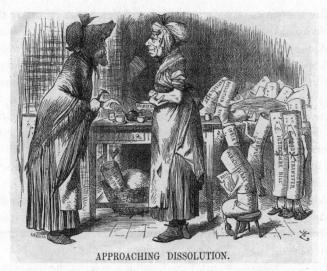

APPROACHING DISSOLUTION.

In drag, Hartington with Disraeli as 'baby farmer' preparing to
'Slaughter the Innocents'. (*From* Punch)

than the Opposition, who knew some of them to be doomed, would
have liked. Merchant Shipping was already head down in a basket
under the table, with its feet waving in the air. The fate of the Merchant
Shipping Bill was therefore uncertain when Eliza climbed the
staircase to the Ladies' Gallery, otherwise known as the Ladies' Cage,
papers in hand, ready to play her part if her husband was thwarted
again. The Cage, separated by a grille from the Strangers' Gallery,
was just above the press gallery and so offered any female ally of
Plimsoll's cause an opportunity Eliza was about to exploit.

Among the Bills that did get an airing that day was the Friendly
Societies Bill. This too was a matter of life and death in which over-
insurance was an issue: it prevented parents from 'making profit of
their babies' deaths by excessive insurance in burial clubs'. (At a time
of widespread poverty and inescapably large families, life insurance was
considered a potential incentive to infanticide for desperate parents.)

At a quarter past four, the hour when the House moved to public
business, the priorities crucial to Plimsoll were revealed. Disraeli
announced that the government, which, he said, had been anxious

to pass the Merchant Shipping Bill during this session of Parliament, could not do so because of unfinished business with the Agricultural Holdings Bill, which it had determined to pass instead.* Failing to anticipate the consequences of this decision, Disraeli expressed 'unfeigned regret' and assured the House that 'If I am in the position next Session which I now occupy, I and my colleagues will take the earliest opportunity of reintroducing the [Merchant Shipping] Bill and pushing it to a safe conclusion.' This was not good enough for the Plimsollites.

One MP beat Plimsoll to an objection. George Goschen, who had been head of the Admiralty, and whose constituency, the City of London, had, as he said, 'a large shipping interest', called attention to the urgency of the case – 'considering that human life is at stake'. He rather moderately postulated: 'I think that interest has some right to complain.' Thomas Eustace Smith also left his seat, but was told by the Speaker, Henry Brand, that this was not the moment to discuss the Bill. Eustace Smith sat down.

Samuel Plimsoll, on the other hand, stood up. By now there were five years of history behind his response. As long ago as 1870 he had argued in the House that every winter that passed while legislation was delayed meant the avoidable loss of five hundred lives. It was three years since his book had made him and the cause famous, and rallied the nation behind him. That same year aristocrats and workers alike had united on the Plimsoll and Seamen's Defence Fund Committee with the intention of bringing about such legislation as this. For years he and his allies had travelled the length and breadth of the country making speeches to raise awareness. He and his wife, who was watching him, had lost their stately home, faced twelve legal suits over the issue and worked late night after night in order to solicit all possible support. Behind Plimsoll were processions and cheering crowds, and rooms thronged with thousands of supporters waving their hats at him in their enthusiasm for more legislative protection for sailors. And he had personally met fearful seamen, sailors' widows and the mothers of

---

* Disraeli was also planning to wind up three other Bills (Supply, Judicature and Land Transfer), allowing the House to adjourn by 10 or 12 August or even earlier.

drowned boys, who had no power to help themselves and looked upon him as their defender. All the accumulated frustrations of an awesome responsibility met in that moment. The eruption was volcanic.

Plimsoll rose, white-faced and trembling, from the cross benches and called out loudly, 'I beg to move the adjournment of the House.' There were immediate murmurs as he was not standing in the proper place for addressing the House. He was in front of the Serjeant-at-Arms' chair, from which spot no one ever spoke. Procedure, still today a powerful force in Parliament, was then sacrosanct, the code that facilitated and defined civilised discourse, and was followed in every detail of the actions and forms of address of the House. Even the formality of the MP's frock coat expressed deference to procedure. The most outrageous thing an MP could do was to flout the rules. Plimsoll's friend, the former naval lieutenant Lord Francis Conyngham, offered a seat closer to the table, which Plimsoll accepted.

Some commentators concluded subsequently that what happened next had all been planned. A Conservative member of the Plimsoll Committee, Lord George Hamilton, later recorded that 'the whole scene had been carefully thought out'. Hamilton was inclined to be disparaging: he held a good many views that were out of sympathy with Plimsoll's extremism. He called Plimsoll a 'whimsical Radical – a curious mixture of philanthropy and self-advertisement', and was ambivalent about the man, although he conceded the value of the cause. Anthony Mundella agreed that the scene was 'clearly premeditated'. He reported that Plimsoll 'told Sullivan *privately* that morning that he should be in a dungeon that night for the course he was about to pursue. He showed his toothbrush, etc in his pockets as in readiness.' The 'etc', according to his son's later account, was six handkerchiefs and a Bible.

Certainly some planning preceded this notorious scene. Plimsoll, who had seen his measures thwarted in the Commons time and again, foresaw the possibility that the Bill might be deferred. Against that contingency he had written and printed a protest, extra copies of which, for distribution to reporters, were Eliza's secret weapon above the Speaker's head.

But the vehemence of Plimsoll's response seems too extreme to have been entirely staged. His words were partly a paraphrase of the protest he had prepared, but he lost his temper spectacularly. He passionately entreated the Prime Minister 'not to consign some thousands of living men to an undeserved and sudden death'. Then he began to make accusations – against the Board of Trade and against shipowning MPs who were listening to him. 'Since 1862,' he said, 'when the commercial marine of this country was committed to the Board of Trade,* they have allowed matters to get worse and worse, and with the aid of ship owners of murderous tendencies outside this House, but who are amply represented inside the House, they have frustrated, and talked to death, every effort to procure a remedy for this state of things.' The 'murderous tendencies' caused a stir. Members began to call out 'Name! Name!' 'I will give the names very soon,' threatened Plimsoll, in a crescendo of anger.

He stood up again, 'raising his arms aloft', and tried to follow the arguments he had planned, starting with the fact that owners never broke up worn-out ships: the secretary of Lloyd's could not think of a single instance in thirty years. This meant they were used until they were dangerous. He cited the figure from Lloyd's Register for ships that had deteriorated over time and were now unclassed – 2654 vessels. Plimsoll was beside himself. One account says he 'hopped about', 'gesticulating madly'. (In his excitement it seems he had a way of standing on one leg, as observed by the parliamentary correspondent Henry Lucy.) 'And what,' he declaimed, 'is the consequence of this? It is that hundreds and hundreds of brave men are continually being sent to their deaths, and their wives are made widows and their children are made orphans, so that' – and by now he was shouting – 'a few speculative scoundrels, in whose breasts there is neither the love of God, nor the fear of God, may make unhallowed gains.' (This seems to have been a slip. His prepared speech said 'neither the love of man, nor the fear of God'.)

There was uproar, with angry members shouting too. When Plimsoll then announced that he had heard on good authority (from

* Board of Trade inspectors were first appointed in 1846 but their powers were increased in 1862.

a secretary to the Treasury) a member of the House described as 'nothing more than a ship-knacker', the Speaker intervened on a point of order, insisting that Plimsoll was 'not at liberty to discuss, on a Motion for Adjournment, the merits of any Bill'.

This only fuelled Plimsoll's indignation, and prompted him to step outside not only his planned text but also the boundaries of parliamentary decorum. Giving notice of a question the following Tuesday to the President of the Board of Trade about five ships wrecked in 1874 with the loss of eighty-seven lives,* he declared, not entirely losing his sense of humour in the heat of the moment: 'I will ask if he will tell the House whether the registered owner of these ships is Edward Bates, the Member for Plymouth, or some other person of the same name. And, Sir, I shall ask some questions about Members on this side of the House also.' Plimsoll took half a dozen strides into the centre of the floor, in front of the mace at the table, and opposite the Speaker's chair stamped his foot and 'cried out at the top of his voice': 'I am determined to unmask the villains who send our seamen to death and destruction!'

The Speaker rose, as calls for 'Order!' became a 'continuous roar'. ('It was no use shouting "Order, order", or "Send for the Serjeant-at-Arms",' wrote one MP some years afterwards. 'Samuel Plimsoll all alone meant to save the sailormen, and he called out to all England.') Plimsoll, overwrought, stood in the middle of the noisy room and shook his fist at members who shouted at him. Newspapers later reported the gesture as shaking his fist at the Speaker, or even in Disraeli's face. This image took hold of the popular imagination, probably because with hindsight it summed up the political impact of the outburst.

Meanwhile it was basic etiquette in the House that two members should not be standing at once, and, since the Speaker, Henry Brand, Liberal MP for Lewes, was on his feet, Plimsoll's friends tried unsuccessfully to make him sit back on the bench. The Speaker, formal in robes and wig, with a 'calm manner and deliberate accents' that 'formed

---

* The *Thetys*, which sank in January 1875 on a voyage from Sydney to Singapore, with the loss of twenty-six men, the *Melbourne* and the *Norah Greame*. Plimsoll also mentioned the *Foundling* and the *Sidney Dacres*, both of which were abandoned.

a strange contrast to the excited demeanour of Mr Plimsoll', who was shaking violently, his head 'moving spasmodically', asked Plimsoll to withdraw the use of the word 'villain' as applied to any member of the House. Plimsoll refused, despite the Speaker's urgings, four times, and, advancing to the table, drew out a large sheet of white paper.

At this the Speaker said, 'If the Honourable Gentleman does not withdraw the expression, I must submit his conduct to the judgment of the House.' Plimsoll retorted, 'I shall be happy to submit to the judgment of the House – and this', he said, slapping his document down beside the mace, 'is my protest.'

Even then, Plimsoll did not sit. 'Indescribable confusion reigned' as he reportedly continued to shake his fist at the Treasury Bench, where Disraeli made to stand up. Plimsoll still would not be silenced, but his words were inaudible over the din. Disraeli stood at the table for some moments waiting to speak, while Plimsoll gesticulated towards the Board of Trade President, Sir Charles Adderley, 'who

'Indescribable confusion': Plimsoll shakes his fist at Disraeli; Alexander Sullivan tries to restrain him; Hartington, seated, Leader of the Opposition, looks on.
(*London Illustrated News*)

occupied a safe position at the remote end of the Treasury Bench'. Only with great persuasion was Plimsoll urged into a seat among friends in the Opposition, who tried to pacify him.

As Plimsoll sat down, Disraeli expressed his 'deep pain' that 'a brother member should have conducted himself in a manner almost unparalleled'. 'And so has the Government,' heckled Plimsoll, his friends' attempts to placate him obviously unsuccessful. Disraeli courted the sympathy of Plimsoll's supporters with his 'reluctance' to take this step to uphold the dignity of Parliament, but, in a response that would later rebound on him, and which some thought showed that he too had lost his temper, moved that the Speaker should 'reprimand the Honourable Gentleman for conduct so disorderly and violent'. While this motion was before the House, Plimsoll, meanwhile, was persuaded to leave, which he did in agitated haste, still talking excitedly to himself.

Captain Gosset, a kindly soul and the Deputy Serjeant-at-Arms, whispered, 'All right, Plimsoll, you'll get your Bill. Take it quietly, man. Have a rest. You'll get your Bill.' Charles Lewis, the member for Londonderry, standing with a group of MPs at the Bar, spoke a few words to Plimsoll as he rushed by. Plimsoll responded with such suddenness and ferocity that Lewis recoiled: 'Good God!' shouted Plimsoll. 'Don't you know that thousands of men are dying for this?' Plimsoll left the Chamber in a state of excitement 'that seemed little less than that of an actual maniac', thus affording his American witness his surprising impression of the workings of British democracy.

At this point Plimsoll gave his friend Alexander Sullivan, the Irish Catholic Home Ruler and MP for Louth, a letter, ready prepared to deliver to his wife (according to Mundella, who said Sullivan told him about it). The letter was presumably Plimsoll's signal to Eliza to drop copies of his protest into the House and on to the gentlemen of the press in the reporters' gallery on the level below. She was perfectly placed to ensure the protest was widely published in its entirety in the following day's papers, and her action that day was remembered for years along with her husband's outburst.

Reports do not tell us whether Eliza, having played her part in the dramatic scene, was in the lobby to meet Plimsoll or to accompany him home. She would surely have chosen to be with her husband and his friends if she could, but in 1875 women were not permitted to wait with the men to enter the Chamber. The Ladies' Gallery was reached by its own staircase from the Speaker's Court, which had a small ladies-only waiting room. The lobby where her husband sat quivering and distraught seems to have been out of bounds for her.* Sullivan (before or after he delivered Eliza's letter) walked his friend up and down the terrace of the House of Commons by the Thames to calm him down in the open air. Then, as one report put it, Plimsoll, 'frantic with grief and despair', was taken home by his friends to Eliza's care at Harrington Square. In fact Eliza was among those, including Lord Francis Conyngham, who escorted him there.

Although Plimsoll had expected the rejection of the Bill, it seems that the shock of having his goal snatched once again from his reach was fresh upon him. One account says that Plimsoll heard earlier that day that he was to be disappointed. If so, he knew just long enough in advance for his indignation to build up steam.

Moncure D. Conway, American-born freethinking minister and protégé of the poet Emerson, then living in London and writing a weekly letter for the *Cincinnati Commercial Gazette*, reported in the issue of 6 August that:

> a week ago he [Plimsoll] was one of the happiest men in England. At a dinner, where I had the pleasure of meeting him, he said that he had been privately informed by a member of the Government that they had substantially adopted his bill, and meant to put it through. The crowning success of his cause appeared just at hand. The dragon of cruel mercantile selfishness seemed already to be dead at his feet.

Conway was sympathetic to Plimsoll's outburst and described it thus: 'Mr Plimsoll's madness was not that of the intellect; it was a

---

* Gentlemen were allowed on the stairs to the Ladies' Gallery at least. On 8 July 1864 Lord Palmerston, after the defeat of an attempt to censure the government over the Danish War, raced up the stairs to the Ladies' Gallery and on the first landing flung himself into the arms of his wife, Lady Palmerston, who was coming down.

sort of divine passion, breaking out with thunder and lightning. This man has dwelt on the scene of poor wretches struggling amid the waves to an extent hardly appreciable by the gentlemen of England who live at home at ease.'*

Disraeli, meanwhile, was not as regretful as he purported to be. He had had no wish to see the Bill through. On the very morning of 22 July he had received a letter from 11 Downing Street, necessarily marked 'private', from his Chancellor of the Exchequer, Sir Stafford Northcote, suggesting a strategy for delaying the Merchant Shipping Bill. (Northcote, remember, was the brother-in-law of Plimsoll's opponent, Thomas Farrer of the Board of Trade.) 'My Dear Mr Disraeli,' Northcote had written, sounding like an executioner: 'May I offer the following suggestions as to the process of massacre?' Disraeli had taken heed.

> When the orders of the day are called you might rise and say that, after carefully considering the state of public business, you had come to the conclusion that it would be impossible to find time for a full discussion of the Merchant Shipping Bill; that you thought it undesirable to attempt to pass a mere fragment of so important a measure; and that you therefore moved to discharge the order, promising, at the same time, that the bill should have a first place among the measures of next session. (This would be quite in order, but, of course, it might lead to some debate both on merchant shipping in particular and on the course of business in general; but I do not see how you can avoid this under any circumstances.)

This letter takes it entirely for granted that the government *wanted* to delay the Shipping Bill. Northcote, writing to Disraeli two days later, revealed the reasons. He said: '[Plimsoll's Bill] was not a bill for applying a direct and simple remedy to an admitted evil. The direct and simple remedy of authorising the Board of Trade to stop unseaworthy ships had already been applied by the Act of 1873; and

---

* 'Ye gentlemen of England, who live at home at ease,/How little do you think upon the dangers of the seas.' From the song 'The Bay of Biscay, O!'

the other direct and simple remedy which Plimsoll desired, of insti-
tuting a Government survey of all seagoing ships, we were not
prepared to adopt.'

The government, as Northcote spells out, wished to put responsibility for the maintenance of ships into the hands of shipowners.
This was not what Plimsoll wanted. So he was fobbed off with
excuses. The truth was that Disraeli did not believe in being pre-
scriptive. He had said in the course of the Agricultural Holdings Bill
debate in the House a month earlier:

> Permissive legislation is the characteristic of a free people. It is easy to
> adopt compulsory legislation when you have to deal with those who
> only exist to obey. But in a free country, and especially in a country
> like England, you must trust to persuasion and example as the two
> great elements, if you wish to effect any considerable change in the
> manners and the customs of the people.

Their excuses got Northcote and Disraeli into trouble, because
the two of them justified the government's decision with different
reasons. Disraeli failed to pick up on the bit of Northcote's advice
that urged him to say it was 'undesirable to attempt to pass a mere
fragment of so important a measure'. Instead the Prime Minister had
pleaded the prior claims of the Agricultural Holdings Bill. This was
an unfortunate and unpopular choice that suggested that the government valued property more highly than human life, which was
exactly the accusation levelled against shipowners. Setting up this
particular Bill against Plimsoll's did Disraeli's government a great
deal of damage. (Disraeli had hoped the Bill would have quite the
opposite effect. It was a measure to give tenants compensation for
improvements they had made to their farms, and intended to prove
that the Tories were not, as some critics thought, just self-interested
landed gentry.)

Meanwhile Northcote, late on the night of 22 July, made the
mistake of following his original script and saying that the government had deferred Merchant Shipping because there was no time to
discuss it properly in the remainder of the session. He argued that the
postponement of the Bill 'would forward the solution of the ques-

tion rather than hinder it'. The Leader of the Opposition was quick to point out that Northcote's excuse 'was totally at variance' with the Prime Minister's.

Northcote had shown some insight, recognising that both the plight of sailors in particular and the conduct of government in general would become matters of debate, but he drastically underestimated the extent of that debate.

The moment that Plimsoll made his exit must have been the moment when Disraeli realised he had underestimated the strength of feeling in favour of the member for Derby. He could no longer count on his own considerable authority and powers of conciliation to carry the day. Before a reprimand could be agreed upon, Plimsoll's friends defended him.

The Marquess of Hartington came to Plimsoll's rescue, and also, unintentionally but certainly, to Disraeli's.* The Prime Minister was on the brink of a conflict with a defiant member of the House which would in the long run have undermined his own authority. Hartington, whose 'frigid accents' were a 'strong contrast with Mr Disraeli's tremulous tones of wrath', suggested that instead of a reprimand, Plimsoll be given a short time to cool off, and was greeted with loud cheers. Hartington advised that 'before taking any strong measures against a man so universally respected, it would be more consonant with the dignity of the House to [let him] put himself right'. And Alexander Sullivan, 'pale and breathless', hastened back in from ministering to his over-excited friend also to plead the strain that Plimsoll had been under as a mitigation of his impropriety. 'I hold in my hand', said Sullivan, 'documents which . . . have wrought him to the pitch of excitement we have seen today . . . I only plead this for him, that his is a nature eminently unselfish.' He spoke of an 'overstrain acting on a very sensitive temperament' and an agitated state of mind that had worried his friends over the previous few days.

Disraeli, realising that Hartington's course would extricate him from the dangerous position into which he was leading the House,

---

* The Marquess of Hartington was Spencer Compton Cavendish, Gladstone's successor as Leader of the Liberal Opposition.

caught the lifeline that was thrown to him by the Opposition and moved that Plimsoll should attend the House again in a week. Henry Fawcett spoke briefly in support of Plimsoll, as did Michael Bass, the brewer who had stood with Plimsoll as an MP for Derby back in 1865 and had proposed Plimsoll in April 1875 for membership of the Reform Club. The motion was agreed. After so much drama, the House moved quietly on to the clauses of the Agricultural Holdings Bill.

When Sullivan told the House that Plimsoll was ill, he was credible. Moncure D. Conway, the man who had dined with Plimsoll just before this scene, also wrote that: 'He is a nervous gentleman, too; thin, pale-faced, with an affection of the eyes which makes it necessary for him to wear coloured spectacles. He has often reminded me of the portraits of Washington.'

Plimsoll had been a stocky man, excitable but robust; now he was thin, pale and nervous. The cause had cost him more than money. (The comparison to Washington must have been a tribute to Plimsoll's sincerity more than an identification of a real physical likeness; it is hard to see in white-wigged, clean-shaven Washington much resemblance to whiskered Plimsoll.)

Disraeli not only misjudged Plimsoll's support inside the House but underestimated the support the MP commanded outside it. Although there were politicians who thought that Plimsoll's tempestuousness had done his cause irreparable harm, it swiftly became clear that this was not the case. The following week showed that the nation was on his side. On 31 July this account of the incident was published in *Punch*:

Mr Disraeli rose to announce the withdrawal of the Merchant Shipping Bill, overlaid by the Agricultural Holdings Bill. What are losses of life to leases for life? The scene which followed is no subject for comic comment. Mr Punch will only express his deep sympathy with Mr Plimsoll, whose indignation at seeing once more dashed from his lips the hope of remedying a great wrong, to the righting of which he has devoted his heart and soul and strength, overcame his self-control, and led him into a fierce defiance of the rules of the House of Commons, for which, in his cooler moments, he will be the readiest to ask pardon. The House behaved well throughout the painful scene. But what does Mr Plimsoll mean by being so terribly in earnest?

And in the same issue *Punch* ran this verse entitled 'A Plea for Plimsoll':

What though the passion in him tore away
The dams and dykes of senatorial phrase?
What though the words that spoke his mind outweigh
The weights of Parliamentary dispraise?
What though, brain-wrung by stress of ruth and rage,
And sudden-baffled hope of help, long nursed;
Against all rules of the St Stephen's stage
Forth in accusing earnest wrath he burst –
Of greed that, ghoul-like, feeds from watery graves,
Of homes and hearts that desolate abide;
Of brave men's lives foredoomed for gain of knaves –
And, so denouncing, flung his charges wide,
And gave his enemies a scoff and boast,
'Lo! you, the Sailors' champion!' Through their sneers,
Still let his bitter cry ring in our ears –
'They drown by hundreds round our England's coast!'

The government, complained the *Penny Illustrated Paper*, 'had outraged the feelings of the nation – had lied and truckled'. It went on:

The bitter agony of anger which moved the member for Derby when he uttered a protest for which no words could be too strong, may be blamed for want of cold and calculating etiquette; but his ringing words have found an echo all over Britain, and will form a rally cry which may, after all, hoot the present Government out of office in spite of the support which it may expect from shipowners who blandly deprecate plain language and appeal pathetically on behalf of their own eminent respectability.

Hansard recorded every word of the tumultuous exchange. But the Votes and Proceedings of the House, the immediate public record, censoring controversial accusations, said only this: 'Breach of Order (Mr Plimsoll). Mr Plimsoll, the Member for Derby, having used expressions in Debate, which, when called upon by Mr Speaker, he refused to withdraw, and having otherwise conducted himself in a disorderly manner: – Motion made and Question proposed, that Mr Plimsoll for his disorderly conduct be reprimanded in his place by Mr Speaker.'

But the country, which promptly heard everything from the newspaper reports, was unperturbed by bad language in the inner sanctum of government, and by politicians calling one another names. Clearly then, as it would now, it delighted in the idea. It also recognised that strong terms were warranted on behalf of the weak, and that they might have an effect that civilised discourse had never achieved. 'The numerous meetings of sympathisers which were held during the next few days proved that the people understood the noble instinct of the man who dared to throw etiquette aside when the question was one of life and death,' said the *Graphic*.

It was an eventful week. The papers published Plimsoll's protest in full. No less vehement, insulting to shipowning MPs and controversial than his utterances in the House, it insisted on both the inadequacy of the present Bill and the urgency of some adequate legislation. It began, like his speech, with the numbers of unclassed ships likely to be coffin-ships, and the possibility of arrest without warrant for 'British subjects who, having carelessly agreed to sail in them, find when it is too late, that the only alternative before them is gaol or death'. It charged the Government:

that they are wittingly and unwittingly – for there are both – playing into the hands of the maritime murderers inside the House and outside the House, to secure a further continuance of the present murderous system. What is demanded by humanity is that rotten ships should be broken up or repaired; that ships should not be overloaded; that grain cargoes should not be carried in bulk, so as to expose the lives of those on board to deadly peril; and deck cargoes, the source of unutterable agony to many and death to so many more,

'The Sailor's Friend': 'a man bold enough to tell what he believes to be the truth', Samuel Plimsoll MP caricatured in *Vanity Fair*, March 1873.

Reflecting on the fate of *Our Seamen*: a rare cartoon from the *London Sketch Book*, a supplement to the *Figaro*.

THE
LONDON SKETCH BOOK.

SAMUEL PLIMSOLL, M.P.
Save your ship from wreck.
The Two Gentlemen of Verona, act 1, sc. 1.

A famous face: colour lithograph from a photograph by the London Stereoscopic and Photographic Company, July 1875.

HARPER'S WEEKLY.
A JOURNAL OF CIVILIZATION

VOL. XIX.—No. 972.]   NEW YORK, SATURDAY, AUGUST 14, 1875.   [WITH A SUPPLEMENT. PRICE TEN CENTS.

Entered according to Act of Congress, in the Year 1875, by Harper & Brothers, in the Office of the Librarian of Congress, at Washington.

THE BRITISH LION LOOSE IN THE HOUSE OF COMMONS.—[See Page 659.]

"Now put your Head in, if you dare."

'Now put your Head in, if you dare': Disraeli and the lion of British public opinion, front cover of *Harper's Weekly* by Thomas Nast, 14 August 1875, New York.

Making his mark: Woodburytype photograph by Lock and Whitfield of Samuel Plimsoll in 1876, from *Men of Mark* (1878), a collection of portraits of prominent men.

London Feb 18/92

My dear Nellie

It is quite your turn to have a letter.

It will resemble proceedings in Parliament generally that is to say — it will look to be very important indeed but will not have much in it.

Give my dearest love to everybody — all is well —

Your loving father

Samuel Plimsoll.

Miss Ellen Plimsoll

'Your loving father': handwritten letter on House of Commons mourning notepaper from Samuel Plimsoll to his adopted daughter Nellie in 1892.

Professor Henry Fawcett MP,
Plimsoll's defender, blinded in his youth
by a shotgun. (*Mary Evans*)

Charles Bradlaugh, Plimsoll's atheist ally,
denouncer of the 'ship-knackers'.
(*Mary Evans*)

Annie Besant, later President of the
Indian National Congress, who
demonstrated for Plimsoll in July 1875.
(*Mary Evans*)

James Hall, shipowner, the first advocate
of a load line. (*From Hayward*, James Hall
of Tynemouth)

Vanity Fair cartoon (1888) of Edward 'Bully' Bates, shipowning MP for Plymouth and the target of Plimsoll's accusations in the Commons in July 1875.

Charles Adderley, President of the Board of Trade, 'always a day behind the world'. (*Getty*)

Charles Morgan Norwood, Liberal MP for Hull, who sued Plimsoll for libel. (*Association of British Chambers of Commerce*)

Samuel Plimsoll in his late sixties, the father of three young children. (*Popperfoto*)

The *Samuel Plimsoll* wool clipper of the George Thompson Aberdeen line, launched in 1873, bore a figurehead of Plimsoll. (Watercolour by A Chidley, from a print in the author's collection)

should be put an end to. The Government Bill provides for none of these things; it provides only heavier penalties and severer punishments against our unfortunate fellow-subjects whose necessities take them to sea.

Urging 'in the name of our common humanity' the immediate adoption of the Merchant Shipping Bill, and desiring 'to unmask the villains who sit in the House, fit representatives of the more numerous, but no greater villains who are outside the House', Plimsoll laid 'upon the head of the Prime Minister and his fellows, the blood of all the men who shall perish next winter from preventible causes'. He concluded with a characteristically extreme fire-and-brimstone condemnation, reminiscent of the awful deprecations of *Our Seamen*, threatening 'the wrath of that God who has said: "Ye shall not afflict any widow, or fatherless child. If thou afflict them in any wise, and they cry at all unto Me, I will surely hear their cry; and My wrath shall wax hot, and I will kill you with sword and your wives shall be widows and your children fatherless" (Exodus 22: verses 22–34).' And, as if that were not enough, he added intemperately: 'How much hotter, then, shall be His indignation and wrath against those who reduce unhappy women and children to that deplorable condition, and who leave their own fellow-creatures, guilty of no crime, to a violent and sudden death.'

Encouraged either by fear of divine retribution or, more rationally, by the appeal to common humanity, the public united in an outbreak of Plimsoll fever aided by the Plimsoll Demonstration Committee, which orchestrated meetings throughout the country. The 'spontaneous' outburst of feeling did represent genuine public passions, but it required a certain amount of organisation. Plimsoll and his friends knew that a wide public reaction was a way to achieve their ends and did all they could to make sure there was one. On Sunday 25 July 1875 three thousand people gathered to express their sympathy for Plimsoll on Clerkenwell Green, a secluded quadrangle in an area of north London which Dickens had referred to as a den of thieves and ruffians, now emptied of its labyrinth of ill-reputed alleys by mid-nineteenth-century development. Its airy, cobbled enclave made an ideal arena for public demonstrations and it was already a centre for radicalism. (To this day marchers convene there, in front of the Marx Memorial Library.)

The countrywide meetings were full of rebellious spirit, righteous indignation and a good deal of humour at the expense of government and shipowners. On each of the evenings of Tuesday 27 and Wednesday 28 July outrage was being expressed simultaneously in many British cities. The general reaction was well represented by this remark made on the 28th at a meeting in the Temperance Hall in Sheffield, where Plimsoll had lived and worked and had friends: 'If one Member went mad every year upon some similar subject, the legislation of the country would proceed a great deal better. If Mr Plimsoll is mad, the sooner he bit a few other MPs the better.'*

A meeting held by Liverpool Working Men's Conservative Association on Tuesday 27 was advertised with this notice: 'ROTTEN SHIP OWNERS SPECIALLY INVITED.'

A great outdoor demonstration in support of Plimsoll took place on the afternoon of Tuesday 27th in Poplar, east London, in the open space in front of the gates of the East India Docks, an entrance in the form of a clock-crowned triumphal arch, stepped like a pile of child's building bricks. The demonstration was partially led by two notable activists and reformers whose fame was yet to grow: Charles Bradlaugh and his intimate associate Annie Besant, who were, as it happened, first introduced by the wife of Moncure D. Conway, at the start of a long and controversial partnership. Later, in 1886, Besant and Bradlaugh were prosecuted together and acquitted on appeal, exonerated of corrupt motives, for republishing an American pamphlet, 'The Fruits of Philosophy', which advocated birth control. Besant was the former wife of a vicar who had banished her from her home when she began to doubt her faith; she had been for the past year vice-president of the National Secular Society, which

---

* The speaker was Percy Rawson, perhaps one of the family of Thomas Rawson, owner of the Old Pond Street Brewery in Sheffield where Plimsoll had a job at seventeen. Thomas Rawson had been an agitator for parliamentary reform and universal suffrage; the local gentry had called him 'dangerous'.

Bradlaugh had founded in 1866. (Besant's beloved son had been given into the care of her ex-husband because of her unorthodox views; she still had care of her daughter, but the vicar claimed custody of her too after the birth-control pamphlet.) Besant went on to organise a celebrated strike of match girls, and to have a hand in huge demonstrations against coercion in Ireland in the autumn of 1887 and in the Dock Strike of 1889. George Bernard Shaw thought her the finest orator, man or woman, of the age. Later still, she became a theosophist under the influence of the mystic Madame Blavatsky, went to India and was elected president of the Indian National Congress, serving from 1917 to 1923.

Bradlaugh, atheist lecturer and proprietor of the *National Reformer*, which he co-edited with Besant, was to enjoy a cycle of elections to Parliament, as Radical MP for Northampton, followed by expulsions from the House because of his refusal between 1880 and 1886 to take the loyal oath. He was attacked for his atheism by Winston Churchill's father, Randolph, and defended by Gladstone. A. N. Wilson has said of him: 'he belongs to the good old English political tradition of cussedness . . . He stood for the little man being allowed to speak his mind, and for the poor man having as much say in the scheme of things as the rich.' (He was, along with Plimsoll, another Radical disapproved of by the Tory MP George Hamilton, and Hamilton and Bradlaugh once very nearly came to blows in a public encounter.)

On that July afternoon in 1875, when Annie Besant was only twenty-eight, she and her cussed atheist comrade stood among the poor sailors who needed a voice. The wrath of God, as threatened by Plimsoll, did not motivate unbelieving Bradlaugh and Besant, but the love of man did. They listened to letters from the constituency politicians, who were quick to assure the crowd of their own solidarity with Plimsoll's cause: missives were read out from the members for Tower Hamlets, Samuda and Ritchie, expressing their regret at not being able to attend in person and citing their support in Parliament of Plimsoll's Bill.

The meeting ended with defiant resolutions. It was Bradlaugh who proposed:

> That we (the meeting) desire to testify our deep admiration for and sym-
> pathy with Mr Plimsoll for his brave protest in the House of Commons
> on behalf of our merchant sailors; and while admitting that in strictness
> his expression regarding 'ship knackers' was unparliamentary, we would
> ask him, before withdrawing it, to learn from the Speaker what is the
> parliamentary expression by which to designate men who insure rotten
> vessels above their value, intending that they shall go to the bottom.

The resolution was seconded by a shipwright, supported by Annie Besant and then passed 'amidst rounds of cheers'. The chairman, Mr T. C. Potter, said he would forward Bradlaugh's resolution forthwith to Mr Plimsoll and the meeting broke up with three cheers for the honourable member for Derby.

The town halls of Victorian England were monuments to the prosperity of the Industrial Revolution, built in a neo-classical style that made a grandiose connection between the empires of the ancient world and the British Empire; merchant seamen helped to make the wealth that built them. It is appropriate then that meetings in their defence took place that same night around the country in such vast arenas as the palatial town halls of Birmingham, Leeds and Manchester and in front of St George's Hall, Liverpool's resplendent neo-Parthenon. There were meetings too in huge market places, in Leicester and in Nottingham, which has, at five and a half acres, the largest open space of its kind in England. Even the more modest venues were substantial, such as the Mechanics Institute in Bradford, where the lecture hall on the upper storey seated seven hundred people. These gatherings were generally 'large', 'crowded' and 'enthusiastic'.

The meeting in Birmingham was chaired by Joseph Chamberlain, then the Lord Mayor of the city, and a year away from his election as its Liberal MP, from which platform he went on to become a Cabinet minister and celebrated statesman.* At this meeting in 1875 he demonstrated his skill as a political speaker and his sympathy for

---

* Chamberlain was Lord Mayor of Birmingham from 1873 to 1876 and an MP for Birmingham from 1876 to 1903, becoming, at first, leader of the Radicals and later leader of the Liberal Unionists. He was the father of the British Prime Minister Neville 'peace in our time' Chamberlain.

Mr Plimsoll – a sympathy important for the eventual outcome of this story, since in 1880 Gladstone was to appoint Chamberlain President of the Board of Trade, the post that offered most opportunity to make or break shipping regulations.

At Birmingham Mayor Chamberlain thought, prompting applause, that the matter at hand was one which 'had deeply stirred the hearts of the people' and 'very nearly touched the dignity and honour of the Empire'. He did not think that 'in their great town there was one man or woman, to whatever party he or she might happen to belong, who would not join with them in offering cordial sympathy with the objects of Mr Plimsoll's self-denying sacrifices [loud applause], and a hearty approbation of the man who had devoted his life to the service of his fellow-countrymen, for in this case Mr Plimsoll had sacrificed almost all that most of them held dear.'

He hoped Mr Plimsoll 'would take comfort from the expressions which were pouring in upon him from his countrymen everywhere throughout the land, assuring him of their sympathy with his burning and righteous indignation, assuring him that they were inclined to condone even un-Parliamentary language when it was applied to un-Parliamentary actions, to crimes which were un-English, un-Christian and which deserved the abhorrence of every honest citizen.'

Chamberlain was armed with figures Plimsoll had sent that morning. They concerned a period of six months in which 128 ships had sunk and 177 sailors drowned, and a year in which 633 sailors were imprisoned for refusing to man ships, 'some of which were subsequently lost'. Borrowing from an 1874 publication of his own, Plimsoll commented, so that Chamberlain could quote him to the Birmingham crowd: 'If [these facts] do not stir the hearts of my fellow-countrymen, no words of mine will, but in that case England will have become false to all her history and all faith. Her destiny will have died in my heart.'

Chamberlain and Plimsoll were not the only ones whose rhetoric scaled heights of hyperbole. The Reverend George Dawson, minister of the Church of the Saviour in Birmingham, said that 'if this were his dying speech and confession in public, he should have desired no better theme and no nobler subject than that before them'.

The Reverend Dawson expressed, too, the general criticism that one of the flaws of Disraeli's ministry was that the Prime Minister, who liked to entertain the House with his wit, took things too lightly. 'This Merchant Shipping question has been played with, trifled with, joked with, and we are disgusted. The whole Session has been dis-organised, ill-arranged, frivolous.' A capacity to lighten proceedings had always been Disraeli's strength, especially compared to sober Gladstone (on whom Lady Palmerston's judgement was: 'if you boiled Gladstone I don't believe you would extract an ounce of fun from him'; and Lord Derby's that 'Gladstone's jokes are no laughing matter'). But Henry Lucy compared Disraeli in this term of government to a fading prima donna: 'The PM, aiming to be gaily audacious, misses the exact pitch and becomes simply rude.' Plimsoll's fervour contrasted with the government's increasingly tiresome attempts at 'gay audacity' and demonstrated the importance of being earnest.

It was not long, in Birmingham as elsewhere, before the discussion of the immediate issue of sailors' safety led to a questioning of the competence of Disraeli's government. Dr R. W. Dale, also a minister, from Carr's Lane Congregational Church, and evidently no fan of the Conservative administration, believed that 'no Ministry had done so much within the same time to bring Parliamentary government in this country into contempt as the conservative Ministry . . . their conduct had been humiliating to themselves and pernicious in its influence upon the political life of the country.' Plimsoll had exposed what were thought to be misguided priorities. Not only was favouring the Agricultural Holdings Bill over the Merchant Shipping Bill perceived to show a higher regard for property than for life, but deferring a Bill that was a matter of life and death just because of the holidays suggested reprehensible trivial-mindedness. Dr Dale asserted: 'If Members of the House of Commons are more anxious to kill partridges on August 12, than to discharge their duties to the nation, the country is likely to form its judgment concerning the fitness of such men to be entrusted with Parliamentary duties. Parliamentary Government is on trial in this country.'

Most of the demonstrations that week were organised by the left, but at Bath, in the south-west, two open-air meetings were held on Monday the 26th, hosted by both rival parties. The Conservatives, while they were sure that the Merchant Shipping Bill was a good thing, found someone other than Disraeli to blame for its abandonment. The reason it had been impossible to carry the Bill through this session, contended Fowler, the former MP for Penrhyn, was the fault of a 'seditious and factious' Opposition, for wasting time, particularly on the evening set aside to debate the Agricultural Holdings Bill. It was well known that the government wished to pass the Merchant Shipping Bill, he said, but the Opposition prevented it. But another speaker admitted that 'the scene in the House of Commons and the rejection of [Plimsoll's] bill would do more to make Mr Disraeli uncomfortable than all the efforts of Mr Gladstone, Mr Lowe [Opposition Home Secretary] or Lord Hartington [Leader of the Opposition], for the national feeling was certain to go with a man who was so earnest in a good cause as Mr Plimsoll was.' Meanwhile the Liberal gathering, which Plimsoll had planned to attend before his illness prevented him, passed a resolution condemning the government for withdrawing the Bill.

Protest was also voiced in the following days by the people of Boston in Lincolnshire, the South Yorkshire Miners' Association, and Plimsoll's Derby constituents, when the Mayor praised Plimsoll's self-denial, but added that his idea about a load line 'had been controverted'. Resolutions supportive of Plimsoll were passed in the Stepney Temperance Hall and the Nottingham Mechanics Hall, and by the St Pancras Working Men's Club, the Bradford Liberal Club, the Great Western Railway company in Swindon and Portsmouth's Liberal Party.

Even an evening at the theatre was affected by the popular mood. At London's Globe Theatre, round the corner from Exeter Hall, a double bill of melodramas was punctuated from 26 July by a recitation – 'by desire' – of Arthur Matthison's poem 'Coffin Ships', as heard in 1873 at the Great Plimsoll Meeting. It was performed in the interval by Adeline Billington, an actress admired by Dickens, who was the daughter, niece and sister of sailors. And 'poor, ill-fated

ROUGH & READY

By PAUL MERITT.

On MONDAY, July 26th, 1875, and following evenings, the performances will commence precisely at 7:30, with the successful Yorkshire Drama, in Three Acts, written expressly for Mr and Mrs BILLINGTON, entitled

THE MUSIC ARRANGED BY EDWIN ELLIS.

John Norman	(A Wealthy Mine Owner)	Mr. A. D. ANDERSON
Harry Valentine	(Mrs Valentine's Son)	Mr CECIL BERYL
Mark Musgrave	(A Yorkshire Gamekeeper—	
	"Rough and Ready")	Mr JOHN BILLINGTON
		(His Original Character)
Nathaniel Hickory	(Mrs Valentine's London Agent)	Mr JACKSON
Charles	(Foreman's Servant)	Mr J. COWELL
Mrs Valentine	(A Wealthy Widow)	Mrs BILLINGTON
		(Her Original Character)
Alice Way	... (her Niece)	Miss E MEYRICK
Amelia Norman, an Héirèss—wih/eng. Méllo		CAMILLE DUBOIS

Act 1.

SEEDS OF DISCORD.

Scene—Mrs Valentine's Residence, Yorkshire.

Act 2

DAGGERS DRAWN.

Scene—Norman's House, London.

Act 3.

THE GAME OF LAW.

Scene—Private Hotel, Westminster.

COFFIN SHIPS

MRS. BILLINGTON

Will (by desire) recite Samuel Plimsoll's Poem "Coffin Ships," as given at the GREAT PLIMSOLL MEETING, at EXETER HALL, Every Evening at 9.30.

WEDNESDAY PROGRAMME

GALLERY OF CELEBRITIES

PHOTOGRAPH FROM LIFE

Woodbury Permanent Photograph.

Figaro Office, 35, St. Bride Street, London

The mood of the moment: Globe Theatre programme announcing an interval recitation by Adeline

Gustavus Brooke', who had drowned on the *London,* had once given her a part that made all the difference to her career. Her recitation was 'received with great applause'.

A new song had reached the music halls. 'A British Cheer for Plimsoll' by John Guest deplored the 'wretches/Who to increase their gain,/Send men in rotten vessels/To perish on the main' and went on:

But Plimsoll has aroused us
He pleads the sailor's cause
And by his fearless courage
He wins the world's applause . . .
Then let us do our duty,
Not resting till we save,
By honest legislation
Poor Jack upon the waves.

Public feeling was fuelled by a case that was reported at the same time as Plimsoll's showdown in Parliament. The *Alcedo* was a two-masted sailing ship, a brigantine. It was twenty-six years old and had not weathered well. In some parts it had become so rotten that the wood could be scooped out in handfuls. The owner, an Irish merchant from Waterford by the name of Laughlin Freeman, wrote to his insurance agent, Messrs Begg and Co. in Cardiff, saying: 'I would be inclined to renew the former insurance of £250 at 8 guineas if I thought there would be no danger of Plimsoll.' Found among his papers was the reply from the Beggs, who wrote back: 'We don't think there is any fear of Plimsoll interfering with the *deed* (at all events on this side) as they do not appear to be so much on the look-out over here.' They were mistaken. Mr Freeman was sentenced on 23 July 1875 to two months in prison in Waterford, as well as to a fine of £300, for sending an unseaworthy ship to sea.

This case demonstrated that there was existing legislation that could catch miscreant shipowners, but neverthless the effect of the story was to fuel indignation. Quoting in a private letter a colleague's observation, Disraeli remarked that:

the withdrawal of the Merchant Shipping Bill would have passed without notice by the country, had it not been for two unexpected incidents which we could not have counted on – the Plimsoll scene and the verdict against a wicked shipowner in the Irish Courts. The first showed . . . what a dangerous man Plimsoll was to trust to in legislation – and the second proved that the existing law was an efficient one; and yet, these two incidents, fanned, of course, by faction, have agitated the country.

Disraeli apparently had no qualms about the withdrawal of the Merchant Shipping Bill in itself; what bothered him was not getting away with it. The immediate reaction, from Plimsoll and the public, was a shock to Disraeli, but it was to get worse for him. As the days passed he found himself increasingly beleaguered, and increasingly alone.

7

PLIMSOLL IS KING

The week between Plimsoll's outburst and his apology was one of those long times in politics. Within days 'the undertow of Mr Plimsoll's out-of-doors wave of popularity [was] evidently sweeping the House strong in the direction of Merchant Shipping Legislation'.

Disraeli swiftly wrote, as he regularly did in exchanges in which both correspondents referred to themselves in the third person, to report the remarkable events in the Commons to his sovereign. Victoria had been waiting to hear, and as it turned out, her sympathies, like the rest of the nation's, were with Plimsoll, whom she had invited in the past to Windsor. When Disraeli's letter reached her, she responded in her scrawly hand: 'The Queen has to thank Mr Disraeli for his last kind long letter which came just as she was going to write and ask him about the proceedings in Parliament. She much regrets the giving up for this year of the Shipping Bill and the state in which poor Mr Plimsoll seems to have been.'

A few days later, in the midst of the national outcry, Disraeli wrote again, apparently hoping for some sympathy from the Queen, who was 'devoted' to him – as he said himself. Revealing that the letter was penned at 3 a.m., after he had carried his Agricultural Bill through committee with 'immense majorities', he complained that he had 'literally not an instant of common tranquillity':

The House sat till within an hour of this – all yesterday, night and morn – and, before the House, he [Disraeli himself] was obliged to have a Cabinet. Yet with all this pressure, and the factitious and unjust agitation, he more than hopes to carry everything to a triumphant conclusion . . .

He thinks he shall be able to steer through all the difficulties of Merchant Shipping, though Sir C[harles] Adderley is a weak vessel, and Mr D. ought to have taken the subject out of his hands, but, as your Majesty once deigned to say, 'Mr D. is too good-natured' – that is to say, he cannot bear hurting anybody's feelings, which is a mistake in politics and war . . .

Disraeli's letter reveals no real sympathy for the public reaction, the 'factitious and unjust agitation'. The blame is shifted to Adderley, everybody's scapegoat.

This 'I'm too nice for my own good' approach received short shrift from Her Majesty. While she responded that she was sorry to hear 'how hard-worked and fatigued' Disraeli was, she went on merely to say: 'She trusts that all will be satisfactorily settled. There is no doubt that the state of the Merchant Shipping vessels is very disgraceful and dangerous and many lives are lost thereby.' She thought Plimsoll had a case. Before it fell at the last hurdle, the Merchant Shipping Bill was 'one in which the Queen was said to be as much interested as Mr Plimsoll himself'.

Disraeli had two confidantes, the widowed Anne, Lady Chesterfield, and her sister Selina, seventeen years younger, the married Countess of Bradford, to both of whom, after the death of his wife Mary Anne in 1873, he wrote obsessively, daily, sometimes several times a day, scribbling notes even in snatched minutes during parliamentary debates. Although he proposed marriage to Lady Chesterfield when he and she were both seventy, his romantic attachment was really to unavailable Selina, Lady Bradford: to her he wrote 1100 letters when he was in his seventies and she in her fifties. To both sisters he expressed thoughts about the Plimsoll incident that he concealed from the House and the public and only hinted at to the Queen. He felt besieged. His correspondence with Anne and Selina during this week reveals how close he thought he came to complete defeat, and possible downfall.

The reaction was so general and so vociferous that the government rushed into hasty damage limitation. By Wednesday 28 July, even before Plimsoll's face was seen again in the Commons, a stop-gap Bill had been 'hurriedly knocked up to block Plimsoll's'. Disraeli wrote to Selina about the panicky Cabinet meeting that had decided on this course of action:

A certain person, violent, treating the whole agitation with contempt – would not sacrifice our 'dignity' as a Government, which he saw would be the result [of giving in to Plimsoll's Shipping Bill]. Strange to say, he was supported by one of a totally different temperament, who had proved by inexpugnable logic on a previous occasion that the course then adopted was 'the only one,' and he stuck to it. At one moment, I thought nothing could be effected – but at last, and *with unanimity*, there was a decision.

Which two Cabinet ministers were so determined not to give ground to Plimsoll is not clear, although the second may well have been Northcote.[*] Disraeli was very anxious that these deliberations were kept secret: 'I entreat you not to breathe a word of what I have written above to any human being,' he wrote.

Adderley's stop-gap Bill headed off disaster. As Disraeli wrote: 'There was to have been a fierce attack on the Government on the order of the day, but Sir C. Adderley's announcement stopped all this, and we went quietly into Committee on the Agricultural Bill.'

In the House of Lords, where the 'Plimsoll Breeze' had also 'ruffled the waters', Lord Carlingford – formerly Chichester Fortescue – remarked that the government was about to 'do penance' for its abandonment of the Merchant Shipping Bill by being rushed into what he feared would prove 'hasty, wild and bad' legislation.

---

[*] The other members of Disraeli's Cabinet were: Lord Cairns (Lord Chancellor); the Duke of Richmond (Lord President of the Council); Lord Malmesbury (Lord Privy Seal); R. A. Cross (Home Secretary); Lord Derby (Foreign Secretary); Lord Carnarvon (Colonial Secretary); Gathorne Hardy (Secretary for War); Marquess of Salisbury (Secretary for India); George Ward Hunt (First Lord of the Admiralty); Lord John Manners (Postmaster General).

Penitent Disraeli portrayed in *Punch*, August 1875.

Punch was all along unequivocally on the side of Plimsoll (though it was harder on him in later years). It was inspired by Carlingford's remark to print a cartoon of Disraeli 'Doing Penance', holding a candle, shrouded in a sheet labelled 'Stop-Gap Merchant Shipping Bill' and standing on a barrel. Bearded sailors around his feet asked (with no attention to question marks) 'How About Deck Loads' and 'How About Grain Stowage In Bulk'.

On Wednesday 28th, after the House had spent a few hours on the troublemaking Agricultural Holdings Bill, Sir Charles Adderley, 'the Whipping-boy of the Government, for its big sin of the Session, rose', according to *Punch*, 'to take his punishment meekly after his manner'.

Punch described his announcement of the stop-gap Bill thus:

Judiciously blinking the fact that, but for the universal voice of popular indignation the Stop-Gap Bill would never have been heard of, he proceeded to describe its meagre features, – yet harsh as they are meagre. It will authorize the Board of Trade to appoint surveyors, armed with the full powers of the Board to stop ships they have reason to believe unseaworthy, whether from improper loading or otherwise, and will empower one-fourth of a crew to complain of unseaworthiness, without giving security for costs, or the preliminary desertion of any of their number. Sir Charles gave statistics strongly corroborating the worst Mr Plimsoll has charged against ship-knackers and coffin-ship-owners, and striking away all justification of the Government which abandons a measure called for by mal-practices involving such risk and sacrifice of life.

He did not state how many of the detentions of unseaworthy ships by his Board were due to Plimsoll's persistent poking up.

Punch added disingenuously, 'No man need wish to see his worst enemy in a more humiliating position than the Head of Her Majesty's Government has made for himself in this matter. *Punch* will not aggravate his penance, or embitter his humble-pie. He hates hitting a man when he is down.' Accompanying this statement was the 'Doing Penance' cartoon, a quintessence of gleeful *schadenfreude*.

It was a nervous moment for the government, rife with speculation and uncertainty. On 29 July Disraeli wrote to Selina: 'I send a rapid line after a morning of great excitement, of endless and terrific rumours of all possible events and combinations; Plimsoll tomorrow not to appear; Plimsoll tomorrow to appear and defy the House; to get into the custody of the Sergeant at Arms at all events, but to come down first with brass bands, an open carriage with four white horses and twenty thousand retainers!' He was doubtless exaggerating to entertain Selina, but behind his jest was at last an acknowledgement of the kind of support Plimsoll could muster.

There were rumours too that the government Bill would be resisted and not admitted, but it got through, and Disraeli fixed its second reading for the morning of Friday the 30th. He remained, he told Selina, 'ostensibly at least, perfectly calm amid a sea and storm of panic and confusion', his obsession with the issues of the Shipping Bill apparently creeping into his own metaphors. He was, though, afraid of defeat. 'If I were defeated in the House . . .' he said, 'in the present fever I probably should get worsted.' His only hope was the support of his friends, if they turned up. 'If they stand by me I shall overcome everything and greatly triumph; but does friendship exist in August? Does it not fly to Scotland and Norway and the Antipodes and Goodwood [racecourse]? I have seen some wonderful long faces that used to smile on me.'

Life for Disraeli became ever more fraught, as he spoke of his 'agitated fortunes' and his 'fierce life'. He was short of sleep, though not, he assured Selina, from anxiety. The drama sustained him – 'the excitement', he said, 'carries one on':

> Now I know exactly how a General must feel in a great battle – like Waterloo for example, with aides-de-camp flying up every moment with contrary news, and spies, and secret agents, and secret intelligence, and all sorts of proposals and schemes.
>
> The Plimsollites, in and out of Parliament, are at me; now cajoling, now the reign of terror. Their great object is to get Plimsoll into the custody of the Sergeant at Arms – and on my Motion.

There was a worry that if Plimsoll did not show up to the House a week after his outburst, as ordered by Disraeli, the Prime Minister would be obliged to have him taken into custody for disobedience to the commands of the House, which would only stoke his support and the opposition to the current administration. Disraeli was prepared for this eventuality. If Plimsoll did not appear, he would, he said, 'make a precedent': 'After the declaration of his authorised friend in the House that "he was off his head" &c, I shall hold him as a man not responsible for his conduct and move the adjournment of his case for a month.' But Disraeli did not expect it would come to this. 'I should not be surprised if, after all his bluster, he goes in and makes an unconditional apology.'

Some of Disraeli's contemporaries were pessimistic. The independent MP for Cockermouth, Edward Horsman, thought 'it was all over with the government'. Disraeli reported on 29 July that Horsman's advice was that 'as a last resource . . . that I should deliver a panegyric today in favour of Plimsoll and accept his Bill *pur et simple*'.

Disraeli disagreed, despite the forces massing against him: 'Every
intriguer is trying to make some fortune by the crisis. Plimsoll has a
wonderful number of enthusiastic friends very suddenly . . . My
own judgement of the House of Commons is that a considerable –
and the most reputable – section of the Opposition is against
Plimsoll; I believe, which is the truth, that his Bill would injure, not
to say destroy, our mercantile marine, and that if my friends are
firm to me, I shall entirely triumph.'

Disraeli had a strong sense, however, of the state of public feeling.
He wrote, only partly in jest: 'For aught I know, while I write . . .
the mob may be assembling which is to massacre me. I have had several letters threatening assassination. I shall take no precautions, but
walk down . . . and meet my fate whatever comes.' The Prime
Minister was not the only one who feared that anti-government
feeling might get out of control. On 29 July Disraeli wrote to Selina:
'Mr Secretary Cross [R. A. Cross, the Home Secretary], who is
naturally a brave man, got so frightened about his chief that I believe
there were 1000 constables hid in the bowers of Whitehall Gardens
and about.'

It is possible that the Home Secretary got carried away in his anxiety about security. The nearest meeting to the House of Commons,
planned for Trafalgar Square, 'to protest against a paltry landholders'
bill taking precedence over an Act on whose issue the lives of thousands depends', was aborted because of suspiciously specious official
concern for the lions at the foot of Nelson's Column. A couple of
Scotland Yard detectives paid a visit to the 'Committee of the
Plimsoll Demonstration', which met in a pub, the Barley Mow
Hotel, in Salisbury Court off Fleet Street. They were authorised by
the First Commissioner of Works and Public Buildings and, addressing those responsible for the meeting, raised an objection: 'The
lions in Trafalgar-square were being renovated. The proposed meeting would perhaps be attended with considerable damage. There was
no desire on the part of the authorities to interfere with public
meetings, but still public monuments must be protected. And the
Act relative to meetings within a mile of the Houses of Parliament
was not *de facto* obsolete.'

A hasty committee meeting was called and, proving that the

stop-gap Bill was indeed an effective way of disarming hostility, passed the following resolution: 'That in the face of the present conciliatory policy of the Government in introducing a Bill which seems practically to promise to remedy the evils complained of by Mr Plimsoll and his supporters, and in consequence of an intimation from the police authorities, the Committee unanimously agree to abandon the proposed demonstration.'

The Barley Mow is no longer a pub in Salisbury Court, but the lions, thanks surely to this pre-emptive protection, are just fine.

The events of 22 July had an impact on shipowners too. A matter of weeks before his outburst, Plimsoll had urged the Board of Trade to pursue the owners of 104 vessels that had a black line against them in an 1870 classification, indicating defects or a lack of survey. He drew particular attention to nine ships in a bad state, of which one, the *Thompson*, had already gone missing (on 29 January 1873) and another, the *Queen of the West*, continued to sail without repairs. Two days before Plimsoll's outburst the Board communicated with the owners of the doubtful 104 ships. Two had since been detained by the Board of Trade. Fourteen ships had been reclassed with Lloyd's or foreign registers. Another fifteen had been, ominously, 'sold to Foreigners'. Forty-seven had been repaired since the date of the list, or re-examined or were stated by the owners to be in good condition. Plimsoll's scene and the subsequent agitation doubtless put the fear of God into the respondents. Most of the shipowners who wrote back in the following months were cooperative, polite and respectful, even referring to Mr Plimsoll's 'kind attentions'. Henry Fernie and Sons, owners of the 'ship trussed up like a barn' criticised two years earlier by the Royal Commission, were particularly scrupulous in their documentation of the repairs to the *Lancashire Witch*. Many respondents were quick to point out how little of the value of their ships was covered by insurance.

A few were angry, among them James Robertson of Sunderland, who was 'surprised and annoyed' to be pursued and suggested that Plimsoll was 'a crazy enthusiast'; Edward Hough of North Shields, who referred to Plimsoll's 'absurdities and distortions of facts'; the firm of Thomas Turnbull and Sons of Whitby, who called Plimsoll 'a reckless and an unscrupulous visionary'; and the enraged Davidson and Charlton of Newcastle, who sent a diatribe referring to his 'late ridiculous conduct in the House of Commons' and describing Plimsoll as 'bigoted and prejudiced' and 'a raving sensationalist' acting from 'a morbid desire to get himself talked about or see his name in print, at the cost of no matter how many misstatements'. The letter did, however, include the caveat: 'We don't wish to defend every individual shipowner.' Five more shipowners omitted to respond. In all, sixteen of the unclassed ships had been lost or abandoned, principally, according to the report, through stress of weather or captain's error. Three, including the *Thompson*, were missing, 'cause unknown'.

Shipowners all over the country were feeling the impact of Plimsoll's outburst, but one in particular had been singled out for blame.

What sort of man was Edward Bates, the Conservative MP for Plymouth since 1871, who took the brunt of Plimsoll's hostility on 22 July? This comment appeared in the *New York Herald* on 8 August 1875:

> Rightly or wrongly, Mr Plimsoll regards Mr Edward Bates, the member for Plymouth, as the gentleman immediately interested in the perpetuation of these many abuses . . . Mr Bates is a conservative of the new type – a wealthy one-ideaed merchant, who feels that he has a stake in the country, and that he must protect his interests. The House of Commons is just now swamped with such as these, and Mr Plimsoll's suspicions are at least plausible. But Mr Disraeli can afford to offend Mr Plimsoll, and cannot afford to irritate the pluto-crats, shippers, merchants and others who are the backbone of the conservative party.

Bates, then fifty-nine, was very tall – about six foot four – very rich and 'stern, fierce, merciless, indomitable'. Yorkshire-born, he was a self-made man with a 'somewhat rough and truculent exterior' who had amassed a fortune by lending ships to the government during the Abyssinian Expedition of 1867–8 (a small but costly war against King Theodore of Abyssinia triggered by his taking a group of hostages, including British women and children). An East India merchant, Bates had lived several years in India and established himself in business in

Bombay. He owned the shipping company Edward Bates & Sons of Liverpool, which operated out of the Albert Dock, and he had three addresses to inspire confidence: a country estate in Hampshire, an inauthentic castle in Wales and an eighteen-bedroom town house of 'sham gothic and bogus armorials' in Liverpool, now the home of Everton Football Club. (There was also a house in Bombay that continued to belong to the family until the 1940s.) Bates was no stranger to vulgarity. One of his ships was called *The Bates Family* and had a group figurehead depicting nine of his closest relatives.

When Bates entered Parliament it was 'to the surprise of most people', according to a fellow Liverpool shipowner, William Forwood. Bates evidently enjoyed being in government. He was one of the most regular attendees in the House, passing on the day-to-day running of his Liverpool business to three of his sons: Edward Percy, Gilbert Thompson (known as Tom) and Sydney Eggers (who was less involved because he lived not in Liverpool but in London). Edward Percy and Tom were not known for caution with their ships any more than their father was. Tom as an old man wrote to his nephew: 'We always wanted power and speed . . . the old *Iran* could do her 11 [knots] in fine weather and seldom was much below 10 in the worst of weather and this in 1886 was considered by some absolute folly for a cargo boat'. Faster voyages were, like faster cab rides, more profitable; more journeys could be made in the time. The sons had inherited their father's parsimony.

In Plymouth, where Edward Sr did not live, but depended on the voters, he was known for his charitable contributions – but perhaps too well known. His giving was 'lavish rather than discreet'. He donated two bells to St Andrew's Church in Plymouth in 1874, for instance, and his conspicuous beneficence in the area prompted a sycophantic self-appointed local laureate, Hampden Wotton, to compose a poem in praise of his charitable works.[*]

---

[*] Bates sent the author a 'Handy-volume' set of Shakespeare's plays by way of thanks and earned another four pages of appreciative couplets in January 1875, which had this bathetic climax: 'Before . . . when caprice would tempt me forth to roam,/And I, compelled to leave my book at home,/Constrained, unwilling, forced at last to part,/I've shelved my favourite with a heavy heart!/But now with 'Handy-volume', come what may,/Howe'er disposed – to wander, or to stay, – / . . . No matter . . .' No doubt Bates appreciated the sentiments.

Even Bates's choice of paintings showed off his compassion: he owned *The Mission of Mercy: Florence Nightingale Receiving the Wounded at Scutari*. Bates did not, however, model his own behaviour on Florence Nightingale's. He had been an aggressive youngster, sent by his father to Calcutta at the age of sixteen to work with his elder brother, in the hope that it would make a man of him. Most of the time the brothers fought. Those who knew Edward then said he had an 'ungovernable temper' and called him 'violent, headstrong and quarrelsome', so much so that his behaviour threatened his father's business, exporting cloth and other goods to India. As a grown man, he still admitted to belligerence. He would tell an anecdote about coming across an idle ship's crew, and laying about the sailors with kicks and blows until all but one ran away. This defiant individual was a small shipwright who armed himself with an axe and threatened to use it on Bates, whereupon Bates discharged all the crew but the shipwright, saying: 'I like pluck and do not mind being faced.'

Later, in 1878, when Edward Bates and Samuel Plimsoll were both on a select committee to consider merchant shipping legislation, they voted against each other on every division of the committee but one. Both supported a clause to make sailors in possession of an unauthorised weapon punishable with a fine. If Bates's anecdote was true, it may be that, much as he claimed to admire the shipwright's pluck, he preferred not to be faced with an axe again.

But it seems likely that the tale Bates told against himself was a self-aggrandising embellishment of a somewhat different tale told about him by others. When he was in Bombay he surprised his acquaintance by dealing happily with the same Parsee shipbroker three years in succession, when his usual pattern was to fall out with the Parsees and cease to do business. The story went that eventually he did quarrel with this man, as he had with his predecessors, and threatened to break the Parsee's neck. The broker, who was as short as Bates was tall, 'snatched up a long ruler and brandishing it, cried "Come on you bully, tall as you are, you can't frighten me," which,' as the Indian raconteur told it, 'so tickled the big man that he cooled down and now he is quite fond of the little game-cock.' This story suggests that Bates made up a version in which he was faced with a weapon rather more sinister than a long ruler. He was not ashamed, though, to tell people that he kicked sailors.

In Liverpool, where there were no constituents to please, the epithet 'Bully' stuck, and Bully Bates was not popular. It was written of him: 'he was eminently successful; otherwise he has taken no part in local matters, never shown interest in a local benevolent enterprise and never attempted to become intimately known here.' This was despite owning at least one living near Bellefield, at Knotty Ash Church, which contains a memorial to his youngest son, who died of fever. His own memorial – the act for which he was principally remembered in the vicinity – was an act of meanness. He built a tree-lined carriageway, with wrought-iron gates at the end, from Bellefield to Sandfield Park and asked permission to use the park as an entrance. When he was told he could do so if he paid £200 park dues, he refused and kept his new gates permanently padlocked; they stayed that way for fifty years, even after Bates's death.

This was not the only manifestation of Bates's mean streak. His thrift was held to be the secret of his wealth. He 'introduced hitherto unheard-of devices to keep down expenses on board and ashore'. Consequently he was not best known for his care of the crews of his ships. He had a reputation as a 'starver of men' and this doubtless made Plimsoll reckless with his accusations.

There was another unsavoury part of Bates's history which may have affected the events that followed Plimsoll's outburst. In June 1874 a collier owned by Bates, the *Euxine*, left South Shields bound for Aden the long way round, via the Cape of Good Hope. She was an elderly ship, built in 1847 at Greenock as a paddle steamer, but bought by Bates in 1868 and rebuilt as a sailing ship, with her engines removed. She was 'perfectly seaworthy', though no longer classified A1 by Lloyd's. On 1 August, in heavy seas, the cargo of coal, loaded loose, shifted, and three days of struggle followed in which the crew tried to level it out. On 5 August it 'spontaneously ignited', a known hazard for such cargo (caused by oxidation of the iron pyrites in coal in unventilated spaces). By 9 August the ship had had to be abandoned in flames. The crew left in three boats, aiming for the island of St Helena, 850 miles away. Two boats, with the master and twenty-two men, arrived at the island, having suffered much during two weeks in open boats. It is the terrible fate of the seven sailors in the third boat that has a bearing on Plimsoll's story.

These sailors, who lacked the skills to measure longitude and could not find St Helena, headed desperately for Brazil, which they could not miss but which was two thousand miles away. Their rations were half a biscuit and a glass of water per person per day. The boat capsized twice, drowning two of their number. The second time the five survivors spent a night clinging to the boat before they could right it. When they did, they had lost all supplies, their makeshift sail and all navigating equipment. By Sunday 30 August one crewman was mad from drinking seawater, and, according to the reports of his fellows, suggested that they kill him and eat him. This, they said later, gave rise to the idea of a lottery to choose one man to be sacrificed for the sake of the others. Best of three selections of short sticks, they claimed, condemned the least popular survivor: an Italian of twenty who could say no more in English than 'yes' and 'no', whose first name was understood to be Francis

'The custom of the sea': an episode of cannibalism similar to the
horrors that followed the loss of Bates's ship the *Euxine*.
(*From Hanson*, The Custom of the Sea)

or Franco and whose surname no one could spell – it was probably
Zuffo or Ciuffu, but versions of it in the records included Gioffey,
Gioffous and Shufus. Accounts of what happened after lots were
drawn varied: one suggested that Franco was resigned and acquies-
cent and lay down quietly in the boat to die; another that he tried
to jump overboard and was dragged back. Either way, his throat
was cut, his head severed and thrown overboard, his blood caught in
a bowl and drunk, and his heart and liver consumed – a few hours
before a passing ship, the *Java Packet*, rescued the last four men.

Although the survivors spoke openly to their rescuers about what
had happened, there was much diplomatic toing and froing between
the Colonial Office and the Home Office about whether there
should be a prosecution for murder. The Attorney General in
Singapore saw depositions from the men and decided there was no
need for a judicial inquiry, but the Colonial Office disagreed and
a trial opened in Singapore. Problems with the validity of the evidence caused the prosecution case to collapse. Amid confusion and
difference of opinion about both the legal and moral issues, and with
the various witnesses (from the *Java Packet*, for instance) scattering
with their ships to other parts of the globe, the four surviving crew
members left Singapore in May to be tried in England, although
only one of them, the second mate, James Archer, was English.
Their continued detention was arguably illegal and their arrival on
9 July was an embarrassment to the Home Office, which had tried
too late to stop them being sent.

On 13 July the Home Secretary, R. A. Cross, made a decision
which was communicated thus to the Board of Trade: 'after careful
consideration of all the circumstances the Secretary of State does not
consider that this is a case in which it would be advisable to institute
proceedings against these men'. They were quietly set free, on the
very day that Plimsoll lost his temper, their release attended with some
anxiety that they might sue for false imprisonment. 'Apparently they
never did,' says one authority, the legal historian A. W. B. Simpson, 'and
the press failed to pick up the story. But before they disappeared,
three of the foreign sailors were persuaded to sign an official form
discharging Edward Bates and the ship's officers of any further
legal liability.' Bates's back was covered.

Implicated in the decision to leave the case alone were members of the Marine Department of the Board of Trade: Thomas Gray, then Assistant Secretary, Sir Thomas H. Farrer, Permanent Under-secretary and President Sir Charles Adderley. Gray's opinion was that 'the details are too disgusting to take to court'. Farrer too thought it would only harrow the feelings of the public and that punishment would have no effect on future cases, since only exceptional necessity would prompt such action. Adderley agreed.

The main argument for taking the case to court was to establish once and for all whether eating another human being in order to save your own life was legally acceptable. This was not the first recorded case of its kind and there was a belief among sailors that cannibalism in such circumstances was an unexceptionable 'custom of the sea'. The *Euxine*, as it turned out, was not to be the test case.

Plimsoll had been wrong to claim on 22 July that Bates had lost five ships in the year. He had lost six and the *Euxine* was the one he failed to mention. It is hard to believe that Plimsoll would have kept quiet if he knew about this episode. But there had been accounts in the newspapers as early as the previous November and December. The Prime Minister was certainly in the picture: on 22 July Disraeli would have known of the Home Secretary's decision nine days earlier and of the fact of the sailors' release that same day. And if Plimsoll had not heard the story in July, he did know of it by the following spring. He wrote a preface to a novel about coffin-ships, *The Wreck of the Eglantine (or A Voice from the Sea)*, dated 10 February 1876, which is a veiled attack on Bates:

I have [found] ships sold for less than a ninth part of the sum they originally cost, and having been converted into sailing vessels (which ought never to be done in the case of steamers, because of their extreme length in proportion to breadth of beam), have subsequently foundered, drowning the whole of their crews. In one case a portion of the crew survived, after being in an open boat three weeks; they made land at length, nearly dead, with part of the body of one of their shipmates, whose life had been sacrificed by lot. This is within a recent period.

It was Bates's habit to buy steamers, have the engines removed and convert them to sailing ships. Although this is not an entirely accurate account of the *Euxine*, it is certainly a reference to what happened after the ship went down. Was Plimsoll told the story after 22 July, or was his anger at Bates partly stoked by his repugnance at it?

Bates defended himself to the House later on the evening of Plimsoll's outburst. 'As to the statement made and epithets used by the junior member for Derby – I forgive him,' said Bates, condescendingly, adding that 'he [Plimsoll] was not responsible for his actions or sayings'. He confessed the unfortunate loss between 1873 and 1875 of five ships, four of them coal-laden and one homeward bound from Calcutta. 'All of them were iron ships, and all class A1.' The ship that was not counted, the *Euxine*, was not A1, although Bates later claimed it was. 'I think I can say that as iron ships they were as well found as any that ever went to sea.' Bates pointed out that his own pecuniary loss was 'very severe, as . . . I never insure my ships for more than half or two-thirds of their market value'. (The two upper limits here undermine the argument somewhat.) But the financial loss was not, he argued, what bothered him. 'I did and do deplore the loss of my men ['Hear, hear,' exclaimed the House], and my only consolation is knowing that as far as human foresight could go the ships were as good and safe as man could make them.'

On 29 July Bates asked for a select committee to look into Plimsoll's charges against him. Disraeli did not take this up, and Bates let the matter go. If an inquiry had been instituted, the full story of the *Euxine* would have come out, and embarrassed both Bates and the government. Disraeli would have had to face the full force of public opinion about whether the case should have been dropped. As A. W. B. Simpson speculates, Bates's call for an inquiry 'may have been contrived'; perhaps Bates counted on Disraeli not seeing it through. Simpson adds, 'We can only wonder whether the terrible story of the Italian boy Shufus played some part behind the scenes in Disraeli's desire to appease Plimsoll.' Was Disraeli all too aware of the four tainted men who had only just walked free? Did the government partly make concessions to Plimsoll because it had something to hide?

Speaking again on 30 July, Bates did name the *Euxine*, which had gone unmentioned the week before, and admitted to its loss, but said nothing of the awful consequences. He did say: 'My maxim through life has been, when I found, either from intemperance of language or ignorance, I had done another wrong, to take the earliest opportunity of acknowledging my error and asking for forgiveness,' therefore claiming the moral high ground over Plimsoll, who did not do so. He named the six vessels he had lost that year, claimed (dishonestly or unwittingly) they were all at least A1 at Lloyd's, and produced an affidavit, sworn by Admiralty brokers in 1874 to say that they were worth £105,235 on the market. They had been insured for £64,000. The losses that year were Bates's worst. Over forty-three years, out of one hundred and twenty-nine ships, Bates had lost thirty-one, fourteen of them new built and only three more than twenty years old.

Sometimes Bates took cheese-paring risks: he bought his first ship, the *Cora*, after it had been wrecked and condemned, and then repaired it; he made another, the *Foundling*, out of 'material lying around in the yard'; he owned a paddle steamer, the *Prince of Wales*, that took passengers from London to North Wales, and 'used to sit on the safety valve rather than be beaten by the train.' Bates did seem to pay more attention to economics than to welfare, so that even if in the particulars of certain accusations Plimsoll was unfair, he was accurate about the spirit of a man who made every possible saving and whose philanthropy looked suspiciously like self-interest. We have no proof that Bates ever knowingly sent sailors to sea in an unsafe ship in the hope of profiting from it, but we can infer that he concentrated harder on how to make a journey cheap than on how to make it safe.

Bates was not the only MP who took personal offence at Plimsoll on 22 July. There was another who was moved to retaliate. Charles Morgan Norwood, the shipowning Liberal MP for Hull who had taken Plimsoll to court in 1873 and lost, believed himself to be the target of Plimsoll's shaken fist. This gesture, along with the threat to ask 'questions about Members on this side of the House also' and 'to unmask the villains who send these sailors to death and destruction', seemed to 'make accusations with sufficient directness to render

[Plimsoll] liable to prosecution for criminal libel'. Norwood, defeated over the *Livonia*, was determined this time to get the better of his old adversary. He was not a man to give up easily. So in 1875 he again instituted proceedings against Plimsoll, who was only spared another courtroom ordeal by an encounter in a hotel room in Hull that came close to blackmail.

Norwood subpoenaed the MP Anthony Mundella to give evidence against Plimsoll. Mundella, who had been a hosier in Nottingham, and the town's former Sheriff, entered Parliament with Plimsoll in 1868 as Liberal MP for Sheffield. Plimsoll had been instrumental in helping him win his seat. In August 1868, when fires in nearby moorland had put paid to the miners' day out, Plimsoll hosted a miners' gala in the grounds of Whiteley Wood Hall, his sixteenth-century country seat near Sheffield.* Mundella had been one of the principal speakers.

Mundella and Plimsoll shared a concern for working people. The former was instrumental in the Factory Act of 1875 which limited the working day for women and children in textile factories to ten hours. Publicly, Mundella spoke for Plimsoll's cause, particularly once he had become the nation's darling. Plimsoll counted on Mundella as an ally, so much so that he wrote to his fellow MP asking him to support his own Bill over the government's, with this undated note:

> *Govt. Bill with my amendments written on the text (and interleaved).*
> *This will show you readily what they are.*
> *Even if I am able to attend next week I entreat you to speak on all of them*
> *for there will be so many eager advocates for the Govt. Bill amongst*
> *shipowners because it does nothing but only seems.*
> *I am, Dear Sir*
> *Yours very truly*
> *Samuel Plimsoll*

---

* This meeting was so popular that, ironically given the driving issue of the host's later life, the buses that carried the miners to the Hall were overloaded. One with the capacity for thirty people carried seventy. The wheels collapsed and seven people were injured.

Privately, though, Mundella had been cross with Plimsoll ever since they both entered Parliament. His behind-the-back descriptions of his fellow debutant were spiteful. Of Plimsoll's maiden speech in which he seconded Mundella's case for the legalisation of trade unions, Mundella said: 'Plimsoll disgusted the House, our Liberal friends abuse him roundly for his impudence and *rot*.' And a few days later, when he decided that his own contribution was better than the newspaper reports gave him credit for, he added pettishly: 'Plimsoll was absurd and spoilt the whole thing.' He was piqued when the Leeds Trades Union Congress of 1873, which he could not attend because of illness, wholeheartedly endorsed Plimsoll's agitation, and when his associate George Howell became secretary of the Plimsoll Committee. 'I sympathise with the cause, but not the man,' wrote Mundella, '– and I don't like being on the same platform with him. His wretched vanity and reckless talk make it painful and undesirable to be associated with him.' He wrote of him as a 'poor creature cracked with vanity whose character is tainted with bankruptcy and meanness'.

At the time, Mundella's antipathy came partly from the fact that, with Gladstone in power, Plimsoll's campaign gave ammunition to the Opposition. He thought Gladstone would think so too, and tried to shop Plimsoll by sending a copy of his speeches to Gladstone: 'Our friend Plimsoll will catch it in a day or two,' he wrote. On the contrary, Gladstone rushed through a temporary Bill in sympathy with 'Our Seamen' to ensure that ships were registered before leaving port.

Fortunately, Mundella's impulse to tell tales on Plimsoll did not last. It was his commitment to the unity of the Liberals, and his sympathy for the sailors, that prevented him from being the Judas among Plimsoll's followers. He could have been Plimsoll's downfall. When Norwood subpoenaed him, Mundella fretted that what he would truthfully have to say would impugn Plimsoll and damage not only the man but also the cause and the party. In desperation, he enlisted the help of the trade unionist Robert Applegarth, who had contributed to Norwood's electoral campaign and was known for his diplomacy.

Applegarth took a train to Hull and met Norwood in his room at the Cross Keys Hotel. He came straight to the point and asked Norwood to stop the proceedings against Plimsoll. The reaction was unpromising. 'Never before had I known what it was to meet a really angry man,' said Applegarth. 'He was furious! He almost snapped me up at every word I spoke; but I bided my time.' Applegarth, arguing like Portia, gave Norwood every chance to drop the case for altruistic reasons. He pointed out that imprisoning Plimsoll would be damaging to the Liberal Party. He urged that the cause was greater than the individual offence. 'You will be attacked,' urged Applegarth, 'on platforms all over the country, for the man has simply fought against a glaring evil. Set down his accusations to the bigness of his heart.' But Norwood was not swayed; he wanted his revenge.

So Applegarth introduced a threat. 'The trial of Plimsoll would bring out facts which would lower you in the estimation of your countrymen,' he told the startled Norwood. He then related a story he had been told after one of Plimsoll's meetings by men from a shipbuilding yard about a ship owned by Norwood that had been lengthened by some eighty feet. (Lengthening ships was one of the dangerous practices that Plimsoll had drawn attention to.) The ship in question was old and its plates had to be scraped. These men were the scrapers and one plate had been scraped right through. When they pointed out the hole to the foreman he told them just to paint over it, saying: 'Plate the damn thing with a tarbrush.' They did. It sailed and sank with the loss of all the crew. 'I know that you personally were not responsible,' said Applegarth, 'but such things should be made impossible. If you proceed against Plimsoll I shall have to give evidence for him and those facts will come out.' Suddenly Applegarth, known and admired for his decency, reasonableness and gentleness, was the thug, the bailiff, the Mafioso. Norwood had no choice. He wrote a note to his solicitors to halt the proceedings. Applegarth took it and left the room. He went straight to show it to the lawyers, but refused to leave it behind so that he could use it to prove to Mundella, and then to Gladstone, the success of his encounter.

Mundella went on to address a pro-Plimsoll meeting at Sheffield on 28 August 1875, suggesting that he approved of Plimsoll's outburst, although he did describe the episode as an 'ugly night'. He referred to the fact that on 7 August the wool-clipper named after Samuel Plimsoll had collided with an Italian barque at Falmouth. The pilot of the clipper and two of the Italian crew were drowned. (There was much comment on the irony, just as the MP was trying to save lives. *Punch* called it 'an instance of bad luck going with a good name'.) Mundella was reported as saying: 'With reference to a joke that had been going on in a Tory circle about a ship named Samuel Plimsoll running down another he (Mr Mundella) would only remind them that the Samuel Plimsoll had also come into collision with the Government ship, and had seriously damaged it – (great laughter) – and he might go a little further and say that another such an ugly night would sink that Ministerial barque (renewed laughter).'

To Robert Leader, sly Mundella had written three months earlier: 'Plimsoll is, well – not a gentleman. He has a good cause but manages it very badly. The fact is that the cause sustains him, rather than he it, and when the question is partially settled and the interest subsides, he will be the least influential member of the House.'

Nevertheless, Mundella had saved Plimsoll from a real danger. As George Howell reported it:

> Cases of criminal libel might have involved imprisonment if the allegations could not be legally substantiated. Civil actions for damages might have crippled his resources, if not caused actual financial disaster . . . earnest efforts were made in Parliament by mutual friends and outside of it by the Committee and others to avert trial in the courts. By means of these friendly interventions none of the actions were fought out in the courts of law, nor was Mr Plimsoll called upon to pay any of the costs on the other side.

Meanwhile Norwood was not the only shipowner anxious about a tarbrush. Plimsoll's power and popularity were such that to oppose him was to be tarred with the same brush as villains. Resistance was more damning than resignation, and innocent shipowners suffered to end the suffering of innocent sailors.

★

Disraeli's anxious meetings, Bates's justifications and Applegarth's intervention had all taken place by the time Samuel Plimsoll re-appeared in the House on Thursday 29 July. On 23 July, as the House was still reeling, Plimsoll had received a letter containing sound advice from his wise friend and patron, Lord Shaftesbury.

> *My dear Mr Plimsoll, As chairman of your committee from the commencement, I may express my deep and heartfelt sympathy with you. I can enter into all your indignation and all your fears. Language would fail me to describe the wickedness and folly of giving preference to the Agricultural Holdings Bill over yours — for yours it is — that affects the lives of so many men and the happiness of so many families. But, as you have often listened to me before, pray listen to me now. I earnestly counsel you to appear in the presence of the House and maintain your statements to the full; but express regret that, under the great excitement into which you fell, you offended against the rules and orders laid down for the government of debate. Such a course will prove a real benefit to yourself and to the cause you have in hand. You know how truly I share all your hopes and fears in this matter and how earnestly I pray God to bless and sustain one who has urged it with so much nobleness and sincerity. — Yours truly, Shaftesbury.*

The letter was, unlike Northcote's letter to Disraeli, for public consumption. It was printed in *The Times* on 27 July, so there was a general expectation that Plimsoll would act on it.

Plimsoll followed Shaftesbury's advice scrupulously. He did not, as he had threatened, 'unmask the villains' and put questions to the President of the Board of Trade about ships owned by members on both sides of the House. Yet again his generalisations were not tested.

When Plimsoll entered the House on 29 July, shortly after four o'clock and so exactly a week after his banishment, only his friends on the cross benches greeted him warmly. He sat quietly through notices of motion from five MPs* about the Merchant Shipping Bill, and through the presentation of a report from the Select

---

* Norwood, E. J. Reed, MacIver, Monk and Eustace Smith.

Committee on Foreign Loans. When he rose, only a few Opposition MPs cheered. But when he said what Shaftesbury had advised him to say, apologising for his 'transgression of Parliamentary usages', the applause was general. There was even greater enthusiasm when he said he 'apologised in no grudging or reluctant spirit, but frankly and sincerely'. Again following Shaftesbury's counsel, he said he 'did not withdraw any statement of fact'.

Disraeli, earning his own cheers, moved to withdraw his reprimand. Everyone was in a forgiving mood. Everyone, that is, except Bates's supporters. But when aristocratic George Bentinck pointed out that a member had been personally insulted and Plimsoll should retract his allegations and apologise, his intervention was greeted with silence. Bentinck was a Cavendish, from the family of the Dukes of Portland, and he had recently acquired his own island, Brownsea in Poole harbour, where he was filling the castle with art treasures and antiquaries. But his wealth and status gave him scant authority now. He was known as 'Little Ben' because he was short, and because his late father, 'Big Ben', former Foreign Secretary George Bentinck, who had in 1873 been a member of the Plimsoll and Seamen's Defence Fund Committee, was a force to be reckoned with in the House. One other MP, the Warwickshire colliery owner C. N. Newdegate, known for his gloomy taciturnity as the 'Mute of the House', spoke up for once and seconded Little Ben, but nobody took either of them up on their contribution. Bates's friends were both simply ignored. Disraeli's motion was put again, and the House accepted it unanimously with loud cheering. (Bentinck was sufficiently frustrated to publish in the *Nautical Magazine* later that year his anti-Plimsoll speeches about merchant shipping legislation; they were subsequently reprinted in a pamphlet entitled 'Fact Against Sensation'.)

Apart from this gesture, Bates did not inspire the strength of feeling for much indignation on his behalf. Samuel Plimsoll may have been careless in his claims, but he was not alone in his hostility. According to B. G. Orchard, in *Liverpool's Legion of Honour* (1893): 'during thirty years sailors had not loved [Bates's] ships and their dislike to his management had been shared by others; and so when it transpired that he had "caught it hot" ... everyone smiled, but none appeared sorry'.

Plimsoll had demonstrated that he commanded quite a different degree of allegiance. Disraeli now knew he had made a mistake by seeming to censure a man of such popularity inside and outside the House. He backtracked: 'had he been aware of the circumstances . . . he should not have moved the resolution now before them . . . He should have looked upon Plimsoll's conduct as the result of a condition of mind overstrained by his devotion to a cause of the greatest importance.' He called Plimsoll's 'a complete and satisfactory apology'. A week ago Disraeli had been anxious not to offend shipowners; Plimsoll and his lobby were now the people to please. But for all the lip-service he was obliged to pay to Plimsoll in the House, Disraeli felt no real warmth for him. Privately he described Plimsoll to Selina as 'a Moody and Sankey* in politics, half rogue and half enthusiast . . . one of those characters who live by pandering to passion and fall into an enthusiastic love of themselves'.

Afterwards Disraeli was smug about the events of 29 July: he said they had gone off 'triumphantly'. He believed that Charles Bradlaugh and his rabble-rousers had orchestrated the meetings in the provinces by 'telegraphic orders from the Reform Club', but could not, despite their best efforts, stir up enough opposition to do for Disraeli: 'the people said they would not go against me who had passed the Labour Laws for them'. He congratulated himself that the legislative reforms he had passed in June to the benefit of the working man had earned him a popularity that had saved him. The announcement of the government's Shipping Bill had also, as intended, taken the wind out of the sails of the agitators. Disraeli even persuaded himself that Plimsoll did not like to be allied with the government's opponents: 'Plimsoll got restive,' Disraeli asserted to Selina, 'and did not like the brass bands and flags &c., and said he would not be made a party tool and that he had received more support from the Tories than the Whigs; the consequence of all this was much fiasco.' Somehow in Disraeli's mind the whole episode became a confirmation of the support his party could command.

Disraeli was, incidentally, claiming more credit for his social

---

* A reference to the American revivalist preacher Dwight Moody and his hymn-singing accompanist Ira Sankey, whose evangelism had swept Britain since 1873.

legislation than was probably due. There was never any real
Conservative social programme, just a collection of haphazard laws
described by one Conservative MP as 'suet pudding legislation . . .
flat, insipid, dull, but very wise and very wholesome'. Reflecting
Disraeli's philosophy of a *laissez-faire* government, they were passed
more as recommendations than as regulations, leaving such measures
as the Artisans' Dwellings Act, the Sale of Food and Drugs Act and
the Public Health Act to be implemented only partially and desul-
torily. These laws were inadequate just as previous shipping
legislation had been. Even where there were provisions to protect
sailors in existing Merchant Shipping Acts, there was a tendency for
the authorities not to fret about whether they were enforced.

Meanwhile, as Disraeli patted himself on the back, Lord
Shaftesbury was anxious, recognising that although Plimsoll's apology had been accepted without reservation, he and his cause were
still in peril. Plimsoll had shown a weakness that played into the
hands of his opponents. There were those who thought that if they
needled him they might yet push Plimsoll to do something from
which his campaign could not recover. It was Shaftesbury who saw
the wisdom of keeping Plimsoll away from the third reading of the
government's stop-gap Bill days after his apology. Many of Plimsoll's
followers believed it was now safest for someone else to take charge
of the amendment he sought. Shaftesbury took it upon himself to
talk Plimsoll into this. 'Good deal of negotiation with Plimsoll –',
wrote Shaftesbury in his diary on 30 July, 'I find him reasonable,
honest and self-denying – but I dread his impetuosity; and the efforts
of men in the House who are evidently seeking to goad him into
another excitement.' Plimsoll agreed to stay away from the House
and to entrust his amendment to E. J. Reed. Shaftesbury wrote that
Plimsoll was 'modest, judicious, acceptable yesterday evening in his
apology', but fretted, 'Will he continue so? God give him counsel'.

Disraeli was worried too. His measure was still not safe. Monday 2
August would be the date of 'The battle of Armageddon', as he
described it, 'when in Committee they will try to substitute
Plimsolliana for our proposals. I am sending all over the world for
votes.' During the weekend before the vote he was panicky. He wrote
on Sunday to Selina: 'I am not an alarmist, but affairs are rather

critical here. Pray do all you can to send fellows up for tomorrow. I have my doubts about Randolph Churchill . . .' The letter asking for reinforcements did not arrive in time. (There was such anxiety on his behalf that on Tuesday at 3 a.m. Disraeli wrote a telegram to Lady Chesterfield to reassure her – and left it on his dressing table.)

So it was that Reed proposed the measures Plimsoll wanted: a load line on all ships, the regulation of grain cargoes and deckloading and a compulsory survey of all ships by the Board of Trade. What came out of the meeting was – thanks to a proposal by C. M. Norwood – the completely counter-productive concept of the 'owner's load line', which Plimsoll described as like letting 'a draper fix the number of inches he allowed in a yard'. A load line was, for the first time, compulsory by law, but not only could owners put the line where they chose, there was also no system in place for making them stick to it. However, loading of grain in bulk exceeding a third of a ship's cargo was prohibited. Officers were to be appointed who could detain unseaworthy ships. It became a misdemeanour for any owner or master to send or attempt to send a ship to sea in an unseaworthy condition, to the danger of life. Shipowners were made liable to the crew for keeping and maintaining a ship in a seaworthy condition. And a quarter of a ship's crew could insist that a ship be stopped and surveyed.

The outcome for Disraeli of the debate, as he conceded to Anne, was '"all right" but it was not glorious'. He admitted that he came close to mortification, and that Plimsoll might have secured all the measures he sought. Not all the supporters Disraeli hoped for came to back him up:

and those who came were still Plimsollised *too* much. If the Opposition had been led by a great general they might have inflicted on me much humiliation. Their main attack, which was what I feared, failed, but from their own panic. If they had known the state of our camp, which they ought to have known, they could have run me very hard and might have substituted their own policy for mine. Instead of that, they let me get into Committee where defeats are on matters of detail. Adderley made a terrific blunder; but on the whole I may be content, and carried the bill through without ignominy.

The stop-gap Bill, which might have included Plimsoll's load line and deckloading clause, instead included Norwood's 'owner's load line'. The Opposition was led not by a great general, but by Lord Hartington, on whose reputation the episode also had an impact, but here views were divided. Hartington's friends called him quiet, manly and modest. His detractors thought him dull, ill-mannered and feeble. Both groups admitted he gave long and boring speeches. 'Whenever he rises members are apt to leave, or if they remain it is to talk. He has been repeatedly compelled to end a speech abruptly by the cries of his own party for division,' reported Moncure D. Conway. Even the reporter Henry Lucy, who was a supporter of Hartington, conceded that he would benefit as a speaker from getting 'a firmer grasp on the great truth that it is not necessary to make a long speech in order to express the views which an intelligent commonsense man holds on a given question'. On one occasion Hartington himself acknowledged how boring he was. He was observed yawning in the middle of one of his own speeches. When a friend commented on this, he replied, 'Well, but it was damned dull, wasn't it?'

But Lucy was quite sure that Hartington's conduct during the Plimsoll episode had proved his mettle.

Hartington . . . stands much higher in public opinion than he did when the barren honour of leadership was thrust upon him . . . It should not be forgotten that it was he who, by his presence of mind and ready resource, saved the House of Commons from a hopeless predicament into which no less a person than Disraeli was leading it on the memorable occasion of Plimsoll's dance of defiance. When the member for Derby had been safely piloted over the bar, and out into the cooler air of the lobby, Disraeli, utterly distraught by the excitement of the scene, hurriedly proposed that he should be brought back and reprimanded by the Speaker. The House, not knowing what to do, silently acquiesced, and in a few minutes Plimsoll would have been once more standing on one leg on the floor of the House, and, so ungovernable was his passion at that moment, might even have done something desperate with the Mace – perhaps made a clean sweep of the Treasury bench with it.

Hartington, interposing, suggested that it might be better to adjourn the debate for a week, by which time Plimsoll would have had an opportunity of cooling down, a shrewd and discreet evasion of the difficulty which Disraeli promptly adopted . . .

Lucy gave Hartington credit for seeing 'further and clearer than some of his contemporaries'. 'The incident', remarked another commentator, 'revealed in Lord Hartington a capacity for cool and adroit leadership, the existence of which had hitherto been unsuspected.' Moncure D. Conway couldn't have disagreed more:

> There is another man [apart from Disraeli] who has suffered by the Plimsoll episode; that is the Liberal leader. If there were any force or 'go' in the Marquess of Hartington, the opportunity for showing it was supplied on Thursday . . . All that he said during the Plimsoll excitement was that, while he was prepared to support Disraeli's motion for reprimand, if necessary, he thought Plimsoll ought to be allowed to cool and see the impropriety of his conduct. Liberal leadership by a man who could omit such an occasion to scathe the Tory leader when he richly deserved it is a farce.

The public had scathed the Tory leader in Hartington's stead. The events of the week shook Disraeli's hold on the nation. Even with the action Disraeli took to limit the damage, by the end of the week his government had been nudged a little further along a road that would lead to its ousting from power in the 1880 election.

At a civic dinner at the Mansion House on 4 August, Disraeli recast the threat to his administration as a victory, in which the government had acted not under the pressure of public opinion but with the aid of public opinion, which enabled it to pass a measure it had been eager to carry but which was at the beginning doubtful of success. 'When it was launched it did not glide into the current of the waters with that grace and facility which is a good omen. Sometimes it was crank, sometimes I almost felt it was waterlogged.' The Cabinet, he insisted, had been about to consider how a Bill with 178 amendments, 140 of them proposed by the Opposition, might be properly dealt with. The *vox populi*, he claimed, 'assisted and aided us'. 'We were enabled to do that in ten or twelve hours which otherwise we would not have done in ten or twelve days.'

The Times saw things differently. Calling Plimsoll an 'inspired idiot' who told Disraeli what he thought he knew but didn't – the will of the people – the paper commented: 'Mr Plimsoll has been King during the past fortnight and Mr Disraeli has been the humble henchman. The Prime Minister knew the power of sections of the House of Commons. He knew nothing of the strength of popular impulse.' The Mansion House audience, thought *The Times*, was 'amused but not convinced'.

Henry Lucy reported: 'the incident has been a severe blow to Disraeli. It has called public attention to his remarkable administrative incapacity . . . From all parts of England the shout is coming back on Disraeli, "It's all your fault!"'

Fun magazine portrayed the Prime Minister brought to his knees. It showed Disraeli kneeling to the winged figure of Popular Opinion, the Union Jack on her shield, like Britannia's, and her sword marked 'Retribution'. Captioned 'An All Powerful Supporter', it had Popular Opinion say: 'Ah Mr Ben, you're ready enough to make "concessions" now that I've made you feel my power. Mind I don't have to give you another lesson, or you may not get off so easily.' Plimsoll, apparently rolling up his sleeves for the fight, looks on over his shoulder from the background as Public Opinion brandishes aloft Plimsoll's Shipping Bill.

On 7 August 1875 the *Spectator* quoted a Conservative member saying: 'There is not much left of Dizzy except his cheek.' And as far afield as New York the power of British public opinion to undermine the British government was making headlines. Plimsoll's outburst was front-page news in the *New York Times* and the *New York Tribune* for days. The *New York Herald* of 8 August saw Plimsoll's sincerity as part of a reaction to what it called 'a despotism tempered by jokes'. Disraeli, it scolded, 'chooses to convert what should be merely a season of politic inaction into a period of bland badinage'. The Prime Minister, it went on, 'has already begun to go too far. His fooling is certainly exquisite, but it is excessive, and the British Senate is beginning to rebel against it.' Even in America there was a feeling that Disraeli had better start to sound serious if he were to save his skin.

The front cover of *Harper's Weekly* of Saturday 14 August 1875 was filled with a drawing (by Thomas Nast) of a huge roaring lion louring over Disraeli, front paws in the prime ministerial lap and fangs inches from his forehead. The lion is labelled 'PUBLIC INDIG-NATION AT THE GOVERNMENT'S WITHDRAWAL OF THE SHIPPING BILL. THE PEOPLE AND THE PRESS IN FAVOUR OF THE BILL'. At Disraeli's feet lies Plimsoll's Shipping Bill, and his top hat, beside him on a parliamentary bench, contains a paper that reads '"I move that Mr Plimsoll be removed from the House" – Disraeli.' The Prime Minister, unintimidated by the presence of the lion, seems to have trouble seeing it; he examines its open mouth calmly through his monocle. In the background a whiskered figure drawn from the back – perhaps Plimsoll himself – holds the ceremonial mace with a sailor's hat hanging from it. The caption reads: 'THE BRITISH LION LOOSE IN THE HOUSE OF COMMONS "Now put your Head in, if you dare."'

That the Prime Minister came badly out of this episode seems to have been the opinion of just about everyone except Disraeli him-self, and, for all his braggadocio, there is a hint that he feared that even his closest friends might think less of him. On 10 August he wrote to Selina, '*The Times* may scold, it may rave and rant; but it will not daunt me. I know it greatly influences you, and it rules Anne, and that the confidence of you both in me is greatly shaken; but you will see that I am right – and very soon see it – and that public opinion will decide in my favour.' But public opinion never looked quite so favourably on Dizzy again.

A later biographer, looking back on Plimsoll's career with the hindsight of a few years, summed up the relationship between Plimsoll and Parliament and public pressure thus:

A man has in most cases . . . to make himself a kind of political Ishmael to get any work of this sort accomplished. He must con-centrate himself on the one point, and so much does the House of Commons . . . delight in little 'squabbles' and 'scenes' and that sort of thing, in bits of schoolboy fun and chaff and heavy joking, that a man with a *purpose* of this kind is very apt to be reckoned the worst sort of *bore* in it. Were it not that the healthy instinct of the people comes into play, and shows itself very decidedly in such cases in the long-run, a man like Mr Plimsoll would often fare but badly.

This suggests that Parliament has not changed so much since the 1870s. But there were also long-term consequences of Plimsoll's outburst and its aftermath which affected the way that parliamentary business was conducted from that day to this. The historian R. C. K. Ensor believed that '[Plimsoll's] outburst could be justified by its motive, and in part by its result . . . But the example of success through disorder did immediate injury to parliament, and has ever since furnished the favourite precedent for those desirous of injuring it further.' Charles Stewart Parnell, for instance, who used obstructionism after 1877 in the cause of Irish Home Rule, 'witnessed and pondered the disorderly success of Plimsoll'.

As Ensor says: 'Such performances have since become commonplaces of parliamentarism . . . but then they were almost unheard of and the sensation was immense.' The obstructionist tactics of the Home Rulers 'partly explain why the Disraelian government, after its fruitful start, became so barren of legislation during its later years.'

In 1879, when Turkish atrocities were committed against Christians in Bulgaria, public protest against Disraeli's foreign policy was also inspired by Plimsoll's model and his success. Plimsoll's concentration on the one point had wide reverberations.

8

VICTORY FOR THE PEOPLE

Samuel Plimsoll earned many accolades by losing his temper in the House of Commons. A tribute was published in the *Graphic* in August 1875. The *Illustrated London News* paid homage to him in a special supplement with a full-page engraved portrait. A Plimsoll Memorial Fund was opened, inviting contributions from 'working men connected with shipping and shipbuilding', with the intention of commissioning a sculpture to be raised in London's docklands.* A laudatory medal commemorating the date and place of Plimsoll's outburst was forged in silver by a French artist, Auguste Chevalier, and copied in brass for wider distribution to the public in two sizes, the size of a crown and the size of a halfpenny. It had Plimsoll's profile on the face, like a monarch on a crown, and on the obverse a sinking coffin-ship with a skull and crossbones on its sail and it was surely the only medal ever struck to commemorate an explosion of anger. Civic authorities met in the docklands on 8 October 1875 and decided to rename Manor Street in Poplar, east London: it became Plimsoll Street in his honour.

Plimsoll himself was not in the country to enjoy the nation's compliments. The stop-gap Merchant Shipping Act became law on 10

* See the Postscript, p. 299, for the fate of this statue.

August 1875. Immediately afterwards, when Parliament was in recess, Samuel and Eliza prepared for a voyage, intended by Eliza as a therapeutic respite and by Samuel as an investigative mission to see how cargoes were loaded on British ships in the Baltic. Ten days later, with nine-year-old Nellie left in the care of her aunt Ellen in the principal's house at Rotherham College in Yorkshire, her parents were sailing for Hamburg, aiming first for Germany's ports. Plimsoll was not good at idling on holiday, even when he was meant to be convalescing; nor did the passing of the Merchant Shipping Act lead him to rest on his laurels. There would be more permanent legislation in the next

A tribute to Plimsoll in the *Graphic*, 28 August 1875, with a vignette (top left) of painting the Plimsoll mark. (*Illustrated London News*)

session, and there was preparatory work to do. He and Eliza headed for the Romanian ports of Galatz and Ibraila (now Braila) expressly to make sure that the masters of vessels were complying with the strictures of the Act just passed, especially when it came to securing grain loads against slippage. By the time Plimsoll Street was renamed they were somewhere along the Danube. At the end of October they had reached the Black Sea and the Romanian port of Sulina, where every British vessel 'dressed ship' to welcome them.

Plimsoll spent a week of terrible weather in Sulina, standing in pouring rain, watching the loading of grain cargoes and making notes, while Eliza waited for him in the comfort of a suite in the palatial Hôtel d'Administration, thanks to the hospitality of the British Commissioner. The rooms had a fine view of the harbour so Eliza could watch Samuel come and go as he visited, at the invitation of the captains of almost every British steamer, and a good many foreign ones, in the port.

By this time Plimsoll had an international reputation and had been greeted warmly by sailors all the way from France to the mouth of the Danube. But he also had enemies beyond the shores of Britain. In Sulina he asked a captain what he thought of Samuel Plimsoll, without revealing his identity. 'If I had my way I'd tie a rope round his neck and throw him in the Danube,' said the man. 'That is severe,' said Plimsoll. He walked away a few steps, turned and presented his card. 'I am Samuel Plimsoll,' he said. The captain was too surprised to give him a ducking.

Back in England, the tributes continued. On 5 November, in the Sussex village of Lewes, carpenters boarded over ground-floor windows, and wet straw was placed over coal gratings in anticipation of the village's traditional Bonfire Night celebration. This included revellers in fancy dress, a procession with a band and banners and, that year, a homage to the man whose load line had come into force four days earlier. Every year (since 1853 – and still today) the villagers of Lewes constructed a different effigy or tableau to burn on a site at Cliffe corner. In 1875 the tableau was a boat, 'fitted up with fireballs and coloured fire', bearing a device that read: 'Honour to Mr Plimsoll. The way to treat rotten ships.' The village's spoof 'Bishop of Cliffe', in full canonicals, made a few remarks about conflicts in Herzegovina and Spain, and some traditionally unpleasant anti-Catholic jests, and then reminded the crowd of 'the noble efforts and sacrifices made on behalf of our seamen by Mr Plimsoll. May God grant him strength to carry on his noble work.' The ship produced a 'novel and attractive' conflagration and Plimsoll's righteous indignation, as he took an Austrian steamer from Sulina to Odessa, burnt on. He had seen enough to persuade him that the English government should appoint a surveyor at all foreign ports where British ships regularly received homebound cargoes.

Corresponding with the Board of Trade from Sulina, Plimsoll learnt that no money was provided by the 1875 Act to give British Consuls the power to inspect ships and enforce the terms of the Act. He therefore decided to fund inspections himself, and informed Lord Derby, former Prime Minister and now the Minister for Foreign Affairs, that he would provide the money. Telegrams were sent from the Board of Trade to Consuls in ports on the Black Sea authorising them to spend 'reasonable sums' on the help they needed to make reports on the loading of British ships. Reports, complained Plimsoll, writing to *The Times*, were not enough; he wanted the Consuls to have the authority to *order* compliance with the Act.

Meanwhile the worst shortcoming of the hasty 1875 Act was the owner's self-determined load line. Such load lines were frequently under water. Plimsoll 'very earnestly entreated' Lord Derby, in his letter copied to *The Times*, to give Consuls in foreign ports the power, already conferred at home by Clause 1 of the 1875 Act, to ensure that ships were not loaded below the point even the owner marked as the limit of safety, and to detain ships that received an adverse surveyor's report. Otherwise, 'impudent defiance' of Parliament would continue.

All that standing in the rain, and the unremitting work Plimsoll engaged in while he was away, did little to improve his health. He hoped to visit five Spanish ports and one in France (Huelva, Pomarón, Gijón, Santander, Bilbao and Bayonne) on the way home but found himself laid up in Constantinople in November for too long to hope to make it. Relentless in his preoccupations, he suggested that Lord Derby have the loading from these ports checked on arrival instead, as they brought copper and iron ore principally to Swansea, Cardiff and Bristol.

Eliza and Samuel came back from Constantinople in December via Malta and Gibraltar. The picture below was taken on the way to Malta. Plimsoll published it years later to 'show what good men we allow to be drowned wholesale, and by men'. (In fact the couple travelled this section of their voyage on the Norwegian cargo steamer the *Peterjebsen*, so the point was a general one; these were probably not British sailors.)

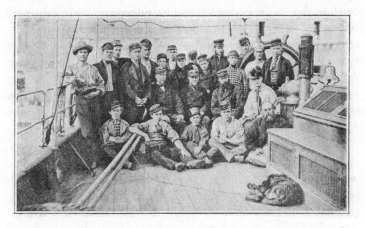

'A souvenir of the kindly men we sailed with', published in *Cattle Ships*. Samuel is seated to the extreme right, with Eliza behind him.

It also reveals more about Plimsoll's character than about the sailors'. He did not sit on chairs with the ship's officers, as Eliza did (any alternative being unthinkable for a woman). He sat cross-legged on the deck (extreme right, front row) with ordinary seamen and the ship's dog. He had been a millionaire and the owner of a stately home. He had been a Member of Parliament for seven years. Streets and ships had been called after him, and songs written in tribute to him. Yet he took his place, partly obscured, on the edge of the group, and lowered himself to the scrubbed planks, at the age of fifty-one, and not entirely well, in a position of humility and solidarity with the least of the mariners, in less of a place of honour than the ship's cook, who stands behind Eliza.

(The circumstances in which this souvenir picture was eventually published also suggest Samuel's lasting feelings for Eliza. It is captioned:

'The crew of a cargo steamer in which I and my wife sailed from Constantinople to Malta.' When this caption appeared, Eliza was dead and Samuel had been married for several years to another woman. It is curious that he did not think it necessary to make this clear.)

Eliza and Samuel were home in time for Christmas 1875 with Nellie. No sooner was Plimsoll back in England than he went to work promoting the safety measures overlooked by the Merchant Shipping Act, in the hope that the government's promised follow-up Bill would remedy omissions. On 10 January 1876 he addressed a meeting of shipwrights in London, making use of his newly acquired expertise, on the subject of the loading of grain ships in Baltic ports; his audience responded by voting him £100 to help bring about legislation against deckloading. Soon afterwards in Liverpool he spoke of the urgent need for the compulsory survey of unclassed ships. And in Bath on 4 February he argued for a fixed load line.

While the Plimsolls were on their way to the Baltic, a British ship was towed into San Francisco harbour on 18 August with a dead man on board. He was the last of thirteen men to die on the voyage from Liverpool, three of them within sight of land. The rest of the crew were 'helpless from scurvy', which had killed their fellows. Twenty-two survivors were sent to hospital, two of whom died there. The ship, the *Bremen*, belonged to Edward Bates.

A fortnight later a court of inquiry was held in San Francisco, at the request of the captain, Lawrence Leslie, to clear himself, he said, of any blame over provisions or care of the men or the use of anti-scorbutics. The court 'mildly censured' Leslie for not stopping in Honolulu where the sick men could have left the ship, and attributed the disease 'to an insufficient quantity of fresh provisions' and the subsequent mortality to 'the refusal of the crew to use anti-scorbutics'. Eleven witnesses were examined who spoke on the side of the captain, while four 'coloured' seamen gave evidence against him. The captain's certificate was returned. A more serious verdict would have confiscated it and interrupted his career. The decision, said the Portland newspaper the *Morning Oregonian*, was 'considered a whitewash'.

A subsequent inquiry in England concluded that provisions were adequate on the ship, although the sailors had thrown some of the beef overboard because it smelt so bad. But the fresh vegetables, principally potatoes and turnips, were not properly distributed – notably not in the first three months at sea. There was conflicting evidence about whether these might also have run out. The report made an assumption that fresh meat could protect against scurvy, when of course it couldn't, but there was, it seemed, more than enough unadulterated lime juice available, which some but not all the sufferers allegedly refused. (This seems to be intransigence of an improbable degree: if there was lime juice to be had, would not sailors who had seen a dozen colleagues die drink it? The captain claimed that he offered double measures of lime juice to the sick. Scurvy affects the back of the throat and tongue, and in some cases the sufferers may already have been too ill to swallow it.) The report attributed four of the deaths on board to diseases the crew were already suffering from when they came on board, in two cases secondary syphilis. The investigator, William Spooner, the Medical Inspector for the port of Liverpool, also surmised that it did not help that the ship was cold and leaky, with no blankets.

But the investigation was so riddled with racism that it is impossible now to trust any of its conclusions. The ship was predominantly manned by sailors of West Indian origin. Doctors were examined and asked: 'Have you ever found negro sailors to be more delicate and more liable to get sick than white men?' There were repeated assertions that black men were weak, dirty, malingering and ignorant. Meanwhile the black sailors' accounts of what vegetables were supplied were much more damning than the captain's: Abraham Scott said he twice had potatoes and twice turnips in a voyage of more than six months. He said that when sailors refused the badly cooked vegetables, which had sand in them, no one pointed out that they gave protection against scurvy. He also reported a conversation in which the captain told the ailing (black) boatswain he had nothing more to give him to eat and said: 'Lie there, damn you, and die.' Joseph Black said compressed vegetables were offered to the sick sailors only when they were too ill to eat them. James Young said he was given a packet of sago to live on for a week and that the captain told him compressed vegetables were not allowed by the ship but came out of his own pocket. The captain and his white supporters insisted that he had given the sick sailors every care, but Philip Every said: 'The way the captain spoke to the sick men was enough to make any one get down-hearted and die.' The evidence of the white witnesses completely contradicted the accounts given by the four black sailors, but black men, even under oath, were held to be so untrustworthy that their evidence was apparently just ignored. 'The testimony of the blacks alone [about the quality of the beef on board] does not appear to me to be a sufficient reason to justify the conclusion that it was bad,' reported Mr Spooner.

Messrs Edward Bates and Sons knew exactly where the blame lay. Expressing no regrets about the deaths, the company wrote to the Board of Trade: 'The whole cause of the outbreak of scurvy was the bad crew, their filthy habits, their refusal to take the limejuice and their foul feeding.' Spooner's principal conclusions were more or less in line with the Bates's; this medical man thought 'negroes' were 'much more susceptible to scurvy than white men; they have less stamina and are more easily affected by cold and exposure, and are extremely dirty in their habits.' The disease was 'accelerated by an absence on the part of the coloured seamen of the moral and physical stamina usually to be found in an ordinary white crew.'

Spooner thought the sailors died because their race made them feeble (and apparently poor morals make you more susceptible to scurvy too). His report even saw fit to point out that the one white sailor who died 'had spent a good deal of time in Africa and was sallow and sickly when he came aboard'. Presumably Spooner thought mere proximity to black men could undermine a white man's constitution.

It was possible to provision a ship in such a way that it could go from Britain to California without fatalities. Since the report's actual conclusions count for nothing, it is hard not to suspect in this grim event the dread effect of Bates's penny-pinching, although the inquiries were more critical of the accommodation on the Bateses' ships than they ever were of the provisions. It was nevertheless the third time a ship owned by Messrs Bates and Sons had been investigated for scurvy. In March 1874 a man died on the *Callirhoe*, contracting scurvy on top of syphilis. The medical investigator, Dr Leach, checked the ship's provisions and wrote: 'I submit that, in the present day, it is utterly inexcusable to send to sea, for human consumption, beef of the kind exhibited to me on board the *Callirhoe*.' On that occasion Bates and Sons replied that the beef was bad 'from want of refilling the casks with pickle', and attached a (surely irrelevant) certificate from its suppliers of port wine and brandy to demonstrate what good medical comforts the company provided for its crew. In May 1875 there was an outbreak of scurvy on the *Sidney Dacres*, on which the sailors also claimed that the salt pork was rotten. William Spooner, investigating, blamed the sailors' diets before they came aboard, and their general health.

It is easy today to see how suspect Spooner's verdicts could be. Plimsoll seems to have doubted them even then, just as he doubted the defence that Edward Bates had presented to the House of Commons in July 1875. Plimsoll's conviction that Bates was one of those guilty men who sent unseaworthy ships to sea had clearly not diminished. In 1876 a novel was dedicated 'by kind permission' to Samuel Plimsoll, and it dramatised precisely the kind of case he condemned. Plimsoll's name, unlike the author's, appeared in gold and in capitals on the royal blue jacket, and he wrote a preface which insinuated a connection between Bates and Sons and the villainous shipowning company that featured in the fiction.

The novel was *A Voice from the Sea*, subtitled *The Wreck of the Eglantine*. The author, Lille Peck, who also wrote under the *nom de plume* Ruth Elliott, was a Methodist with a taste for social justice and a talent for evangelical tearjerkers. Her previous novel, *Margery's Christmas Box* (1875), was a thinly disguised sermon on the subject of the virtuous poor, a quintessence of Victorian sentiment about a pair of pious and cheerful orphaned sisters living in poverty, the elder caring for the younger, who asks: 'Do you think it is Jesus who puts lovely thoughts into my head to keep me from being lonely?' before dying of consumption. Such an author was not ashamed to have a palpable design upon her readers.

A Voice from the Sea was special pleading for the cause, an awful warning about a heartless shipowner, Richard Hilliard, who was in the habit of sending rotten ships to sea. In the story a crew doubts the seaworthiness of one of Hilliard's ships, so his son innocently agrees to join the voyage as a guarantee of his father's good faith.

The boy is the one human being whose life is precious to his father. After the inevitable shipwreck, Hilliard *père* goes into decline and dies hearing the curses of the drowned, in hideous contrast to the good-hearted sailors, who die seeing visions of the Gates of Glory. Shipowners with bad consciences were implicitly invited to consider which kind of death they would choose.

Plimsoll wrote in the preface to *A Voice from the Sea:* 'If I thought there was any statement in this book, or any suggestion of circumstance other than what had its counterpart in real life, and in cases dreadfully numerous, I should not think it right to accept its dedication. The facts, however, are far stronger than any statement in fiction which I have ever read.'

Citing the fact that the chief surveyor of Lloyd's had never known, in his thirty-year career, of a ship being voluntarily broken up, Plimsoll (who assumed that worn-out ships were only bought to sail again, and not, say, for the recycling of parts) was, he said: 'thus driven to a conclusion, which seems to me a very dreadful one, that, even with regard to respectable shipowners, when their ships are worn out, and do not admit of being further repaired, instead of being broken up, they are sold for what they will fetch to anybody who is willing to risk the lives of human beings so long as they can make a profit by it.'

This was followed by a reference to the *Euxine* (see pp. 201–2). It seems fortunate that its publication did not lead to another libel action. The preface might as well have said: 'Edward Bates is a man like the fictional Richard Hilliard.' Plimsoll concluded: 'This book, then, may be safely offered to the public, as containing a truthful representation of the state of things now prevailing in the British mercantile marine; and I shall be glad to think that it will be read by a great number of people, in the hope that it will impress more fully upon the public mind the necessity for a radical change.'

That there were no repercussions is surprising. Was Bates still deterred by not wanting to encourage publicity for the case of the *Euxine*? Or did he not read sentimental novels and their prefaces? Bates was one of the few men Plimsoll named and shamed who never set out to face him and the available evidence in a libel court.

Plimsoll's preface was dated in print 10 February 1876, his fifty-second birthday, and a spoof letter from a shipowner under the same date, possibly a birthday tribute, appeared in *Punch* magazine on 19 February, making fun of Plimsoll's opponents in general and Bates in particular. The news of the deaths from scurvy on the *Bremen* the previous autumn had filtered through to British newspapers and that month more damning stories of Bates ships had broken, including the case of the *Sir Charles Napier*, on which thirteen sailors suffered from scurvy. The Bates family was exonerated as the Assistant Secretary of the Marine Department of the Board of Trade, James Lyons, noted: 'The master informed me that the seamen were very dirty in their habits; they were all coloured men.'

A higher-profile case – thoroughly examined, perhaps because all eighteen of the crew were white, and six of them even British – was that of the *Royal Sovereign*, which arrived in Falmouth with eleven men suffering badly from scurvy and seven others with symptoms. The crew members were cross-examined as they recovered at Falmouth Sailors' Home. A court of inquiry communicated its conclusions to the Board of Trade at the end of February before they were made known to the public, and attributed the outbreak to bad meat, having no problem with the supply of anti-scorbutics. Gilbert Bates gave evidence that 'It is my usual custom in ordering stores to make no reference to price. I only ask that they should be of the best quality.'

Edward Bates, although he said he had had nothing to do with the running of the company for some years, submitted documentary evidence of the high quality of Bates and Sons' provisions. Not surprisingly he thought the first cause of the scurvy was 'the dirtiness of the crew'. Soon afterwards a court found Bates guilty of negligence.

Punch's spoof letter from 'A Shipowner' on 19 February said:

Dear Mr Punch,

Not having had an opportunity of laying my views before the Prime Minister the other day, I send you a brief note of what I intended to have said on behalf of myself and brother Ship-owners.

In the first place, what rights has a fellow like Plimsoll to interfere with me? I wish he'd give me provocation to pull his nose, or smash his spectacles. I've actually had four out of five ships detained in consequence of his meddling. Because one fourth of a crew of sixteen object to be drowned, are they to prevent twelve other honest and daring fellows from risking their lives, as British Seamen ought always to be ready to do at the call of duty. It is perfectly monstrous!

It is true that one or two of my ships have occasionally sailed rather deep in the water, and that one did go down not long after leaving port. But in this case it was solely because the Captain had foolishly forgotten to allow for the weight of the crew, who only shipped at the last moment – the carpenter and boatswain being exceptionally heavy men.

Then, as for saying that Seamen are, as a rule, dissatisfied with their ships, it is all moonshine. The Sailor's attachment to his ship is, on the contrary, proverbial. Why, it was only the other day a man fell overboard from one of my own ships. Did he swim away from it? No, he endeavoured to climb on board again, and expressed the highest satisfaction when he found himself once more among his messmates. Instances of this kind are numerous . . .

And as to a case, lately much commented upon by a scandal-loving Press in which one of my ships came into port with eighteen out of twenty disabled by scurvy, if you only knew the trouble a Captain has to get his men to take the slightest precautions and their rooted prejudice against lime juice and other antiscorbutics, you would, I am sure, agree with me that the owner is the last person to be made responsible . . .

So you see, Mr Punch, there is not the slightest occasion for all this agitation; and all I can say is, that if I am to be interfered with in my business, it will end in my being unable to clear a living profit, and cutting the concern altogether, at whatever cost to the country. I have only expressed in this letter what I know to be the private views of others of my class . . .

Yours indignantly.

A shipowner.

Despite such ongoing media support, and the evidence of wrongdoing collected in his researches and reported in the newspapers, Plimsoll was heading again for disappointment over legislation. On

11 February Sir Charles Adderley presented the government's new Merchant Shipping Bill to the House, the Bill that had been promised after the stop-gap Bill. It wasn't what Plimsoll wanted for his birthday (albeit a day late). Among its inadequacies was the fact that it did not forbid deckloading, nor did it provide for a compulsory survey of ships.

On 27 March Plimsoll moved an amendment to make every British ship qualify for a certificate of seaworthiness before it could sail. Adderley argued that it would make ships uncompetitive, and Plimsoll's amendment was defeated by 247 votes to 110. After all the years, and all the public protest, the same old argument of competition got in the way of making ships safe.

On 8 April 1876 an indignation meeting (a common form of protest in the nineteenth century and into the twentieth) was held at the Cutlers' Hall in Sheffield. Plimsoll's old friend W. C. Leng, the editor of the *Sheffield Telegraph*, said: 'Mr Plimsoll accepts the hatred of evil men as an honour, receives their curses as compliments and wears their epithets as a garland; but, after all, Mr Plimsoll is but one man against hundreds. By himself, he is weak, but with the nation behind him, he is invincible.'

Plimsoll spoke, deriding the owner's load line, and advocating imitation of the Canadians who issued certificates of seaworthiness before vessels left port. He also referred to the case of scurvy on the *Bremen* as he described the state of meat provided for sailors. Doubtless thinking of the *Callirhoe*, he deplored the practice of feeding sailors with food 'they would not give to their dogs'. His hostility to Bates rumbled on.

On 19 January Plimsoll instigated an investigation into the circumstances in 1862 of the repeal of 1839 legislation against deckloading. Always alert to the possibility of conspiracy, Plimsoll alleged that Thomas Milner Gibson and Sir William Hutt, under the mistaken idea that they were advancing the cause of Free Trade, had that year surreptitiously included the number of the deckloading clause in a list of clauses to be repealed from the statute book, when repeal had neither the consent nor the knowledge of Lord Palmerston's Parliament. The investigators, a deputation of Plimsoll's constituents, reported to a February meeting in Derby that all the evidence had undoubtedly been in favour of continuing the prohibition on deckloading. The meeting recorded 'its disapproval of the mode in which the abolition of the prohibition was effected'. This is not conclusive proof that Plimsoll's allegation was accurate; it was not, however, refuted.

Eliza was again put to work for the cause. Plimsoll, convinced by his experiences of the efficacy of public pressure, wrote an appeal to churches asking congregations to get involved. Eliza addressed thousands of envelopes from their flat in Whitehall Court. The appeal read: 'I entreat assistance in getting redress of the sailors' wrongs. My Amendments provide for Survey of Doubtful ships, carefully verified Load line, no Deck-loading and Survey of Grain Cargoes. Will you send up Petitions in support, and write letters to each of your members, or at least do the last?'

In early 1876 trivial distractions from political protest included the new crazes for roller-skating (hindered by the fashion for tight skirts) and spelling bees. Plimsoll needed to continue to publicise the failings of the Merchant Shipping Bill lest the public believe the battle was won and turn its attention elsewhere. Shipowners had lain low during the height of the controversy but now that the storm had subsided they reacted. On 2 February 1876 many met in the London Tavern in Bishopsgate Street (a renowned meeting place close to Liverpool Street Station) to protest at the 'unfounded' accusations which had been made against the fraternity, and to demonstrate that shipowners were 'not to be regarded any longer as a rope of sand', as John Glover put it. He was the shipowner who had penned the refutation *The Plimsoll Sensation: a Reply* back in 1873.

Lord Eslington, who had sat on the Royal Commission, chaired the meeting, declaring, to cheers, what shipowners did not want. 'They do not want a fussy, meddlesome, crochetty interference with their business,' he said, nor 'an artificial stimulus given to foreign trade by the imposition of needless, frivolous and embarrassing restrictions upon their trade'. Above all, he said, 'they do not want to be legislated for in a spirit of suspicion'. The Bills passed in 1875, he argued, had been 'devised in an admirable spirit for the highest of human objects – for the purpose of saving human life'. But he objected to the way they were introduced: 'They were introduced under pressure, and they were passed under pressure ['Hear, hear,' said the assembled shipowners] and they were passed under a great amount of popular excitement out of doors. Now that is, in my humble opinion, not the way to legislate for a mighty shipping nation.' Lord Eslington also spoke highly of Sir Charles Adderley. The meeting argued that the Plimsoll agitation had damaged the shipping industry by making the British seaman perceive his employer as an enemy. But it also characterised the sailor as the culprit for most shipping accidents: his laziness, lack of skill and drunkenness undermined shipowners' best care. Deeply laden steamers, contended Mr Laws of Newcastle, were 'a necessity in order to maintain the maritime supremacy, or even equality, of this country'. The meeting grumbled about the 'vexatious interference of Board of Trade inspectors'.

Seven resolutions were passed. Several urged that merchant shipping legislation should be whittled down and simplified, with the qualification that shipowners would support any legislation that could be demonstrated to save lives. One resolution denied that over-insurance of ships had been 'general or even frequent' and resisted interference with insurance law. One asked that local public courts should hear immediately any accusations of unseaworthiness brought by sailors. Another deplored the clause that permitted a fourth of the crew to detain a ship, which not only brought trouble and loss upon shipowners, but had also diminished the reputation of the British sailor for his 'pluck' (refusal to risk his life being bad for his image). A further resolution wished to remove the following clause from the legislation: 'that every person who sends a ship to sea in such an unseaworthy state as to be likely to endanger the lives of those on board shall be held guilty of misdemeanour, unless he proves that he has used all reasonable means of ensuring the contrary'. This was the only legislation, argued the meeting, that put the onus on the accused to prove his innocence. It was, in effect, a meeting that urged the undoing of all that had already been done.

Disraeli had agreed before the meeting to receive a deputation with its resolutions and duly gave the shipowners a hearing.

Adderley's new Merchant Shipping Bill had the merit of providing for a government survey and a government load line and compulsory classification of unregistered ships. But after it was read on 10 February, the Bill's intransigent opponents (Rathbone, Wilson, Bentinck) retrod the old ground and protested at taking responsibility away from shipowners. Meanwhile Plimsoll defended himself against the charge of making errors of fact: he had on one occasion, he said, slightly overstated the loss of life from wrecks. Three different members had referred to this on different occasions in different places, amounting to eleven attacks for inaccuracy all over one error. His irresistible inference, he said, was 'that those hon. Gentlemen would not have fiddled so long on one string if they had had another on which to play'. He also declared that neglecting to deal with the issue of deckloading in the Bill, or dealing with it 'in an ineffectual manner' was 'very silly'. Plimsoll suggested amendments to the government's Bill. The difference, said Plimsoll, between his proposals and the government's was this – 'that he advocated precaution, while they advocated subsequent inquiry', which was more expensive and less efficacious.

A TUC deputation asked to discuss the Merchant Shipping Bill with Disraeli. The Prime Minister, who had received the shipowners, refused to see the trade unionists. Instead Plimsoll addressed two hundred TUC delegates himself at the Westminster Palace Hotel on 25 April, and told them that the way ministers were dealing with the Merchant Shipping Bill was 'like a child that skips the hard words in its lessons'. 'The Government, when a vital part of the Bill comes to be discussed, either postpones its consideration or leaves it to be dealt with on report.'

If this was true, Disraeli was the child who feigns illness. It seems he had already had too much trouble with the Merchant Shipping Bill. He preferred to dissociate himself from its controversies. He had a fine track record for attendance in the House, but whenever the Bill was discussed he was not there and delegated responsibility to Northcote, his Chancellor of the Exchequer.

On 22 May 1876 all Eliza's addressing of envelopes, all the fictional propaganda and all Plimsoll's speeches seemed to pay off. Plimsoll's amendment to abolish deckloading, debated at length in the House in April, was carried a month later by 163 votes to 142. But victory was snatched away. The Bill went for ratification to the House of

Lords – and came back with the clause about deckloads deleted. The Lords was not, if Shaftesbury's experience is to be believed, easily stirred by the emotions that animated the rest of the populace. Shaftesbury described the second chamber as 'That vast aquarium of cold-blooded life'. He had had trouble there with his legislation to end the misery of chimney sweeps, and found it an extraordinarily impassive body. While the rest of the nation responded fervidly to Plimsoll, the Lords could still be swayed against him, if anyone had the inclination to sway them.

And there was an old enemy in the Lords, who had found a new arena in which to oppose the member for Derby. One of the peers had persuaded the Upper House to insert a clause allowing deck-loads to a height of three feet. And who was this? None other than Lord Carlingford, who before his elevation to the peerage had been Chichester Fortescue, former President of the Board of Trade. The same man who had held out against Plimsoll's reforms as long ago as 1870, and had an angry exchange of letters with him about corruption among Board of Trade officers in 1873. Plimsoll later spoke of 'the malign and homicidal influence of Lord Carlingford' in remov-ing the deckloading clause, and declared him 'morally responsible for the deaths of thousands of men'.

But the Merchant Shipping Act, passed on 12 August 1876 with the Lords' amendments, went further than any previous legislation in safeguarding the lives and welfare of the men who sailed the nation's cargo ships. The Act, which replaced in its entirety the stop-gap Act of 1875 and several clauses of the Merchant Shipping Acts of 1854, 1871 and 1873, had forty-five clauses. Notably it pre-served from the stop-gap Act this clause (no. 4): 'Every person who sends or attempts to send, or is party to sending or attempting to send a British ship to sea in such unseaworthy state that the life of any person is likely to be thereby endangered shall be guilty of a misdemeanor . . .' (to be prosecuted with the consent of the Board of Trade). It also forbade loose loading of grain cargoes and deck-loads of timber in winter and made provision for the detention of unsafe ships. Deck levels were also to be marked on the outside of ships.

But no. 26 was its ground-breaking clause: it made a load line compulsory. It established the famous symbol, of a circle, twelve inches in diameter, with a line through the middle, which popularly took Plimsoll's name.

> The owner of every British ship (except ships under eighty tons register employed solely in the coasting trade, ships employed solely in fishing, and pleasure yachts) shall, before entering his ship outwards from any port in the United Kingdom upon any voyage for which he is required so to enter her, or, if that is not practicable, as soon after as may be, mark upon each of her sides amidships or as near thereto as is practicable, in white or yellow on a dark ground, or in black on a light ground, a circular disk twelve inches in diameter with a horizontal line drawn through its centre:
>
> The centre of this disk shall indicate the maximum load-line in salt water to which the owner intends to load the ship for that voyage.

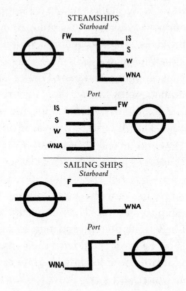

Safety ladder: the long-awaited load line for different conditions: Fresh Water, Indian Summer, Tropical, Summer, Winter and Winter North Atlantic. (*British Library*)

The flaw was that the line showed only the owner's intention. Clause 28 added:

Any owner or master of a British ship who neglects to cause his ship to be marked as by this Act required, or to keep her so marked, or who allows the ship to be so loaded as to submerge in salt water the centre of the disk, and any person who conceals, removes, alters, defaces, or obliterates, or suffers any person under his control to conceal, remove, alter, deface or obliterate any of the said marks, except in the event of the particulars thereby denoted being lawfully altered, or except for the purpose of escaping capture by an enemy, shall for each offence incur a penalty not exceeding one hundred pounds.

Sailors came to refer to the Plimsoll mark as 'the pancake', but also as 'Plimsoll's eye', not only because it looked like an eye but because it meant that attention was being paid to their safety. It was there because of the man who 'kept watch for the life of Poor Jack'.

The circle with the line through it represented eight years of self-sacrificing dedication to other people's lives, and the triumph of popular opinion over self-interest and the manipulations of Members of Parliament. This was the high moment of the period of activism that was the Plimsoll Sensation.

The moment was celebrated in song. In white tie and tails, with moustaches waxed to needle-points, dapper Fred Albert, topical comic songster, known from the Grimsby Varieties in the North to the Collins and Oxford music halls in London, performed his own composition, 'A Cheer for Samuel'. His wife played the piano. This 'infallible mirth-maker', this 'merry minstrel', this 'comical card', as the programmes called him, also had his moments of 'patriotism and pugnacity'. His rousing paean to Plimsoll was one of these.

There was a time when greed and crime did cruelly prevail,
And rotten ships were sent on trips to founder in the gale;
When worthless cargoes, well insured, would to the bottom go,
And sailors' lives were sacrificed, that men might wealthy grow . . .

Our mariners to us are dear, they are the nation's pride,
Rich merchandize to us they bear across the ocean wide;
And so we then, as Englishmen, will honour and respect
The man who raised his voice and pen, our sailors to protect.[*]

Albert had a reputation for forming 'pretty correct estimates of
public opinion' and for 'a good vein of common sense underlying
his comments on burning questions of the day'. Though he was held
to be greatly entertaining, his manner was formal, like his dress – a
certain stiffness apparently giving rise to the widespread, but erro-
neous, rumour that he had a wooden leg.

On 16 August 1876 at the North Western Hotel in Liverpool, still
a monumental turreted edifice with a façade the whole width of a
city square near Lime Street Station, Eliza was called upon by a
deputation from the local committee of the National Lifeboat
Association who made a presentation to her. The working men of
Liverpool had subscribed £500 for a testimonial, and Samuel Plimsoll
had asked that the money be used to buy a lifeboat. It was named
after him. Eliza's gift, a silver model of the boat, was made with the
surplus £50. As usual, Eliza did not speak in public; Samuel spoke
for her. According to the *Liverpool Daily Post*, he said that:

Mrs Plimsoll wished him to state that she thanked them very
heartily for the handsome present they had just now made to her,
and that she received it with feelings of the liveliest gratification,
and would always regard it as one of her most precious possessions.
It was valuable intrinsically, and also because it was a beautiful
specimen of workmanship; but more than that it was chiefly valuable because it was an expression of the kindly feeling towards her
which was entertained by such a vast number of working people,
not only in Liverpool but elsewhere (applause) . . . it would be
impossible for Mrs Plimsoll to look upon it without reflecting that
it was a representation of . . . a real lifeboat (hear hear) which
would probably be the means of rescuing from premature death
some of their fellow-creatures . . . And if sailors were saved from

[*] See p. 312 for complete lyrics.

impending death, husbands restored to their wives, fathers to their little children he put it to them whether that consideration would not be productive of a feeling of happiness inconceivably greater than could have been experienced by Mrs Plimsoll sitting at a table and looking at the finest candelabra or the most beautiful epergnes [a table centrepiece] that the art of man could design (applause).

The newspaper also reported the praise expressed by Mr Whalley MP for Mrs Plimsoll. He said that 'throughout Mr Plimsoll had been sustained in his task by his noble wife (applause). It is not only to Mrs Plimsoll but to the women of England they must look for thorough participation in all movements of this kind, if they desired that they be carried out with success; and he hoped Mrs Plimsoll's example would be largely followed.'

The Times skimped Eliza's worth and sentiments and reported Plimsoll's speech:

The hon. Gentleman then proceeded to refer to the new Shipping Act, and, whilst very far from being satisfied with it, he thought he must now do the best he could in co-operating with those who had charge of its administration in order to get the utmost possible amount of good out of it. In the evening the two hon. Gentlemen, accompanied by Mrs. Plimsoll and several other ladies, visited her Majesty's ship *Eagle*, and witnessed the Royal Naval Artillery Volunteers go through a variety of exercises.

Plimsoll, on observing the Volunteers, confessed his ignorance of the drill and remarked that they looked to him 'as if they were running about the guns in a great deal of confusion', but he was diplomatic enough to praise their 'quickness and facility'.

The lifeboat named after Plimsoll was launched at Lowestoft in December. It went on to bring honour to coxswain Robert Hook, who saved more than two hundred lives in it over the next six years.

Plimsoll battled on for a ban on deckloads, and to keep tabs on the implementation of the new law, travelling with Eliza to Northern ports to watch how ships were loaded. Meanwhile tributes came thick and fast (despite the fact that the nation had another bearded hero to fête that August: the cricketer W. G. Grace, who scored 839 runs in three innings over five days). At Sheffield Plimsoll was presented with a silver cup, only for there to be controversy within days about its provenance, as the company that made it, Walker and Hall, was accused of an irregularity in taking out a licence for the manufacture of silver plate. But the memorial that made his name endure more than all the lifeboats and sailing ships,* more even than the line, was dreamt up in Liverpool in 1876 by a sales representative called Lace, who was, appropriately, in the shoe business.

Philip Lace worked for the Liverpool Rubber Company, who produced shoes with rubber soles and canvas uppers, which were becoming popular beach wear for bank-holiday outings. He called them 'plimsolls' because it was perilous to submerge these black lace-ups beyond their rubber trim. (By coincidence, the Bank Holiday Act, the brainchild of Sir John Lubbock, was passed in 1871 with the help of a vote from Samuel Plimsoll.) The Liverpool Rubber Company failed to copyright the name in 1876 and a competitor, the Harburg and Vienna Rubber Company (based in London), registered the trademark 'Universal Plimsoll' in 1885 and tried to cash in. The Liverpool Rubber Company retaliated, in the hope of reclaiming authenticity, with an advertisement that read: 'See that the name "Liver" is on the sole.' Lace organised a display of the original shoes, with half a window full of sand and shingle and seaweed, at Rabbits and Sons, Boot and Shoe Makers at 2-14 Newington Butts, near the Elephant and Castle in London. 'Rabbits Corner' was just near Plimsoll's office on the New Kent Road. When he walked past in later life he could peer in and enjoy the display. The name caught on as far afield as Jamaica, though it was never used in Scotland, where the footwear is known to this day as a 'sand shoe'.

Plimsoll never really retired from his campaign, but had to slow down for a while. He had made himself unwell from the strain, per-

* Another ship, a dredger, was named for him in 1877.

haps even suffering a nervous breakdown. As early as February 1876 the Hon. Georgina Cowper-Temple of the Ladies' Committee had recorded in her diary how Plimsoll was 'made quite ill' by the terrible suffering of sailors. His health continued to deteriorate. Plimsoll was said for some time to be 'seriously indisposed' and in February 1877 he failed to open a new dock in Bristol because of 'an acute nervous disability'.

It cost him dear, but the 1876 Act was the defining achievement of Plimsoll's career, even if it still permitted owners to put the load line where they pleased. One defiant Cardiff captain placed it on the funnel of his ship as if to say, 'I can load it to here if I like.' It was to take Plimsoll another fourteen years before ships were required to carry a standard load line regulated by the Board of Trade. Yet George Howell said of the 1876 Act, 'It was not all that was desired; still it was a great step. Mr Plimsoll had won a signal victory.' And in Derby, addressing his constituents in 1878, Plimsoll acknowledged that he had passed a landmark: 'An Act of parliament is now on the Statute book, which although not by any means without defects, is still one that, zealously and faithfully administered, will be found to remedy the evils which afflict our sea-going population. My special work, therefore, I regard as done.'

Plimsoll's immortality was assured. Posterity would call this his finest hour. Parliamentary intransigence had succumbed to public pressure; Plimsoll and the people had triumphed. And yet there were those defects. And Plimsoll was not one to ignore unremedied evils, of which there were plenty still to be opposed. There was another two decades' worth of indignation in him, and it found expression in other objects.

9

THE AFTERMATH

After success came a waning of reputation. Even *Punch* magazine, which had been so supportive in its pro-Plimsoll rhymes and spoofs, adopted a more cynical tone towards him. In March 1877 it published, over several weeks, a parody of a novel, *All in the Downs; or The Bottomry Bond!*, recalling the anonymous *Ship Ahoy!* of 1873 (in fact by George Manville Fenn), of which Plimsoll had circulated reprints. (The heroine of *All in the Downs* was called Mary Maybud; the heroine of *Ship Ahoy!* was May, and its coffin-ship the *Merry May*.) The send-up made fun of the opening of *Our Seamen*: 'I have no idea of writing a Novel. I don't know how to do it . . .' Set in the harbour of Newport Pagnell (which is land-bound at the centre of England) with its cliffs and sands and 'gay quay thronged with sailors of all nations', it mocked Plimsoll's lack of nautical knowledge, his assertion that fiction is fact and his capacity for alarmist exaggeration. Here is a fragment of the action, encapsulating several of Plimsoll's preoccupations: 'A number of men, under the command of a Captain who was only seventeen years old [annotated as: 'A fact. I expect him to come to grief next month'] were rapidly cutting a vessel in two, so as to lengthen her fore and aft and thus enable her to carry more grain than she was ever intended to carry, and so enrich the coffers of her proprietors.'

The *Punch* episodes were interspersed with joke letters from

Plimsoll sprinkled with inaccurate attempts at sailors' idiom, such as 'avast heaving!' They ended with this lampoon:

> Ye who read this, help me to do my best to destroy the homicidal system, and never let the two thousand working-men of Derby, who have never seen a ship in their lives, or a sailor, and who don't know a bow from a keel or a jib from a forecastle, and whose conduct, in sending me to Parliament is therefore all the more disinterested and generous, let them, I say, never forget what I have done, what I will do, for the sailor's wrongs; and let them ever, and always, send <u>me</u> to the House as their Member – honest, bluff, hearty and earnest S. P., as they know me to be . . .

Some attacks were stronger. A satirical pamphlet, *Plimsoll's England*, published anonymously in 1878 under the pseudonym 'Ajax' (a disguise used by many writers of the time), concluded its rhyming condemnation:

> Thus England, overweighted and disgraced,
> Soon found her flag by Foreign flags displaced,
> Her sons of commerce more oppressed became
> By unjust laws, and so retired in shame,
> Until at last she wavered in the race,
> Fell back and gave the Foreigner first place,
> England, farewell, for all thy sons are slaves,
> So sink, Britannia – Plimsoll rules the waves!

It satirised *Our Seamen* and accused 'mad Sam' of vanity and ignorance. It attacked him for employing rabble-rousers. (Plimsoll's then unborn son was later to admit that his father 'had an army of paid agitators'.) 'Ajax' deplored the 'many hired/To stump the country o'er and keep up strife/(The proper way to save the Sailor's life.)' He also ranted against the drunkenness of sailors (as well as the unrelated belligerence of miners and the lewdness of writers), against the 'brainless busybodies' who made reformist laws, and against 'Addlepate' and 'Greyhead' – Adderley and Grey of the Board of Trade, who enacted the Bill brought about by Plimsoll's agitation, and gave sailors more power than they deserved. Illogically, it blamed Plimsoll not only for the downfall of the British merchant navy in favour of foreign competition, but also, xenophobically, went on to hold him responsible for the sullying of the purity of British blood by the miscegenation that it predicted would follow.

A more rational target might have been the inadequacies in the new legislation, not least the fact that the load line was unfixed. Furthermore, it remained possible to circumvent the strictures of Plimsoll's law by selling an unseaworthy ship to another country. One such case in 1883 was remembered by L. M. Montgomery, author of *Anne of Green Gables*, in her journals. When the author-to-be was eight, a British ship that had been condemned by the Plimsoll Bill evaded destruction, was sold to a Norwegian firm and sailed with a cargo of deal planks from Canada. The ship sprang a leak and was grounded, and twenty colourful crewmen came ashore to Montgomery's home, Cavendish, on Prince Edward Island, just across the Northumberland Strait from Nova Scotia. They enlivened the quiet village for the summer. The incident was not without its tragedy, though. Later, wreckers who were stripping the ship were caught on board in a storm, and one man drowned before young Lucy's eyes while he was trying to reach the shore.

Meanwhile Plimsoll's zeal for improving the lot of sailors had not ended with the Merchant Shipping Act, and he was unfazed by satire and slights. Wherever he travelled in subsequent years he considered the effect of local conditions on sailors who landed there. When he went to Malta in 1879, en route to India, he wrote a pamphlet, *The Condition of Malta*, that he sent to the editor of *The Times*, in which he identified a risk of cholera in its otherwise impressive and spacious harbours. He traced the danger to the fact that Malta's main source of income was from its taxes on food, which caused poverty and squalor. Change Malta's tax law, he argued, and British sailors would not be susceptible to infection.

The food tax in itself stirred his sense of justice. He discovered that the Maltese poor – who were very poor indeed – subsisted mostly on bread and paid the highest proportion of their income in tax. 'A poll tax would be less iniquitous than this, for this takes more per head from a poor man than from a rich man, and this, too, to pay for many things which are the exclusive possession of the rich'; he thought the funding of the new opera house and the university from this source particularly questionable. (Much as he approved the social intentions of Dickens and Doré, Plimsoll's tastes were not highbrow.) Worse, he discovered that Malta's upper classes were supplied with water for free from pure underground reservoirs, while the country's farmers and agricultural labourers were charged for a supply from 'the surface overflow from open highways'. These iniquities had been reported to Parliament in 1878 by an MP by the name of Rowsell. Plimsoll quotes the facts Rowsell adduced, but remarks on the equanimity with which he reported them: 'I should say that Mr Rowsell must be a very nice man to live with. Nothing seems to rouse him or to disturb his placid pulses.' Evidence of suffering never left Plimsoll so unmoved.

His pulses were disturbed, too, by the living conditions in Maltese homes he visited: cramped cellars hollowed out of rock, three storeys deep, with no windows or chimneys, no natural light or heating, no ventilation or sanitation. He reported that the air was foul and the floors were coated with excrement, and that the sick and the heavily pregnant never managed to climb the precipitous stairs out of the darkness to the fresh air.

I have been in Baldwin's Gardens, in Fulwood's Rents, in Holborn, the blind courts in the south side of the Old Bailey, and parts of Seven Dials; I found the widows and mothers of drowned seamen in sad places in the waterside alleys in South Shields; I have been in the colliery villages in Wales and Northumberland, the slums of Dublin, Glasgow and Edinburgh, the mud and reed huts in Southern Russia, and I have also seen where the poor live in some of the worst parts of Guirghenti, Messina, Taormina, Catania, Syracuse and other parts of Sicily; I have seen squalor enough, filth enough, darkness enough, misery enough and nakedness enough, in these places, to make me very sad in the United Kingdom and wretched in Sicily; but never was I filled with such horror, such loathing, and such panting indignation as when I was in the homes of the poor in this beautiful city in the dominions of our kind-hearted and Christian Queen; for they are taxed and ruled over by British Governors, and, if goaded by the most awful misery and despair they rose upon their oppressors, they would assuredly be stabbed to death by British bayonets, and shot down by British soldiers.

Plimsoll's capacity for resounding rhetoric, albeit more emotive than reasoned, continued to be put to use. His rolling rhythms managed to conjure an act of murder that had not in fact been committed, in the service of a righteous outrage. The suffering he attacked here was not only the sailors'. His reputation as a one-issue politician did not tell the whole story. Wherever he saw injustice he was moved to denounce it.

Sometimes, too, he took up smaller issues: the adulteration of beer, for instance, prompted a speech to a Derby Temperance Society in 1877, in which, with the fervour of a modern real-ale campaigner, he complained of drinks that were intoxicating – in the precise sense of poisoning rather than inebriating. He listed the additives to one beverage: *Cocculus indicus*, darnel seed, chloride of sodium – which is of course common salt – copperas, opium, strychnine, tobacco, extract of logwood, sulphate of zinc or lead, and alum. The French, Plimsoll pointed out, drank wine without getting drunk. Their alcohol, he argued, was not adulterated.

Moderate drinkers though they were, both Mr and Mrs Plimsoll had health problems in the years after the 1876 Act. Samuel's right eye, which suffered some unidentified accident and subsequently painful inflammation, was removed by a distinguished oculist, and he spent the first part of 1879 recovering. Afterwards he would treat other people's children, including his nephews and nieces, to the delightful horror of seeing him take his glass eye out. (Photographs reveal that his false eye was not always precisely parallel to the one that worked.) His various illnesses tempted Plimsoll to retire from politics, but when he broached the possibility, he was urged by his constituents to stay, and agreed.

By the summer of 1879 Plimsoll was hopeful enough about the future to buy a four-storey house with roofed, wrought-iron balconies at 28 Park Lane. It is now a phenomenally expensive address embellished with fancy stonework in a row of buildings just along from the Dorchester Hotel and fronting a dual carriageway; but then it was on a quiet corner of a quiet street overlooking Hyde Park and was described by Plimsoll's friend Havelock Wilson as 'a little old-fashioned but pretty place'. Plimsoll, in an act of uncharacteristic self-aggrandisement (perhaps the gesture was tongue-in-cheek), also purchased a family crest, unauthorised by the College of Arms, with a motto of his own invention. The motto was '*Difficultas Conditio Est Fortuna*': variously translatable as 'Fate is Fickle' and (in jest) 'It's not easy to make a fortune', both of which expressed something of the ups and downs of the Plimsolls' lives. It appeared, as was fashionable, on letterheads with his new address. There were, incidentally, no nautical symbols on his coat of arms, only symbols of Christian piety, wisdom and courage: a pelican, helmet, snake and lion rampant.

Plimsoll's coat of arms.
(*From Peters*, The Plimsoll Line)

The Plimsolls' enjoyment of their status and comforts was short-lived. The summer of 1879 was unusually wet, with weeks of rain in July, and Eliza's health suffered. By December she was unwell with an illness more serious, as it turned out, than Samuel's recurrent disorders, and the couple left London for the warmth that was expected to do her good. They stayed at the Hôtel d'Orient in Algiers (fifteen years before Oscar Wilde and his lover Bosie Douglas stayed there) and travelled on to Malta (their second visit, which inspired the pamphlet discussed above) and then to India. On 24 January 1880 Samuel had a meeting in London with George Howell and the TUC about grain cargoes, which he would not forgo. The missing deckloading clause from his legislation had become the new focus of his ongoing crusade. Eliza insisted on returning home with her husband and 'caught a chill' as they crossed the Channel. A 'chill', in Victorian England, was a serious illness.

It was clear that Eliza needed to avoid the cold, especially of English winters, but there was a general election to contest. Plimsoll campaigned in 1880 under the slogan 'For Gladstone and For Jack' and was re-elected with a handsome majority of five thousand. Election handbills attacked the Tories 'who tried to crush our "Sailor's Friend"/But Plimsoll would not for them bend.' His work for the load line was not forgotten, as was also evident in the electoral campaign against an old enemy. Charles Morgan Norwood, who had proposed the 'owner's load line', was dogged by his conflict with Plimsoll. The opposition's campaign poster depicted in a cartoon two sinking ships owned by Norwood, the *Walamo* and the *Livonia*, and a third with its load line below the water. Norwood was shown floored by a punch from his Tory opponent, Pope. Plimsoll was drawn expressing approval (despite the fact that Plimsoll and Norwood were both Liberals) and saying, 'I've got my eye on yonder load-line, a foot or two below the authorised mark.' (This disparaging reminder was not, however, enough to keep Norwood out of office: he went on to be elected for Hull and sat until his defeat in 1885, continuing to oppose legislative interference in the shipping industry.)

After his celebrated 'Midlothian campaigns', in which he toured Scotland addressing massed gatherings and attacking Disraeli's foreign policy, Gladstone won his seat at Midlothian from the Tories and became Prime Minister on 23 April 1880, with a majority of over a hundred seats. Plimsoll proposed a public reception to celebrate Gladstone's return. On an overnight visit to Hawarden, Gladstone's Welsh home, ostensibly to discuss this, Plimsoll was 'overflowing with his own subject of the mercantile marine', as Gladstone recorded in his diary. He added that Plimsoll 'was however an original & childlike man, full of reality & enthusiasm'. Gladstone expressed his objections to the reception, which he put in writing two days later, and the idea was shelved.

There was a damper on the Liberals' success. William Vernon Harcourt, the Liberal Home Secretary, had lost his Oxford seat. It was thought that Sir Charles Villiers MP would give up Wolverhampton in favour of Harcourt, but Eliza, in poor health and wanting the companionship of her husband, urged him to do so instead. There were several reasons why this seemed like a good idea, and Eliza's illness tipped the balance in favour of Plimsoll's resignation (or 'taking the Chiltern Hundreds', as the form was).* Harcourt had an influence in the House that Plimsoll was never likely to possess, and was induced to promise to take up Plimsoll's fight in exchange for his constituency. Plimsoll had also encountered such resistance in the House of Commons, and enjoyed such popularity outside it, that he was persuaded he might have as much impact on the nation's affairs as an agitator as he had as an MP.

There was another event that is said to have influenced his premature retirement. Eighteen eighty saw a storm on the Yorkshire coast comparable to the Bridlington Great Gale of nine years earlier. Thirteen ships were driven on to the beach at Withernsea, near Hull, alone, and the sands were strewn with bodies. All of Plimsoll's agitation against rotten ships and the introduction of the load line had not prevented the loss of fifty ships and many lives. It was a disheartening moment and led him to think he might do better to refocus his efforts on trying to improve conditions for seamen.

---

* A resolution of 1623 forbade MPs from voluntarily resigning a seat. Instead, those wishing to resign had to apply for a paid office of the Crown, which disqualified them from holding a seat. There are two such offices: Crown Steward and Bailiff of the Chiltern Hundreds.

For all these reasons, on 18 May 1880 Samuel stood with William Harcourt on the balcony of the Midland Hotel, where Queen Victoria had a suite of rooms, opposite the railway station in Derby, and told his constituents that he could serve the sailors' cause as well outside Parliament as inside it, especially with an ally as powerful as the man beside him to take on the responsibility for seamen. A week later Harcourt was elected unopposed and was able to return to the Cabinet as the new Home Secretary. He became the subject of a revised rhyme: 'Harcourt's the cherub who sits up aloft/To keep watch for the life of poor Jack'. *Punch* published a cartoon of Harcourt as 'a man overboard' being thrown a lifebelt labelled 'Wolverhampton'. When it turned out to be 'the sailor's friend' who threw Harcourt a constituency instead, *Punch*, which had cooled towards Plimsoll, warmed to him again, described him as 'Salt of the Earth', congratulated Sir William on the 'agility he has shown in availing himself of the Derby life-buoy' and reported:

Mr Plimsoll thinks the cause he has at heart will be better served by what Sir W. V. Harcourt can do for it in the House than by any efforts of his own there. So he hands over his seat to the Home Secretary, battling with the waves without a spar, and himself goes down, without a spar, to the depths of private life! The act becomes Mr Plimsoll. Impulsive he may have been, but his impulses were always generous and self-sacrificing. The ending of his parliamentary life is consistent with its tenor; it shows more consideration for his cause than for himself.

Harcourt was full of praise for Plimsoll, who, he said, 'has the way of speaking to other men in a manner that comes from the heart and goes straight to it'. He called Plimsoll's surrender of his seat 'a noble act of self-sacrifice. His conduct will surprise no one who has marked the chivalrous and unselfish devotion to the cause of humanity and right to which he has given his life . . . With regard to the welfare of sailors, if it interested me before, you may rest assured that it will occupy my mind still more in the future.'

In Oxford, where there were accusations of electoral irregularity and a petition against Hall, the MP who had defeated Harcourt, the local Liberal Party invited Plimsoll to stand for the constituency if the election were rerun. But it was not.

When Plimsoll resigned, this was the comment in a diary in the *Penny Illustrated Paper*: 'Sir William Harcourt and the Liberal Party I congratulate ye on winning your Derby! . . . Ye danced quite deftly to the hornpipe "The Sailors' [*sic*] Friend" played ye . . . But what reward shall we give to Mr Plimsoll? "Rise, Sir Samuel Plimsoll, Baronet!" I should counsel Her Majesty to say . . . were I in your shoes, Sir William!'

But Plimsoll was not knighted. All the ways in which Plimsoll was recognised in his lifetime came from public enthusiasm: the illuminated addresses, the street names and the statues were grass-roots initiatives. He never received any official recognition. Perhaps Harcourt failed to counsel Her Majesty to honour him, and others who might have done so did not have the favour of the Queen. Maybe Plimsoll had the wrong friends and the wrong enemies. Shaftesbury, despite his earldom, had lost the trust of the monarch back when he was plain Lord Ashley. Having been a friend to Queen Victoria in her youth, he upset her by voting against an allowance of £50,000 a year to Prince Albert and helping to reduce it to £30,000. Victoria was furious for years afterwards. Meanwhile Shaftesbury had said of her: 'She has a small and girlish mind, unequal to the business of government or even of common life.' This contrasts with the flattery of Disraeli, who had too bad a time at the hands of the Plimsollites ever to recommend him for honours.

Plimsoll was the man who had undermined the administration of the Queen's beloved Dizzy, but on the other hand *Our Seamen* had been dedicated to her. She had expressed sympathy for 'poor Mr Plimsoll' and his cause. She had lent her ear, and her son the Duke of Edinburgh to preside over Plimsoll's Royal Commission. Her daughter's mother-in-law had been the president of the Ladies' Committee of the Plimsoll and Seamen's Defence Fund. Still she apparently never rewarded Plimsoll's dedication to saving lives.

Or perhaps she did. Perhaps Plimsoll was offered a knighthood. His granddaughter, Sally Shaw, believes he would have declined one. The names of those who turned down knighthoods were secret. Plimsoll adopted a coat of arms, but would he have accepted a title that set him above the men he had fought all his life to protect? Would Plimsoll, who said, 'I absolutely glory in the working men, and aspire no higher than to merit equal respect with them', have cared for a baronetcy?

Sir Edward Bates, after all, had one. He was knighted, but not before being the subject of more controversy. In 1876 he was accused of bribing the electorate. Bates was in the habit of distributing goods and money to the poor around his places of residence whenever there was a cause for family celebration. He did this in North Wales when his son came of age, when he was elected to Parliament in 1871 and again in 1873 and 1874 when two of his daughters wed. When in 1876 two sons were married, his largesse got him into trouble. Donating gifts and cash in Liverpool and at his Welsh castle, Gyrn, was acceptable, but he also bestowed his bounty in Plymouth, where he did not live but stood for election. Accusations were brought by a local clergyman and members of the Plymouth Liberal Party and the case went to court. He was cleared of bribery at a five-day trial and cheered by supporters inside and outside the courtroom. But by then another impropriety had come to light.

Trawlermen who had landed in Penzance had been offered train fares by one of Bates's agents to come and vote for Bates in Plymouth. This much was legitimate. But when one complained that he would lose a day's fishing, the agent arranged for someone else to take his place and compensated him for the money he lost, which was against the law. Bates claimed no knowledge of his agent's action, but was held responsible and expelled from the House of Commons. Disraeli gave him the baronetcy by way of consolation.*

---

* In fact Sir Edward Bates's career in government was not over. He stood again for Plymouth in 1885 and was elected with an increased majority, and apparently without undue incentives. He ceased to be a partner in Edward Bates and Sons, which had long been run by his three sons, by 1895 and died at eighty in 1896, leaving a clause in his will that used money to exercise posthumous power over a family member, refusing part of his inheritance to a son-in-law if he incarcerated his daughter for more than half the year in his remote Scottish country house.

Now untitled Mr Plimsoll, ex-MP, was free to travel with his wife wherever her health demanded. But in May 1880 Plimsoll's old ally Joseph Chamberlain, who had once declared as Mayor that every citizen of Birmingham must surely be on the side of Mr Plimsoll, was appointed President of the Board of Trade. The day after his appointment, Chamberlain paid Plimsoll the compliment of arranging a meeting to discuss what still needed to be done for sailors. Eliza was then ill in Torquay and expecting her husband to come to her, but he kept her waiting an extra day in order to take advantage of Chamberlain's sympathetic ear.

Chamberlain was practical and efficient and had no history of alienating members of the shipping industry. He quietly and capably began to bring about measures Plimsoll had noisily tried for years to bludgeon the authorities into adopting.

It seems Plimsoll regretted his retirement almost immediately, perhaps because, as he complained, Harcourt's mind seemed little occupied with the welfare of sailors once he found himself again in power. There were issues, too, over which he had cause to wish he still had a parliamentary voice, as, for instance, when an old ally ran into trouble.

Charles Bradlaugh, who had stood with sailors in the docks and denounced the ship-knackers after Plimsoll's outburst in July 1875, fell foul of Parliament for his lack of religious belief. Although elected for Northampton in 1880, he was banished from the House for his refusal to speak four words of the loyal oath: 'So help me God.' It caused a huge controversy. Plimsoll was a man of passionate religious conviction but on 25 June 1880 he wrote this letter to Bradlaugh and sent a copy also to *The Times*, in keeping with his habit of making his views as public as possible:

Your theological beliefs and mine are as opposite as the poles. I believe in God and in His Son Jesus Christ . . . but I do not find that He has anywhere authorized those who do not believe in Him of their natural rights. On the contrary I believe the attempt to do so is not only not the way to obtain adherents to His cause but is diametrically opposed to His saying: 'Whatsoever ye would that man should do unto you, do ye even so to them.'

I think there can be no doubt that the spirit now arrayed against you in the House of Commons is the old spirit of domination and intolerance, which if allowed to gain the upper hand would deprive us not only of our religious liberty but of our civil rights . . .

Had I still been in the House of Commons I should probably have said this there: I should certainly have supported Mr Gladstone's worthy vindication of civil and religious liberty by my vote: as it is I wish to stand if not by his side at least behind him as one willing to do battle for civil and religious liberty no matter in whose person its sacred principles are assailed, more especially as there is great danger of some being beguiled into striking a deadly blow at liberty under a mistaken idea that they are defending the Honour of God.

Plimsoll's ardent faith was not of the intolerant kind. Unfortunately, although his view reflected the thinking of those outside the House, he was once again at odds with the majority inside it. And even Plimsoll's hero Shaftesbury, who had always been evangelical, believed that Bradlaugh should be excluded from the House for his unbelief: letting him in would lead to a dangerous dissociation of Church and State. Bradlaugh found it easier to secure a place in Madame Tussaud's, which admitted him in wax in July 1880, than to be allowed to take the seat his electorate repeatedly voted him into, which did not happen until 1886.*

Plimsoll's change of heart about his retirement was demonstrated in August when he stood as a Liberal candidate for Liverpool, only to be defeated by Lord Claude Hamilton – fortunately for Eliza. That summer she was transported from her bed to a sleeping carriage on the train that took her, with Samuel, via Folkestone to Paris, where she stayed a few days, and then to Royat in the Auvergne, where she spent six weeks. There followed two years in which Eliza and Samuel spent eight months of each year out of the country pursuing good weather and Eliza's recovery. Plimsoll had finally said his farewell to his sweetheart, politics.

---

* Bradlaugh joined Gladstone and Disraeli in Madame Tussaud's – they are still there – and Lord Shaftesbury, who warranted a place until 1915. Samuel Plimsoll never qualified (although the waxworks was temporarily closed at the height of his campaign).

PUNCH'S ESSENCE OF PARLIAMENT.

PLIMSOLL'S ADIEU!
"HIS HEART WAS TRUE TO POLITICS."

(*But it was only an overladen Phantom Ship, that couldn't take him on board.*)

MONDAY, August 2 (Lords).—"Propulty, propulty, propulty!" Pitched battle among the Peers over the Compensation for Disturbance (Ireland) Bill; prodigious press of Peeresses to witness the first round.

"In their gay fal-lal-eries,
They thronged the galleries,
And filled the passages, and choked the floor-ways;
Peers' wives and daughters,
Crushed in closest quarters,
And sat cosmozed in the open doorways."

Fancy a Peeress sitting in a doorway—and probably a draught—to hear an Irish Bill discussed! Patience on a monument smiling at Grief, seems nowhere in comparison.

Plimsoll says farewell to politics, to which 'his heart was true'; in the background a ship named *Liverpool* sails by. (*From* Punch)

In September 1880 an Act was finally passed to provide for safe carriage of grain cargoes. Suddenly legislation that Plimsoll had hoped to bring about was in place and, as he travelled the world with his invalid wife, he was not there to share in the drama and the glory. Through all his foreign adventures Samuel could not leave his other preoccupations alone.

Plimsoll continued to correspond with Chamberlain. In October 1880 he wrote from the Hotel Braganza in Lisbon praising Chamberlain's achievements, but not quite relinquishing his own position as the sailor's first defender. He drew attention to evils that still needed to be remedied: to the bad food and poor sleeping accommodation on many merchant ships, and to the fact that many sailors were obliged to work in all weathers without shoes. In Madeira three weeks later, Plimsoll received a letter from Chamberlain about the still unresolved question of a fixed load line. Chamberlain suggested (as James Hall had back in 1868) that ship-builders should establish load lines, rather than the owners or the Board of Trade – a sensible solution to differences of opinion that had held the measure back.

Although his most immediate concern was Eliza's health, Samuel had philanthropic projects wherever he went, collecting information, considering social improvements and corresponding with the British newspapers. While he was away he worked on a paper which drew on his old expertise in the coal industry. His essay, 'Explosions in Collieries and Their Cure' (dated 'Madeira, 10 November 1880'), appeared in *Nineteenth Century* magazine in December 1880. It was an appeal to chemists to find a solution to the dangers of firedamp or 'light carburretted hydrogen', which caused explosions in mines, a problem he said had preoccupied him for twenty years.

Characteristically, Plimsoll told terrible stories of the suffering caused by colliery explosions he had known. He also recounted the heroism of miners searching for survivors who entered mines where one explosion had occurred, knowing that there was a danger of a second, and who perished when the next explosion came. (At the Oaks Colliery, near Barnsley, 344 miners died on 12 December 1866; the next day a further twenty-seven volunteer rescuers died, including Plimsoll's friend the mining engineer Parkin Jeffcock.)* Evidently it disturbed Plimsoll that the business from which he had made his fortune, which he called the miners' 'beneficent labour', should entail bereavement and anguish. He blamed not a vengeful God, but man, who 'will not learn and will not obey the physical laws of the universe'. Plimsoll's own proposed preventative measure against explosions was a pump to extract the volatile gas.

---

* Between 1860 and 1879 there were eighty-five explosions at UK mines caused by firedamp, resulting in the loss of at least 3190 lives. (Explosions where fewer than five men were killed are not included in these totals.)

Meanwhile for the family there were several crises. From Bordeaux in autumn 1880 Samuel returned home with fourteen-year-old Nellie to fetch Eliza's doctor, W. F. Butt, and brought him back to France, sailing from Liverpool after a few days in England on 20 October 1880. Eliza recovered sufficiently for the party to move on to Lisbon for two months and winter in Madeira, where in November Samuel finished his paper on explosions but Eliza suffered an attack of paralysis. Her life 'seemed to hang by a thread' but she rallied and at Christmas her physician, by now a Dr Graham, recommended travelling nineteen days on a steamer to South Africa. Amazingly, it did her good and through that spring she journeyed up the coast from Wynberg near Cape Town to Natal, Durban and Pietermaritzberg, by which time she was so much better that she headed home.

At the end of May 1881 Samuel and Nellie brought Eliza back to England. June was wet and she relapsed, and the conviction that chasing mild climates would keep Eliza one step ahead of danger led to another peripatetic burst. The family set off again in July 1881 to France (Boulogne, Paris, Bordeaux, Arcachon) and Lisbon. In October Samuel invited his sister Mary Dickinson, then living in Australia, and his niece Alice to join the three of them in India. Eliza, Samuel and Nellie sailed to Karachi (then in India), spent several weeks in Bombay, went down the Malabar Coast (to Vingorla, Goa, Cochin, Quilon) and on to Ceylon (Colombo, Kandy, Newerra Alia). Alice remembered the adventure, and her uncle's generosity:

> He made allowances to a number of his relations who were not well off, my mother being one of them. He was always kindness itself, and gave us many treats, including taking us to the Continent one summer and some years later to India. I think his generosity and his religion are what impressed me most. He was a truly religious man and always had family prayers in the morning. He was a great smoker and when sitting in his chair or lying down, he moved his head from side to side with the cigar in his mouth. He was a good deal affected by the weather, a bright day having a very cheering effect on him.

In Ceylon in 1882 he made a decision he was to regret. He elected to go back to England, not in fact for any urgent business on behalf of sailors, but because of a personal financial project. He hoped to organise a fish market in London, on the site of houses he had bought and demolished in the New Kent Road in the 1860s. The trip to India was partly to research a supply for the market. Eliza was by then in the company of Nellie and her sister-in-law Mary, who was to take her home to Brisbane for a visit. Plimsoll said goodbye to Eliza, intending to follow her to Australia as soon as he could complete his errand. He had convinced himself that his wife's life was not in danger, but this was the last time he saw her and they spent the final months of her life apart.

In the middle of March 1882 Eliza sailed for Java accompanied by Mary, Alice and Nellie. She went on to Melbourne, where she visited Mrs Chambers, the widow of her stepfather's brother Thomas, and another of Samuel's sisters, Caroline Barnes. On 14 April Eliza and Nellie arrived in Brisbane and stayed at Mary's house. She telegraphed Samuel to say she was well, and again in June, by which time she had made up her mind to make her way home, sailing on the *Roma*. By July it was obvious that the journey would be too much. On 11 July 1882 she telegraphed her husband to say she would stay in Australia and await his arrival. (The shortest sailing time in the 1880s from England to Australia was some eight weeks.) Eliza had swapped a British winter for an Australian winter and found herself trapped. When Samuel received the telegram of 11 July he booked himself a passage – for a ship that sailed on 28 August. By 8 August Eliza had pneumonia. Four days later she sent a plaintive telegram: 'Very poorly. Are you coming soon?' On 17 August she died in Brisbane, half a globe away from the partner and soulmate to whom she had demonstrated such selflessness and dedication. A telegram was sent to W. F. Butt: 'Tell Samuel Plimsoll that his wife died today.'

Eliza's Australian death certificate gives ten days of pneumonia as the cause of her death. Her longer-term illness – perhaps tuberculosis – is still unexplained. Her obituary in *The Times* gives no clues: the only diagnosis referred to is a neuralgia brought on, in the opinion of the doctor, by washing her hair. A bad case of wet hair would not seem to justify a two-year pursuit of healthy climates.

Some years later Samuel's fish-market project failed: his guilt at abandoning his wife in order to set it up seems to have overshadowed it, though he did take one more related trip to India in 1884 before he gave up on the venture. He had left Parliament at Eliza's urging in order to be at her side, then wavered over this choice and been with her only because of the contrariness of the Liverpool voters. Ultimately he had been as far away as it was possible to be at the moment when she needed him most.

Eliza was buried in Brisbane with pomp and official recognition: the funeral at Toowong was attended by eminent dignitaries including the Governor General and the Premier. But three days later Plimsoll had sent an exhumation order via the Colonial Secretary. He could not bear his wife to be buried so far away. Her corpse left Australia on 12 September, on a ship (the *Manora*) that sailed via Batavia in Java, and Samuel went part of the way to meet it. Eliza, who had fled the threatening chill of an English winter sixteen months earlier, arrived home at Plymouth Sound on board the Indian steamer *Leonora*, accompanied by Samuel and sixteen-year-old Nellie, in the middle of a November night. The body was transferred at midnight on to a steamer for London. A week later Eliza Plimsoll, who gave up as much for the cause of the sailor as her husband did, was interred in the family vault at Highgate Cemetery in north London, to lie with Samuel's mother Priscilla and his youngest sister Victoria, both of whom she had nursed in her own home. Then the sad event became even sadder: the very day of Eliza's funeral Samuel's favourite sister, Ellen Falding (who had looked after Nellie for months in 1876 when her parents went travelling), died at the age of sixty-five.

Eliza's obituaries were full of praise (and much less equivocal about her merits than her husband's were to be about his). They included one apparently written by Ellen's husband (just before his own bereavement), which gave her credit for 'entering heart and soul into [her husband's] work', 'sharing his solicitude' and 'laudably seconding his efforts for the good of seamen'. She had, said this tribute, 'a love of plain living and high thinking' and valued her husband's life 'more than her own'. She was 'lovely in person, most loving in disposition, a wise counsellor, grateful to excess for that love which none who knew her could withhold, marvellously unselfish; perfect as daughter, sister, wife, mother and friend'.

Eliza's grave is now unmarked. It once took the rectangular form of a casket, but in the late 1990s the memorial was so broken and dilapidated, with the stone smashed in from above, that the Friends of Highgate Cemetery, not knowing that anyone significant lay there, removed the pieces for safety and tidied up. No one now remembers if there was an inscription. But there was something unusual about the location: this was the only private plot in an area of common graves. The site was purchased by Plimsoll in April 1863, when his mother died. At the time, this eastern section of the cemetery had been open for burials for only three years. Then it would have been airy and green and orderly, a hillside haven away from the stink and noise of the City – giving the Victorians the impression that they were already a step nearer to Heaven. Highgate Cemetery, which was run as a private business, offered prestigious burial places to the rich, including the vaults of the resplendent Egyptian Avenue in the western section. But Plimsoll, with Eliza still alive to plan this with him, chose a plot for his family among the poor. He was the only private purchaser to do so.

When Samuel buried Eliza, having brought her body halfway round the world, no doubt he expected that when his time was up he would be beside her till the Last Trump. Together they would lie with the needy, and be resurrected with them. The separation of the last months of Eliza's life was to be compounded by the fact that their mortal remains were never in fact to share the Plimsoll vault.

Something of what Samuel felt about losing Eliza perhaps found its way into a passage he wrote in 1890, appealing (again) for help for sailors' widows from readers who knew what it was to be bereaved. His words evoke an ailing wife more than they suggest a drowned husband.

Can't you remember how you felt – as if a knife had gone through you – when you were first startled by the thought – as day by day your loved one seemed to get no better, and the confidently (hith-erto) expected improvement had not taken place – that perhaps the improvement was never coming at all; that this was to end in

separation – in death? What! is the long and pleasant companionship which has made your life so happy, ending? Are you to lose the
faithful friend, the wise counsellor, the cheerful companion, the
unselfish, the self-sacrificing partner of your life?

His bereavement cost Plimsoll some aimless years. In 1883 he did
not travel, or write, or campaign. In 1884 he found it in himself to
go to India taking Nellie, whose diary of the trip is now lost, and to
America, to see his brother Henry in Brooklyn, though while he
was away there were two more blows. His Irish republican friend
Alexander Sullivan died on 27 October 1884, and on 6 November
Henry Fawcett, another loyal friend who had calmed him down
when disappointment got the better of him in the House, died too.*
Only in 1885 did signs of Plimsoll's old spirit return.

Just as Plimsoll was returning to form, one of his old opponents
came to grief. The career of Thomas Eustace Smith was done for by
scandal. In 1885 the husband of one of his daughters, Virginia
('Nia'), filed for divorce, citing Sir Charles Dilke as co-respondent.
Dilke was not only known to have been the lover of Virginia's
mother Eustacia, but was also now related by marriage to the Smiths:
his brother Ashton had married Nia's sister Margaret in 1876. Nia's
husband Donald Crawford had received a series of anonymous notes
about his wife's infidelity, naming Charles Dilke, who was then both
Gladstone and Chamberlain's favourite as successor to the party
leadership, and therefore likely to be a future Prime Minister. The
court case that followed included revelations of Dilke's affair with
Eustacia, as well as salacious accusations of promiscuity, including a
story of a *ménage à trois* with Nia and a servant girl, Fanny Grey. These
accusations were found not proven by the court, but Dilke now had no
hope of the highest office.

Equally destroyed was Eustace Smith, who resigned his seat in
1885, sold his art collection secretly, handed the running of the
family business to his son and decamped with his wife to a life of

---

* In his lifetime Henry Fawcett did so much for women's rights that in 1886 a commemorative
fountain 'from his grateful countrywomen' was installed in Victoria Embankment Gardens,
where it still stands.

obscure exile in Algeciras in Spain. All sorts of theories have been put forward since about the truth of the scandal, among them the suggestion that Nia Smith was covering up for a different affair, with a Captain Henry Forster, and trying to take revenge on the overbearing mother who had locked her in her room on bread and water when she declined the proposal of Duncan Crawford, the third man she had refused to marry. Whatever the whole truth, Dilke was certainly a womaniser; Eustacia had certainly been his lover; and Eustace Smith could not hold up his head in English society for years. Later even the provenances of the paintings he had owned tended to omit his name from the records. Five years on, he slunk home to England and had a house, High Coxlease, built near Lyndhurst in Hampshire's New Forest, where he was little known. It was decorated with a simple austerity that contrasted with the opulence of Prince's Gate – perhaps following the new modernist Arts and Crafts trend for comparative minimalism, or perhaps a contrite gesture appropriate to the ignominy in which he lived.

After Plimsoll retired from politics and failed to win Liverpool, he had been offered, according to some reports, candidacies in thirty constituencies, at all of which he demurred. In 1885 he changed his mind and stood again for Parliament, this time for Sheffield Central. In the speech that led to his adoption as the Liberal candidate he spoke rousingly in favour of the Criminal Law Amendment Act, which proposed penal servitude for life for rape (notably of poor women by rich men), and against the 'crawling creatures' and 'wooden-headed old gentlemen' in the House of Lords, which he thought needed reform. But his old ally W. C. Leng of the *Sheffield Telegraph* failed to back him, favouring the Tories. For all his admiration of the man, Leng could not agree with Plimsoll's politics and used his newspaper to depict him as a man once free, as a sitting MP, to criticise his own party, but now, as a candidate, gagged. When Plimsoll said that only a fool could trust the Tories to pass beneficial social legislation, Leng portrayed him as a liar. Plimsoll lost the election. (Leng went on to become one of Lord Salisbury's 'Jubilee Knights' in 1887.)

Plimsoll was then a widower of sixty-one, five years out of

Parliament and ten years past his finest hour, a losing candidate at two elections, with no title, one eye, a history of nervous illness, a failing fish market and a good many enemies. It might have seemed that the erstwhile national champion had nothing to look forward to but a slow decline in health and reputation. Then, at the house of a Hull JP, Joseph Armitage Wade, where Charles Morgan Norwood was a regular guest, Samuel Plimsoll found a new lease of life. He met Wade's daughter, Harriet Frankish Wade, a woman twenty-seven years his junior, who had followed his campaign and his conflict with Norwood with admiration (perhaps she disliked Norwood) and was as dedicated to the cause of the sailor as Eliza had been. Young Harriet did not have Eliza's original prettiness, but she had youth and largeness of heart. Later she would give money from her own purse to sailors' widows who came to her door seeking help.

Samuel married Harriet in Hornsea church on 8 October 1885, when he was sixty-one and she was thirty-four. He called his first daughter Eliza. Harriet was only her middle name.

With his second wife, and his children Samuel Junior, Eliza and Ruth,[*] Plimsoll found domestic happiness again, and would be seen strolling contentedly in Hyde Park with his babies and their mother. There were friends again about him. Thomas Brassey, who had argued that 'the law on marine insurance urgently needed reform', lived two doors down, at 24 Park Lane. And although Plimsoll's parliamentary career was over, he had other public roles still to play.

In 1888 Plimsoll met Havelock Wilson, a young radical from Sunderland, a former sailor who had founded the National Amalgamated Sailors' and Firemen's Union of Great Britain and Ireland. Wilson persuaded Plimsoll to become its first president. From offices based near the House of Commons, Plimsoll would dash into the House and harangue members in the lobbies about seamen's issues, pressuring them by showing photographs of a multitude of hands raised at indignation meetings in their own

---

[*] Samuel Richard Cobden Plimsoll (b. 15 December 1887), Eliza Harriet Plimsoll (b. 1 December 1888) and Ruth Wade Plimsoll (b. 17 February 1891).

constituencies. As Wilson told it, 'Plimsoll with the aid of George Howell and others would have as many as three or four Bills concerning ships and seamen before the House at the same time', and would determine to get as many MPs as possible to ballot for a place for these Bills, the MPs representing sea ports being 'our special prey'. Plimsoll would send Wilson 'at a moment's notice' to sea ports to hold the indignation meetings against the member, and Wilson would, as he admitted, 'hold forth on the horrors of the sea and the iniquities of the shipowners'. Plimsoll gave instructions to have a photographer present to take the show of hands in favour of the resolution. The picture would be swiftly developed, and Wilson would rush back to Westminster with it.

> If the meeting was a large and successful one, the old gentleman would almost do an Irish jig in the outer lobby of the House of Commons; then he would send for the unfortunate member, read him a lecture and show him a photograph. In this manner Plimsoll so alarmed many of the members that they became very attentive in their duties when Plimsoll had any shipping matters before, or likely to come before, the House.

Plimsoll and Wilson would plot strategy as they dined at Samuel's favourite restaurant, the still thriving Simpson's on the Strand (just across the road from the scene of his triumph in Exeter Hall). Once Plimsoll considered paying the train fares of all the sailors' widows and orphans in the country and bringing them to demonstrate outside the Houses of Parliament, which would have been illegal and have caused his arrest. But he restrained himself from the extravagance of the gesture.

In 1888 Plimsoll visited his late friend Alexander Sullivan's brother Timothy Daniel Sullivan on his release from Tullamore Jail in County Offaly, where he had been incarcerated for his Home Rule activism. Plimsoll told Sullivan, 'I would rather have seen Mr Balfour [Secretary for Ireland] in there than you,' and was rewarded with this speech from Sullivan to the small crowd of sympathisers:

Gentlemen, this is a famous and beloved and respected Englishman, Mr Plimsoll, who has come down here as a mark of sympathy not merely with myself, but with the Irish people and the Irish cause. Thank God we now have what we had not in other times – as our greatest friends, Englishmen and Englishwomen, with whose aid Irishmen and Irishwomen will free Ireland, and then we may have pleasant and peaceable times between the two countries, with God's help.

Then the object which Plimsoll had pursued for thirty years came about. In the year of Eliza's death the British government and the shipping classification societies had gathered data to publish tables of freeboards to be used as guides to overloading and by the insurers.

For decades one argument against a load line had been that no single rule could apply to the various sizes and conditions of different ships. A voluntary rule of thumb had existed since the 1830s, based on a recommendation by the committee of Lloyd's Register and known as 'Lloyd's Rule': 3 inches of freeboard per foot depth of hold. The less straightforward guide for an average merchant ship was this: a ship of 600–1400 tons, five or six times longer than it was broad, needed a freeboard of 28 per cent of the depth of the hold to make it reasonably safe in heavy weather. It was necessary to find out if such general principles could be applied, with appropriate variations, to any vessel.

At Chamberlain's instigation, a committee chaired by Sir Edward Reed was convened in 1882 to decide 'whether it is now possible to frame general rules concerning freeboard, which will prevent dangerous overloading without unduly interfering with trade'. The Board of Trade asked for the assistance of Lloyd's Register. When the committee met, Benjamin Martell, the Register's chief surveyor, who had worked on this issue since 1873 and consulted with Plimsoll, used research collected by Lloyd's surveyors about the immersion of vessels at various ports to frame tables of freeboard that were suitable for every type of vessel.

While the committee was sitting, Chamberlain pursued a fixed load line, resorting to Plimsollesque rhetoric. As President of the Board of Trade in 1883 he said:

If Mr Plimsoll should choose to engage in another crusade, such as that he was engaged in some years ago, I will undertake to say that he can find facts more heartrending, cases more disgraceful than any of those which he included in his celebrated book which created so great a sensation at the time of its publication. I myself could furnish him with facts which, if they were known and appreciated by the people of this country, would rouse a cry of indignation from one end of the land to the other.

Chamberlain had taken on Plimsoll's mantle, and *Punch* versified: 'There's a sweet little Chamberlain sits up aloft/To keep watch o'er the life of poof Jack . . .' In 1884 Chamberlain delivered a speech three hours and forty-five minutes long in defence of a Bill to prevent overinsurance of ships. After two and a half hours Norwood 'had to be carried out and laid on two chairs in the library'. Such Plimsollesque tactics intensified opposition.

It took until 1885 for the committee to conclude that a fixed load line was possible. Discussions with shipowners and shipbuilders led to modifications of Martell's proposals, which did their best to accommodate variations of length and breadth, but they were at last adopted and issued by the Board of Trade in 1886.

Still a fixed load line was not compulsory. In 1887 another Royal Commission, in which William Harcourt had been instrumental, looked into the safety of sailors. Plimsoll, for all his grumbling, was still breakfasting with Harcourt in 1889, and giving him facts and figures which the latter quoted in his speeches in support of a Merchant Shipping Bill to fix a load line based on Martell's tables.

This long-overdue safety measure finally came into being when the Merchant Shipping Act received Royal Assent on 9 June 1890. To protect British ships against competition, the 1890 Act required all foreign ships leaving British ports to bear the same load lines, and so encouraged the international standardisation that was eventually to come about.

At this moment of climactic success after the long years of agitation, Plimsoll was already engaged with another issue. In 1886 he had gone with Harriet to visit his brother Henry again in Brooklyn and enlisted his help in another cause, which found expression in a new book. It was published in 1890, when Plimsoll was sixty-six. He had planned to take up where *Our Seamen* left off with a second appeal for sailors against all the shortcomings of their working conditions. The new book was described on its title page as 'the fifth chapter' of his appeal, published out of order because of the urgency of the case. The 'fourth chapter', the book revealed, was to have been about provisions on merchant ships. The missing chapters with their unknown subjects were never written, but instead Plimsoll espoused the surprisingly modern cause of conditions for animals transported live on transatlantic ships, and also for the men who crewed them. Henry Plimsoll took photographs of the loading of cattle ships, principally belonging to the London Steamship Company. He also triggered an investigation by one 'Berry' of *The Press* in New York, published on 24 March 1890, which Plimsoll quoted in his book.

If *Our Seamen* was eccentric, *Cattle Ships* (1890) was even more so. It was a mishmash of evidence and surmise, real letters and personal anecdote, of railing and lament. Some sections, perhaps revealing the absent-mindedness of age, appeared more than once. It was also not a book for the squeamish. It described the horrors of live cattle, penned too closely together to lie down, goring and trampling one another to death when a ship heaved in a storm. And it revealed the tortures inflicted upon sick and exhausted beasts to make them stand up again if they had fallen (including pouring petroleum into their ears). Its thesis was that the only advantage of transporting live cattle was that it gave middlemen the chance to pass off foreign meat as British and charge accordingly, while the transport was not only cruel but dangerous, since cattle stalls were routinely built on deck and often, still more hazardously, in a higher layer above the deck.

This book was inspired by a cattle-ship disaster. The steamer *Erin* was lost on 6 January 1890 with its seventy-four crew members. Samuel and Harriet went to meet ten of the sailors' widows, who told their sad stories as they sat around a table in the cold, dimly gaslit and fireless vestry of a congregational chapel near the London docks. *Cattle Ships* contained photographs of the bereaved and, most poignant of all, two long, loving and pious letters from the ship's carpenter, Charles Fields, to his darling wife 'Tetsey' and his three beloved children.

Some of the mothers and widows of men drowned after the *Erin* was lost,
published in Plimsoll's *Cattle Ships*.

God grant me a safe passage home to my pets, and the remainder of
my life shall be consecrated to His service on shore. *No more sea* for
Tetsey's Charlie. Farewell to aching hearts caused through part-
ings . . . My darling I cannot find words to express my love for you.
Pen could not write that. It is engraven on my heart. Your dear face
is ever before me. My thoughts are continually of you.

Charlie, and his brother Harry, never came home. 'Compare such
a man as this,' wrote Plimsoll, the vehemence of old undiminished,
'with the broad-clothed and button-holed moral carrion who swarm
into the City every forenoon from Villadom to scheme the capture
of the savings of industry and thrift by lying prospectuses and bogus
companies, or to send gallant and daring – alas! often too daring –
men to death in their overloaded and unseaworthy ships.'

He was especially indignant at the callous response of the owners
of the *Erin*, who refused to give the sailors' dependants the men's
unpaid earnings.

As in *Our Seamen*, Plimsoll personalised his appeal with anecdotes
about himself, including stories of how he would visit Smithfield
Market at 4 a.m. to learn the difference between meat slaughtered

abroad and at home. (He recommended wearing a cardigan and a light overcoat for the purpose, so that the coat could be removed if you were jostled and smeared by passing carcasses.) He told how he had worked so hard, morning and evening, on this issue that once, having strolled from the docks at Deptford, he fell asleep on the grass of Greenwich Park. And he revealed his own state of mind as he threw himself again into a cause, and how the misery of others revitalised him:

> Deeply depressed by a sense of unaccomplished purpose, weary of work-ing, discouraged by the smallness of the work done, the volume of work to do, I went to Tidal Basin to renew my sympathy with contact with the suffering and the helpless ... and, seeing around me those weeping women, I felt weariness fall off me, purpose renewed, hope inspired, courage fortified; and as at midnight we [Samuel and Harriet] were walking on the platform at Bishopsgate Station on our return, with feet cold as lead, but hearts on fire, I wished I could then have spoken my mind to the callous men whose greed causes this suffering, for I would have poured upon them such a torrent of fiery indignation and blazing scorn as would have caused sleep to depart from their eyelids ...

As *The Times* commented, 'serene impartiality of judgement' was not among Plimsoll's most conspicuous characteristics.

In 1891 Plimsoll took this cause to the other side of the transatlantic cattle trade, finding a mixed reception on his tour of North America. He went to Toronto, Quebec and Montreal, where he attended a three-day investigation. It ended with an angry voice from the floor protesting that Plimsoll wished to annihilate the Canadian beef trade, an ill-treatment of a colony that could only lead to 'independence or annexation'. Three days later he addressed the Auditorium in Chicago, to a warmer reception. For all his efforts, cruelty to transported animals remained an issue long after the publication of his book.*

---

* This, for instance, is from the Irish Ministry of Agriculture in 1995: 'No person shall transport animals by sea, air, road or rail, or cause or permit animals to be so transported, in such a way as is likely to cause injury or unnecessary suffering to the animal.' And: 'Animals shall be provided with adequate space to stand in their natural position and, when necessary, with partitions to pro-tect the animals from motion of the means of transport. Unless special conditions for the protection of animals require otherwise, room to lie down shall be provided.'

Plimsoll's radical ally Havelock Wilson managed to get himself arrested for 'unlawful assembly and riot' and imprisoned for six months in Cardiff during the seamen's strike of 1891, at which he talked imported labourers from Newcastle out of strike-breaking. Plimsoll visited him twice in prison and was there, sharing a carriage with Sir Charles Dilke (undeterred by scandal) and accompanied by twenty thousand supporters, when Wilson came out of jail. He found himself shaking hands with various of Wilson's fellow inmates.

(This was not the first time Plimsoll had had contact with criminals. The notorious burglar and murderer Charles Peace, who was hanged in 1879, met Plimsoll in the House of Commons in 1877 to show the MP his patented design for an invention for raising sunken vessels by filling them with gas. At the time Peace was wanted for murder, but was living under another name, John Thompson, as a respectable gentleman in Peckham, while spending his nights breaking into other people's houses – one of which was, as it happens, Lord Shaftesbury's Wandsworth home. Fortunately Plimsoll declined to introduce Peace and his co-inventor Henry Brion to the head of the Admiralty as requested and, perhaps suspecting that he was untrustworthy, would have nothing to do with him.)

The reception breakfast for Wilson also marked Plimsoll's resignation from the presidency of the seamen's union, 'on the ground that the office he has held neither confers authority nor gives power'.

It was not long before Wilson was elected to Parliament, with the help of a deposit from Plimsoll, and as MP for Middlesbrough he became a spokesman in the Commons for Plimsoll, who could only watch proceedings from the Strangers' Gallery.

This did not stop him trying to interfere. Close to his heart now was the issue of sailors' appalling provisions, which included meat rejected by butchers as unfit but still sent to sea. Plimsoll had done much to promote the Seamen's Inspection of Provisions Bill, and had spent some two thousand pounds doing so outside the House. Now he watched as, in a painful reprise of July 1875, the government dropped the Bill at the end of the summer session. Horrified, he ran from the House, dragging Wilson with him, hailed a cab to go to St Pancras and took a train to Chamberlain's home in Birmingham without so much as a toothbrush. Chamberlain was not at home when Wilson and Plimsoll arrived; they were obliged to stay overnight at a hotel and call again at 7 a.m., when Plimsoll urged that the Bill should be put back on the books. Chamberlain, irritable in his dressing gown, said at first there was nothing he could do. But he succumbed eventually, perhaps because Plimsoll offered, if the Bill went through, to issue a manifesto urging the working class to support Chamberlain's Unionist Party at the next election. Chamberlain sent a telegram to Arthur Balfour, by then Leader of the House of Commons, the Bill reappeared on the order paper and it was passed. Plimsoll wrote the manifesto, which the Tories circulated.

The strength of Plimsoll's opinions did not wane. He continued, throughout 1891, to be vociferous about the iniquities of the cattle trade. He gave inspiring talks to the young, as at the YMCI in Regent Street in London. He went into print, in May in the *Nineteenth Century Review*, arguing against US President William McKinley's protectionism. He went on writing about sailors' victuals to the press for years. And in January 1892 he gave evidence before a Royal Labour Commission about over-insurance and provisions for sailors, and made the case, again, against deckloading. Many of the arguments and much of the controversy of the 1870s were revisited.

Then, in 1892, Samuel Plimsoll was found to be diabetic. In those days, before insulin (which was not discovered until 1921), the only treatments were opium and a diet – either, according to opinion, over-eating or starvation. He nominally retired from public life and moved to Folkestone, where his homes, first at 31 Clifton Gardens and then at 35 Augusta Gardens, were a short walk from the sea, by a famously picturesque stretch of English coast, the Leas. Here wooded slopes descend from an elegant promenade to small, curving beaches, and it is reminiscent, when the weather is good, of the French Riviera.

Plimsoll's reclusiveness did not last long. In 1894 he sat on a Royal Commission to investigate labour relations, in the wake of a series of traumatic strikes, including the 1889 Dock Strike and the 1891 Seamen's Strike, and consider what legislation if any might help.* Its

---

* On this Commission, for the first time ever, four women served as assistant commissioners. They were praised for their efficiency. The Commission was also served by twenty-seven clerks, all but six of them women. One of these subsequently sued for unfair dismissal.

secretary, Geoffrey Drage, published a book, *The Unemployed*, based on the Commission's findings, which – revisiting an old battleground of Plimsoll's – caused controversy by being critical of the Board of Trade.

In 1894, when his father was seventy, Plimsoll's fourth child, Sidney Kingsley Cox Plimsoll, was born. He lived only four months, and died of seven days' colic followed by convulsions. Despite this grief of his own, Plimsoll was supportive of old allies to the last. His friend George Howell had been MP for North East Bethnal Green from 1885 until he was defeated in 1895, during which time he was a mouthpiece for Plimsoll in the House. In 1895 he was replaced by an Indian barrister and journalist, Mancerjee Merwanjee Bhownaggree, and took it ill. 'After ten years' hard labour in Parliament, I was kicked out by a black man, a stranger from India, one not known in the constituency or in public life,' complained Howell grudgingly, and in terms that were all of a piece with widespread contemporary assumptions about the superiority of the white man. Howell's only income had been from journalism and he spent fifteen years of retirement in poor health and obscurity, suffering initially from the increasing alcoholism of his wife, who died in 1897. An appeal for a civil list pension for Howell was denied but his closest friend, Applegarth, organised a testimonial fund in his honour. Plimsoll, Harcourt and Rothschild contributed and £1650 was raised for an annuity. Howell's papers were given to the Bishopsgate Institute at the suggestion of its librarian, and in 1906 he was finally awarded a civil list pension of £50 a year 'in recognition of his merits as a writer upon labour questions'. When he died, on 16 September 1910, *The Times*, with the awful dismissiveness of a medium dedicated to novelty, said, 'Mr Howell, who was in his 78th year, was a familiar figure in Labour politics 20 years ago.'

In March 1896 it made the news not just at home but in the papers of small-town America that Plimsoll was seriously ill. He made his will, taking particular care to allocate the popular tributes he had received to his children. Those that honoured Eliza were given to Nellie. Then he rallied and was ready to work again.

The Americans took Samuel Plimsoll to their hearts and were in his later life much less cynical about him than his compatriots. He found in their affection the possibility of making another difference to history – one little acknowledged, but which had enormous international consequences. As the *Middletown Daily Argus* in New York reported his ambitious plan on 27 June 1896: 'Samuel Plimsoll, in whose honour the safety load line of British ships is called "The Plimsoll Mark" has just arrived in New York with the avowed intention of studying and trying to cure America's alleged dislike of England. Plimsoll deprecates the so-called prejudice and says he believes it starts among schoolchildren who gather it from their history books. His object is to reform such books, cutting out the unkind allusions to the mother country.'

The Americans had better reason than we generally now acknowledge to hate Britain. The war of 1812–14 with the British Empire was only a lifetime in the past, and among the many brutalities of that campaign was the burning by British troops of the White House and all the government buildings in Washington. Animosity towards Britain had lasted as a powerful force in American politics into the 1880s. As John E. Moser, an American academic specialising in the field, pointed out in a 2002 lecture, this hostility was a feature of all parties in America in the late nineteenth century and 'the Populist Party, which formed in the 1880s [disbanding in 1896] . . . represented the high water mark of anglophobia in the United States. The party dedicated itself to ridding the country of British influence, referring to England as a "monster" that had "seized upon the fresh energy of America and is steadily fixing its fangs into our social life."'

In 1896 this antagonism made the Americans threaten the British over a disputed border in Venezuela. Throughout the 1890s it was not by any means a matter of course that in international politics the US and Britain would be on the same side.

Nevertheless, in towns across America, the response to Plimsoll was sympathetic. Widely syndicated in local papers from the *Fort Wayne Sentinel* in Indiana to the *Steubenville Daily Herald* in Ohio was a piece by Franklin Price that said: 'If all Englishmen were like Samuel Plimsoll, he would not have the slightest difficulty in achieving his object, and if all Americans were as good as he, this would be a great and glorious nation. A great big heart has Mr Plimsoll –

a heart that beats for all humanity. You know this as soon as you have seen the kindly, benevolent way in which he beams through his glasses at the world.'

With the help of Nellie, Plimsoll gathered all the references he could find to Americans in British textbooks, and compared them with references to the British in American textbooks, pointing out to the US Commissioner for Education, William T. Harris, that the hostility was all one-way. In 1896, under the Democratic presidency of Grover Cleveland, this pressure secured the withdrawal of anti-British history books from American day schools. Thus Samuel Plimsoll can be credited as the father of the Special Relationship. By the twentieth century, Americans who intervened in the First World War belonged to a generation that had grown up without learning an antipathy to Britain in the classroom.

Plimsoll was incapable of giving up. In 1897 he was campaigning to prevent 'a landing of the American Armada of trusts [conglomerates] upon British shores', alarmed by the economic power they wielded, and by the Americanisation of the world.

This prescient cause was to be Plimsoll's last. At the end of May 1898, at seventy-four, he became seriously ill. By 1 June it was news even in American regional newspapers that he was dying. He took a little nourishment with difficulty, declined a second medical opinion, and went into a coma. One of his last wishes had been to ask his family to sing him Charles Wesley's hymn 'Jesu, lover of my soul', which contains words of maritime resonance: 'While the tempest still is high:/Hide me, O my Saviour, hide,/Till the storm of life be past!' Nellie was with him when the end came on 3 June.

She registered the death that day. Describing the informant, the registrar wrote half a word – 'Daug' – on the death certificate, before being corrected, crossing this out, and writing 'Great Niece' instead. Nellie's adoption, it seems, was never formalised. The cause of Samuel's death, according to the certificate, was diabetes and albuminuria,* with '6 years chill followed by coma, 4 days 12 hours'.

---

* Albuminuria (or protein in the urine) is a symptom of diabetic kidney damage.

Shortly after Plimsoll's death all the ships' flags in Folkestone harbour flew at half mast. On the day of his funeral a crew of sailors from vessels in the harbour arrived at Plimsoll's home in Augusta Gardens and removed the horses from the hearse. They drew the coffin several miles to the churchyard themselves. The service was conducted 'on a breezy hillside in sight of the sea' by the Reverend John Solloway of York, husband of Plimsoll's niece Alice, with the help of the local congregational minister. Harriet, Nellie, young Eliza and Ruth were the chief mourners, along with members of Harriet's family and Plimsoll's sister, Mary, who had been with his first wife when she died. Several other churchmen and representatives of sailors' organisations were present. Samuel Jr was too ill to attend his father's funeral.

It was reported, with the sunshine, and corn waving on the hillside, the laburnum and hawthorn blossom, to be 'a glorious scene'. One old salt remarked: 'He is now beneath the load-line.' Among the wreaths were some from sailors' societies, and both the hymns used metaphors of storms at sea. One was the Wesley hymn; the other – 'O God our help in ages past,/Our hope for years to come/Our shelter from the stormy blast/And our eternal home' – Isaac Watts's eighteenth-century composition. The hymn now known as 'The Sailor's Hymn', with the chorus 'for those in peril on the sea', written by William Whiting in 1861, was not used, although it was quoted and sung by Plimsoll in his lifetime.

Plimsoll's obituary in *The Times* was lukewarm. It described him as 'One whose sole stock-in-trade was to become fervidly indignant on hearsay evidence' and said:

> He leaves behind him a reputation for sincere attachment to a cause which many wiser men may envy. We forget his absurdities, we draw a veil over his lack of self-control, we almost pardon his exaggerations (which continued to the end), and his recklessness of accusation, when we remember that the evil he attacked was real and gigantic, and that the ferocity of his attack was the outpouring of the indignation of a sincere, if not always well-regulated mind.

Seamen felt there was less to forgive. Harriet, writing a thank-you letter for a vote of sympathy from the sailors' union, and acknowledging that 'thousands have mourned with us', called Samuel 'the kindest and best of husbands and fathers, a most beautiful Christian example to all in his home'. In losing him, she wrote, 'the seamen have lost a true friend. To the last he took the warmest interest in all that concerned them and his heart burnt within him, as of old, when he heard of any case of wrong or injustice.'

To a branch of the union she wrote: 'If the Plimsoll mark were ever taken from you, it would take years of hard work to gain it again, and hundreds of valuable lives would be lost. I cannot think that the sailors of Great Britain will ever allow their chief safeguard to be taken from them.'

Yet, from the moment the load line was fixed, it was under threat.

10

THE LEGACY

The law of 1890 had given the Board of Trade the power to alter the freeboard without reference to Parliament. Even when the load line was fixed, Plimsoll's legacy was still not safe from the pressure to increase profits. The Plimsoll mark was graded from 'Tropical Fresh' at the top for the calm waters of rivers near the equator, through 'Fresh', 'Summer' and 'Winter', down to 'Winter North Atlantic' for the stormiest ocean routes between October and March which needed the greatest safety margin.* One way of eroding the efficacy of the load line was to adjust, qualify or even do away with some of these levels. In 1896, to the chagrin of the grain shippers of New York, the Board of Trade dictated that the Plimsoll mark for Winter North Atlantic on ships sailing south of Baltimore could be higher than for destinations north of the city. At the same time, the Board conceded that Plimsoll was 'undoubtedly entitled to the gratitude of sailors the world over'.

Shippers argued that the transatlantic route to all US East Coast ports was the same. So, in December 1898, mere months after the death of Samuel Plimsoll, the Board of Trade abolished the Winter North Atlantic mark altogether for vessels more than 330 feet long.

---

* Ships carrying timber sometimes have the letter L before the initials of the levels, indicating 'lumber'.

They could now sail at a depth of loading previously considered safe only in summer. Smaller vessels too had a reduced the margin of safety. A medium-sized vessel (7000–8000 tons) could carry 150 tons more cargo. In the first three months after this change in the legislation, nine steamers were reported missing in the Atlantic.

In 1906 a committee of the Board of Trade met quietly to consider whether the Winter North Atlantic load line might be abolished for all ships, and announced another adjustment of the mark of 'six to twelve inches'. The change was authorised by the future Prime Minister David Lloyd George, then President of the Board of Trade. It increased the potential load of cargo ships by 5 per cent.

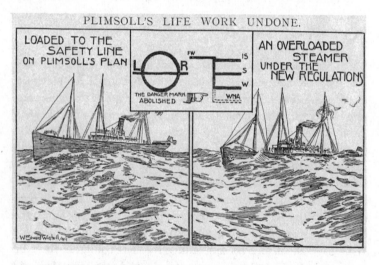

'The danger mark abolished'. (From Hopkins, *Altering Plimsoll's Mark*)

At last the erosion of the load line was accompanied by a resurgence of the anger that Plimsoll had aroused. Havelock Wilson of the Seamen's Union – who always had his late friend Samuel Plimsoll's picture over his bed – was indignant and raised questions in the House. He was obliged to go on doing so through 1907 and 1908 without any opportunity being given for the change to be reconsidered by Parliament. Randolph Churchill remarked of the quiet alteration: 'As the matter was one purely for technical experts, it was not considered necessary to consult representatives of officers or seamen with regard to it.'

Lloyd George's fond biographer E. T. Raymond in 1922 had a favourable view of the adjustment of the load line.

> Mr George called into consultation the shipowners and the seamen's representatives . . . From the owners' point of view the load-line put British ships at a disadvantage; foreign vessels, using our ports, were enabled, while our own ships were forbidden, to carry dangerously heavy cargoes, and could thus underbid in freights. Mr George's measure, it was claimed, put the matter right without sacrificing the interests of the seaman. The British load-line was slightly modified, but no foreign vessel was allowed to enter our ports without conforming to this amended standard. All the 'interests concerned' were satisfied. The safety of the sailor was not jeopardised, the owner was given protection against the foreigner, the humanitarian could even rejoice that sailors under other flags were benefited. Thus it was natural that Mr George should receive general congratulation.

The truth was he also received a good deal of condemnation. It was rash to assert that the safety of the sailor was not jeopardised, and to argue in favour of keeping pace with foreign ships that were permitted to carry 'dangerously heavy cargoes'. The argument about foreign competition was the same one that had been used against the load line ever since the birth of the idea.

Seven years of protest followed Lloyd George's adjustment, the agitation reaching a head in 1913. Matters were exacerbated by the fact that although the amended load level was intended to apply only to new ships, increasingly old ships took advantage of it as well. Among the casualties that resulted was the *North Briton*, a ship whose freeboard, formerly one foot four inches, had been reduced to a lamentable ten inches in 1906. Twenty sailors drowned when it was lost off Ushant on 4 March 1912. The only survivor, the boatswain, gave 'insufficient freeboard' as the reason. The *Daily Mail* reported that 'When her condition was hopeless, the crew . . . stayed together on the deck with their pipes in their mouths, silently, calmly and dauntlessly facing death. Without a murmur or a cry they perished in the sea. Their lives were sacrificed to 130 tons additional freight.'

There was general pressure to reconsider the revised load line tables, and the reprise of Plimsoll's campaign led to the establishment of a Load Line Committee in 1912 to decide whether Plimsoll's mark should be reinstated. Contrary to the recommendations of the 1890s, it included no representatives of sailors. Two vehement treatises followed, arguing against Lloyd George's measure. One was *Altering Plimsoll's Mark* (1913) by Father Charles Hopkins, then chaplain to the mercantile marine and a trustee of the seamen's union. He wrote: 'The great work for humanity which has made the name of Plimsoll world-renowned and saved the lives of thousands, if not millions, of British seamen, has been undone by the stroke of a pen. "Plimsoll's mark", which in every harbour of the world is the synonym for safety and the stamp of wise legislation, has now by the recent action of the Board of Trade lost all its significance and value.'

The second treatise, entitled with less restraint, was *The Murdering of British Seamen by Lloyd George, the Liberal Cabinet and the Board of Trade*. This was the transcript of an address, in the Memorial Hall in Farringdon Street, London, in April 1913, to the British Socialist Party (at a time when Lloyd George was Chancellor of the Exchequer and embroiled in a shares scandal*). The speech was delivered by Henry Mayers Hyndman, the cricket-playing stockbroker and improbable socialist leader who founded the Social Democratic Federation, forerunner of the Communist Party. Influenced by Marx, he had been active in the Dock Strike of 1889, was one of the first proponents of an eight-hour day, formerly edited the *International Review* and had taken it upon himself to be a Plimsoll for his own time.

In his Farringdon Street speech, and his pamphlet, Hyndman said:

The life of the ordinary seaman or fireman is very hard even on a well-laden vessel. But when this occurs on an overladen vessel, the anxiety,

---

* Lloyd George was accused of profiting from government policy by buying shares in the Marconi company just before Parliament granted it a contract to build a chain of wireless stations.

horror, trouble of it, is something quite terrible ... This horror got
hold of Plimsoll. I met him once, and I know the man was full of this
one subject ... He brought it forward in the House of Commons, and,
as you know, strode forward when the members rejected his measure,
damned them all – very bad language, but very bad people ...

Hyndman's own language was no less forceful: he spoke of
'cowardice and treachery' in the House of Commons, and of 'official murdering'. He also voiced his anger in Trafalgar Square and
lamented that his agitation had prompted only feeble debate in the
House. His pamphlet argued that the raising of the load line had an
impact not only on sailors' safety, but on their employment. An extra
twenty million pounds' worth of cargo could be transported under
the new regulations without using any more ships: sailors stood idle
in the docks while those who were employed faced greater risks.
Angry correspondence followed between the British Socialist Party
and the Board of Trade. History repeated itself.

The 1912 committee concluded in 1915 that no change was necessary. There is still no Winter North Atlantic level for vessels over
330 feet, but the level does exist for smaller ships.

The world came round to the measure in the end, but not without resistance in some quarters. Germany adopted a load line in
1908, France in 1909, and Holland in 1910. American vessels continued to be loaded according to the old formula of three inches of
freeboard per foot of depth of hold until 1917, when the US
Shipping Board required ships to follow the British Board of Trade's
freeboard tables, which took account of the variables that always
handicapped the notion of a load line: structural strength; compart-
mentalisation, or number of bulwarks dividing the ship; hull form,
fullness and length and the nature of the cargo, some being more
buoyant than others. (All these factors affected a ship's 'reserve buoyancy' – or volume of the watertight portion above the waterline.)

Load line legislation was introduced to Congress in the United
States in 1920 and failed. Then in 1929 the US adopted the Load
Line Act for international voyages. On 5 July 1930 an international
convention providing for a fixed Plimsoll line was signed in London
by thirty nations. In 1931 an American commentator remarked: 'I feel

sure that Samuel Plimsoll must have looked down with a twinkle in his eye upon the conference in London which accomplished that result and he must have been filled with glee when the President of the United States ratified the convention on May 1 of this year.'

In 1935 the Americans went further and passed a Load Line Act making the Plimsoll line compulsory for domestic trade. Over the subsequent years other nations adopted the line. In 1966 sixty nations from Malta to Nicaragua that already used the line agreed a revised measure adopted by the International Maritime Organisation to meet new conditions at sea. Larger ships could load somewhat more deeply than the existing standard, but smaller ships had the load line lowered. (The load line now reveals the nationality of ships; the initials at each end of the central line stand for each country's shipping registry: in Britain this was LR for Lloyd's Register; in France BV for Bureau Veritas; in Germany GL for Germanischer Lloyd; in the US, AB for American Bureau of Shipping, and so on.)

Since the first convention in 1930 the load line regulations have been continually adapted to accommodate changes in ship design. In 1988 there was a revised Load Lines Protocol (amended in 1995 and 2003); the rules now in place were established in January 2005.

Plimsoll's literal legacy was a fortune of £40,000, left to his wife and children. He also left £100 'in recognition of his integrity and devoted service' to Russell Spencer, who had managed Plimsoll's coal business while his attention was elsewhere. Plimsoll's descendants went on to play their parts in history in other ways, several of them manifesting an interest in social welfare. Samuel Jr became an administrator at the Middlesex Hospital, as well as a poet and the author of a novel (using the *nom de plume* Gabriel Wade) and a translator (from French). He was awarded two Military Crosses for heroism in France and Belgium during the First World War. One of his daughters, Enid Barbara, was in the Philippines in 1941 (where her husband, Charles Agnew, worked for Shell) when the Japanese arrived, and became a prisoner of war; she weighed six stones when she was released, and although she survived, the physical damage contributed to her early death in 1971. Her sister Sally (Mrs Shaw), had her grandfather's empathy with the poor and became a city councillor for a 'slum' ward in Manchester, with a special interest in education.

Of Samuel Sr's other daughters, Eliza studied at Oxford, married J. H. Rose, a professor of Greek, lived in St Andrew's in Scotland and had seven children, before dying at forty-nine. Ruth took a medical degree and, though once engaged to an American Rhodes scholar at Balliol, never married, but served in maternity and child welfare clinics around England, including in Derby and London, where her father had lived. When Nellie was forty she met the Reverend C. E. Raven at the house of her cousin Alice in York, and married him; she lived a long, childless life as the wife of a school chaplain in Essex (at Bancroft's School) and died at the age of ninety-one.

Meanwhile Plimsoll's mark emerged as the logo of the London Underground. Until 1907 stations were labelled by a solid red circle, with a horizontal band bearing the name, a coincidental echo of the mark. Frank Pick, the traffic development officer whose belief in the importance of good design led the architectural historian Nikolaus Pevsner to praise him as a great patron of the arts, was responsible for turning this echo into a direct imitation of the Plimsoll mark, which he cited as an inspiration. The logo was eventually registered as a trademark for London Transport in 1918. This shape, variously called the eye, disc, pancake, bullseye and roundel, also suggested other associations: a 1939 poster by Man Ray, for instance, identified its similarity to a ringed planet or a flying saucer.

While his mark lived on and thrived, Plimsoll's reputation in posterity waxed and waned. In his later life, as in all his career, he had continued to be both idolised and vilified. In 1890 he was held up as an example for schoolboys to emulate by A(lexander) H(ay) Japp in his *Good Men and True: Biographies of Workers in the Fields of Beneficence and Benevolence*. Japp was unequivocal about his merit:

> The tricks of the trade of shipowning were very well known before
> Mr Plimsoll emerged prominently into public view . . . [but] general
> statements somehow made no more impression on the public mind
> than the blow of a baby's hand on a feather pillow. It seems to yield
> easily to the impact, but no lasting impression is produced . . . If you

are to do any good in a case where vested interests are so directly involved, you must come to very close quarters indeed. The scattered rays of the sun, hardly felt on a May-day, concentrated through a glass, will burn a whole right through broadcloth. You want a powerfully concentrating glass to burn into the public mind and conscience. Such a glass was found in Mr Plimsoll's mind and inflexible purpose.

The policy of the peccant shipowners was to give the impression that Mr Plimsoll was a hare-brained enthusiast, a notoriety-hunter, a sensation-monger, and unreliable man; that he knew nothing practically of the subject he talked about, and that his object was simply to gain public notice. He took the best way to stop their mouths. He showed that, as regards knowledge of facts, he had mastered that with which he dealt; that he was fully alive to the difficulties in the way; and that he did not come forward declaiming against an evil for which he was not able to provide some practical remedy. He showed, and satisfactorily showed, that compulsory survey and prevention of overloading, by the adoption of a load-line, if applied to all merchant ships, would result in the saving of all the lives proved to have been lost from these causes . . .

The indomitable and persistent effort, the complete indifference to all personal interests and considerations, which Mr Plimsoll has shown, certainly entitle him to be regarded as one of the devoted philanthropists and reformers of our time.

The novelist Joseph Conrad was not so enthusiastic about Plimsoll. He gives him an unflattering walk-on part as an 'old coon' who deserves a ducking in *The Nigger of the Narcissus*, published, before Plimsoll's death, in 1897. Conrad, who came to England in 1878 and spent twenty years at sea himself, might have been expected to sympathise with the cause. But lame Knowles with the unwashed face, who 'had the distinction of being the dirty man of the forecastle', an apparently down-to-earth, though not absolutely reliable, narrator, regales his crewmates with the following story:

I mind I once seed in Cardiff the crew of an overloaded ship – leastways she weren't overloaded, only a fatherly old gentleman with a white beard and an umbreller came along the quay and talked to the hands. Said as how it was crool hard to be drownded in winter just for the sake of a few pounds more for the owner – he said. Nearly cried over them – he did; and he had a square mainsail coat, and a gaff-topsail hat too – all proper. So they chaps they said they wouldn't go to be drownded in winter – depending upon that 'ere Plimsoll man to see 'em through the court. They thought to have a bloomin' lark and two or three days' spree. And the beak giv 'em six weeks – coss the ship warn't overloaded. Anyways they made it out in court that she wasn't. There wasn't one overloaded ship in Penarth Dock at all. 'Pears that old coon he was only on pay and allowance from some kind people, under orders to look for overloaded ships, and he couldn't see no further than the length of his umbreller. Some of us in the boarding-house, where I live when I'm looking for a ship in Cardiff, stood by to duck that old weeping spunger in the dock. We kept a good look-out, too – but he topped his boom directly he was outside the court . . . Yes. They got six weeks' hard . . .

On another occasion Conrad criticised Plimsoll's methods. On 29 May 1914 a Canadian Pacific liner, the *Empress of Ireland*, collided in the St Lawrence with a Norwegian collier, the *Storstad*. Of the 1476 people on board the *Empress*, 1024 were drowned. The death toll was the worst yet on a passenger ship, only ever to be exceeded by the *Titanic*. On 10 June Conrad had a letter published in the *Daily Express*. He recommended, in the spirit of Samuel Plimsoll, that all seagoing ships should have a buffer or stern-fender. Some objected to his suggestion. In the ensuing correspondence Conrad said in a letter to the editor of the *Globe*:

I remember Mr Plimsoll's load line campaign which saved so many sailors' lives. It was based on a very outrageous assumption. If one were to believe the statements he (and even more his followers) made in the course of their propaganda every second British shipowner was a heartless ruffian ready to send men to their death for the sake of the extra freight – two hundred pounds or thereabouts. How much indignation (and pain which had to [be] gulped down before the state of the then public feeling) have those statements caused.

Conrad may have had a character say that Plimsoll was a weeping sponger who worked sailors up into misguided rebellion, and may have accused him of an 'outrageous assumption', but in some ways Plimsoll and Conrad were kindred spirits. Conrad also responded to shipwrecks with an impulse to find ways to protect those on board. In his essay 'The Titanic Inquiry' he wrote that the owners who scorned to provide enough lifeboats on the *Titanic* disclosed 'the psychology of commercial undertakings. It is the same psychology which fifty or so years ago, before Samuel Plimsoll uplifted his voice, sent overloaded ships to sea. "Why shouldn't we cram in as much cargo as our ships will hold? Look how few, how very few of them get lost, after all."'

In 1928 Havelock Wilson, at the age of seventy, asked his friend Captain Edward Tupper, later his successor as president of the seamen's union, to search for the grave of a 'forgotten man'. That man was Samuel Plimsoll, thirty years buried 'in some churchyard on the Kentish coast'. Tupper's quest ended with a stone cross not far from the medieval north wall of picturesque St Martin's Church at Cheriton, near Folkestone. The grave was 'completely overgrown and neglected', like Plimsoll's reputation. Tupper cleared away the green moss from the stone, revealing a familiar circle with a line through it.

Today, the grave, once in open ground, lies under a plane tree, and is only somewhat unkempt. The three-tiered plinth of the cross is enduringly inset, under the Plimsoll mark, with capitals that read:

SAMUEL PLIMSOLL
THE SAILORS FRIEND
BORN AT BRISTOL FEB 10TH 1824
DIED AT FOLKESTONE JUNE 3RD 1898
HE GIVETH HIS BELOVED SLEEP

LORD MY STRENGTH AND MY REDEEMER

In early June, the anniversary of Plimsoll's death, the grave of the forgotten man sits in a blue haze of forget-me-nots.

The grave that was overgrown in 1928 was still neatly kept in 1911,

Plimsoll's grave at St Martin's Church, Cheriton, Kent, the cross
carved with a Plimsoll mark. (*author*)

as shown in a photograph from the *Home Counties Magazine* of that
year. But this did not guarantee that Plimsoll was appreciated everywhere. By the time Samuel Plimsoll Jr went up to Balliol College,
Oxford, before the First World War, the boy was looked down upon
by fellow undergraduates as a social inferior. His family was not considered to be distinguished. A father who had once been a national
hero counted for little compared to rigorous criteria of pedigree.

Sailors remembered Plimsoll longest: his granddaughter Sally
Shaw recalls that as a child in the 1930s she had an enthusiasm for
ships, and that her father, by then Captain Plimsoll, would take her
visiting docks, where the name was an instant passport into any
bridge or engine room.

And it had been sailors who paid for a memorial to Samuel
Plimsoll in the 1920s, when Edward Tupper, at Havelock Wilson's
instigation, commissioned the monument to him that now stands in

London, overlooking the Thames and in sight of the House of Commons, between Westminster Bridge and Charing Cross on Joseph Bazalgette's Victoria Embankment. The site, allocated by the Board of Works, was where Plimsoll had persuaded the Duke of Buccleuch to open a stretch of garden to the public, and had fought to stop ventilation holes from the Underground from punctuating it. The sculptor was Ferdinand Victor Blundstone. Plimsoll's memorial bears, in bronze on a granite base, a life-size barefoot sailor in a knitted jersey and a scantily clad figure of Justice with a sword, both carrying laurel wreaths; a plaque adorned with a sailing ship; and a bust of Plimsoll, in a woollen waistcoat, based on the photograph that hung over Havelock Wilson's bed. The iron railings beside the monument were cast to include Plimsoll marks and, charmingly, seahorses. Wilson died before the memorial was finished, but it was unveiled on 21 August 1929, in the presence of representatives of government, shipowners and seamen, of Havelock Wilson's widow and children, and of Plimsoll's son, who was (along with Nellie)

Justice and the sailor: the unveiling of F. V. Blundstone's Plimsoll memorial, Victoria Embankment, 21 August 1929. (*Illustrated London News*)

not convinced of the bust's likeness to their father. He spoke of his father's tireless energy and his sacrifices. The unveiling was performed by Walter Runciman, a shipowner and former sailor, who had been Plimsoll's friend. He said: 'It was only at long intervals that men of Plimsoll's massive gifts were brought into existence. He never aimed at rhetoric, but wherever he saw the power of wrongs he took a fierce determination to destroy it. This he did by a rugged, fearless eloquence, and roused public opinion into wrath on his side.'

Blundstone's work was the first memorial ever erected to Plimsoll, thirty years after his death. Tupper wrote:

> Thus there stands upon Thames bank a monument to a great man who loved Seamen, and it stands there because another great man who loved Seamen [Wilson] could not bear the neglect his country had apportioned to Samuel Plimsoll. The Plimsoll mark, painted on the sides of every ship afloat, is a boon, indirectly, to all humanity; but it was the British Seamen who paid honour to the creator of it – every penny of the cost of the Plimsoll Memorial was borne by the National Union of Seamen.

Thereafter the twentieth century generally appreciated Plimsoll. In 1927 Derby had got its Plimsoll Street on a newly built estate, adding to the streets that had been named after Plimsoll in his lifetime – including the two in London,* one in Kidderminster, and three in Nottingham. He was also commemorated in street names in Hull, Birmingham, Liverpool, Penrith, Folkestone, Wakefield and Bristol. A plaque (recently stolen) was placed by the Society of Merchant Venturers on the site of Plimsoll's birthplace in Bristol – the house itself had been demolished in 1868; the bronze tablet was unveiled in a dense fog on 20 December 1935. (Bristol also still has a plaque with a brief biography in its Floating Harbour,

---

* Plimsoll Road in Islington, London, formerly Templeton Road (which included Albion Terrace, Florence Terrace and Lorne Terrace), was renamed in 1881 in a clutch of streets named in tribute to philanthropic Victorian politicians, also including Romilly, who was responsible for the abolition of the capital punishment of hanging, drawing and quartering.

near the Neptune Statue.*) References in novels around this time were sympathetic, as in this one from Hugh Walpole's *Vanessa* (1933), in which the irony is all in Plimsoll's favour: 'They [the stuffy and conservative Herries family] knew, they had always known, that Adam Paris failed at anything that he tried. What could you expect of a fellow who had once been a Chartist and approved of these Trades Unions, was always on the wrong side, against Disraeli, in favour of tiresome agitators like Mr Plimsoll? (They disliked any and every agitator. They disapproved of agitation.)'

By the mid-twentieth century Plimsoll had become a worthy legend taught to schoolchildren, and coffin-ships were part of the national heritage of stories, alongside such unexamined snippets of Victorian history as Florence Nightingale's lamp and the difficulty of amusing Queen Victoria. Joan Aiken's pseudo-Victorian children's novel *The Wolves of Willoughby Chase*, for instance, published in 1962, had the heroine's parents come back from the dead after being shipwrecked victims of a villain's overinsured coffin-ship.

But Plimsoll was not immune from denigration. R. H. Thornton's *British Shipping* (1939) took the cynical line that never entirely died out:

> Most of us have been brought up to believe that an enlightened and benevolent gentleman, named Samuel Plimsoll, fought a single-handed and triumphant battle with an industry ruthlessly exploited by human greed. Like most nursery stories, it suffers from a disarming simplicity which is seldom true to life. The facts are that throughout the whole period from 1850 to 1906 Parliament was actively concerned with the improvement of conditions in the mercantile marine and scarcely a year passed in which a Commission was not sitting or

---

* A bronze plaque on the fourth bench from the cascade on the western end of the Floating Harbour reads, in raised Roman capitals: 'SAMUEL PLIMSOLL/ORIGINATOR OF THE LOAD LINE KNOWN AS/THE PLIMSOLL LINE ON SHIPS/BORN AT 9 COLSTON PARADE BRISTOL 10TH FEBRUARY 1824/MEMBER OF PARLIAMENT 1868 TO 1880/ IN 1872 PUBLISHED 'OUR SEAMEN – AN APPEAL' IN WHICH HE/SHEWED THAT A LARGE PROPORTION OF SAILORS IN THE/MERCHANT SERVICE WHO PERISHED AT SEA LOST THEIR LIVES/FROM PREVENTABLE CAUSES SUCH AS OVERLOADING/INITIATED AND CARRIED THROUGH ALMOST SINGLE HANDED/THE MERCHANT SHIPPING ACT OF 1876/DIED AT FOLKESTONE IN 1898. BURIED AT CHERITON/A VILLAGE NEARBY'. Then centred below the Plimsoll mark is: 'THE SAILOR'S FRIEND'.

a Bill was not in course of preparation. Plimsoll's agitation was little more than an incident in that process. He was the sincere but hysterical member for Derby, a constituency as far removed from a British seaport as it is possible to be. He believed, what was generally admitted, that many British ships, especially in the coastal trades, were sent to sea in a condition which endangered the lives of those on board and in order to keep the subject in the public eye he adopted the familiar method of grossly overstating his case . . . But he was not a reformer.

No one would suggest now that Plimsoll was not a wily manipulator of opinion. He was described by Gladstone as 'childlike', but he was not an innocent. His son, at the unveiling of his Embankment monument, said he 'ran "special" trains to his meetings and kept an army of paid agitators'. There was planning and strategy in the apparently spontaneous outpouring of public feeling that he engendered. His tactics – for instance, showing photographs of meetings of their constituents to MPs – were sometimes close to blackmail. He played a carefully orchestrated game.

His detractors have tended to see all this as self-interest and to believe that Plimsoll was a man who deliberately stole the credit that should have been James Hall's; who interfered with the shipping industry by stirring ill-feeling between sailors and shipowners; who lied about his own history and motives and who possibly even delayed reform that was already progressing. They think he manipulated events for his own fame and glory.

Surely this is not so. Certainly Plimsoll must have been exasperating. No one could keep pace with his fervour and determination, nor could he forgive those who were not ignited as he was by injustice. He made hyperbolic, unchecked allegations, and men who were probably guiltless were caught in the crossfire. But, if anything, these were symptoms of moral conviction rather than of vanity. His vehemence may have worked upon the crowds, but it was not a way to ingratiate himself personally with those in power. *Punch* remarked just after his outburst in 1875: 'Mr Plimsoll's worst fault as a strategist is his readiness to make and endorse specific accusations. It shows his good faith as a man; but gives a powerful handle against him as a Parliamentary tactician.'

The self-interest in Plimsoll's character was this: he thrived on righteous outrage. He needed a cause. He enjoyed not the acclamation of the mob, but the sense of purpose in channelling his energies to a greater good. As he admitted in *Cattle Ships*, the suffering of others invigorated him, not because he delighted in it, but because he was fulfilled by fighting it. When one crusade expired, he found another. He looked at injustice on any scale – from the closure of a footpath or the misery of cold feet in a third-class carriage to widespread manslaughter though greed and negligence – and took upon himself the responsibility to end it. He was, you could argue, addicted to philanthropy. And he had to find a worthier object for his indignation than the restrictions of the halfpenny toll on Waterloo Bridge.

His biographer of the 1950s, David Masters, believes Plimsoll was duplicitous and knew and confessed his own guilt when he said, at a Congregational meeting in Derby in 1878: 'I believed when I was a boy that my minister hoped that I would also become a minister . . . but I never thought I was fit for the work of the ministry, as it seemed to require a higher standard of purity of life and motives and therefore I did not presume to put myself forward for such an office.' Masters concludes that this is evidence of the self-knowledge of a flawed man. It might also be modesty. Plimsoll wrestled with his own weaknesses, like the rest of us. If he had expressed the conviction that he was unusually pure, we would not have liked him better.

Credit for shipping reform has fairly been given since to James Hall, and to other enlightened shipowners, including, as Thornton listed them, 'families like the Thompsons, the Holts and the Bibbys and men like McIver, of the Cunard, Ismay of the "White Star" and the two Andersons of the P and O and the Orient Line.' Thornton argued that they (passenger shipowners among them) 'did far more to raise the general level of safety of life at sea than did the efforts of Samuel Plimsoll'.

There are even those, Adderley included, who have given the honour of establishing the load line to Charles Adderley. In 1876 he wrote: 'I had to fight Plimsoll on several clauses . . . and I carried my load-line against him, though it goes by his name'. And Geoffrey Alderman of the University of Reading, in his authoritative paper

'Samuel Plimsoll and the Shipping Interest', points out the load line that was adopted in 1876 was not Plimsoll's measure but (to its detriment) Norwood's – the man who introduced the Bill on 23 March 1875 for a voluntary load line to be fixed by the shipowners. Alderman has reiterated the point that Plimsoll's agitation occurred at a moment when shipping reform was already much under discussion. And that he was himself dissatisfied with the legislation of 1876, which still did not truly fulfil his aims.

Ironically, part of the legacy of Plimsoll, first president of the seamen's union, is that shipowners became a united body. It was the need to band together against the excesses of the 'Sensation' that led to the formation of the Chamber of Shipping in 1878. It is still going strong.

In old age Plimsoll self-depreciatingly (or self-knowingly?) told a visitor, as he looked out to sea, 'How little I have done for these dear fellows. I have done nothing for God or for man.' Yet he deserves honour for not relenting in the pursuit of aims that he knew could help where help was needed. And he recognised an important truth about the relationship between profit and risk. If the person who profits is not the person who takes the risk, the one with the profit will tend to increase the risk. It is a truth that still applies. The website of the National Union of Marine, Aviation and Shipping Transport Officers contained this observation in 1999:

> It was not for nothing that the term coffin ship was coined just over a century ago to describe in vivid terms the appalling scale of losses at sea. What a shocking indictment of our industry that, on the verge of the 21st century, we still find ships that fit such a description, with inspectors still finding ships infested with rats and cockroaches, or ships lacking adequate food and water supplies. For example, more than 20% of the foreign ships checked in UK ports last year were found to fall short of food and hygiene standards.

The site goes on to denounce registrars 'who blatantly flout any notion of adherence to accepted civilised standards'.

And a report in 2004 from the Maritime and Coastguard Agency reported the detention of twenty-six ships for breaches of safety regulations in the month of March alone, including a general cargo ship from the Bahamas detained for overloading in Glasgow. 'The winter load line mark was submerged 13 centimetres after allowing for dock water density. Ship allowed to sail following discharge of excess cargo.' The mark is still policed but there is an issue that has lingered since Plimsoll's day. Safety regulations, and their enforcement, vary from country to country. Ships still register under foreign 'flags of convenience' to avoid restrictions they dislike.

In Britain, by and large, although pockets of enthusiasm for him survive, the nation has forgotten about Plimsoll. Even the cockney rhyming slang he gave rise to is obsolete. Once Londoners could stroll through the Plimsoll in plimsolls (Plimsoll mark = park), but they don't any more. The narrator of John Banville's 2005 Man Booker Prize-winning novel *The Sea* says: 'Plimsoll. Now there is a word one does not hear any more, or rarely, very rarely. Originally sailors' footwear, from someone's name if I recall, and something to do with ships.' And he's not even right about the sailors' footwear.

Tony Benn MP, making one of those rare references to Samuel Plimsoll, in the House of Commons in 1995, during a debate about the hunting ban, remarked:

> We like to think that [social progress] is made by an amendment from a Back Bencher, and accepted by the Government. It is not like that at all. Social progress is made when public pressure builds up . . . My experience is that when people come along with some good idea, in the beginning it is completely ignored; nobody mentions it at all. If people go on, they are mad, and if they continue, they are very dangerous. After that, there is a pause and then nobody can be found who does not claim to have thought of it in the first place. That is how social progress is made.

That is how Plimsoll made social progress. And, as the good-hearted shipowner David McIver said of him:

> Many vessels have been lost which ought not to have been lost; and as that means that a great many lives have been lost which should not

have been lost, I think this sad truth amply justifies Mr Plimsoll in having compelled attention to the subject. Let all credit, then, be given to Mr Plimsoll; for, although wrong sometimes, it is now only too clear than in the main issue he has, unhappily, been right.

So too were Eliza and the members of the Victorian public who rallied to the cause. And if anyone doubts that Plimsoll and his associates did some good, it is worth bearing in mind that we do not now see, as photographs from the 1870s showed, cargo ships loaded as low in the water as canal boats. Freeboard is no longer a matter of a few inches between the deck and the waterline on ocean-going vessels. No one who leaves the deck of any kind of freight-bearing ship ever takes a step *up* into a rowing boat lying alongside.

In his lifetime Plimsoll believed that the load line had already made a difference to mortality. On 20 October 1891 he wrote to *The Times*:

Sir, A year and eight months ago, when we fervently urged the Government to assist us in passing the Load-line Bill, we showed that, according to the evidence accumulated by the late Mr Rothery, the annual loss of life at sea from overloading was 434 men; that this deplorable loss was entirely preventable; that the passing of the Bill would immediately and greatly check it . . .

That check has been applied, and now, while circumstances are fresh, I ask your readers . . . if they ever remember a gale of equal suddenness, violence and duration which was not the cause of very, very much greater loss of life than that recorded of the gale which has recently passed away.

Plimsoll's letter ended with a stanza of praise from a hymn. Unfortunately, a month later, more gales did cause severe loss of life. Nevertheless, the annual death toll at sea was never again as high as it was before Plimsoll alerted the world to the dangers of greed and neglect. A report in the *Star* in 1898 stated that the mortality rate at sea was then twelve per thousand – lower than on land.

Plimsoll's load line has been a UK standard for nearly 120 years, and a global standard for about 80. If we take his own estimate that 400–500 lives a year were lost from preventable causes on British ships alone, his measure has since protected hundreds of thousands. Thanks to Samuel and Eliza's determination, the sea is even now a safer place. And in a world where profit is still made out of other people's suffering, their moral conviction and self-sacrifice continue to set us an example.

POSTSCRIPT

Belt and the Bristol Bust

There is a mystery about the white marble bust of Samuel Plimsoll that commemorates him in Bristol, the city of his birth. Its origin, date and creator are unknown. The statue, evidently carved by a nineteenth-century hand, was spotted in a Nottingham junkyard in 1939 and acquired by a dealer in Stratford-upon-Avon who sold it for £25 in May 1940 to Bristol Art Gallery. Now it stands in the district of Hotwells near the mouth of the Severn, high above the edge of the river on one side with the traffic hurtling by on the other, and Plimsoll gazes, not out to sea but, with a kind of civic pride, in the opposite direction up the Clifton Gorge at Isambard Kingdom Brunel's elegant Suspension Bridge. Although there is no record of who made the bust of Plimsoll, it was surely intended to be a public memorial: it is three times life-size.

The history of plans for the memorial is like the history of Plimsoll's load line: it was a long time between the first proposal and the execution of the idea. A tribute was first suggested in Bristol in 1929, when the Plimsoll monument sculpted for the Thames Embankment was to be copied in Bristol. In the end an overdue memorial to the soldiers of the First World War took precedence. The idea was debated again in 1946. Eventually the bust that had been in the city gallery for more than twenty years was placed on its modern Cornish granite plinth in 1962 with an unveiling accompanied by the hooting of a sand ship.*

---

* The statue was unveiled on 24 July 1962. It bears a bronze plaque that says, in raised Roman capitals: 'SAMUEL PLIMSOLL, M.P./BORN IN THIS/CITY AND PORT OF BRIS-TOL/1824/DIED IN/1898/HIS UNTIRING EFFORTS LED TO THE/MERCHANT SHIPPING ACTS OF 1875/AND 1876 WHICH FIRST MADE LOAD/LINES COMPUL-SORY FOR THE SAFETY/OF SHIPS'. Centred below this is a Plimsoll mark.

Meanwhile there is a trail of clues that suggests a provenance for this statue, indicating that it was inspired by the national outcry of summer 1875, and connecting it with a curious history.

Both the *Graphic* and the *Art Journal* reported the commissioning in August 1875 of a tribute to Samuel Plimsoll to be made by one R. Belt. Richard Claude Belt was a twenty-five-year-old sculptor who was well on the way to becoming fashionable. 'Working men connected with shipping and shipbuilding' had contributed to the Plimsoll Memorial Fund, in the aftermath of his parliamentary outburst, intending their tribute to be raised near the London Docks.

Belt invited Plimsoll to come and sit for him in 1876. Plimsoll attended what he later described as 'probably not less than six sittings' at Belt's Hugh Street studio while the sculptor worked in clay. Immediately afterwards Plimsoll asked Belt to make a bust of his daughter Nellie. Belt in turn prevailed upon Plimsoll to pose standing on a dais with his arm outstretched in a declamatory attitude, and made a statuette in this form. But eight years after the sittings Plimsoll said: 'I do not recollect ever seeing the bust.'

When Plimsoll made this remark he was one of eighty-two witnesses giving evidence in support of Belt in a celebrated court case (sixty-one witnesses gave evidence on the other side). It was the second-longest libel case to date and the last trial ever heard at Westminster Hall, the five-hundred-year-old courtroom in which Anne Boleyn, Guy Fawkes and Charles I were condemned to death. The trial that Plimsoll attended went on for forty-three days, not counting subsequent appeals, and the proceedings attracted crowds of spectators. On every day of the hearing, room had to be made for the titled ladies and gentlemen who had come to see its drama unfold. Richard Belt was suing a rival sculptor and former friend, Sir Charles Bennet Lawes (later known as Lawes-Wittewronge), for libel. An anonymous author had written in *Vanity Fair*, and Lawes had repeated the alleged libel in a letter to the Lord Mayor of London, that Belt was not capable of producing his own work but depended on drawings by others, including Thomas Brock, who 'worked up' a statuette of Dean Stanley (later accidentally destroyed) and memorial

The Bristol bust of Samuel Plimsoll, carved by an unknown hand?
(*Bristol City Council*)

busts of the novelist Charles Kingsley and Plimsoll's supporter
Moncure D. Conway, all of which Belt claimed to have made.[*]

The *Vanity Fair* piece called Belt 'a purveyor of other men's work,
an editor of other men's designs, a broker of other men's sculpture . . .
He presents himself as a sculptor and an artist when in reality he
is but a statue-jobber and a tradesman . . . Mr Belt has been guilty
of a very scandalous imposture and those who have admired and
patronized him as a heaven-born genius are the victims of a monstrous deception.'

Belt was assisted in the execution of his works, said the article, by
more skilled practitioners: Brock, Lawes and Belt's former partner,
François Verheyden, who was allegedly responsible for the drawings

---

[*] Brock, later Sir Thomas Brock, elected an RA in 1891, was a prolific sculptor of portrait busts
and public statues, including the tomb of Lord Leighton in St Paul's and W. E. Gladstone in
Westminster Abbey. 'Mr Brock, equally with Mr Lawes, declares that Mr Belt was incapable of
doing anything in the shape of artistic work,' said *Vanity Fair* in August 1881.

that secured the commission for the Conway memorial. Belt was by then credited with a catalogue of important works including a colossal memorial to Byron for Hyde Park, a gift from the people of Greece. It now stands by the park on a traffic island and shows Byron – or, according to one commentator, someone quite unlike him – sitting on rocks and looking out to sea, his dog Boatswain at his side. Belt had won the commission in competition with thirty-eight other proposals in 1877 and the statue was erected in 1880. Verheyden, said the article, had in fact done the winning Byron sketch and modelled the memorial himself.

Just weeks before the trial opened, Belt's bust of Disraeli, commissioned by Queen Victoria, had been unveiled in London's Guildhall. If Belt was passing off others' work as his own, the deception was at a very prestigious level. His wealthy sitters came to court to give evidence that they had seen him at work, even when they chanced to drop by his studio unannounced. But Lord Frederick Leighton, president of the Royal Academy, gave his judgement that some of the works attributed to Belt could not be his. He recognised, he said, in the bust of Plimsoll, among others, the hand of Brock. He thought too the earlier work (which would have included this bust) much better than the later and doubted that a young artist could deteriorate so quickly. Belt v. Lawes put the authority of the Royal Academy itself on trial and raised issues of aesthetics – what constituted artistic skill, how authorship could be judged and where the line was drawn between technical help and creative ownership. Two social worlds clashed in the course of the trial: 'Fashion was for the plaintiff, art for the defendant.'

Tempers were lost in court, one bust among the profusion of works of art around the room had its head accidentally knocked off by a lawyer taking a book off a shelf and, most bizarre of all, Belt was given the task of sculpting a head of one of his assistants in clay in an adjacent closed room while the trial was going on, to prove his unaided ability. When the work was finished Leighton argued that it was unlike, and inferior to, a previous work attributed to Belt of the same sitter.

Meanwhile some newspaper coverage was unsympathetic to Belt on personal grounds. The *Penny Illustrated Paper* thought the 'petty case' a 'waste of valuable time' and, with its populist suspicion of the aesthete, blamed the plaintiff: 'Had Mr Belt not exercised his effeminate manner on "swell" persons of note, it may be doubted whether the Baron [Huddleston, the judge, who had also tried the famous Whistler v. Ruskin case] would have allowed the case to continue so long.'

But the court found for Belt, fining Lawes for damages of £5000, and Belt was carried in triumph on the shoulders of his friends out through the corridors of Westminster Hall.*

During the trial the statuette of Plimsoll declaiming and the bust of Nellie were produced in court. Both occasioned merriment – the statuette, unveiled beside its seated subject as he gave his testimony, because of its pontificating stance, and Nellie's bust because of a mistake: it was announced and 'when the work was uncovered it turned out to be a melancholy bronze bust of Lord Beaconsfield' (the title taken by the now deceased Disraeli).

Belt was a blacksmith's son who had worked for Lawes before setting up his own studio, and come from obscurity in the course of a few years. He admitted his humble origins in court: his first head had been made with a nail and a handbrush out of a piece of a clock tower. He was apprenticed to a Royal Academician, Foley, who had been dissatisfied with his previous protégé: one Charles Lawes. Lawes's hostility to Belt was felt by many to be a classic case of a mentor's jealousy of his upstart pupil.

The case went to two retrials in another court, on the grounds that the verdict contradicted the weight of evidence, and that the damages were excessive. The original fine was confirmed, and Lawes was bankrupted. Then new evidence was volunteered by Belt's assistant, Charles Louis Schotz, who said he had been induced by Belt to produce preliminary drawings for the Byron memorial, copying Verheyden's, to be presented to the court as Belt's originals. In return, he alleged, he was promised a third of any damages secured.

* Belt's career was unharmed. In 1886, for instance, he made the copy of the original eighteenth-century statue of Queen Anne that still stands in front of St Paul's Cathedral (after Francis Bird's original had been damaged by a 'mad lascar' who thought for some reason it was an insult to his mother).

This confession of perjury was never tested in court, but Belt came to grief in a different courtroom anyway, convicted in 1886 for conning a breathtakingly gullible aristocrat, Sir William Neville Abdy, into buying modern jewellery at an inflated price by passing it off as a sultan's diamonds. Belt was found guilty of fraud and sentenced to twelve months' hard labour. His career, surprisingly, recovered from the conviction and he lived on to enjoy such honourable commissions as a bust of Kitchener for the grand staircase of the War Office at Whitehall.

In all this drama there is no account of what became of Plimsoll's bust. That he had not seen it before the court case suggests that it was not immediately erected. And there is no record of a statue of Samuel Plimsoll ever being put up in London's docklands, despite the contributions of working men on a national scale. During the famous trial Westminster Hall became an art gallery as Belt's works were lined up to be brought in as evidence. Among the works listed in *The Times* as part of this exhibition, as well as the statuette of Plimsoll and the bust of Nellie, was the bust of Plimsoll. We know from the testimony in court that Belt followed the common practice of working in clay and then casting in bronze. He also regularly copied his clay busts in white marble, the stone from which Plimsoll's bust at Hotwells in Bristol is carved.

It is strange that Plimsoll's evidence did not explain why he had never seen a work which was commissioned by subscription to be a public memorial. Something prevented it from finding the home that had been intended for it. Possibly Plimsoll asked for the subscribed funds to go to another cause more immediately beneficial to sailors, and then paid for the bust himself, which would be consistent with his response to other subscriptions in his honour. But we do know from the trial records that the bust was made. It is just possible that Richard Belt's bust – made by his hand alone or possibly with more than a little assistance from Brock – is one and the same as the Hotwells foundling, having taken an unrecorded route, in the forty-six years since it was seen at Westminster Hall or the nineteen years after Belt's death, to the Nottingham junkyard. The pennies of workers from the East End of London may eventually have resulted in a monument after all. In fact, indirectly, they may have led to two: the Hotwells statue was copied in bronze in 1968 by Ernest Pascoe of the Royal West of England Academy, to adorn a dining society in New Orleans called the Plimsoll Club. And if the Hotwells original was all Belt's own work, it would, by chance, have found a suitable home. After Belt had been exonerated in the Lawes trial, he married one Georgina Lane. The wedding took place in the seaside town of Weston-Super-Mare, home of his bride, which is just along the Severn estuary from the city of Bristol.

AFTERWORD

O ne of the joys of publishing a book is that people bring you more information about its subject. Here are some late discoveries I wish I had known about for the hardback:

Many thanks to Francesca Simon (and, independently, Nicholas Tucker) who drew my attention to Henrik Ibsen's play *The Pillars of the Community*, published in 1877 and apparently influenced by Samuel Plimsoll's far-reaching campaign. The play concerns a hypocritical shipowner, Karsten Bernick, who, for his own ends, is tempted to send a hastily and inadequately repaired coffin ship to sea. Ibsen's inspiration was a ship that proved unsafe after it had been declared seaworthy, a case he heard about on a visit to Norway in 1874 (he was then living in Germany). The text shows clearly that Ibsen was familiar with the wider issue of unseaworthy ships,* and the programme notes for the 2005 National Theatre production refer to Plimsoll and therefore suggest a debt.† *The Pillars of the*

---

* 'Börlund: Look at all our fine ship-owners. Name me a single one of them who, for mere gain, would sacrifice a human life. And then think of those scoundrels in the big countries who, just to make money, send out one unseaworthy ship after another.' Act Three, *The Pillars of the Community* translated by Una Ellis-Fermor (Penguin Classics, 1980).

† Programme notes by Gunilla Anderman for National Theatre Production of *The Pillars of the Community* which opened in November 2005: 'The danger of unsafe vessels or "floating coffins" was brought to public attention in the United Kingdom by the efforts of Samuel Plimsoll [. . .] who, having tried unsuccessfully to legally prevent the unscrupulous sacrifice of human lives at sea, in 1875 created a furore in Parliament by referring to ship-owners as murderers and the politicians supporting them as scoundrels [. . .]. In Norway, another sea-faring nation, the problem of unseaworthy ships and their risks to human life was also a familiar subject; during Ibsen's visit to Christiana in 1874, newspapers gave prominent coverage to the story of a ship proving unsafe while at sea after having been declared unseaworthy.' (With thanks to Matt Wolf.)

Community opened in Copenhagen in November 1877 and became, in translation, the first Ibsen play to be performed in Britain, at the Gaiety on the Strand in December 1880. (The verdict of *Theatre* was that the villainy of Bernick, who is redeemed at the end, was 'inadequately punished'.) The second performance was at the Opéra Comique on the Strand in 1889. Both productions were in Plimsoll's lifetime, and close to his stamping grounds.

I am very grateful to Courtenay Latimer, great-grandson of Plymouth newspaperman and JP Isaac Latimer, who told me about his great-grandfather's feud with Plimsoll's enemy, Edward Bates MP. Isaac Latimer was Mayor of Plymouth 1871–2 and contested the 1885 election against Bates. According to family legend, Bates employed a gang of thugs to beat Isaac up on the steps of Plymouth Guildhall. This corroborates other evidence of Bates's bad character, while letters from Plimsoll to Isaac in the Latimer family archive reveal that Bates had a reputation for corruption, and that Plimsoll, whose hostility to Bates never waned, conspired with Latimer to expose him. In 1880 he wrote to Latimer: 'I hope that you will use every effort to turn out Bates – I felt morally certain that he . . . had been bribing as soon as I saw the state of the Poll.'[*]

Roy Palmer sent me four more street ballads and shanties about Plimsoll and the Merchant Shipping Act. One is now added to the Appendix. The others (excluded for lack of space) are: 'God Bless Plimsoll, The Sailor's Friend'; 'The Merchant Shipping Act'; and 'The Limejuice Ship'.[†] The streets and quays must have rung with Plimsoll's name.

Bristol surveyor Christina Raddon told me of plans to move the Plimsoll bust in Bristol from its long-standing home at Hotwells to the docks, by the SS *Great Britain*, which may soon make the current text out of date. Readers who fail to find the statue beneath Clifton Suspension Bridge are advised to look there.

---

[*] Letter marked 'Private' from Samuel Plimsoll to Isaac Latimer, 14 Sept 1880. In Courtenay Latimer's collection.

[†] These songs can be found in the following books edited by Roy Palmer: *Room for Company: Folk Songs and Ballads* (Cambridge University Press, 1971); *Boxing the Compass: Sea Songs and Shanties* (Herron Publishing, 2001), *A Ballad History of England* (BT Batsford, 1979) and *The Oxford Book of Sea Songs* (Oxford University Press, 1986)

Details of characters who played a part in this tale came to light. I was informed by Mary Taylor, great-granddaughter of quartermaster William Daniels, the quartermaster who survived the wreck of the *London*, that this was his third shipwreck. Afterwards, he said 'no more', and applied for a job on the North London Railway, where he became a guard. He worked on the railway for the rest of his life, and went on to father seven children. Daniels, who came from a village in Norfolk and never learned to read or write, gave evidence to the Board of Trade enquiry about the *London* (signed with a cross). A picture of the shipwreck by British maritime artist Francis Maltino is inscribed 'From information supplied by William Daniels'.

Helen Clappison passed on family research about the unfortunate Clappisons who lost their son John in the Great Gale in Bridlington in 1871: John was the youngest of the five children of Henry and Hester Clappison and they had already lost another boy, Tom, at the age of eleven in 1858. Caroline Shaw revealed that Mr Rowsell MP, whose placid pulses were not disturbed by the conditions endured by the poor of Malta, was Francis Rowsell who played an important part in the Suez Canal negotiations, and appreciated simple pleasures.* And Alan Stears wrote to me about his stonemason grandfather George Stears, who worked for Hambrook and Johns in Folkestone and, at the age of twenty-eight, carved the headstone of Samuel Plimsoll's grave. It was a lasting source of pride to George's son.

Expert reviewers made helpful contributions. Richard Gorski in *The Mariner's Mirror* quoted Marine Department papers at Kew in which Gray and Farrer of the Board of Trade called Plimsoll 'silly' and 'embarrassing'. Piers Brendon of the *Sunday Telegraph* and Sam Leith of the *Spectator* pointed out two minor errors of fact and a typo that have now been corrected.

Meanwhile, it was hard for me to leave the subject alone and I found, as I had failed to earlier, that the *Sea Queen* had been 'sold to

* Caroline Shaw 'Egyptian Finances in the Nineteenth Century: A Rothschild Perspective' *The Rothschild Archive Annual Review April 2005–March 2006* pp34–38 www.rothschildarchive.org/ib/articles/AR2006Egypt.pdf

E T Gourlay [*sic*]' in 1864.* That Gourley was the owner of the overloaded ship explains Plimsoll's hostility towards him in *Our Seamen*; the *Sea Queen* had been the subject of Plimsoll's poignant Manchester meetings in 1871.

I also discovered an error: the houses on London's Park Lane have been renumbered, and although there is still a number 28 which has a roofed, wrought-iron balcony like the one in a photograph of Plimsoll's residence from 1877 to 1896, his home, built in 1726, was demolished in 1928, along with the house next door. It is a different building that has now taken the number.†

I learnt too of the beautiful Plimsoll Viaduct, built by Plimsoll behind Kings Cross Station in London to carry his rail trucks to the coal unloading yards, and was dismayed to hear that an application has been submitted for its demolition.‡

I acquired a copy of the *English Mechanic and World of Science* of 17 May 1872, in which a miner's safety lamp patented by Plimsoll is described. The flame was designed to go out in the presence of gas.

And I was entertained to learn a tangential anecdote about Fred Albert, composer and singer of the song on the endpapers of this book. He employed a teenager to cycle between the two or three music halls where he performed in an evening, bringing with him a bouquet of flowers. The teenager was required to sit beside the prettiest girl he could, and throw the bouquet onto the stage at the end of the performance. Albert would then blow kisses to the girl, earning himself another round of applause. The teenager was George Foster who grew up to be Charlie Chaplin's agent.§

Finally, I owe particular thanks to Andrew Linington of the NUMAST *Telegraph*, who sent me eyebrow-raising statistics from the European and Canadian ship inspection authorities that revealed 3,197 breaches of load line regulations internationally in 2005, and slightly more in each of the two preceding years.

This story is not ended yet.

---

* www.theshipslist.com/ships/lines/hartlepool.html
† 'Park Lane', *Survey of London: Volume 40: The Grosvenor Estate in Mayfair*, Part 2 (The Buildings) (1980), pp. 264–89. URL: www.british-history.ac.uk/report.asp?compid=42151
‡ www.rsaum.co.uk/weblog/archives/2006/02/plimsoll_viaduc.php
§ Richard Anthony Baker *British Music Hall: An Illustrated History* (Sutton Publishing, 2005) p 233

APPENDIX: SONGS AND POEMS

COFFIN SHIPS

or A Tale of the Day

Arthur Matthison

As told by the Author at the great Plimsoll Meeting (chaired by the Earl of Shaftesbury) at Exeter Hall, London, in March 1873. From The Little Hero, and Other Stories, *adapted for recitation by Arthur Matthison.*

In the great London Parlyment House, lads,
They're a talkin' about us Jack Tars;
'Bout us, and the ships as we sails in,
Bolts, timbers, sails, riggin' and spars.

An' it's pretty nigh time as they did talk,
Them big wigs as settles it all!
Tho' I wish we could tell 'em what we think,
In that lingo ship, Westminster Hall!

D'ye know what they calls them old hulks, lads,
As all on us know, and all curse?
'Coffin ships' is the name as they gives 'em
An' I don't want to give 'em a worse!

For, mates, we might just as well all be buried,
As sail in them thin ribb'd old craft!
As ain't got a sound timber in 'em
From the hold to the mast, fore and aft!

I shipp'd in a coffin myself, lads,
From a port in the North, years ago;
An' back'd out – 'Sail you must!' says the Owner,
'If you don't, man, to prison you go!'

I went as if it 'ad bin to the gallows;
But what can a poor fellow do?
Then – liefer than mould in a prison
A true salt 'ud be drown'd in the blue!

You, most on you, know'd young Bill Severn,
The heartiest blue jacket afloat,
He was one of the crew of that ship, lads –
'Ship'! – it waren't strong enough for a boat!

Her bolts wasn't fit for a hencoop,
She'd a swamp'd in a breeze on the Tyne,
Though she look'd trim and seaworthy too, lads,
And as bold as a ship o' the line!

Look'd so spick, and so span, and so new, lads,
They insur'd her for double her worth!
But them innocent chaps as insure ships
Thinks they're safer at sea than on earth!

In a week comes a gale as we'd laugh at,
In the stout ship, as holds us all now;
It stove that in, as if the *Great Eastern*
Had struck her midships with her prow!

She went down, lads, as quick an' as easy,
As a bucket with holes in a pool!
Or as them little cockboats, all paper,
The land-sailor boys make at school!

When the day broke there me and Bill Severn
Lay floating about on the mast,
Of the short muster roll of the living
In that doom'd bark, that man-trap, the last!

Poor shipmate! He was to bin married,
When the vessel came back, that same Spring!

An' she'd giv'd him to wear for her sake, lads,
The half of a little gold ring!

And there he lay dying afore me;
For he'd hurt hisself bad, in the wreck;
An' he takes off his half of the ring, mates,
As always hung round his brown neck.

And his big hand, now weak as a babby's,
Tremblin', plac'd the gold token in mine:
'Carry this – Ben – to Mary – and tell –'
Quick and dead were alone on the brine!

If the Owner, that minute, before me,
Had stood with his throat near my hand! –
But there – thank the Lord as he didn't;
Thank the Lord, I aint mark'd with his brand!

I was pick'd up, getting on towards nightfall,
By a lugger bound out from South Wales;
But the rest of the crew in that 'Coffin' –
They can't – poor fellows – tell tales!

Mates, I've spun this yarn often and often,
Widows, mothers and sweethearts have cried.
But in vain to make old England listen,
England's sea sons, and daughters, have tried!

Coffin ships they yet sail o'er the waters;
Death sneaks in his salt water den!
Ship Owners! – Ship Slayers! I calls 'em,
And sea-devil slayers of men!

But they're talking about us in London,
England's big heart at last, mates, is stirr'd:
An' though we can't speak for ourselves, lads,
Them as *does* talk, thank God! will be heard!

OUR SAILORS ON THE SEA

Respectfully dedicated to Mr Plimsoll MP. Written by F. W. Green Esq., 1874.
Music composed by Alfred Lee.

At night when we are lying in
Our beds secure and warm,
We hear the moaning wind that tells
The coming of the storm . . .
Then thunder roars and lightning plays
Around with fiendish glee,
On such a night may God protect
Our sailors on the sea,
On such a night may God protect
Our sailors on the sea.

Chorus:
Amid the raging of the storm
We humbly ask of Thee
Oh! Father in thy mercy save,
Our sailors on the sea.

The sailor little dreams when he
Sets out upon the wave
The worn-out ship in which he sails
Will bear him to his grave.
Should storms arise, her rotten planks.
To pieces soon would go,
Yet ships like this are sent to sea
That men may richer grow,
Yet ships like this are sent to sea
That men my richer grow. *Chorus*

Such things we often hear of, and
The wealthy merchant thrives,
But what about the priceless freight
Of precious human lives . . .
Poor honest Jack from such a fate
Protected ought to be,
So let each do his best to help

Our sailors on the sea,
So let each do his best to help
Our sailors on the sea. *Chorus*

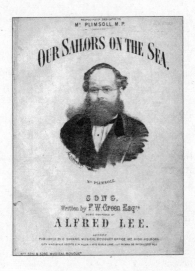

A BRITISH CHEER FOR PLIMSOLL

Written and composed by John Guest, 1875.

A British Cheer for Plimsoll
The sailor's honest friend
In spite of opposition
Their rights he dares defend
Tho' wealth and pow'r united
To put him down have sought
His valor has defeated
The forces 'gainst him brought.

'Britannia rules the ocean'
We've sung with thoughtless pride
Whilst thousands of our seamen
Through rotten ships have died.

But Plimsoll has aroused us
He pleads the sailor's cause
And by his fearless courage
He wins the world's applause.

'Tis not for gold he labours
A nobler aim has he,
The widow and the orphan
And the sailor out at sea
Their dangers and distresses
His heart of pity moves
His singleness of purpose
Day by day he proves.

Oh shame upon the wretches
Who to increase their gain,
Send men in rotten vessels
To perish on the main;
Then let us do our duty,
Not resting till we save,
By honest legislation
Poor Jack upon the waves.

A CHEER FOR SAMUEL PLIMSOLL

Written, composed and sung by Fred Albert, 1876.

In well known lays we sing the praise of men renown'd in war,
How heroes brave on land and wave have fought for us of yore;
But I will sing of one who fought, though not in deadly strife,
The noble object that he sought was saving human life.

Chorus:
So a cheer for Samuel Plimsoll, and let your voices blend,
In praise of one who, truly, has proved the sailor's friend;
Our tars upon the ocean, he struggled to defend,
Success to Samuel Plimsoll, for he's a sailor's friend.

There was a time when greed and crime did cruelly prevail,
And rotten ships were sent on trips to founder in the gale;
When worthless cargoes, well insured, would to the bottom go,
And sailors' lives were sacrificed, that men might wealthy grow. *Chorus.*

Full many a boat, that scarce could float, was sent to dare the wave,
Till Plimsoll wrote his book of note, our seamen's lives to save;
His enemies then tried to prove the pictures false he drew,
But with English pluck to his task he stuck, that task he deem'd so true.
    Chorus.

Our mariners to us are dear, they are the nation's pride,
Rich merchandize to us they bear across the ocean wide;
And so we then, as Englishmen, will honour and respect
The man who raised his voice and pen, our sailors to protect. *Chorus.*

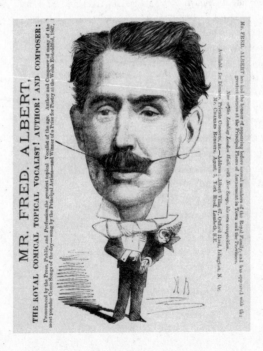

Cheering for Plimsoll: Fred Albert, music-hall comedian
(without a wooden leg). (*Footlight Notes/John Culme*)

A COFFIN-SHIPOWNER'S LAMENT

Author unknown

I bought up an old rotten ship
And filled it with boxes of earth,
I swore they were boxes of Indian silk
And insured them for ten times their worth.
At sea, of course, she went down,
Ten thousand I got for my greed;
But Plimsoll is putting a stop to my game,
And hang it, I think he'll succeed,

HERE'S SUCCESS TO MR PLIMSOLL

Folk ballad, date unknown. Recorded by Bill Cameron, St Mary's, Scilly, 1956.

Here's success to Mr Plimsoll
A sailor's friend you all must know
He proved that many of our shipowners
Religious men profess to be.
They go to church to pray for sailors
Whilst they have rotten ships at sea.
Now they'll go and buy old worn-out vessels
And paint them up again as good as new
They'll sell them for double of their value
And sail them in another name.
And when they get out upon the ocean
Their timbers then to pieces fly,
And they're left to the mercy of the waters,
And that's why our British seamen die.

MORE POWER TO PLIMSOLL

(Air – 'Poor Jack')
From Punch, *15 March 1873.*

Here's more power to Plimsoll, for Derby MP,
His pluck and his bottom I like,
That at rotten old ships, sent o'erloaded to sea,
Not too soon he's determined to strike.

With a cargo of rails in an old hull stowed tight,
And a deck-load, how pleasant to scud;
While loose bolts, leaky seams, Father Neptune invite,
And the pumps fight in vain with the flood.
Let horrified shipowners never so oft,
His charges, indignant, fling back,
I call him the Cherub, who sits up aloft,
To keep watch for the life of Poor Jack!

We've heard Reed* and his rivals, this many a day,
Discussing builds, riggings, and such,
On flotation, stability, jabb'ring away,
In what sounds to landsmen High Dutch.
But whatever the ship of the future may be –
What a ship that will be when it's seen! –
The ship of the past (hear a voice from the sea!)
Too often a coffin has been.
So says Plimsoll, says he, though our tars aren't so soft
At sea-risks to be taken aback,
There's room for a Cherub to sit up aloft,
And keep watch for the life of Poor Jack!

Underwriters at Lloyd's, now their risks wax so high,
Are beginning cantank'rous to be,
As with undertakers they don't want to vie
For performing of fun'rals at sea.
The cost of your cargo, as well as your hull,
'Tis but safe to insure, – if no more –

---

* The naval architect.

And if weather is bad, and nights dark, and freights dull,
Of course there'll be wrecks to deplore.
What then? All's a hazard: Compunction is soft:
Suppose a few tars ne'er come back! –
Leave them to the Cherub that sits up aloft
To keep watch for the life of Poor Jack!

Hearts of oak in old times were our ships, every inch,
And our men the same stuff as the ship:
But now from the cost of live oak builders flinch –
The point is to make a cheap trip.
And as cheap trips on shore in a smash often end,
Thanks to old engines, axles, or springs,
So your cheap trips at sea oft to Davy Jones send
All but what grist to shipowners brings.
Well, as life's breath is not like a coat to be doft,
Which owners, when lost, can give back,
I say, more power to Plimsoll, who sits up aloft,
To keep watch for the life of Poor Jack!

THE UNSEAWORTHY SHIP

Broadside printed by T Pearson, Manchester
(From Strike the Bell *edited by Roy Palmer, CUP 1978)*
To the tune of 'Driven from Home'

The doomed ships weighs anchor, out she is bound,
With cargo too heavy and timbers unsound;
A storm overtakes her, reef, reef, ev'ry sail,
But all to no purpose, she's lost in the gale.
See the old vessel, now tossed on the waves,
Telling her crew to prepare for their graves;
Sent out insured, with a hope she'd go down,
Not caring for widows and orphans at home.

Chorus:
Honour to Plimsoll, his labour will save
Thousands of brave men from watery graves.
May his movement all sour support adorn;
HIs work will save thousands of lives yet unborn.

Out on the wild waves sailors must go,
Earning bread for their children – what perils they know.
In old, rotten craft, which ship agents procure,
Brave men they are lost, in those vessels insured.
The captain is anxious the vessel to save
From the tempest which threatens a watery grave,
But all human efforts can't keep her afloat;
Oh, God! she is sinking, out, out with the boat.

Down with the life-boat, out on the waves,
Hoping to find land or sight some vessel's sail;
They pray to be saved but what can they do,
Surrounded by wild waves, that boat, and her crew?
The storm it is raging, the billows they roll;
No help is near for to save those poor souls.
The boat is upset, that brave crew is lost;
This, this is the price which our rotten ships cost.

Out, out, ye landsmen, out with a will,
Stand up in justice for Plimsoll's great Bill;
Don't be rejected, it's on God's mission sent,
But up, all as one man, before Parliament.

The nation demands it, 'tis the widows' cry;
The sailors' poor orphans we can't pass them by.
Let us work, every soul to help brave Plimsoll through,
And then we may boast of our ships and their crews.

CHRONOLOGY

28 August 1785   Thomas Plimsoll born in Ashburton.

9 February 1789   Priscilla Willing born in Hooe.

21 May 1809   Thomas Plimsoll and Priscilla Willing marry at St Andrew's Church, Plymouth.

Births of SP's siblings: 21 July 1810 Thomas Jr; 26 April 1812 John; 24 April 1815 Priscilla Willing; 17 June 1817 Ellen; 13 August 1819 Walter Rowse; 21 June 1821 Sarah Cranch; 18 November 1825 Caroline; 8 August 1828 Henry Davidson; 1830 Fanny Isabella; 1832 Mary Sophia; 1836 Victoria Nightingale.

2 May 1820   Thomas Plimsoll transferred to Bristol.

10 February 1824   Samuel Plimsoll born in Bristol at 3 Colston Parade, seventh surviving child of Thomas and Priscilla Plimsoll.

30 January 1825   Baptised at Bridge Street Congregational Church, Bristol.

1827   Plimsoll family moves to Sion Place, Bristol.

November 1828   Family moves to Penrith, Cumberland.

7 September 1830   Eliza Ann Railton born.

22 January 1838   Family moves to 50 Regent Street, Sheffield.

1839   Leaves school aged fifteen, works for Henry Waterfall, Sheffield solicitor.

1841   Clerk at Old Pond St Brewery – Thos Rawson & Co.

1842   Enrolled at Robert Bayley's the People's College, which is founded that year in Sheffield.

1 August 1844   Thomas Plimsoll (father) dies near Rugby, aged fifty-nine. SP and five younger siblings (the six elder children not living at home) move to Glossop Road, then 7 Sheaf Gardens.

1851   Honorary secretary to Sheffield Great Exhibition Committee; organises Sheffield Pavilion, including three inventions of his own.

5 January 1852   Raises subscriptions for relief after Rawmarsh Colliery explosion for widows and orphans, while still a brewer's clerk and living at 7 Sheaf Gardens.

Summer 1853   Follows brother Thomas, manager of Sunderland and Hartlepool Coal Co., to London, hoping to make his fortune as coal merchant; rents a room in the Coal Exchange, Lower Thames Street.

1854   Opens office at 55 New Kent Road.

7 February 1855   Files for bankruptcy.

21 April 1855   Certificate issued by Chief Bankruptcy Registrar.

1 August 1855 Suspended from membership of his church, the Nether Congregational Church, because of bankruptcy.

22 January 1856   Arrested for assault of tollkeeper on Waterloo Bridge.

1856   Opens coal office at 32 Hatton Garden, advertised in *The Times*, 1 April 1856.

2 April 1856   Restored to church membership.

19 February 1857   Organises relief effort after Lund Pit disaster.

1 October 1857   Marries Eliza Ann Railton at Ecclesfield Parish Church; living in room above office at 32 Hatton Garden

1861   Buys 9 Harrington Sq nr Mornington Crescent, north London, where he and Eliza look after his mother and ill sister Victoria.

17 March 1863   Thomas Plimsoll (brother) dies at 6 Brownlow Street, aged fifty-three.

6 April 1863   Priscilla Plimsoll (mother) dies, aged seventy-four.

27 June 1863   Victoria Plimsoll (sister) dies of consumption, aged twenty-six. (Of SP's eleven siblings, two emigrated to Canada, one to America and one to Australia; two died before SP was forty.)

1864   Buys Whiteley Wood Hall, a mansion near Sheffield.

11 April 1864   Welcomes Garibaldi at Nine Elms Station, London; escorts him to Barclay and Perkins Brewery, Southwark.

13 April 1864   On platform with Garibaldi at Crystal Palace for 'the people's reception' attended by 24,000–25,000. Garibaldi later visits the Plimsolls in Harrington Square.

20 April 1864   Garibaldi given the freedom of the City at the Guildhall; SP and Eliza in leading carriage in procession.

27 June 1865   Addresses the Liberals of Derby at the Athenaeum Club in Derby.

12 July 1865   Stands unsuccessfully for Parliament.

24 July 1865   Eliza (daughter) dies at four hours old of imperfect respiration at Whiteley Wood Hall.

27 July 1865   Eliza buried at Fulwood Chapel.

23 July 1866   Writes in support to George Howell, secretary of Reform League, offering to pay for damage to Hyde Park railings during a demonstration; pays fines of £2 for each of five demonstrators.

October 1866   SP and Eliza adopt six-month-old great-niece, Nellie
   Plimsoll.

November 1867   James Hall advocates independent inspections for
   seaworthiness.

January to June 1868   Charles Reade's novel, *Foul Play*, serialised in *Once
   a Week*.

2 July 1868   Announced as Liberal candidate for Derby.

1868   Elected MP for Derby. Maiden speech in favour of legalising trade
   unions reported by the *Telegraph* and the *Daily News* as 'tiring the
   patience of the house'.

8 June 1869   Father-in-law dies, aged sixty-four.

1869   Votes for disestablishment of Irish Church.

9 August 1869   Merchant Shipping Code Consolidation Bill introduced
   by Lefevre, MP, though not passed; reintroduced 1870, giving seamen
   the right to an automatic survey.

2 March 1870   Introduces Railway Travelling Bill.

March 1870   Encouraged by Eliza to meet James Hall, shipowner, to discuss load line.

13 April 1870   Opens parliamentary campaign for sailors, prompting
   media support.

10 February 1871   Great Gale, Bridlington.

1872   Writes *Our Seamen*.

January 1873   *Our Seamen* published.

10 February 1873   Bill against unseaworthy ships and overloading proposed.

1 March 1873   Plimsoll Defence Fund prompted by letter from Walter
   Farquhar to *The Times*.

4 March 1873   Proposes motion calling for a Royal Commission.

22 March 1873   Great Exeter Hall meeting, chaired by Lord Shaftesbury.

26 March 1873   Plimsoll and Seamen's Defence Fund opened by Lord
   Mayor of London.

28 March 1873   Chichester Fortescue announces Royal Commission on
   Unseaworthy Ships, which sits until July.

14 May 1873   Second reading of Plimsoll's Bill in the House.

14 June 1873   Judgement in libel case about the *Livonia*, owned by
   Charles Norwood MP.

16 July 1873   Florence Nightingale declines invitation from Plimsolls,
   claiming illness.

6 September 1873   *Samuel Plimsoll* launched at Aberdeen.

24 September 1873   Unanimous support for load line at Association of
   Chambers of Commerce of the UK meeting in Cardiff (reiterated
   every year until 1876).

December 1873   Serialisation in *Once a Week* of novel about coffin-ship owners, *Ship Ahoy!*, with introduction by Plimsoll, prompts libel case.

12 January 1874   Fanny (sister) dies, aged forty-three.

17 February 1874   Chichester Fortescue loses his seat at Louth to Alexander Sullivan; Sir Charles Adderley becomes President of the Board of Trade.

1874   Disraeli becomes Prime Minister; Plimsoll re-elected MP for Derby.

1 April 1874   Houghton and others v. Plimsoll tried at Liverpool; found in SP's favour.

24 June 1874   Plimsoll's Bill rejected in the House: 173 votes against; 170 votes for.

1 July 1874   Final report of Royal Commission fails to recommend a load line.

4 February 1875   Plimsoll abandons his own Bill and accepts the government's Merchant Shipping Bill, proposed by Sir Charles Adderley, despite its faults.

6 April 1875   Second Exeter Hall meeting, organised by Ladies' Committee.

15 April 1875   Elected to membership of the Reform Club, proposed by Michael Bass, Liberal MP and brewer of Burton-on-Trent, Staffs, seconded by Charles Pelham Villiers, MP for Wolverhampton, lawyer and Cabinet minister.

22 July 1875   Outburst in the House of Commons, prompted by delay to shipping legislation.

28 July 1875   National outcry at delay sparks indignation meetings at the East India Dock Gates, Sheffield Temperance Hall, Leicester market place, Nottingham market place, St George's Town Hall, Liverpool, Leeds Town Hall, Birmingham Town Hall, Stepney, St Pancras, Derby Town Hall, Bath and Swindon.

29 July   Apologises in the House.

6 August 1875   Stop-gap Bill proposed by Sir Charles Adderley.

7 August 1875   *Samuel Plimsoll* collides with an Italian barque at Falmouth; Falmouth pilot and two of the Italian crew drown.

7 and 9 August 1875   Hostile correspondence in *The Times* between SP and Charles Adderley. SP blames Board of Trade for not putting existing Acts into practice.

10 August 1875   Temporary Merchant Shipping Act passed, introducing Britain's first Plimsoll Line, to be applied from 1876.

20 August 1875   SP and Eliza sail for Hamburg.

August 1875   Plimsoll Memorial Fund set up for monument to SP in the East End.

October 1875   SP and Eliza at Sulina in Romania on the Black Sea.

30 October 1875   SP and Eliza travel by Austrian steamship to Odessa.

13 December 1875   SP and Eliza arrive in Malta from Constantinople.

17 December 1876   Leave Malta for Southampton on P&O steamer *Poonah*, calling at Gibraltar.

10 February 1876   First reading by Charles Adderley in the House of the Merchant Shipping Bill that was to become law; SP introduces amended Shipping Bill.

27 March 1876   Moves amendment to Adderley's Bill to enforce a survey; Adderley argues it would make ships uncompetitive. Amendment defeated.

22 May 1876   Amendment to abolish deckloading carried 163 votes to 142; subsequently reversed by the Lords, who permit deckloading to a height of 3 feet.

1876   Plimsoll shoes so named by Philip Lace, sales representative of the Liverpool Rubber Co.

21 December 1876   *Samuel Plimsoll* lifeboat launched at Lowestoft.

February 1877   Too ill to attend opening of new Bristol Port and Channel Dock because of 'acute nervous debility'.

9 September 1878   Addresses constituents: 'My special work, I regard as done.'

Between September 1878 and June 1879   Right eye removed.

Summer 1879   Buys 28 Park Lane and acquires coat of arms.

December 1879   SP and Eliza, who is unwell, stay at Hotel d'Orient, Algiers.

1879   Travel to Malta en route to India.

24 January 1880   Return to London for meeting with George Howell and TUC regarding grain cargoes. Eliza catches a chill in the English Channel and is advised to go south to Madeira.

3 May 1880   Joseph Chamberlain becomes President of the Board of Trade.

4 May 1880   Chamberlain writes to SP to solicit a meeting.

18 May 1880   Gives up his seat to William Harcourt, Home Secretary, who had lost his Oxford seat.

25 May 1880   Harcourt elected unopposed for Derby.

August 1880   Loses by-election in Liverpool against Lord Claude Hamilton.

September 1880   Act passed to provide for safe carriage of grain cargoes.

Summer 1880   Eliza transported to Folkestone, Paris and Royat in the

Auvergne, where she spends six weeks. Travels via Vichy, Limoges, Bordeaux (whence SP returns home in September with Nellie to fetch Eliza's doctor) and Lisbon to Madeira. Winters in Madeira.

14 November 1880   Eliza suffers an attack of paralysis in Madeira.

Christmas 1880   Eliza travels to the South African Cape and back up the coast; health improves.

End of May 1881   Plimsolls return home; Eliza relapses during wet June.

July–October 1881   SP, Eliza and Nellie travel to Boulogne, Paris, Bordeaux, Arcachon, Lisbon, India and Ceylon.

Spring 1882   Returns to England, parting from his wife in Java.

14 April 1882   Eliza arrives in Brisbane to stay with her sister-in-law, planning to return in June, but her health deteriorates.

17 August 1882   Eliza dies in Brisbane and is buried the next day at Toowong.

21 August 1882   Sends exhumation order via Colonial Secretary.

12 September 1882   Corpse transported to London, arriving in November.

15 November 1882   Eliza interred in family vault at Highgate Cemetery.

24 May 1884   Chamberlain introduces Merchant Shipping Insurance Bill.

October 1884–January 1885   Visits brother Henry in New York.

1885   Stands for Sheffield Central and loses.

8 October 1885   Marries Harriet Frankish Wade.

January–May 1886   SP and Harriet visit New York.

1888   Becomes first president of the National Union of Seamen.

6 January 1890   Cattle-ship *Erin* disaster inspires publication of *Cattle Ships*.

1890   Merchant Shipping Act; load line fixed by Board of Trade.

January 1891   Visits Canada to research beef trade.

27 January 1892   Gives evidence before Royal Labour Commission following seamen's strikes of 1891.

1892   Retires from public life, moves to Folkestone.

27 June 1896   Arrives in New York to try 'to cure America's alleged dislike of England'; secures withdrawal of anti-British books from American schools.

3 June 1898   Dies at 35 Augusta Gardens, Folkestone; buried at Cheriton, Kent. Harriet and children move to Penrith Gate, Duchy Road, Harrogate.

1906   Lloyd George, President of the Board of Trade, raises load line.

20 May 1911   Harriet dies at 15 Reynolds Close, Hampstead Garden Suburb.

21 August 1929   Plimsoll monument, paid for by sailors, erected on the Victoria Embankment.

29 December 1935   Plaque unveiled at Plimsoll's Bristol birthplace.

1930   International load line convention signed by thirty nations.

1966   Sixty nations revise Plimsoll line to meet new conditions at sea.

1988   Revised Load Lines Protocol published; amended in 1995 and 2003.

2005   Latest load line regulations issued by International Maritime Organisation.

NOTES

INTRODUCTION

1. *'Farewell, father, brother'*: Henry Dennis's letter, quoted by his brother-in-law, W. Gilbert Highton in 'A Voice from the London and its echoes, to which is prefixed an Address to those who have suffered by the calamity, etc'.

1. *These three messages*: washed-up messages reported in *The Times*, 1 March 1866.

2. *'It'll be her last voyage'*: Highton, p. 13.

2. *the pierman at Woolwich*: Highton, p. 21. The pierman told three concurring seamen that he wouldn't sail in her for £100 because she was 'far too deep'.

2. *'he did not like his ship'*: Highton, p. 14.

2. *'gradually disappeared'*: as recorded in a letter from Alexander Burrell to *The Times*, 22 January 1866.

3. *'a remarkable and unanimous spirit'*: reported in the *Western News*.

4. *'a beautiful shipwreck'*: Reverend H. N. Wollaston, 'Death's Warning Voice: Loss of the SS London, a Sermon preached at Trinity Church, East Melbourne on Sunday evening 25 March 1866', pp. 17–19.

4. *'if the passengers had exerted themselves'*: letter to *The Times* quoted in Wollaston, ibid.

6. *hers was one of the few bodies found*: letter from Henry Debenham to *The Times*, 11 March 1866.

6. *Several ballads of meagre literary merit*: John Abraham Heraud, 'The Wreck of the London: A Lyrical Ballad', and Edward Tomlin, 'The Wreck of the London, In Memory of G. V. Brooke', T. Barrett, 'The Wreck of the "London"' (in verse) and Gerard Moultrie, 'The Wreck of the "London"' (a poem).

7. *'when the London's awful end is told'*: song lionising Captain Martin, W. C. Bennett, 'The Wreck of the London', *Songs for Sailors*, p. 99.

8. *'It cannot be denied'*: letter to *The Times*, Monday 27 January 1866, p. 6.

8. *'the deep load line should be permanently marked'*: *The Times*, 28 February 1866, p. 9.

8–10. Other sources for story of the wreck of the *London*: *The Times* 18, 19, 21, 22, 24, 25, 27 January, 5, 7, 8, 14, 28 February, 1, 21 March 1866; *Wreck of the 'London' (with illustrations)*; Edward Gilbert Highton, *A Voice from the London and Its Echoes*; William Baird, 'Sermon given at St Gabriel's Mission Church, Bromley, Middx January 25 1866'.

10. *It promptly folded*: Kay Grant, *Samuel Cunard: Pioneer of the Atlantic Steamship*, p. 144.

10. *the Board of Trade was much more reluctant to intervene*: Philip S. Bagwell, *The Transport Revolution*, pp. 73–4.

10. *The Board of Trade's Annual Report*: facsimile of 1871 report, p. 7, in Samuel Plimsoll, *Our Seamen*, opposite p. 3.

11. *Between 1861 and 1870 . . . 8105 people died*: Richard Larn, *Shipwrecks of Great Britain and Ireland*, p. 158.

11. *half of the 17,086 wrecks . . . occurred in 'very fine weather', and about one in twelve resulted in loss of life*: from *Lecture by Mr Brassey MP Given at Hastings 17 November 1873* in pamphlet *Our Merchant Ships*.

11. *these deaths were preventable*: 1871 Board of Trade Report, p. 3, in Samuel Plimsoll, *Our Seamen*, opposite p. 2.

11. *In 1850, the British mercantile marine*: Henry Mayhew, *Morning Chronicle*, 7 March 1850.

11. *postings of wrecks*: Peter Cunningham, *Hand-Book of London*, quoted in Lee Jackson, *The Victorian Dictionary*, www.victorianlondon.org.

12. *As early as 1836, 11,226 ships carried coal . . . were lost at sea*: George Patterson, 'Victorian Working Life in Sunderland', in *River, Town and People*.

12. *'coal from the Tyne to London alone'*: ibid.

12. *'the millionaire, warm from his wine'*: quoted in Highton, p. 29.

13. *In another terrible instance*: from Samuel Plimsoll speech, Amphitheatre, Leeds, March 1873.

13. *One wooden sailing vessel, the* Kingsport: Mick Mulligan's yarn recounted in Sir James Bissett, *Sail Ho!: My Early Years at Sea*, pp. 117–19, quoted in Ronald Hope, *Poor Jack*, pp. 259–60.

14. *Plimsoll argued that insurance companies*: Samuel Plimsoll, *Our Seamen*.

15. *'The appearance of a seaman in a court of law'*: Charles Plomer Hopkins, *Altering Plimsoll's Mark*, p. 8.

15. *'If the ship-owner and merchant be so amply protected'*: *Nautical Magazine*, quoted in William Henry Higman, 'Thoughts on Shipwrecks'.

15. *the rise of steam*: Valerie Fenwich and Alison Gale, *Historic Shipwrecks*, p. 104.

16. *removed from the statute books by stealth*: Samuel Plimsoll, *Cattle Ships*, pp. 126-8 and pp. 145-8, Appendix: 25 & 26 Victoriae, cap. 63, 1862, Merchant Shipping Acts, &c., Amendment. Table (A) 'Enactments to be repealed'.

16. *a series of public bodies*: A. W. B. Simpson, *Cannibalism and the Common Law*, pp. 101ff.

17. *Among those who contributed*: letter to *The Times*, 15 February 1861, from William Keane, curate of Whitby, listing donors to the lifeboat appeal, including £5 from Charles L. Dodgson of Christ Church.

17. *A flurry of papers . . . in Manchester and London*: Thomas Gray (Assistant Secretary of the Board of Trade), 'On the Condition of Merchant Seamen', read at the Society of Arts, London 1867; Captain Henry Toynbee, 'The Social Condition of Seamen: A Paper read at the Royal United Service Institution', London, 1867, and 'On Mercantile Marine Legislation: A Paper Read before the Society of Arts', London, 1867; Royal United Service Institution, 'The Loss of Life at Sea, with report of a special committee of members of the council to the Vice-President of the Board of Trade', London, 1866.

17. *'a deep load-line . . . is not recommended here'*: Report of the Committee of the Society for Improving the Condition of the Merchant Seaman, p. 33.

17. *'The majority of merchant seamen'*: ibid., and quoted in Patterson.

17. *cases of scurvy were becoming 'very common'*: ibid., p. 8.

18. *The 1867 report's recommendations*: ibid., pp. 14–17.

19. *Sailors were each allotted*: Joseph Havelock Wilson, *My Stormy Voyage Through Life*, pp. 31–5.

20. *'dandy funk' . . . 'cracker hash'*: Sir James Bissett, *Sail Ho!: My Early Years at Sea*, pp. 55-6.

20. *A sample of this was once presented*: Wilson, *My Stormy Voyage Through Life*, pp 32-3.

22. *'their dress varied according to their taste and pocket'*: Ian Jack, review of Peter Padfield, *Rule Britannia: The Victorian and Edwardian Navy*, in *London Review of Books*, vol. 25, no. 1, 2 January 2003.

22. *Boys were assigned the most dangerous tasks*: Ronald Hope, *Poor Jack*, p. 256.

22. *'What, only a boy? Keep her as she goes'*: Frederick William Wallace, quoting his father's experience in the 1860s, *Under Sail in the Last of the Clippers*, p. 173; also quoted in Hope, p. 255.

22–3. *'I've got seamen aboard my ship'* . . . *'I like my fellows to understand'*: quoted in James Greenwood, *In Strange Company*, p.197.

23. *Davy Jones was an evil spirit*: Brewer's *Dictionary of Phrase and Fable*, p. 302.

23. *The bottom of the sea was a locker*: explanation from W. H. Smyth, *The Sailor's Word-Book* p. 451.

23. *Fiddler's Green*: ibid., p. 293.

24. *'This great inequality was most felt . . . on the coast'*: F. L., *Our Merchant Seamen: Their Importance and Their Claims*, p. 10.

24. *'and thus the Merchant Seamen of the country were left'*: ibid, p.11.

24. *One such was the Sailors' Orphan Girls' Home*: Thomas Archer, *The Terrible Sights of London: and labours of love in the midst of them*, ch. 1, part 4, www.victorianlondon.org.

24. *Another was the Merchant Seamen's Orphan Asylum*: James Thorne, *Handbook to the Environs of London*, pp. 558–9.

25. *'in this island . . . the sailor's orphan'*: Archer, *The Terrible Sights of London*, ch. 1, part 4.

25. *'widow-and-orphan-manufacturing system'*: Plimsoll, *Our Seamen*, pp. 85–6.

1: A LOVING SPIRIT

27. *At the age of thirty-two*: Plimsoll's arrest on Waterloo Bridge on the evening of Tuesday 23 September, reported in the police (law) column, *The Times*, 26 September 1856.

27. *One September evening*: on Monday 22 September 1856 Plimsoll represented Yorkshire coal owners at the Congress of some four hundred delegates in the Hotel de Ville in Brussels, reported in *The Times*, 24 September 1856. The Congress published Plimsoll's paper, 'The Export Coal Trade of Britain' (later followed by a second publication on the inland coal trade).

29. *'the Cinque Port of Newport-Pagnell'*: from a spoof novel, *All in the Downs; or The Bottomry Bond! A Nautical Novel by S. PL-MS-LL MP*, *Punch*, 3 March 1877, p. 93.

29. *spelt 'Plimsall' in the church records*: from Bridge Street Congregational Church records on film 0099151059 0593816 (RG4 338).

29. *known to invite the hungry*: G. H. Peters, *The Plimsoll Line*, p. 3.

30. *'wanted to do a great work for the Lord'*: told to George Nettleship of the Ebenezer Church, Penrith, as reported in Peters, p. 8.

30. *received his basic education*: David Masters, *The Plimsoll Mark*, p. 23; Peters, p. 7.

30. *'a glorious panorama'*: William Furness, *History of Penrith*, p. 176.

30. *'lofty and ponderous' railings*: Samuel Plimsoll objects to Regent's Park railings, *The Times*, 19 March 1870.

30. *to protest against the closing of public footpaths*: *Monthly Chronicle*, December 1888, vol. 2, p. 573.

30. *That year . . . Samuel was inspired to write a pamphlet*: Peters, p. 12.

31. *'Left with five younger than me'*: Samuel Plimsoll, *Cattle Ships*, p. 130.

31. *a bundle of hareskins*: story of Samuel Plimsoll's early business venture, Masters, p. 33; Peters, p. 11.

31. *He supplemented his abbreviated formal schooling*: Peters, pp. 11–12.

31. *the irascible Dr Samuel Eadon*: from S. R. C. Plimsoll's notes for a biography of his father in Sally Shaw's private collection.

31. *Plimsoll's first jobs*: Peters, p. 11; 'Samuel Plimsoll, Brewer's clerk, living at 7 Sheaf Gardens, Sheffield', from *White's Directory of Sheffield*, 1852.

32. *The surviving daguerreotype*: daguerreotypes of Samuel Plimsoll and J. Ridge Simpson in the *Sheffield Daily Telegraph*, 23 February 1928, with article by C. Ridge Simpson, editor of the *Weekly Telegraph*.

32. *the excellence of its cutting instruments*: *Hunt's Handbook to the Official Catalogues*, cited in the frontispiece of *The Great Exhibition: a Poetical Rhapsody* by 'A Visitor', Sheffield, 1851.

33. *'a mine of bad taste'*: Augustus Pugin bracketed Birmingham and Sheffield together as 'inexhaustible mines of bad taste', quoted in Asa Briggs, *Victorian Things*, p. 22.

33. *'coromandel-wood cases'*: *Official Descriptive and Illustrated Catalogue of the Great Exhibition of the Works of Industry of All Nations* by authority of the Royal Commission, Vol. 2.1 Part III Class 22 General Hardware, including Locks and Grates, no. 149, made by John Nowill & Sons, Sheffield.

33. *'ladies' steel busks'*: ibid., Class 22 no. 177, made by John Wright, New George Street, Sheffield.

33. *system . . . for straining impurities*: 1852, Samuel Plimsoll, Patented invention no. 513 for 'cleansing and fining malt liquors'; also 1853, Patented invention no. 1009 for 'cleansing, extracting and separating or fining ale, beer etc from yeats, bottoms, barm, sediment etc'.

33. *three inventions by Plimsoll*: *Official Descriptive and Illustrated Catalogue of the Great Exhibition of the Works of Industry of All Nations*, Vol. 2.1 Part III Class 22 General Hardware, including Locks and Grates no. 185: 'PLIMSOLL, Samuel, Sheffield – Inventor. Improved warming and ventilating apparatus, which can be forced by means of a wheel-fan, adapted, by means of a white enamel upon the exterior surface of the hot-air piping, casing, &c., to retain and conduct heat. A

pocket-umbrella to attach to a walking stick, or any other handle. Improved surface-file handles. Concave and convex surface-files; exterior and interior angle files. Moulding-file.'

Also listed in Vol. 1.2 Class 6 Manufacturing Machines and Tools item 631 Plimsell [*sic*] S, Sheffield, Improved Warming Apparatus (perhaps the same as above).

And Asa Briggs, *Victorian Things*, p. 55: 'among the exhibits there was a pocket umbrella submitted by Samuel Plimsoll, who was to press for load-lines on ships'.

33. *In January 1852 he raised subscriptions*: Rawmarsh explosion report, *The Times*, 5 January 1852.

33. *another relief effort*: Lund Hill fire, Peters, pp. 21–2; reports in *The Times*.

34. *In 1867 . . . a huge public meeting*: *The Times*, 3 September 1867, p. 10.

34. *His only motive . . . 'the great loss of life'*: *The Times*, 24 February 1865.

34. *a 'vital matter'*: ibid.

34. *a business venture sabotaged*: story of coal transportation and Seymour Clarke, Peters, pp. 16–17.

35. *Years later . . . living among . . . the hungry*: Samuel Plimsoll, *Our Seamen*, p. 79.

36. *suspended from his membership*: resolution passed at Church meeting, 1 August 1855, cited in Peters, p. 19.

36. *A matter of months after . . . he was able to pay dividends*: bankruptcy certificate issued 21 April 1855; dividends declared in *The Times*, 30 June 1855, p. 5.

36. *He would never*: 'But for the help given me by the Press, I could not have succeeded', speech at Barnsley Corn Exchange, 6 July 1859, quoted in Peters, p. 24.

37. *she had loved him from the first*: according to Peters, who does not give his source.

37. *She admired his 'zest for living'*: Peters, p. 22.

38. *'His good wife was not at all behind her husband'*: George Howell, handwritten account of the Plimsoll and Seamen's Defence Fund, Howell Collection, Bishopsgate Institute Library.

38. *her 'patience and mature deliberation'*: Eliza Plimsoll's obituary, 26 August 1882, in the *Rotherham Advertiser*, possibly written by the Reverend Falding, Principal of Rotherham College and Samuel Plimsoll's brother-in-law; quoted in Peters, p. 148.

38. *A note in the Hon. Georgina Cowper-Temple's diary*: 25 February 1876.

40. *'Several of the principal coalmasters'*: Report on the South Yorkshire Coal Trade, *The Times*, 19 September 1857, p. 10.

40. *he invented a sloping grille*: patent for coal chute, no. 2430, 1 August 1868.

40. *A timely property purchase*: Nellie Plimsoll writes of this in a letter in Sally Shaw's private collection.

40. *'I absolutely glory in the working men'*: Samuel Plimsoll, *Our Seamen*, p. 82.

40. *'If the lives of nearly a thousand of our ministers'*: ibid., pp. 78–9.

41. *It was the . . . middle classes he found tiresome*: Samuel Plimsoll's granddaughter Sally Shaw, in conversation with author.

41. *It was here that Garibaldi came to call*: sources of Garibaldi story include Peters, p. 25; Minute Books of the London Trades Council, which took a prominent part in organising the popular welcome of Garibaldi; *Giuseppi Garibaldi in London, 1864–1964* Centenary, British–Italian Society.

42. *The baby died at four hours old*: death certificate Eliza Plimsoll June–Sept 1865 Ecclesall Bierlow.

42. *The family wisdom*: from S. R. C. Plimsoll's resumé of his aunt Nellie Plimsoll's life in Sally Shaw's private collection.

42. *Instead she adopted one*: marriage certificate Thomas Joseph Hatch Plimsoll to Elizabeth Margaret Palmer Apr–June 1865 W London 1c 91; birth certificate Ellen Mary Ann Plimsoll Apr–June 1866 St Pancras 1b 159; death certificate Thomas Joseph Hatch Plimsall [*sic*] Apr–June 1866 Pancras 1b 111.

43. *'Mrs Plimsoll had waited many hours'*: Samuel Plimsoll, speech at Exeter Hall, 22 March 1873.

43. *'I mingled my tears with hers'*: ibid.

44. *'My dear Nellie'*: letter 18 February 1892, author's private collection.

44. *Howell reported that he 'could not refer to some of the incidents'*: George Howell, *Labour Legislation, Labour Movements and Labour Leaders*, p. 265.

44. *'he is made quite ill'*: Georgina Cowper-Temple, *Diary*, Southampton University, BR58/6, 21 February 1876. Traced by James Gregory.

44. *'Do you hear the wind? . . . at home'*: Samuel Plimsoll, London, June 1873, quoted in Peters, p. 91.

45. *He even cultivated his empathy*: Samuel Plimsoll, *Cattle Ships*, footnote p. 54.

45. *The ticket he then stood on*: *Derby Ram*, 1865.

45. *Bass was to speak*: report of pelting with dead animals, *The Times*, 10 July 1865.

46. *He went on to defend sailors*: defence of sailor's drinking in *Punch*. Also, he drank himself: 'Plimsoll and I then proceeded to Simpson's in the Strand, his favourite place of dining when in town, and we had a very excellent repast, washed down with a little wine', Wilson, p. 254

46. *One protest took place*: Justin McCarthy, *A History of Our Own Times*, vol. IV, pp. 154–8.

47. *Plimsoll . . . wrote to George Howell*: letter 23 July 1866, Howell Collection, Bishopsgate Institute Library.

47. *Plimsoll chaired a gathering of twelve thousand people in Sheffield*: *The Times*, 8 August 1866, p. 9.

48. *'I went to London . . . with £18 10s'*: speech in Temperance Hall, Sheffield, 2 June 1873, quoted in Peters, p. 82.

48. *the average cost per candidate*: J. A., *The General Election: Campaigning Papers, being the first part of A Political Handbook for the People*, 'The Cost of a Seat in Parliament', p. 105.

48. *levée of the Duke of Edinburgh*: at St James's Palace, *The Times*, Court Calendar, 14 May 1872.

48. *The brewery owner Thomas Rawson*: Peters, p. 11.

49. *Mundella . . . thought Plimsoll . . . 'talked rot'*: A. J. Mundella to Robert Leader, Leader Correspondence, Sheffield University Library, quoted in W. H. G. Armytage, *A. J. Mundella, 1825–1897: The Liberal Background to the Labour Movement*, pp. 70–1.

49. *'Our New Members of Parliament'*: *The Times*, 8 December 1868.

49. The Times *called the new intake 'an ugly rush'*: 7 December 1868, p. 8.

50. *'I have just been elected to Parliament'*: from Fulwood Chapel speech to celebrate the chapel's 139th Anniversary, after the singing of the hymn 'Eternal Father, strong to save', Peters, p. 44.

50. *Plimsoll's former role as a defender of miners*: pit lock-out and consequences, Peters, p. 34.

50. *Plimsoll's first cause as an MP*: Railway Travelling Bill, reported in *The Times*, 3 March 1870, p. 6.

51. *Newcastle shipowner called James Hall*: William Hayward, *James Hall of Tynemouth*, vol. 1.

51. *In March 1867 the* Utopia: story of the *Utopia*, Peters, pp. 40–1.

52. *a collector of art*: Hall owned Holman Hunt's painting *Isabella, or The Pot of Basil*, half of Millais's *The Widow's Mite* (which had been split into two: Hall's half was called *Christ Teaching Humility*) and Alma Tadema's *Young Lovers*.

53. *'Every practical authority'*: James Hall, letter to the editor, *The Times*, 17 December 1869.

54. *at Westminster Hall . . . Hall proposed resolutions*: Lorraine Gray, 'The Fight for Shipping Reform in the 1870s', *Sea Chest*, Journal of the Tyneside Branch of the World Ship Society, no. 43, March 1971, p. 13.

54. *'How will that tell in the House of Commons!'*: Hayward, ch. IV, 'The Plimsoll Agitation', p. 243.

55. *'I felt like one who was groping in the dark'*: W. C. Leng, *Memoirs*, quoted in Peters, p. 45.

55. *Leng was already a public figure*: A. H. Millar, *Oxford Dictionary of National Biography*, vol. 33, p. 346.

56. *Plimsoll, addressing fifteen thousand colliers*: *The Times*, 3 September 1867, p. 10.

56. *'If you have ever stood'*: *Hull Free Press*, 13 December 1856, quoted in Peters, p. 45.

56. *'chafed at heart'*: ibid.

57. *one of the 'most remarkable' novels of the year*: *The Times*, 4 January 1869, p. 5.

58. *'a middle class gentleman with . . . more conscience'*: George Orwell, 'Books in General', *New Statesman*, 17 August 1940, quoted in Wayne Burns, *Charles Reade: A Study in Victorian Authorship*, p. 310.

58. *'It is only a month or two . . . running like a West End hotel'*: Orwell, quoted in Burns, p. 310.

59. *'There's not a day passes that ships are not scuttled'*: Charles Reade and Dion Boucicault, *Foul Play*, Act 1, scene 1, pp. 10–11.

59. *'more or less a failure'*: Lee Jackson, *The Victorian Dictionary* (www.victorianlondon.org).

59. *Foul Play was the subject of a small controversy*: *The Mask: A Humorous and Fantastic Review of the Month*, February 1865.

59. *'The Sham-Sample Swindle'*: *Once a Week*, 22 August 1868, and Charles Reade, *Readiana*, p. 302.

59. *'a hideous gorilla in knickerbockers'*: frontispiece 'Companions of the Bath', *The Mask*, August 1868, described in Elwin, p. 199.

60. *'It was our bullion and you're bullyin' us'*: F. C. Burnand, *Fowl Play*, p. 8.

60. *The actors were extravagantly dressed*: from costume notes for *Fowl Play*.

2: THE POWER GAME

62. *'When Plimsoll was fifteen'*: G. H. Peters, *The Plimsoll Line*, p. 11.

63. *A chest containing Plimsoll's correspondence*: from S. R. C. Plimsoll's notes for a biography of his father in Sally Shaw's private collection.

64. *'I have long been regarded as a monomaniac on these subjects'*: Shaftesbury's speech to amend the Ten Hour Bill, 10 May 1844, from www.historyhome.co.uk.

65. *At the same time Sir John Pakington*: *Pall Mall Gazette*, 18 April 1870.

65. *Prolonged newspaper coverage ensued*: *Sheffield Daily Telegraph*, 23 April, 30

July 1870; *Pall Mall Gazette*, 8, 18, 21, 24, 27 April, 4, 5, 19, 31 May 1870, *Shipping and Mercantile Gazette*, *Suffolk Gazette*, *Sheffield and Rotherham Independent* and other cuttings April–July 1870 in Working Class Movement Library, Salford.

66. *The* City of Boston *was considered . . . 'dangerously overloaded'*: from *The Times*, 1870, undated cutting from the uncatalogued Plimsoll collection in Working Class Movement Library, Salford.

66–8. *A five-day inquiry by the Board*: 'Proceedings of the court of inquiry into the loss of the steamer Sea Queen with the minutes of evidence before the court', Parliamentary Papers 1870, vol. LX, pp. 408–11.

68. *It was against this backdrop*: Hansard, 28 July 1870; Peters, p. 49.

69. *In their black weeds the tearful widows*: account of Manchester meetings, special edition of *Sheffield Daily Telegraph*, 14 February 1871.

70. *Recently snowdrop bulbs*: the initiative of local historians Mike and Diane Wilson.

71. *There were those, Plimsoll among them, who believed*: *Leeds Mercury*, 13, 14 February 1871; *Newcastle Daily Chronicle*, 11 February 1871, etc., Plimsoll Papers, Working Class Movement Library, Salford.

71–82. *It was a balmy, early spring day*: sources for account of the Great Gale include *Scarborough Express*, 17 February 1871; *Shields Gazette*, 11 February 1871; *Leeds Mercury*, 13 February 1871; *Sheffield Daily Telegraph*, 18 February 1871, John Dickinson, *The Storm at Bridlington Bay or God's Voice in the Tempest*, William Sharrah and John William Day, *Tales of the Sea: being an account of the great storm in Bridlington Bay etc. 10th February 1871*, Mike Wilson, 'The Great Gale of 1871', in *Bridlington's Historic Heritage No. 2*, Mike Wilson, *Full Fathom Five*, Sydney T. Thompson, former Bridlington Borough Librarian, 'The Great Gale 1871 and the Funerals of the Drowned Men', transcript of lecture, 1996, Joseph Benjamin Braithwaite, *The Priory Church, Bridlington: A Short History*, Bridlington, 1923, David and Susan Neave, *Bridlington: an introduction to its history and buildings. Bridlington Memories*, Bayle Museum Trust, 1995, L. H. E. Whitaker, *Men of the Storm: The Story of Bridlington's Lifeboats*.

71. *'presented an animated scene'*: Thomas Cape, *Brief Sketches Descriptive of Bridlington Quay*.

3: THE INSANE FARRAGO

83. *the general indignation against unseaworthy ships*: Plimsoll quoted in *Newcastle Daily Chronicle* and *Leeds Mercury* on the lessons of the Bridlington gale in a letter to the *Daily Telegraph*, 8 April 1871.

83. *'all this fuss about losses at sea is nothing more than a "humanity dodge"'*: Hansard, 22 February 1871; *Pall Mall Gazette*, 23 February 1871.

84. *'was desirous of enlisting the Trades Union Congress'*: George Howell, 'The Plimsoll Movement' MS, Howell Collection, Bishopsgate Institute Library.

84. *Our Seamen: An Appeal*: Virtue & Co., 1873.

84. *'Few books . . . have ever moved a generation of British people so widely and deeply'*: G. H. Peters, *The Plimsoll Line*, p. 54.

84. *a bound-in note*: 'the more fully you may think fit to quote or transfer any portions of the Appeal . . . the better he [Mr Plimsoll] will be pleased, as his object is more to get the facts before the public than to sell the book', insert bound into early editions of *Our Seamen*.

84. *'a book jumbled together in the fashion of an insane farrago'*: *Vanity Fair*, 15 March 1873.

86. *'Shipowners, as a class, are really careful'*: Samuel Plimsoll, *Our Seamen*, p. 13.

86. *'There are in every class of men'*: ibid., p. 14.

87. *He cited the bravery and altruism of miners, common soldiers and sailors*: ibid., pp. 78–82. (These descriptions of the poor helping one another contributed to Kropotkin's theory of Mutual Aid in human societies: William P. Kropotkin, *Mutual Aid: A Factor of Evolution*, pp. 288–9.)

87. *'abandoned to the tender mercies of unchecked irresponsibility'*: Plimsoll, *Our Seamen*, p. 87.

88. *The 1871 census identifies William Wilks*: 1871 Census RG 10 5119 fo. 72 p. 24; from the research of Eric Hollerton of North Shields Central Library.

88. *drawn by Harry J Cornish*: *Lloyd's Register: A History 1760–1999*, pp. 24–5. Cornish's drawings of the construction of ships won prizes at exhibitions in Moscow and Paris.

88. *'I tell you, you who read these lines'*: Plimsoll, *Our Seamen*, pp. 85–6.

89. *The Leeds papers that week*: *Leeds Mercury*, *Yorkshire Post* and *Leeds Intelligencer*, 13–20 January 1873.

90. *All pledged their support*: *Leeds Mercury*, 20 January 1873.

90. *'a trader may leave port in midwinter'*: *The Times*, 12 February 1873.

92. *'Everyone – for surely everyone has read Mr Plimsoll's appeal'*: J. Ewing Ritchie, *Days and Nights in London*, ch. 6, 'The Low Lodging House', www.victorianlondon.org.

92. *'Mr Plimsoll's "Appeal" has excited a storm'*: *The Times*, 13 February 1873.

92. *'I can assure you that we require on board . . . a barrister'*: C. M. Norwood, addressing the Royal Commission on Unseaworthy Ships, and quoted in Robert Frump, *Until the Sea Shall Free Them*, p. 153.

93. *'For God's sake don't send us into the Baltic'*: Plimsoll, *Our Seamen*, p. 49.

93. *a letter to* The Times *countered*: *The Times*, 15 February 1873, p. 12.

94. *'Plimsoll, worthy man, is growing wiser'*: Shaftesbury's diary, 23 April 1873, quoted in Peters, p. 175.

94. *'Mr Plimsoll's reasoning seemed to be'*: *The Times*, 16 June 1873, p. 13.

94. *'In our opinion, for the time of year'*: stevedores Anderson and Campbell, *The Times*, 16 June 1873, p. 13.

94. *The court decided*: The Queen vs Plimsoll verdict, 14 June 1873, reported in ibid.

95. *'There was one ship-owner whose name was often mentioned'*: Plimsoll, *Our Seamen*, p. 47.

96. *'Mr Gourley is a thin spare man'*: 'Mark Rutherford' (William Hale White), 'Our London Letter', *Norfolk News*, 4 May 1872.

97. *'Hon. Members who had received the book'*: Hansard, 10 February 1873, and letter to *The Times*, 13 February 1873, p. 6.

97. *In the following days coverage and correspondence*: *The Times* leader February 1873; letters from Charles Mercier and James Goodenough, *The Times*, 16 February 1873, p. 6. See also *The Times*, 12, 13, 15, 17, 18 and 21 February 1873.

97. *'Bill to provide for the Survey of Certain Shipping and to Prevent Overloading'*: Tracts 1779–1873 BL 8806BB23; first reading reported in *The Times*, 12 February 1873.

98. *'a breach of parliamentary privilege'*: *The Times*, 20 February 1873.

98. *one study has concluded*: Geoffrey Alderman, 'Samuel Plimsoll and the Shipping Interest', *Maritime History*, vol. 1, no. 1, April 1971,footnote 35 p. 91.

98. *'Owing to the fact that two or three of . . . the "greatest sinners in the trade"'*: Plimsoll, *Our Seamen*, p. 71.

99. *'That to accuse in a printed book'*: Eustace Smith's motion, Plimsoll's apology and Eustace Smith's defeat, *The Times*, 20 February 1873, p. 8.

100. *including those of teenage sailors*: *Penny Illustrated Paper*, 8 March 1873, p. 2.

100. *the earnest pages of the* Christian World: 21 February 1873, quoted in Peters, pp. 72–3.

100. *a motley gathering of seamen . . . in North Shields*: *Penny Illustrated Paper*, 8 March 1873.

100. *Plimsoll's Derby constituents were noisy*: *The Times*, 1 March 1873.

100. *he was lauded in Liverpool Town Hall*: 3 March 1873, *The Times*, 4 March 1873.

100. *This points a finger at Tate & Lyle*: as pointed out by George Patterson of the University of Durham in conversation with the author.

NOTES 343

100. 'the meeting approved of a load line and a Royal Commission': *The Times*, 24 February 1873, p. 5.

100. *He spoke in language that was 'not that in common use'*: W. L. Rutton, 'Samuel Plimsoll, Cheriton Church and the Vicinity', *Home Counties Magazine*, vol. 13, 1911, p. 211.

100. 'It is enough to say that Mr Gladstone': *The Times*, 19 March 1873, p. 9.

100. *the captain shot a passenger*: 'The Wreck of the Northfleet', *Ballads of Britain and Ireland, Storm and Shipwreck* CD (Folktrax 512).

101. The Times . . . *reported the case of the Peru*: *The Times*, 4, 7, 18 March 1873.

101. 'All the crew were saved, except three': *The Times*, 7 March 1873.

101. 'Plimsollism is another word for terrorism': J. W. Mitchell, letter to *Shipping Gazette*, April 1873, quoted in E. S. Turner, *Roads to Ruin*, p. 170.

101. *In Whitby shipowners . . . crammed into the Talbot Hotel*: meeting 23 April 1873, *The Times*, 24 April 1873.

102. *In Sunderland shipowners met*: *Penny Illustrated Paper*, 8 March 1873.

102. *a deputation of leading Baptists went to see Gladstone*: led by Charles Haddon Spurgeon, London, 28 April 1873, Peters, p. 73.

102. 'If "Little Bethel" would look after': *Nautical Magazine*, quoted in Peters, p. 74, and E. S. Turner, 'Plimsoll Rules the Waves'.

103. *the Mayor of Plymouth, was critical*: 28 April 1873 in the New Guildhall, Peters, p. 74.

103. 'On one occasion I was with him': George Howell, *Labour Legislation, Labour Movements and Labour Leaders*, quoted in Peters, p. 72.

103. Punch *paid tribute*: Tenniel cartoon, *Punch*, 15 March 1873, p. 108.

105. 'no right to exclude others': Samuel Plimsoll letter to *The Times*, 3 March 1873, p. 12, and to *Penny Illustrated Paper*, 8 March 1873, p. 14.

106. 'Four children' who raised six shillings: donations reported in *The Times*, 8 March 1873.

106. 'the small but earnest offerings': letter to *The Times*, 1 March 1873, p. 7.

106. *The contribution of Samuel Plimsoll's own family*: George Howell, 'The Plimsoll Movement' MS, Howell Collection, Bishopsgate Institute Library.

106. 'the story of the brig Demetrius, from which three lives were lost': *The Times*, 19 March 1973, p. 10.

106. *a report of the statistics of Maritime Disasters*: of 221 European sailing ships lost in January, 137 were English, and in February 147 out of 312 were English. Of steamers, in January, of 32 totally lost 11 were English (19 were American) and in February 12 out of 19 totally lost were English (and one American), *The Times*, 22 March 1873.

107. *'The British Tar'*: J. V. Bridgeman, 'The Music Composed expressly for Mr Santley by J. L. Hatton', Boosey & Co., London, 1873.

107. *Lilian Dundas*: David Stone, from the D'Oyly Carte, 'Who Was Who' website.

107. *Henry Smart*: Henry Smart was a composer of hymn tunes, notably 'Angels from the Realms of Glory' and 'The Lord is My Shepherd', as well as songs including 'Curfew Bell' and 'Twilight'.

107. *George Howell recorded*: Howell's handwritten account of The Plimsoll Movement, Plimsoll Papers, Howell Collection, Bishopsgate Institute.

107. *He circulated a pamphlet*: Samuel Plimsoll, *A Bill to provide for the Survey of Certain Shipping and to Prevent Overloading* [Tracts 1779–1873 BL 8806 BB23].

108. *a letter written in 1934*: from the World's Fair, cited at thegalloper.com and by John Turner, circus historian, in correspondence with the author.

108. *the Ampitheatre music hall*: the Amphitheatre was between Briggate and Albion Street, but no longer exists. This arena was an apt venue for Plimsoll. One of the successes in this theatre had been, six years earlier, a play called *The Mariner's Compass* by Henry Leslie – which, like *Foul Play*, raised public awareness of the dangers sailors faced. To add to the drama, real rocket apparatus was used on stage to reconstruct a rescue. The title came from the saying that 'a mariner's compass is grog'. Symptomatic of contemporary revisionism about sailors, this pious tale of nobility and courage demonstrated that 'a mariner's compass is DUTY'.

108. *He gave examples of cases*: Leeds speech in *The Times*, 17 March 1873; also published in pamphlet 'A Speech delivered in the House of Commons, March 4, 1873 . . . in moving for a Royal Commission to inquire into the condition of the Mercantile Marine of the United Kingdom. Also a notice of a speech delivered at Leeds, March 16, London 1873.'

110. *'dwelt upon the constant and extreme perils'*: *The Times*, 21 March 1873.

4: THE GREAT PLIMSOLL MEETING

111. *'banisters of cedar, curiously inlaid with gold'*: *Punch*, Jan–June 1842, quoted in victorianlondon.org.

111. *This was the headquarters*: John Timbs, *Curiosities of London*, quoted in victorianlondon.org.

111. *John Stuart Mill, 'no orator but merely a reciter'*: *Vanity Fair*, 29 March 1873.

111. *Land Tenure Reform Association*: Margot Finn, *After Chartism: Class and Nation in English Radical Politics 1848–1874*, p. 267.

112. The Times *reported that 'all classes of Londoners'*: report of Exeter Hall meeting, including following quotes from Shaftesbury's and Plimsoll's speeches, *The Times*, 23 March 1873.

113. *'glorious defence of the wretched, oppressed seamen'*: Shaftesbury's diary, 24 March 1873, quoted in Edwin Hodder, *The Life and Work of the Seventh Earl of Shaftesbury K.G.*, vol. III, p. 32.

113. *Shaftesbury, then seventy-two*: sources on Shaftesbury: John Pollock, *Shaftesbury, The Poor Man's Earl*; Edwin Hodder, *The Seventh Earl of Shaftesbury K.G. as Social Reformer*; John William Kirton, *True Nobility: or the Golden Deeds of an earnest life*.

114. *'purest, gentlest, kindest, sweetest'*: quoted in Dorothy M. Williams, *Shaftesbury: The Story of His Life and Work as the Emancipator of Industrial England (1801–1885)*, p. 53.

114. *'Never was a death so joyous, so peaceful'*: Shaftesbury's diary, 16 December 1872, Hodder, *The Life and Work of the Seventh Earl of Shaftesbury K.G.*, vol. III, p. 316.

114. *'We have heard much about unseaworthy ships'*: Eustace Smith, Hansard, 17 June 1875, p. 102.

116. *'Mr Plimsoll is a popular as well as an excitable speaker'*: R. J. Hinton, 'Political Agitators', in T. W. Higginson (ed.), *Brief Biographies: English Radical Leaders*, vol. 2, p. 207.

118. *Doré was acquainted*: Joanna Richardson, *Gustave Doré: A Biography*, p. 118.

118. *there was also a recitation*: Arthur Matthison, 'Coffin Ships aka A Tale of the Day As told by the Author at the Great Plimsoll Meeting . . . at Exeter Hall', Arthur Matthison, *The Little Hero, and Other Stories*.

119. *'Walking round St Katherine's Dock'*: handwritten affidavit of J. Harris 'riggar [*sic*] of 2 Garden Cottages, New Street, Valkshall [*sic*] St, Lambeth', Plimsoll Papers, Howell Collection, Bishopsgate Institute Library.

120. *Plimsoll brought a complaint*: *Parga* story, G. H. Peters, *The Plimsoll Line*, p. 76.

120. *'Sirs, Yours of the 22nd inst'*: letter written from 111 Victoria Street, 24 March 1873; copy in Plimsoll's handwriting in Plimsoll Papers, Howell Collection, Bishopsgate Institute Library.

120. *One account says that Plimsoll was proved wrong*: David Masters, *The Plimsoll Mark*, p. 171.

120–1. *But Chichester Fortescue . . . thanked Plimsoll*: *Punch*, 5 April 1873, 'Essence of Parliament', p. 138.

121. *'We only hope . . . that an earnest word'*: Penny Illustrated Paper, 29 March 1873.

121. *George Odger, who volunteered*: George Howell, 'The Plimsoll Movement' MS, Howell Collection, Bishopsgate Institute Library.

121. *'object of ridicule'*: 'Sir Charles Dilke and Mr Odger were held up to perhaps undeserved ridicule in burlesques at this and other theatres', letter from M. Litton, Royal Court Theatre, The Times, 10 March 1873.

121. *the Liberal Party itself . . . opposed his candidature*: Sidney and Beatrice Webb (eds.), The History of Trade Unionism, note p. 238.

122. *one of his own biographers, who concluded that he was vain*: F. M. Leventhal, Respectable Radical: George Howell and Victorian Working Class Politics, p. 215.

122. *'Mr Plimsoll was a man in earnest'*: Howell, 'The Plimsoll Movement' MS.

122. *He claimed credit*: George Howell, Labour Legislation, Labour Movements and Labour Leaders, 2nd edn. 1905, vol. ii, ch. 27.

123. *George Howell . . . circulated*: draft Petition item 23, Plimsoll Papers, Howell Collection, Bishopsgate Institute Library.

124. *'tired of German princes'*: Daphne Bennett, Queen Victoria's Children, p. 107.

124. *Two admirals' daughters*: sources for details of members of the Ladies' Committee, and donors to the cause: Plimsoll Papers, Howell Collection, Bishopsgate Institute Library; Penny Illustrated Paper; wikipedia.com; Dictionary of National Biography; website of the Centre for Whistler Studies, University of Glasgow; national archives.gov.uk; scouting.milestones.btinternet.co.uk (Henrietta Baden-Powell); 1881 Census (Mrs Pennington); peerage.com (Duchess of Argyll, Countess of Airlie, Georgiana Cowper-Temple, Miss Cazalet, Baroness Rothschild); Jewish Chronicle, 16 March 1877, obituary; Rothschildarchive.org; correspondence with Caroline Shaw of Rothschild Archive (Baroness Rothschild); emails from James Gregory, biographer; Southampton University Broadlands Archive (Georgiana Cowper-Temple); emails from Marjory Harper; University of Aberdeen (Countess of Aberdeen, Katherine Gordon); McMaster University website/Bertrand Russell Gallery; University of Iowa English Department website (Lady Amberley).

124. *'The draught of water'*: 'load line' entry, Admiral W. H. Smyth, The Sailor's Word-Book.

125. *she had a smile which 'was the result'*: A. C. Benson, quoted in email by James Gregory, biographer of Georgiana Cowper-Temple.

126. *wife of Peter Rylands*: Louis G. Rylands, Correspondence and Speeches of Mr Peter Rylands MP.

127. *the Ladies' Committee . . . organised . . . a marching band*: 6 April 1875, *The Times*, 7 April 1875.

127. *She declined politely*: letter from Florence Nightingale to Samuel Plimsoll, 16 July 1873, D6018/1/1 and D3181/1-2, Derbyshire Record Office.

128. *a matter-of-fact appeal*: item 21, Plimsoll Papers, Howell Collection, Bishopsgate Institute Library.

128. *'The Lass that Loves a Sailor'*: *Penny Illustrated Paper*, 'The Ladies' Column', 21 June 1873; donors also listed item 21, Plimsoll Papers, Howell Collection, Bishopsgate Institute Library.

129. *giving her son . . . charge*: Duke of Edinburgh's involvement in the Royal Commission, British History online, 'List of commissions and officials 1870–1879'.

129. *'the glorious task'*: *Penny Illustrated Paper*, 29 March 1873.

5: ROYAL COMMISSION: CELEBRITY AND SETBACKS

131. *Plimsoll proposed the second reading*: Hansard, 14 May 1873, p. 1991.

132. *He shamelessly read aloud*: ibid., pp. 1988–9.

132. *'that his head was turned'*: ibid., p. 1990.

133. *'The compulsory survey'*: ibid., p. 1992.

134. *This opponent was a man of great wealth*: Dianne Sachko MacLeod, *Art and the Victorian Middle Class*, p. 279.

134. *'painted by G. F. Watts'*: Watts's portrait of T. E. Smith, Tate Gallery, also reproduced in Timothy Wilcox, 'The Aesthete Expunged, The Career and Collection of T. Eustace Smith MP', *Journal of the History of Collections* 5, vol. 1.

134. *'a long-bearded little man'*: sources on Thomas Eustace Smith and his collection: F. G. Stephens, 'The Private Collections of England', no. III, 'Gosforth House, Tynemouth', *Athenaeum*, no. 2395, 20 September 1873, pp. 372–3; Wilcox, pp. 43–57.

135. *'la respectable Smith'*: letter from F. R. Leyland at Speke Hall, Liverpool, to J. M. Whistler, 19 August 1875, Glasgow University Library, Centre for Whistler Studies, MS Whistler L102.

135. *'The affair with Dilke'*: sensual and unconventional Eustacia, wealthy in her own right from her landowning father's fortune, patronised painters and writers to give herself social standing as a hostess. She entertained Henry James at her home and inspired admiration from Robert Browning. She claimed, titillatingly, to have been the model for the goddess's feet in Leighton's daring nude *Venus Disrobing*, which

belonged for a while to Leyland. He sold it in 1872, perhaps not wanting the feet of 'la respectable' in his house. The Smiths bought it, and displayed it conspicuously in their drawing room, first at Gosforth and later in London. *Venus Disrobing* is described in Stephens, p. 372, and Wilcox, p. 52.

135. *an interior-design competition*: Linda Merrill, *The Peacock Room*, p. 222, and footnotes on pp. 141–4; MacLeod, pp. 291–4.

135. *'a wretched debate on occasional sermons'*: Samuel Plimsoll, speech at Colston Hall, Bristol, 21 June 1873, *Western Daily Press*, 23 June 1873.

135. *At a private meeting . . . at the Westminster Palace Hotel*: Plimsoll and Seamen's Defence Fund Committee Report, Plimsoll Papers, Howell Collection, Bishopsgate Institute Library.

135. *Councillor Jesse Collings*: G. H. Peters, *The Plimsoll Line*, footnote p. 74.

136. *'eagerness itself'*: Jesse Collings, *Life of Rt Hon. Jesse Collings*, Part 1, p. 98.

136. *He said then that he would go on*: The Times, 17 May 1873.

136. *'A wave of popular feeling'*: George Howell, *Labour Legislation, Labour Movements and Labour Leaders*, p. 269.

136. *Arriving in Hull in April*: Hull meeting reported in *Penny Illustrated Paper*, 5 April 1873, p. 2, and *The Times*, 5 April 1873.

137. *'I was never more astonished'*: Shaftesbury, *Speech of the Earl of Shaftesbury at the Annual Meeting of the Church Pastoral Aid Society, at St James's Hall, London, on Thursday May 8 1873*, pp. 10–11.

138. *Subscriptions of a shilling a head*: Peters, p. 72.

138. *Eliza was with her husband in June*: 18 June 1873, as reported in *The Times*, 20 June 1873, p. 10.

138. *There had been objections*: Plimsoll's presence at Royal Commission, Hansard, 20 May 1873, p. 167.

138. *as he told a Sheffield audience*: speech to Sheffield Trades Council, 28 June 1873, Peters, p. 82.

139. *Nowhere was this truer than in Bristol*: Bristol speech and visit, 21 June 1873, reported in *Western Daily Press*, 23 June 1873.

140. *But Gladstone had refused to meet a deputation*: Peters, p. 82.

140. *'You are mistaken in supposing'*: J. A. Roebuck, quoted in ibid.

142. *'Immense and enthusiastic meetings'*: Liverpool Town Hall, 3 March 1873. Manchester, 21 April 1873, reported in *Penny Illustrated Paper*, 26 April 1873, p. 2. The meeting was presided over by the Bishop of Manchester, with the mayor, Joseph Bright MP, Hugh Mason and William Fairbairn speaking. Leeds Amphitheatre (Music Hall), 16 March 1873, addressed by the Reverend William Thomas Adey and Samuel Plimsoll. Birmingham, 14 May 1873, addressed by Jesse

Collings, Mayor of Birmingham Ambrose Biggs, Alderman Hawkes, George Howell and Samuel Plimsoll. Hull, Hengler's Circus, 31 March 1873. Grimsby Town Hall, 18 June 1873, reported in *The Times*, 20 June 1973. Bristol, 21 June 1873. An address to the Sheffield Trades Council, 28 June 1873. Meetings reported by George Howell, 'The Plimsoll Movement' MS, Bishopsgate Institute Library.

142. *a bitter correspondence with Chichester Fortescue*: exchange between Plimsoll and Board of Trade reproduced in *The Times*, 2 August 1873.

143. *a vast miners' demonstration in Chesterfield*: 23 August 1873, reported in *The Times*, 24 August 1873.

143. *the same company might rename a ship after Mrs Plimsoll*: Duncan Haws and David Savill, *Merchant Fleets: The Aberdeen and Aberdeen & Commonwealth Lines*, p. 50.

143. *'Built in 1873'*: Haws and Savill, *Merchant Fleets: The Aberdeen and Aberdeen & Commonwealth Lines*, p. 50

144. *In October and November civic receptions were held*: public meeting at the Beneficial Societies Hall, Portsea, near Portsmouth, and banquet on the *Samuel Plimsoll*, reported in *The Times*, 23 October 1873.

144. *'They can call me an agitator'*: Samuel Plimsoll, 14 November 1873, *The Times*, 21 November 1873.

144. *Thomas Brassey . . . argued . . . David McIver wrote*: *Our Merchant Ships* pamphlet containing: *I Letter from David MacIver to The Times 2 December 1873/II Lecture by Mr Brassey MP Given at Hastings 17 November 1873 etc.*

145. *One biographer wrongly speculates*: Malcolm Elwin, *Charles Reade: A Biography*, p. 317.

145. *Plimsoll had written to Reade*: letter (with Reade's annotation), 4 March 1874, Charles Reade Letterbook, Robert H. Taylor Collection, Princeton University Library, vol. 1, fo. 35 RTC01, no. 89.

145. *The 1874 tour that included* Our Seamen: Ellen Terry, *Memoirs*, pp. 71–2

145. *the first of several tribute songs*: 'Our Sailors on the Sea', written by F. W. Green, music composed by Alfred Lee.

146. *Sometimes the stalwarts of his Committee stood in*: George Howell, 'The Plimsoll Movement' MS.

147. *Meanwhile the Royal Commission*: Report of the Royal Commission on Unseaworthy Ships with minutes and digest of evidence and appendix, 1874.

147. *One Plimsoll enthusiast*: George Reid's evidence, ibid., pp. 2–3.

149. *Ships were sold to foreign owners*: ibid., p. 12.

149. *he had written contemptuously elsewhere of Plimsoll's campaign*: 'Farrer and his civil service colleagues were contemptuous of Plimsoll and his patent cure, the load line', Edgar J. Feuchtwanger, *Disraeli*, p. 176.

153. *'several thousand copies of which were circulated anonymously'*: Plimsoll and Seamen's Defence Fund Committee Report, Plimsoll Papers, Howell Collection, Bishopsgate Institute Library.

153. *A spoof in* Punch: *All in the Downs; or The Bottomry Bond! A Nautical Novel by S. PL-MS-LL MP*, *Punch*, 3 March 1877.

153. *a note in George Howell's account*: 'The Plimsoll Movement' MS, p. 10.

153. *'Heav'ly insured – rotten old hulk'*: George Manville Fenn, *Ship Ahoy!: A Yarn in Thirty-Six Cable Lengths*, p. 12.

153. *The prosecution in Liverpool*: Houghton vs Plimsoll trial, reported in *The Times*, 2 April 1874.

153. *A solicitor's letter*: letter from Messrs Harvey and Alsop, Castle-street, Liverpool, and Samuel Plimsoll's reply, *The Times*, ibid.

154. *A preliminary report*: Preliminary Report of the Royal Commission on Unseaworthy Ships, Parliamentary Papers.

154. *'There is no apparent probability'*: *The Times*, 18 March 1873, 'Election Intelligence', p. 5.

155. *'a dull man'*: John Bright on Adderley, quoted in Peters, p. 99.

155. *'would have made an admirable'*: Henry W. Lucy, *A Diary of Two Parliaments*, quoted in Peters, pp. 102–3.

155. *Adderley . . . announced that he had no intention*: 13 April 1874, quoted in Peters, p. 97.

155. *In one case Adderley's caution*: case of *Thornaby*, recounted in Peters, p. 101.

155. *'To lose the Bill by a majority of three'*: 'Essence of Parliament', *Punch*, 4 July 1874, p. 2.

156. *'Mr Plimsoll need not be discouraged'*: *Western Daily Press*, quoted in Peters, p. 100.

156. *'though [Plimsoll] failed the other night'*: 'Plimsoll: A Commercial Eclogue', *Punch*, 11 July 1874, p. 19.

156. *Correspondence between the Board of Trade and shipowners*: *Merchant Ships* (draught of water records): 'correspondence between Mr. Plimsoll . . . and the Board of Trade, on the draught of water records furnished to him by the Board of Trade', January 1875, Parliamentary Papers.

157. *Adderley received a deputation of shipowners*: reported in *The Times*, 29 January 1875, p. 6.

157. *'Oh! Sir Charles Adderley'*: 'From our London correspondent', *Staffordshire Sentinel*, 10 February 1875.

158. *'struggling for five hours with the ship owners'*: H. W. Lucy, quoted in Peters, pp. 102–3.

158. *The Commons had not been amused*: story of Russell placards, *The Times*, 18 February 1875.

158. *'Every day brings me so many letters'*: letter circulated as a flyer by Edward Baines in July 1875, Plimsoll Papers, Working Class Movement Library, Salford.

159. *The* International . . . *later lightened*: *The Times*, 24 March 1875, p. 6.

159. *When the Ladies' Committee*: Exeter Hall meeting, 6 April 1875, *The Times*, 7 April 1875.

160. *the Defence Fund Committee . . . decided . . . to disband*: minutes of meeting of 12 May at 16 St James's Street, Plimsoll Papers, Howell Collection, Bishopsgate Institute Library.

160. *On 28 May Plimsoll went to witness a curious feat*: *The Times*, 28 May 1875, p. 5.

6: DISRAELI'S ERROR

161. *a young American . . . visited the House of Commons*: Richard Henry Dana III, 'Seventy-Six Years After', in Richard Henry Dana, *Two Years Before the Mast*, 1911 edn., p. 521.

161. *they both gave papers at the Social Science Congress in Sheffield*: recorded on omnesamici.co.uk.

163. *Disraeli announced*: principal sources for description of outburst are: Henry W. Lucy, *A Diary of Two Parliaments*, vol. 1, 1874–1880, pp. 105–18, printed first in *Daily News* and then in *Penny Illustrated Paper and Illustrated Times*, 31 July 1875, pp. 1–7; and Hansard, 22 July 1875, pp. 1822ff.

164. *George Goschen . . . called attention to the urgency*: Hansard, 22 July 1875, p. 1822.

165. *'the whole scene had been carefully thought out'*: Lord George Hamilton, *Parliamentary Reminiscences 1868–1885*, pp. 95–6.

165. *'whimsical Radical – a curious mixture of philanthropy and self-advertisment'*: ibid.

165. *'clearly premeditated . . . told Sullivan'*: W. H. G. Armytage, *A. J. Mundella 1825–1897: The Liberal Background to the Labour Movement*, p. 158.

165. *'The 'etc', according to his son's later account'*: from S. R. C. Plimsoll's notes for a biography of his father in Sally Shaw's private collection.

166. *'hopped about', 'gesticulating madly'*: *Penny Illustrated Paper*, 31 July 1875.

166. *standing on one leg*: Lucy, p.107.

167. *'It was no use shouting "Order"'*: Frank Hugh O'Donnell MP, in the *New Witness*, 1912, quoted in Charles Plomer Hopkins, *Altering Plimsoll's Mark*, p. 2.

167. *Plimsoll . . . shook his fist*: 'Still remembered to this day is the Plimsoll incident, when in July 1875 Samuel Plimsoll, the member for Derby, shook his fist at Disraeli in the House', Edgar J. Feuchtwanger, *Disraeli*, p. 176.

167. *The Speaker, in 'calm manner'*: Lucy, p. 107.

167. *Plimsoll also mentioned the* Foundling: *Telegraph*, 22 July 1875.

168–9. *Sir Charles Adderley, 'who occupied a safe position'*: ibid., p. 108.

169. *Captain Gosset . . . whispered*: as remembered by Frank Hugh O'Donnell MP in *New Witness*, 1912, and quoted in Hopkins, p. 6.

169. *'that seemed little less than that of an actual maniac'*: Justin McCarthy MP, *A History of Our Own Times*, vol. V (originally published 1880), 1932 edn., pp. 144–50.

169. *Plimsoll gave his friend Alexander Sullivan*: Armytage, *A. J. Mundella, 1825–1897: The Liberal Background to the Labour Movement*, p. 71.

169. *the gentlemen of the press in the reporters' gallery on the level below*: details of layout of the House of Commons in 1875 from parliamentary historian Chris Pond.

169. *her action that day was remembered for years*: mention in Eliza's obituary, *The Times*, 26 August 1882.

170. *Plimsoll, 'frantic with grief and despair', was taken home . . . to Eliza's care*: Moncure D. Conway, 'London Letter', *Cincinnati Commercial*, 6 August 1875.

170. *One account says that Plimsoll heard earlier that day*: R. J. Hinton, 'Political Agitators', in T. W. Higginson, (ed.), *Brief Biographies: English Radical Leaders*, vol. 2, p. 193.

170. *'a week ago he [Plimsoll] was one of the happiest men in England'*: Conway, 'London Letter', *Cincinatti Commercial*, 6 August 1875.

170. *flung himself into the arms of his wife, Lady Palmerston, who was coming down*: Andrew Lang (ed.), *Life, Letters and Diaries of Sir Stafford Northcote, first Earl of Iddesleigh*, p. 128.

171. *'May I offer the following suggestions as to the process of massacre'*: Lang, letter 22 July 1875, pp. 77–8.

171. *'[Plimsoll's Bill] was not . . . a direct and simple remedy'*: Lang, letter 24 July 1875, p.78.

172. *'Permissive legislation is the characteristic of a free people'*: Disraeli, Hansard, 24 June 1875, p. 525.

172. *It was a measure . . . intended to prove that the Tories were not . . . just self-interested*: K. Theodore Hoppen, *The Mid-Victorian Generation 1846–1886*, p. 616.

172–3. *'would forward the solution of the question rather than hinder it'*: Hansard, 22 July 1875, p. 1867.

173. *The Leader of the Opposition was quick to point out*: 'The Marquess of Hartington said he could not allow the debate to close without pointing out that the statement just made by the Chancellor of the Exchequer was totally at variance with that which had been made by the Prime Minister,' Hansard, 22 July 1875, p. 1867.

173. *Disraeli, realising that Hartington's course would 'extricate him'*: R. Wilson, *The Life and Times of Queen Victoria*, vol. II, p. 486.

174. *'He is a nervous gentleman'*: Conway, 'London Letter', *Cincinnati Commercial*, 6 August 1875.

174. *'Mr Disraeli rose to announce' Punch*, 31 July 1875, p. 3.

175. *'A Plea for Plimsoll'*: ibid., p. 44.

175. *The government had . . . 'lied and truckled'*: *Penny Illustrated Paper*, 31 July 1875.

176. *'The numerous meetings of sympathisers'*: *Graphic*, 28 August 1875, p. 175, col. 3.

176. *The papers published Plimsoll's protest in full*: as in *The Baker and Plimsoll Number of the Penny Satirist*, special edition, London, 1875.

177. *Clerkenwell Green*: William Dawson, *A Mid-London Parish: Short History of the Parish of St John's Clerkenwell*, ch. V, London, 1885.

178. *'If one Member went mad every year'*: Frederick Percy Rawson, quoted in G. H. Peters, *The Plimsoll Line*, p. 11. (Rawson was a plant owner employing 126 men.)

178. *'introduced by the wife of Moncure D. Conway'*: Annie Wood Besant, *An Autobiography*, pp. 133–4.

179. *'he belongs to the good old . . . tradition of cussedness'*: A. N. Wilson, *The Victorians*, pp. 447–8.

179. *On that July afternoon in 1875*: *The Baker and Plimsoll Number of the Penny Satirist*, London, 1875.

180. *meetings . . . took place that same night around the country*: *The Times*, 29 July 1875, p. 5.

180. *The meeting in Birmingham*: ibid.

181. *'If [these facts] do not stir the hearts'*: Samuel Plimsoll's appendix to George Manville Fenn, *Ship Ahoy!*, and *The Times*, 29 July 1875.

181. *'if this were his dying speech'*: ibid.

182. *'if you boiled Gladstone'*: Lady Palmerston, quoted in Malcolm Pearce, *British Political History, 1867–2001*, p. 32.

182. *'Gladstone's jokes are no laughing matter'*: Lord Derby, quoted in Joseph S. Meisel, 'The Importance of Being Serious: The Unexplored Connection between Gladstone and Humour', *History:*

The Journal of the Historical Association, vol. 84, issue 274, 1999, pp. 278–300.

182. *fading prima donna . . . 'aiming to be gaily audacious'*: Henry W. Lucy, quoted in Feuchtwanger, pp. 176–7.

182. *questioning of the competence of Disraeli's government*: *The Times* report of Birmingham and other meetings, 28 July 1875, and Peters, p. 115.

183. *Even an evening at the theatre*: Globe Theatre programme in the author's collection.

183–4. *'poor, ill-fated Gustavus Brooke'*: Adeline Billington in *Life Stories from Lloyd's*, 1912, p. 4.

184. *'received with great applause'*: *Penny Illustrated Paper*, 31 July 1875, p. 7.

184. *Public feeling was fuelled by a case*: case of the *Alcedo,* Conway, 'London Letter', *Cincinnatti Commercial*, 8 August 1875, p. 4, and *Penny Illustrated Paper*, 31 July 1875, p. 10.

185. *'the withdrawal of the Merchant Shipping Bill'*: Disraeli to Lady Bradford, 27 July 1875, Marquis of Zetland (ed.), *The Letters of Disraeli to Lady Bradford and Lady Chesterfield*, vol. 1, *1873–5*, p. 266.

7: PLIMSOLL IS KING

187. *'the undertow of Mr Plimsoll's out-of-doors wave of popularity'*: 'Essence of Parliament', *Punch*, 7 August 1875, p. 46.

187. *whom she had invited*: S. R. C. Plimsoll reported that his father visited the Queen at Windsor more than once to explain his ideas, from his notes for a biography of his father in Sally Shaw's private collection.

187. *'The Queen has to thank Mr Disraeli'*: letter from Queen Victoria to Disraeli from Osborne House, 25 July 1875, Bodleian Library, Hughenden Papers 79/1 fos. 1–52 B/XIX/B319/37.

187. *'immense majorities'*: 'The Agricultural Bill was carried through the Committee with immense majorities; only one – but an important clause – remains for – though night – he must say to-day – at 12 o'clock': Disraeli, letter to Queen Victoria from Whitehall Gardens, 3 a.m., 28 July 1875. From George Earl Buckle (ed.), *Letters of Queen Victoria, second series 1870–1878*, 1926.

188. *While she responded that she was sorry*: letter from Queen Victoria to Disraeli from Osborne House, 29 July 1875, Bodleian Library, Hughenden Papers 79/1 fos. 1–52 B/XIX/C/32/49.

188. *'one in which the Queen was said to be as much interested'*: R. Wilson, *The Life and Times of Queen Victoria*, vol. II, p. 48.

188. *He felt besieged*: as the scale of the reaction grew, Disraeli's notes to Anne and Selina grew less confident. To Lady Bradford, in response to a sympathetic note after Plimsoll's outburst, 23 July: 'One can get through anything with such celestial messengers!' To Lady Chesterfield, on 24 July, he wrote during 'a pause in a time of great labor [*sic*] and some anxiety'; and on 25 July: 'The storm is high but I think I shall direct it'. To Lady Bradford, 27 July: 'The Cabinet was an anxious one'. Marquis of Zetland (ed.), *The Letters of Disraeli to Lady Bradford and Lady Chesterfield*, vol. 1, *1873–5*, pp. 263–4.

189. *stop-gap Bill . . . 'hurriedly knocked up to block Plimsoll's'*: to Lady Bradford, 27 July, Zetland, p. 265.

189. *'A certain person'*: ibid.

189. *'There was to have been a fierce attack on the Government'*: ibid.

189. *'do penance' . . . 'hasty, wild and bad' legislation*: quoted in ibid.

190. *'the Whipping-boy of the Government'*: *Punch*, 7 August 1875.

191. *'I send a rapid line after a morning of great excitement', 'ostensibly at least, perfectly calm', 'If I were defeated', 'If they stand by me'*: Disraeli to Lady Bradford, six o'clock, 29 July, Zetland, p. 267.

192. *'Now I know exactly how a General must feel'*: Disraeli to Lady Bradford, ten o'clock, 29 July 1875, Zetland, p. 268.

192. *'After the declaration . . . that "he was off his head"'*: ibid.

192. *'I should not be surprised if, after all his bluster'*: ibid.

192. *'it was all over with the government'*: Horsman, quoted in ibid.

193. *'Every intriguer'*: ibid.

193. *'For aught I know . . . the mob may be assembling'*: Disraeli to Lady Bradford, 29 July 1875, Zetland, pp. 269–70.

193. *'Mr Secretary Cross . . . who is naturally a brave man'*: 29 July 1875, Zetland, p. 268.

193. *The nearest meeting . . . was aborted*: *Penny Illustrated Paper*, 31 July 1875, p. 7.

193. *'The lions in Trafalgar-square'*: *The Times*, 29 July 1875, p. 5.

194. *'That in the face of the present conciliatory policy'*: ibid.

194. *Plimsoll had urged the Board of Trade to pursue*: correspondence relating to ships detained as unseaworthy. Parliamentary Accounts and Papers (25), vol. LXVI 8 February–15 August 1876 BS Ref1 66.

195. *'Rightly or wrongly, Mr Plimsoll regards Mr Edward Bates'*: 8 August 1875, probably written by Edmund Yates, proprietor of the *New York Herald*.

195. *'stern, fierce, merciless, indomitable'*: B. G. Orchard, *Liverpool's Legion of Honour* (1893), quoted in Alan H. Rowson in P. E. Bates, *Bates of Bellefield, Gyrn Castle and Manydown*, p. 10.

195. 'somewhat rough and truculent exterior': Vanity Fair, 12 May 1888.

196. a group figurehead depicting nine of his closest relatives: A. W. B. Simpson, Cannibalism and the Common Law, p. 129.

196. 'We always wanted power and speed': Tom Bates, quoted in Bates, Bates of Bellefield, Gyrn Castle and Manydown, p. 27.

196. 'lavish rather than discreet': Vanity Fair, 12 May 1888.

197. he had an 'ungovernable temper': the opinion of Bates's father's partner, Mr Elliott, quoted by Alan H. Rowson, in Bates, Bates of Bellefield, Gyrn Castle and Manydown, p. 8. Elliot complained too of Edward's 'quarrelsome disposition' and of conduct 'attaching discredit to us'. Elliot wrote to Bates Sr that his son's 'most prominent feature' was 'unreasonableness': ibid., pp. 7–8.

197. He would tell an anecdote: J. G. Cooper and A. D. Power, A History of West Derby, p. 219.

197. Later, in 1878: Report of the Select Committee on Merchant Seamen Bill, together with the Proceedings of the Committee, Minutes of Evidence and Appendix, House of Commons, 31 May 1878, pp. 1–330 BS Ref1 Reports, Committees vol. XVI 1878.

197. a somewhat different tale told about him: story of Parsee in Rowson in Bates, Bates of Bellefield, Gyrn Castle and Manydown, p. 9.

198. Bully Bates was not popular: Cooper and Power, p. 219.

198. He built a tree-lined carriageway: old lantern slide, Liverpool Record Office, Cooper and Power, p. 220.

198. they stayed that way for fifty years: Cooper and Power, p. 220.

198. 'introduced hitherto unheard-of devices to keep down expenses': 1863 article reprinted in Orchard, Liverpool's Legion of Honour, and quoted in Rowson in Bates, Bates of Bellefield, Gyrn Castle and Manydown, p. 10.

198. In June 1874 a collier owned by Bates: story of Euxine from Simpson, Cannibalism and the Common Law, pp. 177ff.

200. 'after careful consideration': Simpson, p. 191

200. 'Apparently they never did': ibid.

201. It is hard to believe that Plimsoll would have kept quiet: Simpson speculates that Plimsoll may not have known about the Euxine, p. 193.

202. 'As to the statement made . . . I forgive him': Bates, Hansard, 22 July 1875 p. 1858, and Penny Illustrated Paper, 31 July 1875, p. 6.

202. the full story of the Euxine would have come out: as Simpson points out, pp. 192–3.

202. 'We can only wonder': Simpson, p. 193.

203. 'My maxim through life has been': Bates, quoted in Rowson in Bates, Bates of Bellefield, Gyrn Castle and Manydown, p. 13.

203. 'material lying around in the yard': ibid., p. 11.

203. *'used to sit on the safety valve'*: allegation quoted in ibid.

203–7. *Charles Morgan Norwood believed himself to be the target of Plimsoll's shaken fist*: story of Norwood, Applegarth and Mundella, A. W. Humphrey, *Robert Applegarth: Trade Unionist, Educationist, Reformer*, pp. 188–90.

204. *'Govt. Bill with my amendments'*: Samuel Plimsoll to Anthony Mundella, Mundella Papers, Sheffield University Library MS6-9 MS22.

205. *'Plimsoll disgusted the House'*: Anthony Mundella to Robert Leader, Leader Correspondence, Sheffield University Library, quoted in W. H. G. Armytage, *A. J. Mundella, 1825–1897: The Liberal Background to the Labour Movement*, pp. 70–1.

205. *'Plimsoll was absurd and spoilt the whole thing'*: ibid.

205. *'our friend Plimsoll will catch it in a day or two'*: Mundella quoted in ibid., p. 128.

207. *'an instance of bad luck going with a good name'*: *Punch*, 21 August 1875, p. 76.

207. *'With reference to a joke'*: *Penny Illustrated Paper*, 28 August 1875, p. 4.

207. *'Plimsoll is, well – not a gentleman'*: Mundella, Leader Correspondence, 15 April 1875, quoted in Armytage, *A. J. Mundella, 1825–1897: The Liberal Background to the Labour Movement*, pp. 158–9.

207. *'Cases of criminal libel'*: from George Howell, *Labour Legislation, Labour Movements and Labour Leaders*, vol. ii, quoted in G. D. H. Cole and A. W. Filson, *British Working Class Movements: Select Documents 1789–1875*, p. 614.

208. *'My dear Mr Plimsoll, As chairman of your committee'*: Shaftesbury's letter to *The Times*, 27 July 1875, and *Penny Illustrated Paper*, 31 July 1875, p. 6.

209. *a pamphlet entitled 'Fact Against Sensation'*: Rt Hon. George Augustus Frederick Cavendish Bentinck, *Fact Against Sensation, Mr Cavendish Bentinck's speeches on Merchant Shipping Legislation, 1875, Reprinted, with notes, from the Nautical Magazine*.

209. *'during thirty years sailors had not loved his ships'*: Orchard, *Liverpool's Legion of Honour*, quoted in Rowson in Bates, *Bates of Bellefield, Gyrn Castle and Manydown*, p. 14.

210. *He backtracked*: Disraeli, Hansard, 29 July 1875.

210. *'a Moody and Sankey in politics'*: Disraeli, letter to Lady Bradford, 30 July 1875, Zetland, p. 270.

211. *'suet pudding legislation'*: Hansard, 7 July 1875, p. 1064.

211. *Reflecting Disraeli's philosophy of a* laissez-faire *government*: K. Theodore Hoppen, *The Mid-Victorian Generation*, p. 615.

211. *'Good deal of negotiation with Plimsoll'*: 'Have persuaded [Plimsoll] not to go to the House, but to entrust his amendment to Mr Reed . . . Many MPs concurred with me'. From Shaftesbury's diary, quoted in Edwin Hodder, *The Life and Work of the Seventh Earl of Shaftesbury K.G.*, vol. III, p. 328.

211. *'modest, judicious, acceptable'*: Shaftesbury quoted in Georgina Battiscombe, *Shaftesbury: A Biography of the Seventh Earl 1801–1885*, p. 316.

211. *'The battle of Armageddon'*: Disraeli, letter to Lady Bradford, 30 July 1875, Zetland, vol. 1, p. 271.

211. *'I am not an alarmist'*: Disraeli, letter to Lord Bradford 1 August 1875, ibid.

212. like letting *'a draper fix the the number of inches he allowed in a yard'*: Samuel Plimsoll, quoted in *The Times*, 17 August 1876, p. 4.

212. *A load line was, for the first time, compulsory*: *The Times*, 6 August 1875.

212. *'"all right" but it was not glorious'*, *'and those who came were still Plimsollised too much'*: Edgar Feuchtwanger, *Disraeli*, p. 176, quoting Zetland, vol. 1, pp. 268–71, letters of 29, 30 July and 3 August 1875.

213. *'Whenever he rises, members are apt to leave'*: Moncure D. Conway, 'London Letter', *Cincinatti Commercial*, 6 August 1875.

213. *he would benefit as a speaker*: Henry W. Lucy, *A Diary of Two Parliaments*, vol. 1, entry for 1 August 1875, p. 111.

213. *'Well, but it was damned dull, wasn't it?'*: George W. E. Russell, *Portraits of the Seventies*, p. 95.

213. *'Hartington . . . stands much higher in public opinion'*: Lucy, p. 111.

214. *'The incident . . . revealed in Lord Hartington a capacity'*: R. Wilson, *The Life and Times of Queen Victoria*, vol. II, p. 486.

214. *'There is another man . . . who has suffered by the Plimsoll episode'*: Conway, 'London Letter', *Cincinatti Commercial*, 6 August 1875.

214. *'When it was launched it did not glide'*: Disraeli, reported in *The Times*, 5 August 1875, p. 8.

215. *'Mr Plimsoll has been King'*: *The Times*, 6 August, 1875, p. 9. Also quoted in Neil Hanson, *The Custom of the Sea*, p. 68.

215. *'There is not much left of Dizzy except his cheek'*: quoted in George Carslake Thompson, *Public Opinion and Lord Beaconsfield*, vol. 1, p. 202.

215. *'a despotism tempered by jokes'*: *New York Herald*, 8 August 1875, quoted in R. J. Hinton, 'Political Agitators', in T. W. Higginson (ed.), *Brief Biographies: English Radical Leaders*, vol. 2, p. 202.

216. *'The Times may scold'*: Disraeli, letter to Lady Bradford, 10 August 1875, Zetland, vol. 1, p. 273.

216. *'A man has in most cases'*: A. H. Japp, *Good Men and True*, p. 408.

217. *'[Plimsoll's] outburst could be justified'*: R. C. K. Ensor, *History of England 1870–1914*, p. 37.

217. *'Such performances have since become commonplaces'*: ibid., p. 56.

8: VICTORY FOR THE PEOPLE

219. *A tribute was published*: Graphic, 28 August 1875, p. 196.

219. *'working men connected with shipping and shipbuilding'*: ibid., p. 195, col. 3; Mr H. T. Humphry of Kennington, London, was the treasurer of the Plimsoll Memorial Fund.

219. *Auguste Chevalier*: Chevalier (1823–98) lived in Paris and also engraved the reverse of the 100- and 50-franc pieces of Napoleon III: L. Forrer, *Biographical Dictionary of Medallists*.

219. *It had Plimsoll's profile on the front and a sinking coffin-ship*: cited in Laurence A. Brown, *A Catalogue of British Historical Medals 1837–1901*, pp. 306–7, no. 3015 (BL HLR 737.22). Samples of the medal are to be found in the National Maritime Museum, the Victoria & Albert Museum, the Museum of London and, in both sizes, in the author's private collection.

219. *Civic authorities met*: the renamed Manor Street included Jeeves Terrace. Source: Malcolm Barr-Hamilton, Borough Archivist, Tower Hamlets, London.

221. *He and Eliza headed for the Romanian ports*: The Times, 19 November 1875.

221. *'If I had my way I'd tie a rope round his neck'*: story told by Walter Runciman, *The Times*, 22 August 1929; also a version in David Masters, *The Plimsoll Mark*, p. 230.

221. *On 5 November, in the Sussex village of Lewes*: Sussex Express, 9 November 1875.

222. *Reports, complained Plimsoll . . . were not enough*: The Times, 9 December 1875, p. 10.

223. *to 'show what good men we allow to be drowned'*: Samuel Plimsoll, *Cattle Ships*, p. 95.

223. *In fact the couple travelled this section of their voyage*: 13 December 1875 the Plimsolls arrived in Malta on the Norwegian steamer the *Peterjebsen*. They left on 17 December aboard a P&O steamer, the *Poonah*, bound for Southampton via Gibraltar: *The Times*, 14, 19 December 1875.

224. *On 10 January 1876 he addressed*: meetings reported in G. H. Peters, *The*

Plimsoll Line, p. 122, including Liverpool (29 January 1876) and Bath (4 February 1876).

224. *He was the last of thirteen men to die*: *Atlanta Constitution*, 19 August 1875, p. 1.

224. *The ship, the* Bremen, *belonged to Edward Bates*: *Western Daily Mercury*, 8 February 1876, cited in Peters, footnote p. 125.

224. *a court of inquiry was held in San Francisco*: *Morning Oregonian*, 3 September 1875.

224. *A subsequent inquiry*: papers relating to recent cases of scurvy on board British Merchant Ships, Case 2 'Bremen', p. 34 of the original document, p. 488 of the bound volume Parliamentary Papers BS Ref LXVII 1876.

226–7. *'I submit that . . . it is utterly inexcusable'*: ibid., 6 March 1874, pp. 56–8, 510–12.

227. *William Spooner, investigating*: ibid., 1 May 1875, pp. 84–5, 538–9.

228. *Plimsoll wrote in the preface*: preface by Samuel Plimsoll MP to *A Voice from the Sea* 'by the author of Margery's Christmas Box', dated 10 February 1876 from 35 Victoria Street, Westminster.

229. *A higher-profile case*: *Staffordshire Sentinel*, 26 February 1876.

229. *'It is my usual custom in ordering stores to make no reference to price'*: Parliamentary Papers relating to recent cases of scurvy on board British Merchant Ships LXVI 1876, pp. 153, 607.

229. *submitted documentary evidence of the high quality of Bates and Sons' provisions*: ibid., including receipts for supplies from the ship's chandler Burnyeat and Dalzell (a firm to whose founders the present author is related by marriage).

229. *'the dirtiness of the crew'*: Edward Bates's evidence from ibid., pp. 159, 613.

229. *a court found Bates guilty of negligence*: *Western Daily Mercury*, 8 February 1876.

231. *On 8 April 1876 an indignation meeting*: Peters, p. 122.

231. *he deplored the practice of feeding sailors with food 'they would not give to their dogs'*: Samuel Plimsoll at indignation meeting at Cutlers' Hall, Sheffield, 8 April 1876, reported in *Sheffield Telegraph* and quoted in Peters, p. 125.

231. *Always alert to the possibility of conspiracy, Plimsoll alleged*: Plimsoll, *Cattle Ships*, p. 125.

232. *'I entreat assistance'*: Samuel Plimsoll, quoted in Peters, p. 126.

232. *trivial distractions*: as recorded in *Punch*, Jan–Mar 1876.

232. *On 2 February 1876 many met*: Report of meeting of shipowners of the United Kingdom, held at the London Tavern, on . . . 2nd February,

1876 . . . With account of the proceedings at the interview of the deputation to the Right Hon. B. Disraeli, . . . 5th February, 1876: General Shipowners' Society, London 1876.

233. *'a necessity in order to maintain the maritime supremacy, or even equality, of this country'*: ibid., p. 35.

234. *Meanwhile Plimsoll defended himself*: Hansard, 17 February 1876, p. 442.

234. *neglecting to deal with the issue of deckloading . . . was 'very silly'*: ibid., p. 446.

234. *'like a child that skips the hard words'*: Samuel Plimsoll to TUC delegates at Westminster Palace Hotel, 25 April 1876, quoted in Peters, p. 127.

234-5. *The Bill went for ratification to the House of Lords – and came back with the clause about deckloads deleted*: Peters, p. 128; Plimsoll, *Cattle Ships*, p. 127.

235. *'That vast aquarium of cold-blooded life'*: Shaftesbury on the House of Lords

235. *'the malign and homicidal influence of Lord Carlingford'*: Plimsoll, *Cattle Ships*, p. 127.

235. *the Merchant Shipping Act, passed on 12 August 1876*: Merchant Shipping Act 1876 39 & 40 Vict ch. 80, pp. 503–5.

237. *'A Cheer for Samuel Plimsoll'*: written, composed and sung by Fred Albert, 1876.

237. *'infallible mirth-maker', Fred Albert's real name*: *New York Clipper* (theatrical magazine), 30 October 1886, p. 523, col. 1, obituary of Fred Albert, 9 November 1845–12 October 1886; John Culme, footlight-notes.tripod.com; playbills from the Templeman Library theatre collection, University of Kent.

238. *'pretty correct estimates of public opinion'*: *The Entr'acte*, 1 January 1881, p. 5b cited at John Culme, footlightnotes.tripod.com.

238. *'a good vein of common sense'*: *The Entr'acte*, 29 January 1881, p. 13a cited at ibid.

238. *his manner was formal*: 'his method was very stereotyped and formal', *The Entr'acte*, 16 October 1886, p. 5b cited at ibid.

238. *It was named after him*: 21 December 1876, lifeboat the *Samuel Plimsoll* launched at Lowestoft, Peters, p. 133.

238. *According to the* Liverpool Daily Post: 17 August 1876, p. 6.

239. *Robert Hook, who saved more than two hundred lives*: *Graphic*, 20 January 1883, p. 61.

240. *At Sheffield Plimsoll was presented with a silver cup*: *Liverpool Daily Post*, 18 August 1878, p. 4.

240. *its provenance*: controversy over cup, *Liverpool Daily Post*, 25 August 1875, p. 4, quoting *Sheffield Telegraph*.

240. *Philip Lace worked for the Liverpool Rubber Company*: Peters, p. 179

240. *black lace-ups*: as depicted in *Shoe and Leather Record*, 17 June 1898, p. 1326.

240. *'See that the name "Liver" is on the sole'*: ibid.

240. *The name caught on as far afield as Jamaica*: plimsolls advertised in *The Daily Gleaner*, 7 June 1892.

241. *Plimsoll was 'made quite ill'*: Georgina Cowper-Temple, *Diary*, Southampton University, BR58 21 February 1876.

241. *'an acute nervous disability'*: *Derby and Chesterfield Reporter*, 16 March 1877.

241. *One defiant Cardiff captain placed it on the funnel of his ship*: reported by Samuel Plimsoll at the indignation meeting at Cutlers' Hall, Sheffield, 8 April 1876, reported in *Sheffield Telegraph* and quoted in Peters, p. 122.

241. *'It was not all that was desired; still it was a great step'*: George Howell, *Labour Legislation, Labour Movements and Labour Leaders*, p. 280.

241. *'An Act of parliament is now on the Statute book'*: 9 September 1878, quoted in Peters, p. 139.

9: THE AFTERMATH

243. *All in the Downs; or The Bottomry Bond!*: 'A Nautical Novel by S. Plimsoll MP', *Punch*, 3 March 1877, pp. 93–5; 10 March 1877, pp. 105–7; 17 March 1877, pp. 118–19; 24 March 1877, p. 131.

245. *One such case . . . was remembered by L. M. Montgomery*: *The Selected Journals of L. M. Montgomery*, ed. Mary Rubio, vol. 1, *1889–1910*, p. 354.

245. *'A poll tax would be less iniquitous than this'*: Samuel Plimsoll, *The Condition of Malta*, p. 5.

246. *'the surface overflow from open highways'*: ibid., p. 8.

246. *'I should say that Mr Rowsell must be a very nice man'*: ibid.

246. *'I have been in Baldwin's Gardens'*: ibid., p. 14.

247. *he complained of drinks that were intoxicating*: Samuel Plimsoll, quoted in *Punch*, 24 November 1877, p. 229.

247. *the delightful horror of seeing him take his glass eye out*: as recounted by his niece, Mrs M. Hemmings, quoted in David Masters, *The Plimsoll Mark*, p. 244.

248. *'a little old-fashioned but pretty place'*: Joseph Havelock Wilson, *My Stormy Voyage Through Life*, p. 163.

249. *The Plimsolls' enjoyment . . . was short-lived*: G. H. Peters, *The Plimsoll Line*, p. 139.

249. *Election handbills*: election flyer in verse from the Plimsoll Papers, Working Class Movement Library, Salford.

249. *The opposition's campaign poster*: Peters, p. 140.

249. *he went on to be elected for Hull*: Norwood chaired the 'Norwood Committee on the Sea Fishing Trade in 1882 to Inquire Into and Report Whether Any and What Legislation is Desirable with a view to placing the relations between Owners, Masters and Crews of Shipping Vessels on a More Satisfactory Basis'. He thought more legislation was undesirable.

250. *On an overnight visit to Hawarden*: The Gladstone Diaries, ed. H. C. G. Matthew, 9 April 1880, vol. 9, pp. 499–500.

250. *'taking the Chiltern Hundreds'*: from parliament.uk factsheet no. 11.

251. Punch *published a cartoon of Harcourt*: 'Man Overboard' cartoon, Punch, 22 May 1880.

251. *described him as 'Salt of the Earth'*: Punch, 5 June 1880, p. 281, included this brief would-be witticism: 'An Oxford Mixture. Pepper and Salt (of the Earth) – Harcourt and Plimsoll.'

251. *'agility he has shown in availing himself of the Derby life-buoy'*: ibid., p. 264.

251. *'Mr Plimsoll thinks the cause . . . will be better served'*: Punch, 29 May 1880, p. 241.

251. *'has the way of speaking to other men', 'a noble act of self-sacrifice'*: Harcourt, Derby speech, 21 May 1880, The Times, 24 May 1880, p. 10, partly cited in Masters, The Plimsoll Mark, p. 249.

251–2. *the local Liberal Party invited Plimsoll to stand*: The Times, 26 May 1880.

252. *'"Rise, Sir Samuel Plimsoll, Baronet!"'*: Penny Illustrated Paper, 29 May 1880.

252. *'She has a small and girlish mind'*: Shaftesbury on Queen Victoria, quoted in A. N. Wilson, The Victorians, paperback edn., p. 55.

253. *'I absolutely glory in the working men'*: Samuel Plimsoll, Our Seamen, p. 82.

253. *In 1876 he was accused of bribing the electorate*: Rowson in Bates, Bates of Bellefield, Gyrn Castle and Manydown, p. 15.

253. *'refusing part of his inheritance'*: Bates's will in ibid., p. 19.

254. *'Your theological beliefs and mine are as opposite as the poles'*: Samuel Plimsoll, letter to Charles Bradlaugh, 25 June 1880, Bradlaugh Papers 173, Bishopsgate Institute Library.

255. *Madame Tussaud's . . . admitted him in wax in July 1880*: Punch, 31 July 1880.

256. *Plimsoll continued to correspond with Chamberlain*: The Times, October 1880.

257. *He blamed not a vengeful God, but man*: Samuel Plimsoll, 'Explosions in Collieries and their Cure', Nineteenth Century, December 1880, p. 903.

257. *Between 1860 and 1879 there were eighty-five explosions*: dmm.org.uk/names.

258. *Meanwhile for the family there were several moments of crisis*: details of Eliza's travels and last months from her obituary, *The Times*, 19 August 1882, and Peters, pp. 147–8.

258. *Alice remembered the adventure*: Alice M. Solloway (née Dickinson), writing from Selby in Yorkshire to Nellie Plimsoll ('Aunt Nellie') in response to questions about her uncle from J. W. Knight of the National Union of Seamen, 10 July 1928, Sally Shaw's private collection and quoted in Peters, p. 172.

259. *neuralgia brought on . . . by washing her hair*: Eliza Plimsoll's obituary, *The Times*, 19 August 1882.

260. *Some years later Samuel's fish market project failed*: document establishing fish market, Southwark Local Studies Library, Parish of St Mary Newington; papers re establishment of the South London Market, Stmarynew/2/Box 13 1882–88; winding-up, *The Times*, 8 August 1888, p. 3.

260. *'entering heart and soul'*: Eliza Plimsoll's obituary, *Rotherham Advertiser*, quoted in Peters, p. 148.

261. *'Can't you remember how you felt'*: Samuel Plimsoll, *Cattle Ships*, p. 92.

262. *Nellie, whose diary of the trip is now lost*: Nellie mentions this diary in a letter to Samuel Jr. ('Dick'), among the private papers of Sally Shaw.

262. *to America, to see his brother Henry in Brooklyn*: *New York Times*, 10 November 1884, p. 5. Plimsoll stayed at the Gilsey House Hotel.

262. *one of his old opponents came to grief*: a full account of the Dilke episode appears in David Nicholls, *The Lost Prime Minister: A Life of Sir Charles Dilke*, ch. 11, 'A Personal Tragedy 1885–86'.

263. *Later even the provenances of the paintings*: Timothy Wilcox, 'The Aesthete Expunged, The Career and Collection of T. Eustace Smith MP', *Journal of the History of Collections* 5, vol. 1.

264. *at the house of a Hull JP*: Peters, p. 153.

264. *would be seen strolling contentedly in Hyde Park*: Masters, p. 255.

264. *Thomas Brassey . . . lived two doors down*: from address in Stenton & Lees.

264. *In 1888 Plimsoll met Havelock Wilson*: Wilson, *My Stormy Voyage Through Life*, p. 84.

265. *If the meeting was a large and successful one*: ibid., pp. 204–5.

265. *In 1888 Plimsoll visited*: story of T. D. Sullivan's release from Tullamore Jail, *The Times*, 2 February 1888, p. 6.

266. *The Board of Trade asked for the assistance of Lloyd's Register*: Lloyd's Register: A History 1760–1999, p. 29.

267. *'If Mr Plimsoll should choose to engage in another crusade'*: Chamberlain, quoted in Charles Plomer Hopkins, *Altering Plimsoll's Mark*, p. 9.

267. *Plimsoll . . . was still breakfasting with Harcourt*: from Harcourt speech in Salisbury, *The Times*, 4 October 1889.

267. *In 1886 he had gone with Harriet*: January 1886 Samuel Plimsoll and Harriet sailed from Liverpool to New York on the White Star *Celtic*, as reported *New York Times*, 18 January 1886, arriving 31 January, *New York Times*, 1 February 1886. In May they stayed at the Gilsey House, *New York Times*, 11 May 1886.

269. *'God grant me a safe passage home to my pets'*: Plimsoll, *Cattle Ships*, p. 102.

269. *'with the broad-clothed and button-holed moral carrion'*: ibid., p. 107.

270. *'Deeply depressed by a sense of unaccomplished purpose'*: ibid., p. 92.

270. *'serene impartiality of judgement'*: *The Times*, 28 January 1892.

270. *It ended with an angry voice from the floor*: *Manitoba Daily Free Press*, 13 January 1891.

270. *he addressed the Auditorium in Chicago*: *Decatur Morning Review*, 16 January 1891.

271. *The reception breakfast . . . also marked Plimsoll's resignation*: *The Times*, 30 May 1891, p. 14.

271. *The notorious burglar and murderer*: Kynaston N. Gaskell, *The Romantic Career of a Great Criminal: A Memoir of Charles Peace*.

271. *had spent some two thousand pounds doing so*: Edward W. Matthews, secretary of the British and Foreign Sailors' Society, letter to *Chart & Compass Sailors' Magazine*, August 1898, p. 250.

271. *Horrified, he ran from the House*: Wilson, *My Stormy Voyage Through Life*, p. 252.

272. *at the YMCI in Regent Street*: *The Times*, 8 May 1891, p. 11.

272. *Many of the arguments . . . of the 1870s were revisited*: *The Times*, 28, 30 January, 1, 11 February 1892.

272. *In 1894 he sat on a Royal Commission*: Institute of Historical Research, *Office-holders in Modern Britain*, vol. 10, no. 77.

273. *in the papers of small-town America*: *Salem Daily News*, 30 March 1896, reported: 'Samuel Plimsoll is seriously ill.'

274. *'the Populist Party'*: John E. Moser, 'The Decline of American Anglophobia Or, How Americans Stopped Worrying and Learned to Love the English', talk at Université de Rouen, France, November 2002; online at <personal.ashland.edu/~jmoser1/anglophobia.html>.

274. *'If all Englishmen'*: *Fort Wayne Sentinel*, 15 July 1896; *Steubenville Daily Herald*, 7 November 1896.

275. *'a landing of the American Armada of trusts'*: Chester MacArthur Destler, *Henry Demarest Lloyd and the Empire of Reform*, p. 342.

275. *news . . . that he was dying*: *Portsmouth Herald*, 2 June 1898.

275. *He took a little nourishment*: 'Court Circular', *The Times*, 2 and 3 June 1898.

275. *One of his last wishes*: report in *Chart & Compass Sailors' Magazine*, August 1898, p. 252.

275. *She registered the death that day*: Samuel Plimsoll's death certificate, 3 June 1898.

276. *On the day of his funeral*: *The Times*, 8 June 1898.

276. *'a glorious scene'*: report in *Chart & Compass Sailors' Magazine*, August 1898, p. 251.

276. *Plimsoll's obituary . . . was lukewarm*: *The Times*, 4 June 1898.

276. *Harriet, writing a thank-you letter for a vote of sympathy*: Harriet Plimsoll, letter to Mr E. Cathery of the National Union of Seamen, 16 July 1898, written from Germany, quoted in Peters, p. 170.

277. *'If the Plimsoll mark were ever taken from you'*: Harriet Plimsoll, letter to the secretary of the Green's Home branch of the National Union of Seamen, quoted in Peters, p. 171. Green's Home in London's East End was founded in 1840 as a lodging for seamen.

10: THE LEGACY

279. *'undoubtedly entitled to the gratitude of sailors the world over'*: *Stevens Point Daily Journal*, 23 November 1896.

279. *the Board of Trade abolished the Winter North Atlantic mark*: Charles Plomer Hopkins, *Altering Plimsoll's Mark*, p. 13.

281. *'As the matter was one purely for technical experts'*: Randolph Churchill, quoted in Hopkins, p. 33.

281. *'Mr George called into consultation'*: E. T. Raymond, *Mr Lloyd George*, p. 97.

282. *'The great work for humanity . . . has been undone'*: Hopkins, pp. 13–14.

282. *Henry Mayers Hyndman, the cricket-playing stockbroker*: E. J. Hobsbawm, *Labouring Men: Studies in the History of Labour*, ch. 12, 'Hyndman and the SDF'.

282. *'The life of the ordinary seaman or fireman is very hard'*: Henry Mayers Hyndman, *The Murdering of British Seamen by Lloyd George, the Liberal Cabinet and the Board of Trade*, p. 7.

283. *All these factors affected a ship's 'reserve buoyancy'*: from deepcreekyacht-club.com/Plimsoll mark and tpub.com/content/combat Buoyancy v Gravity.

283–4. *'I feel sure that Samuel Plimsoll'*: Manly O. Hudson, *Progress in International Organization*, p. 79.

284. *In 1935 the Americans went further*: Carl E. McDowell and Helen M. Gibbs, *Ocean Transportation*, p. 437.

284. *Since the first convention in 1930*: 'Ship Safety', *Nonstop* magazine, January 2005, p. 27.

284. *'using the* nom de plume *Gabriel Wade'*: Gabriel Wade (Samuel Richard Cobden Plimsoll), *Three Ways*.

284. *a translator (from French)*: Pierre Loti, *Madame Prune*, translated by S. R. C. Plimsoll.

285. *'though once engaged to an American Rhodes scholar at Balliol'*: Ruth was engaged to Arthur Garfield Cameron, G. H. Peters, *The Plimsoll Line*, pp. 173–4.

285. *a solid red circle, with a horizontal band*: the art historian E. H. Gombrich, in his *Art and Illusion*, pp. 197–9, surmised that the emblem was a simplified depiction of the idea that the Underground crossed London, but other commentators agreed that the symbol was not a literal representation of its function: David Lawrence, *A Logo for London: The London Transport Symbol*, p. 35.

285. *a direct imitation of the Plimsoll mark*: Frank Pick 'cited the Plimsoll line as an inspiration for the Underground Group bullseye': from a conversation between David Lawrence and Pat Schleger (Hans Schleger's wife) in 1995 referred to in ibid., p. 35, quoting London Transport Public Relations Office press release TAN 633, 17 February 1950.

285. *'The tricks of the trade of shipowning'*: Alexander Hay Japp, *Good Men and True*, pp. 404–20.

286. *had the distinction of being the dirty man of the forecastle*: Joseph Conrad, *The Nigger of the Narcissus*, Dent 1945 edn., p. 27.

286. *'I mind I once seed in Cardiff'*: ibid., p. 80.

287. *On 10 June Conrad had a letter published in the* Daily Express: a revised version also appeared in an *Illustrated London News* special supplement, 'Protection of Ocean Liners', 1914.

287. *'I remember Mr Plimsoll's load line campaign'*: letter to the editor of the *Globe*, June 1914: Joseph Conrad, *Letters*, ed. Frederick R. Karl and Laurence Davies, vol. 5, *1912–1916*, pp. 387–9.

288. *In his essay*: Joseph Conrad, 'The Titanic Inquiry', in *Notes on Life and Letters*, p. 326. One Conrad scholar has suggested, sadly without illustration, that Conrad borrowed his imagery from Plimsoll. 'The historical source for [the depiction of the ship as a space of death] is almost certainly the reformist speeches of the MP for Derby, Samuel Plimsoll . . . Though Conrad alludes to Plimsoll himself as an officious meddler, he still uses Plimsoll's imagery': Beth Sharon Ash, *Writing in*

Between, ch. 1, note 30. It is satisfying to think that Plimsoll's undoubtedly spine-tingling rhetoric had an influence on the prose of one of the most important novelists of the twentieth century. Another Conradian sees the 'fatherly' figure of Plimsoll as not specifically an attack on Plimsoll but as an encapsulation of Conrad's general view that 'paternity, for one reason or another, is not to be trusted': Catharine Rising: *Darkness at Heart*, p. 72.

288. *grave of a 'forgotten man'*: Edward Tupper, *Seamen's Torch: The Life Story of Captain Edward Tupper*, pp. 287–8.

289. *Samuel Plimsoll Jr . . . was looked down upon*: according to his daughter Sally Shaw, in conversation.

290. *a bust of Plimsoll*: a clay original appears in the *Northern Telegraph*, 15 January 1929; the artist with a preliminary model in *Sunday Graphic*, 19 February 1929.

290. *fought to stop ventilation holes*: Nellie Plimsoll letter to Dick Plimsoll, 1928, from Sally Shaw's private collection.

290–1. *He spoke of his father's tireless energy and his sacrifices*: 'Sacrificing His All', undated cutting, Plimsoll Papers, Working Class Movement Library, Salford.

291. *'It was only at long intervals that men of Plimsoll's massive gifts'*: Walter Runciman, *The Times*, 22 August 1929.

291. *'Thus there stands upon Thames bank'*: Tupper, p. 288.

292. *'the bronze tablet was unveiled in a dense fog'*: Peters, p. 183.

292. *'Most of us have been brought up to believe'*: R. H. Thornton, *British Shipping*, pp. 83–4.

293. *His son . . . said he 'ran "special" trains'*: from undated and unattributed newspaper cutting c. 1929, uncatalogued Plimsoll Papers, Working Class Movement Library, Salford.

293. *'Mr Plimsoll's worst fault as a strategist'*: *Punch*, 7 August 1875.

294. *'I had to fight Plimsoll on several clauses'*: Charles Adderley, quoted in Geoffrey Alderman, 'Samuel Plimsoll and the Shipping Interest', *Maritime History*, vol. 1, no. 1, April 1971.

294. *his authoritative paper*: ibid.

295. *'the formation of the Chamber of Shipping in 1878'*: ibid., pp. 90–1.

295. *'How little I have done for these dear fellows'*: reported by Edward W. Matthews, secretary of the British Foreign and Sailors' Society, *The Times*, 6 June 1898, and *Chart & Compass Sailors' Magazine*, August 1898, p. 250.

295–6. *the detention of twenty-six ships for breaches of safety regulations*: report of Maritime and Coastguard Agency, 14 May 2004, quoted in Merseyshipping.co.uk/news.

296. *Safety regulations . . . vary*: William Langewiesche, *The Outlaw Sea*, p. 4.

296. *'Plimsoll. Now there is a word one does not hear any more'*: John Banville, *The Sea*, p. 11.

296. *'We like to think that [social progress] is made'*: Tony Benn speaking in the House of Commons, 3 March 1995, Hansard, col. 1317. He credited the argument to E. S. Turner, in his book *Roads to Ruin*.

296. *'Many vessels have been lost'*: David MacIver, letter to *The Times*, 2 December 1873.

POSTSCRIPT

299. *Its origin, date and creator are unknown*: the National Recording Project of the Public Monuments and Statues Association based at the Courtauld Institute records what is known of the history of the Bristol statue.

299. *'the Plimsoll monument sculpted for the Thames Embankment was to be copied in Bristol'*: the fact that the Thames Embankment memorial by Blundstone was to be copied in Bristol was reported as far afield as Jamaica, in the *Kingston Daily Gleaner*, 26 August 1929.

300. *'Both the* Graphic *and the* Art Journal *reported the commissioning in August 1875'*: the *Graphic*, 28 August 1875, p. 195; and 'A Statue of Mr S. Plimsoll, MP, is in the hands of Mr Belt for execution. The movement in favour of this work originated with working men of London, who propose to make it the testimonial of the estimation in which they hold this gentleman for his exertions in the cause of the British Sailor': the *Art Journal*, 1876, vol. 38, p. 350.

300. *'Working men connected with shipping and shipbuilding . . . intending their tribute to be raised near the London Docks'*: the *Graphic*, 28 August 1875, p. 195, also *New York Times*, 27 September 1875, Foreign Notes, p. 7.

301. *'Mr Brock, equally with Mr Lawes'*: quoted in *The Times*, 23 June 1882, p. 10. Brock's history: Colonel Maurice Harold Grant, *Dictionary of British Sculptors*, p. 42.

302. *Belt's bust of Disraeli, commissioned by Queen Victoria*: on 1 November 1883.

302. *doubted that a young artist could deteriorate so quickly*: Joseph Dean, *Hatred, Ridicule or Contempt: A Book of Libel Cases*, 'The Last Trial in Westminster Hall', p. 249.

302 . *'Fashion was for the plaintiff, art for the defendant'*: ibid.

303. *'would have allowed the case to continue so long'*: *Penny Illustrated Paper*, 11 November 1882, p. 11.

303. *'when the work was uncovered'*: *The Times*, 23 June 1882, p. 4.

303. *the title taken by the now deceased Disraeli*: other sources for details of Belt v. Lawes trial are *The Times*, 23 June 1882, p. 10, 11 November 1882, p. 4 and 26 May 1883, p. 11.

303. *'Belt was a blacksmith's son'*: according to Grant, *Dictionary of British Sculptors*, p. 42, Belt was a blacksmith's son; though when he married in 1884 his father George Belt was described on the marriage certificate as a gentleman.

303. *a mad lascar*: *The Times*, 9 February 1965.

304. *as well as the statuette of Plimsoll and the bust of Nellie*: *The Times*, 11 November 1882, p. 4.

APPENDIX

314. *'A Coffin-Ship Owner's Lament'*: quoted in G. H. Peters, *The Plimsoll Line*, p. 67, as a popular music-hall song.

BIBLIOGRAPHY

I am much indebted to the Reverend George Hertel Peters for the invaluable starting point of his biography of Samuel Plimsoll, *The Plimsoll Line* (Barry Rose, 1975), a ten-year labour of love. Peters was the grandson of the master of a 'coffin-ship' who was lost at sea.

Samuel Plimsoll's own words survive not only in the books, pamphlets, papers, letters and articles listed below, but also in the newspapers that quoted or reproduced his speeches and printed his correspondence, and in Hansard (on the open shelves of the British Library's Social Sciences Reading Room).

The following websites were especially useful:
The Times Digital Archive (at the British Library); the British Library's generally accessible Collect Britain website, offering access to the *Penny Illustrated Paper and Illustrated Times*; and newspaperarchive.com. (Other websites are cited in the footnotes.)

The following newspapers were consulted:
The Times, Penny Illustrated Paper and Illustrated Times, Punch or the London Charivari, Illustrated London News, Pall Mall Gazette, Vanity Fair, Fun, London Sketch Book, Graphic, New Witness, Nineteenth Century Review, Nonconformist, Nautical Magazine, Shipping Gazette, Fairplay, Lloyd's List, Germanischer Lloyd Nonstop, New Statesman, London Review of Books, Morning Chronicle, Derby Ram, Scarborough Express, Shields Gazette, Sheffield Daily Telegraph, Leeds Mercury, Liverpool Daily Post, Derby and Chesterfield Reporter, Hull Free Press, Staffordshire Sentinel, Norfolk News, Western Daily News, Western Daily Mercury, Sussex Express, Daily News, Monthly Chronicle, Sunday Graphic, Sunday Companion, Northern Telegraph, Yorkshire Post and Leeds Intelligencer, Jewish Chronicle, Art Journal, Shoe and Leather Record, Daily Gleaner (Kingston, Jamaica), *New York Times, New York Herald, Harper's Weekly, Cincinnati Commercial, Salem Daily News* (Ohio), *Fort Wayne*

Sentinel (Indiana), *Steubenville Daily Herald* (Ohio), *Atlanta Constitution* (Georgia), *Manitoba Daily Free Press* (Canada)
Also:
Sedalia Daily Democrat, Missouri, 9 April 1875
Decatur Morning, Illinois, 16 January 1891
Fitchburg Sentinel, Massachusetts, 27 January 1892
North Adams Evening Transcript, Massachusetts, 1 June 1899
Middletown Daily Argos, New York, 27 June 1896
Lincoln Evening News, Nebraska, 11 July 1896
Stevens Point Daily Journal, Wisconsin, 23 November 1896
Placerville Mountain Democrat, California, 23 November 1896
Portsmouth Herald, New Hampshire, 2 June 1898
Coshocton Tribune, Ohio, 13 August 1930

A., J., *The General Election: Campaigning Papers, being the first part of A Political Handbook for the People* (London, 1880)

Aiken, Joan, *The Wolves of Willoughby Chase* ([1962] Red Fox, London, 1992)

Albert, Fred, 'A Cheer for Samuel Plimsoll' (song) (H. D'Alcorn & Co., London, 1976)

Alderman, Geoffrey, 'Samuel Plimsoll and the Shipping Interest', *Maritime History,* vol. 1, no. 1, April 1971 (David & Charles, London, 1971)

Armytage, W. H. G., *A. J. Mundella, 1825–1897: The Liberal Background to the Labour Movement* (Ernest Benn, London, 1951)

Ashton, Agnes, *The Mark of Safety* (The Ebworth Press, London, 1961)

Bagwell, Philip, *The Transport Revolution* (Routledge, London, 1988)

Baird, William, 'Sermon given at St Gabriel's Mission Church, Bromley, Middx January 25 1866' (Jesse Salisbury, London, 1866) [BL 4477.aa.6]

The Baker and Plimsoll Number of the Penny Satirist, special edn. (London, 1875)

Banville, John, *The Sea* (Picador, London, 2005)

Barrett, T., of Skipton, 'The Wreck of the London, January 4 1866' (in verse), (Edmonson & Co., Skipton, 1866)

Bates, P. E., *Bates of Bellefield, Gyrn Castle and Manydown* (P. E. Bates, Liverpool, 1994)

Battiscombe, Georgina, *Shaftesbury: A Biography of the Seventh Earl 1801–1885* (Constable, London, 1974)

Bayle Museum Trust, *Bridlington Memories* (Bridlington, 1995)

Baylen, Joseph O., and Grossman, Norbert J., 'Samuel Plimsoll', *Biographical Dictionary of Modern British Radicals,* vol. 3, *1870-1914,* Part 2 (Harvester Press, Brighton, 1988)

Benford, Harry, 'Samuel Plimsoll: His Book and His Mark', *Seaway Review*, vol. 15, no. 1, January–March 1986

Bennett, Daphne, *Queen Victoria's Children* (Gollancz, London, 1980)

Bennett, W. C., 'The Wreck of the London', *Songs for Sailors* (London, 1872)

Bentinck, George Augustus Frederick Cavendish, Rt Hon., *Fact Against Sensation, Mr Cavendish Bentinck's speeches on Merchant Shipping Legislation, 1875, Reprinted, with notes, from the Nautical Magazine* (Simpkin Marshall & Co., London, 1875)

Besant, Annie Wood, *An Autobiography* (London, 1891)

Billington, Adeline, interviewed in *Life Stories from 'Lloyd's News'* (London, 1912)

Bissett, Sir James, *Sail Ho!: My Early Years at Sea* (Angus & Robertson, London, 1959)

Board of Trade, Annual Report for 1871, facsimile in Samuel Plimsoll, *Our Seamen*

Braithwaite, Joseph Benjamin, *The Priory Church, Bridlington: A Short History* (Bridlington, 1923)

Brassey, Thomas, MP, MacIver, David, etc., 'Our Merchant Ships', pamphlet containing: *I Letter from David MacIver to The Times 2 December 1873/II Lecture by Mr Brassey MP Given at Hastings 17 November 1873/III Extracts from Preliminary Report of the Royal Commission on Unseaworthy Ships/IV Extract from Returns Made to the Board of Trade of Wrecks, Casualties and Collisions Which Occurred on and Near the Coast of the United Kingdom during 1872* [BL 8829.d.2/13] (obtainable from Mrs Henry Kingsley at Samuel Plimsoll's office, 4 Victoria Street, Westminster, 1874)

Brewer's Dictionary of Phrase and Fable, centenary edn. (Book Club Associates with Cassell, London, 1977)

Bridgeman, J. V., 'The British Tar Song' – 'The Music Composed expressly for Mr Santley by J. L. Hatton' (Boosey & Co., London, 1873)

Briggs, Asa, *Victorian Things* (Batsford, London, 1988)

Brown, Laurence A., *A Catalogue of British Historical Medals 1837–1901* (Batsford, 1987)

Burnand, F. C., *Fowl Play, or a Story of Chikkin Hazard* (Phillips, 1868) [BL RB.23.a.17679]

Burns, Wayne, *Charles Reade: A Study in Victorian Authorship* (New York, 1961)

Cape, Thomas, *Brief Sketches Descriptive of Bridlington-Quay* (Bridlington-Quay, 1868)

Chambers Biographical Dictionary (Chambers, London, 2002)

Cole, G. D. H., *British Working Class Politics 1832–1914* (Routledge, London, 1941)

Collings, Jesse, *Life of Rt Hon. Jesse Collings*, Part 1 (Longmans Green & Co., London, 1920)

Conrad, Joseph, *Letters*, ed. Frederick R. Karl and Laurence Davies, vol. 5, *1912–1916* (Cambridge University Press, Cambridge, 1996)

— 'The Titanic Inquiry', in *Notes on Life and Letters* (Dent, London, 1921)

— *The Nigger of the Narcissus* ([1922] Dent, London, 1945)

Conway, Moncure D., 'London Letter', *Cincinnati Commercial*, 6 August 1875

Cooper, J. G., and Power, A. D., *A History of West Derby* (Bellefield Press, Liverpool, 1988)

Cowper-Temple, Georgina, *Diary* (Southampton University, BR 58/6)

Cunningham, Peter, *A Hand-Book for London, Past and Present* (London, John Murray, 2nd edn., 1850), cited in Jackson, Lee, *The Victorian Dictionary* (www.victorianlondon.org)

Dana, Richard Henry III, 'Seventy-Six Years After', preface to Dana, Richard Henry Jr, *Two Years Before the Mast* (Houghton Mifflin, New York, 1911)

Dawson, William, *A Mid-London Parish: Short History of the Parish of St John's Clerkenwell* (London, 1885)

Dean, Joseph, *Hatred, Ridicule or Contempt: A Book of Libel Cases* (Constable, London, 1953)

Destler, Chester MacArthur, *Henry Demarest Lloyd and the Empire of Reform* (University of Philadelphia Press, Philadelphia, 1963)

Dickinson, John, *The Storm at Bridlington Bay or God's Voice in the Tempest* (Bridlington, 1871)

Elwin, Malcolm, *Charles Reade: A Biography* (London, 1931)

Ensor, R. C. K., *History of England 1870–1914* (Oxford University Press, Oxford, 1936)

Ewald, Alex Charles, *The Earl of Beaconsfield and His Times* (Chatto & Windus, London, 1881)

Farnie, D. A., 'John Rylands of Manchester', reprinted from the *Bulletin of the John Rylands University Library of Manchester*, vol. 56, no. 1, Autumn 1973

Fenwich, Valerie, and Gale, Alison, *Historic Shipwrecks* (Tempus, London, 1998)

Feuchtwanger, Edgar J., *Disraeli* (Arnold, London; Oxford University Press, New York, 2000)

Finn, Margot, *After Chartism: Class and Nation in English Radical Politics 1848–1874* (Cambridge University Press, Cambridge, 2004)

Forrer, L., *Biographical Dictionary of Medallists*, vol. 1, *A–D* ([1904] A. H. Baldwin, London, 1979)

Fournier, Narcisse and Meyer, Horace, *Le Portefeuille Rouge: drame en cinq actes,* in *Théatre contemporain illustré,* Liv. 581, 582. (1852)

Frump, Robert, *Until the Sea Shall Free Them: Life, Death and Survival in the Mercantile Marine* (Arrow, London, 2003)

Furness, William, *A History of Penrith* (Penrith, 1894)

Gaskell, N. Kynaston, *The Romantic Career of a Great Criminal: A Memoir of Charles Peace* (London, 1906)

General Shipowners' Society, *Merchant shipping legislation. Report of meeting of shipowners of the United Kingdom, held at the London Tavern, on . . . 2nd February, 1876 . . . With account of the proceedings at the interview of the deputation to the Right Hon. B. Disraeli, . . . 5th February, 1876* (London, 1876)

Gladstone, W(illiam) E(wart), *The Gladstone Diaries,* ed. H. C. G. Matthew (Oxford University Press, Oxford, 1986)

Globe Theatre programme for Paul Meritt's *Rough and Ready,* including notice of the recitation of Arthur Matthison's 'Coffin Ships', July 1878 (author's collection)

Glover, John, *The Plimsoll Sensation: A Reply (to the pamphlet entitled 'Our Seamen')* (London, 1873)

Grant, Kay, *Samuel Cunard: Pioneer of the Atlantic Steamship* (Abelard-Schuman, 1967)

Grant, Colonel Maurice Harold, *Dictionary of British Sculptors* (Rockliff, London, 1953)

Gray, Lorraine, 'The Fight for Shipping Reform in the 1870s', *Sea Chest,* Journal of the Tyneside Branch of the World Ship Society, no. 43, March 1971

Gray, Thomas, 'On the Condition of Merchant Seamen' (read at the Society of Arts, London, 1867)

Green, F. W., 'Our Sailors on the Sea', music by Alfred Lee (C. Sheard, London, 1874)

Greenwood, James, *In Strange Company, being the experiences of a Roving Correspondent* (London and Edinburgh, 1873)

Grey, Michael, 'The Sailor's Friend', *Maritime Heritage,* vol. 23, September–October 1998 (Binnacle Publications)

Guest, John, 'A British Cheer for Plimsoll' (song) (London, 1875)

Hall, Nick, 'The Sailor's Friend', *Fairplay,* 21 February 2002

Hamilton, George Francis, Rt Hon. Lord, *Parliamentary Reminiscences 1868–1885* (John Murray, London, 1917)

Hanson, Neil, *The Custom of the Sea* (Corgi, London, 2000)

Harrison, Elaine, *Officials of Royal Commissions of Inquiry 1870–1939, Office-holders in Modern Britain,* vol. 10 (Institute of Historical Research, London, 1995)

Haws, Duncan and Savill, David, *Merchant Fleets: The Aberdeen and Aberdeen & Commonwealth Lines of George Thompson* (TCL Publications, Hereford, 1989)

Hayward, William, *James Hall of Tynemouth: A Beneficent Life of a Busy Man of Business*, vol. 1 (Hazel, Watson and Viney, London, 1896)

Heraud, John Abraham, 'The Wreck of the London: A Lyrical Ballad' (C. W. Stevens, London, 1866) [BL 11650 e.5 (8)]

'Here's Success to Mr Plimsoll', song on *Ballads of Britain and Ireland, Storm and Shipwreck* (Folktrax 512), performed by Bill Cameron, Scilly Isles, 1956

Highton, Edward Gilbert, *A Voice from the London and its echoes, to which is prefixed an Address to those who have suffered by the calamity, etc* (London, 1866)

Higman, William Henry, 'Thoughts on Shipwrecks, Description of a Newly Invented Life-buoy etc' (Bath, 1838), pamphlet from *Tracts on Nautical Matters* [BL8805 bbb31 1–20]

Hinton, Richard Josiah, 'Political Agitators', in Higginson, T. W. (ed.), *Brief Biographies: English Radical Leaders*, vol. 2 (New York, 1875)

Hobsbawm, E. J., *Labouring Men: Studies in the History of Labour* (Weidenfeld & Nicolson, London, 1964)

Hodder, Edwin, *The Life and Work of the Seventh Earl of Shaftesbury K.G.*, vol. III (Cassell, London, 1886)

— *The Seventh Earl of Shaftesbury K.G. as Social Reformer* (James Nisbet & Co., 1897)

Hope, Ronald, *Poor Jack* (Chatham Publishing, 2001)

Hopkins, Charles Plomer, *Altering Plimsoll's Mark* (Simpkin, Marshall & Co., London, 1913)

Hoppen, K. Theodore, *The Mid-Victorian Generation 1846–1886* (Clarendon Press, Oxford, 1998)

Howell, George, *Labour Legislation, Labour Movements and Labour Leaders* ([1901] T. Fisher Unwin, London, 1905)

— Handwritten account of 'The Plimsoll Movement', Howell Papers, Bishopsgate Institute Library

Hudson, Manly O., *Progress in International Organization* (Stanford University Press, Stanford, 1932)

Humphrey, A. W., *Robert Applegarth: Trade Unionist, Educationist, Reformer* ([1913] Garland, New York and London, 1984)

Hyndman, Henry Mayers, *The Murdering of British Seamen by Lloyd George, the Liberal Cabinet and the Board of Trade. Verbatim report of a speech on this subject delivered . . . April 14, 1913, etc.* (British Socialist Party, London, 1913)

'The Influence of Samuel Plimsoll on the Coal Trade of London', *Manufacturer and Builder*, vol. 20, issue 12, December 1888

Irving, H. B., *A Book of Remarkable Criminals* (Cassell, London, 1918)

Jack, Ian, review of Peter Padfield, *Rule Britannia: The Victorian and Edwardian Navy* (Pimlico, 2003), in *London Review of Books*, vol. 25, no. 1, 2 January 2003

Japp, Alexander Hay, *Good Men and True: Biographies of Workers in the Fields of Beneficence and Benevolence* (T. Fisher Unwin, London, 1890)

Jenkins, Roy, *Gladstone* (Macmillan, London, 1995)

Jerrold, Blanchard and Doré, Gustave, *London: A Pilgrimage* (Grant & Co., London, 1872)

Kirton, John William, *True Nobility: or the Golden Deeds of an earnest life. A record of . . . Anthony Ashley Cooper, seventh Earl of Shaftesbury* (London, 1886)

Kropotkin, William P., *Mutual Aid: A Factor of Evolution* (Heinemann, London, 1902)

L., F., *Our Merchant Seamen: Their Importance and Their Claims* (pamphlet) (London, 1868)

Lang, Andrew, *Life, Letters and Diaries of Sir Stafford Northcote, first Earl of Iddesleigh* (Wm Blackwood & Sons, London, 1890)

Langewiesche, William, *The Outlaw Sea: Chaos and Crime on the World's Oceans* (Granta, London, 2005; paperback edn., 2006)

Larn, Richard, *Shipwrecks of Great Britain and Ireland* (David & Charles, London, 1981)

Lawrence, David, *A Logo for London: The London Transport Symbol* (Capital Transport, Harrow Weald, 2000)

Leslie, Henry, *The Mariner's Compass*, playbill, the Royal Amphitheatre, Leeds, 1867

Leventhal, F. M., *Respectable Radical: George Howell and Victorian Working Class Politics* (Weidenfeld & Nicolson, London, 1971)

Leyland, F. R., letter to J. M. Whistler, 19 August 1875, Glasgow University Library, Centre for Whistler Studies, MS Whistler L102

Lindsay, W. S., *History of Merchant Shipping from 1816–1874* (Sampson, Low Marston & Co., London, 1874)

Lloyd's Register: A History 1760–1999 (unpublished, provided by Lloyd's Register Information Services)

Loti, Pierre (Louis Marie Julien Viaud), *Madame Prune*, trans. S. R. C. Plimsoll (London, 1919)

Lucy, Henry W., *A Diary of Two Parliaments*, vol. 1, *1874–1880* (Cassell, London, 1885)

MacCarthy, Desmond, MS notes for *Makers of History*, Lilly Library, University of Indiana

McCarthy, Justin, *A History of Our Own Times*, vols. IV and V (Chatto & Windus, London, 1880, and 1932 edn.)

McDowell, Carl E., and Gibbs, Helen M., *Ocean Transportation* (McGraw Hill, New York, 1954)

MacLeod, Dianne Sachko, *Art and the Victorian Middle Class* (Cambridge University Press, Cambridge, 1996)

Manville Fenn, George, *Ship Ahoy!: A Yarn in Thirty-Six Cable Lengths* (Harper & Bros, New York, 1874)

Marsh, Arthur and Ryan, Victoria, *The Seamen: A History of the National Union of Seamen* (Malthouse Publishing, 1989)

Masters, David, *The Plimsoll Mark* (Cassell, London, 1955)

Matthews, Edward W. (secretary of the British and Foreign Sailors' Society), 'Mr Plimsoll and Our Sailors', *The Chart & Compass Sailors' Magazine*, August 1898

Matthison, Arthur, 'Coffin Ships or A Tale of the Day. As told by the Author at the great Plimsoll Meeting (the Earl of Shaftesbury in the Chair) at Exeter Hall', in *The Little Hero, and Other Stories, adapted for recitation* (Samuel French, London 1879) [BL 11653 DE18 Poems 1877–79]

Mazzini and Garibaldi Club, *Giuseppe Garibaldi in London, 1864–1964 Centenary* (British–Italian Society, 1964)

Meisel, Joseph S., 'The Importance of Being Serious: The Unexplored Connection between Gladstone and Humour', *History: The Journal of the Historical Association*, vol. 84, issue 274, 1999

Merchant Shipping Act 1876 39 & 40 Vict ch. 80

Merrill, Linda, *The Peacock Room* (Yale University Press, Yale, 1998)

Millar, A. H., entry on Samuel Plimsoll in *Oxford Dictionary of National Biography*, ed. H. C. G. Matthew and Brian Harrison (Oxford University Press, Oxford, 2004)

Montgomery, L. M. (Lucy Maud), *The Selected Journals of L. M. Montgomery*, ed. Mary Rubio and Elizabeth Waterston, vol. 1, *1889–1910* (Oxford University Press, Oxford, 1985)

Moser, John E., 'The Decline of American Anglophobia; Or, How Americans Stopped Worrying and Learned to Love the English', talk at conference 'The "Special Relationship" between the United Kingdom and the United States, 1945–1990', Université de Rouen, France, November 2002 (www.personal.ashland.edu/~jmoser1/anglophobia.html)

Moultrie, Reverend Gerard, 'The Wreck of the London' (G. J. Palmer, London, 1866)

Neave, David and Neave, Susan, *Bridlington: An Introduction to its History and Buildings* (Otley, 2000)

Nicholls, David, *The Lost Prime Minister: A Life of Sir Charles Dilke* (The Hambledon Press, London, 1995)

Nightingale, Florence, *Letter to Samuel Plimsoll 16 July 1873*, Derbyshire Record Office [D60181/1]

Osmánczyk, Edmund Jan, *Encyclopedia of the United Nations and International Agreements* (Taylor and Francis, London, 1985)

The Oxford Companion to Ships and the Sea, ed. Peter Kemp (Oxford University Press, Oxford, 1976)

Parliamentary Papers:

Board of Trade inquiry into the loss of the Sea Queen: 'Proceedings of the court of inquiry into the loss of the steamer Sea Queen with the minutes of evidence before the court' vol. LX, 1870

Report of the Royal Commission on Unseaworthy Ships with minutes and digest of evidence and appendix, 1874

Correspondence between Mr Plimsoll and others writing on his behalf, and the Board of Trade, on the draught of water records furnished to him by the Board of Trade, January 1875

Correspondence relating to ships detained as unseaworthy, vol. LXVI, BS Ref 166, 8 February–15 August 1876

Papers relating to recent cases of scurvy on board British Merchant Ships, BS Ref LXVI and LXVII, 1876

Report of the Select Committee on Merchant Seamen Bill, together with the Proceedings of the Committee, Minutes of Evidence and Appendix, House of Commons 31 May 1878, BS Ref 1 Reports, Committees vol. XVI, pp. 1–330, 1878

Patterson, George, 'Victorian Working Life in Sunderland', ed. G. R. Batho, in *River, Town and People* (Sunderland, 1998)

— 'J Havelock Wilson', *Durham Biographies*, vol. I, ed. G. R. Batho, (Durham, 2000)

Pearce, Malcolm and Stewart, Geoffrey, *British Political History, 1867–2001: Democracy and Decline* (Routledge, London, 1992)

Peck, Lille, a.k.a. Elliott, Ruth, *A Voice from the Sea or The Wreck of the Eglantine* (London, 1881)

— *Margery's Christmas Box* (London, 1875)

Peters, Rev. George H., *The Plimsoll Line: The Story of Samuel Plimsoll, Member of Parliament for Derby from 1868–1880* (Barry Rose, Chichester and London, 1975)

Plimsoll, Nellie and Samuel Jr, letters and notes from Sally Shaw's private collection

Plimsoll Papers: Howell Collection, Bishopsgate Institute Library; Working Class Movement Library, Salford (uncatalogued)

Plimsoll, Samuel, *Our Seamen: An Appeal* (Virtue & Co., London, 1873)

— *A Bill to provide for the Survey of Certain Shipping and to Prevent*

Overloading, 10 February 1873 (Virtue and Co., London, 1873) [Tracts 1779-1873 BL 8806 BB23]

— *A Speech delivered in the House of Commons, March 4, 1873 . . . in moving for a Royal Commission to inquire into the condition of the Mercantile Marine of the United Kingdom. Also a notice of a speech delivered at Leeds, March 16* (London, 1873)

— *Letter to Charles Reade (with Reade's annotation), 4 March 1874,* Charles Reade Letterbook, Robert H. Taylor Collection, Princeton University Library, vol. 1, fo. 35 RTC01, no. 89

— *Correspondence between Mr Plimsoll and the Board of Trade, Parliamentary Papers, 1874*

— *Letter to Anthony Mundella* (1875?), Mundella Papers, Sheffield University Library MS6-9 MS22

— Preface to *A Voice from the Sea 'by the author of Margery's Christmas Box'*, dated 10 February 1876, from 35 Victoria Street, Westminster (Hodder, London, 1876)

— *Our Seamen: Speeches and Facts* (G. Kelly & Co., London, 1876)

— *The Condition of Malta ('To the Editor of the Times')* (G. Kelly & Co., London, 1879)

— Appendix to Manville Fenn, George, *Ship Ahoy!: A Yarn in Thirty-Six Cable Lengths* (Harper & Bros, New York, 1874)

— *Letter to Charles Bradlaugh 25 June 1880,* Bradlaugh Papers 173, Bishopsgate Institute Library

— 'Explosions in Collieries and their Cure', *Nineteenth Century*, December 1880

— 'Twelve Millions Per Annum Wasted in the Sea', *Nineteenth Century*, March 1889

— 'A Rejoinder', *Nineteenth Century*, June 1889

— *Cattle Ships* (Kegan Paul & Co., London, 1890)

— Letter to daughter Nellie, 18 February 1892 (author's private collection)

Patents:

1852, Patented invention no. 513 for cleansing and fining malt liquors

1853, Patented invention no. 1009 for 'cleansing, extracting and separating or fining ale, beer etc from yeats, bottoms, barm, sediment etc'

21 Dec 1859 patented invention no. 2909 for unloading railway waggons

1 August 1868 patented invention no. 2430 coal chute

Public records:

Certificates of Marriage:

Samuel Plimsoll to Eliza Ann Railton 1 Oct 1857 Ecclesfield, Wortley, Yorks (Oct–Dec 1857 9c 213)

Thomas Joseph Hatch Plimsall to Elizabeth Margaret Palmer W. London (Apr–Jun 1865 1c 91)

Samuel Plimsoll to Harriet Frankish Wade 8 Oct 1885 Skirlaugh, E. Yorks (Oct–Dec 1885)

Birth:

Ellen Mary Ann Plimsoll 7 April 1866 St Pancras (Apr–June 1866 1b 159)

Samuel Richard Cobden Plimsoll 15 Dec 1887 St George Hanover Square (Jan–Mar 1888 1a 420a)

Eliza Harriet Plimsoll 1 Dec 1888 St George Hanover Square (Jan–Mar 1889 1a 412)

Ruth Wade Plimsoll 17 Feb 1891 St George Hanover Square (Jan-Mar 1891 1a 436)

Sidney Kingsley Cox Plimsoll 12 Dec 1894 St George Hanover Square (Oct–Dec 1894 1a 414)

Death:

Priscilla Plimsoll 6 Apr 1863 Pancras (Apr–June 1863 1b 53)

Victoria Nightingale Plimsoll 27 June 1863 Pancras (July–Sept 1863 1b 55)

Eliza Plimsoll 24 July 1865 Ecclesall Bierlow (Jun–Sept 1865)

Thomas Joseph Hatch Plimsoll 9 Apr 1866 Pancras (Apr–June 1866 1b 111)

Eliza Plimsoll 17 August 1882 Brisbane, Queensland State Archives

Sidney Kingsley Cox Plimsoll 30 April 1895 Dorking (Apr–June 1895 2a 90)

Samuel Plimsoll 3 June 1898 Elham, Folkestone, Kent (Apr–June 1898)

1871 Census RG 10 5119 fo. 72 p. 24

Pollock, John, *Shaftesbury: The Poor Man's Earl* (Hodder, London, 1985)

Raymond, E. T., *Mr Lloyd George* (W. Collins, 1922)

Reade, Charles, *Foul Play* (novel) (London, 1868)

— *The Scuttled Ship* (drama, a version of *Foul Play*) (Stepney, 1880)

— *Readiana* (Chatto & Windus, London, 1883)

— and Boucicault, Dion, *Foul Play* (drama) (New York, 1870)

Richardson, Joanna, *Gustave Doré: A Biography* (Cassell, London, 1980)

Rising, Catharine, *Darkness at Heart: Fathers and Sons in Conrad* (Greenwood Press, New York, 1990)

Ritchie, James Ewing, *Days and Nights in London, or Studies in Black and Gray* (Tinsley Brothers, London, 1880)

Rowson, Alan H., 'Edward Bates – Shipowner', in P. E. Bates, *Bates of Bellefield, Gyrn Castle and Manydown* (P. E. Bates, Liverpool, 1994)

Royal United Service Institution, *The Loss of Life at Sea, with report of a Special committee of members of the Council . . .* (Harrison & Sons, London, 1866)

Russell, George W. E., *Portraits of the Seventies* (T. Fisher Unwin, London, 1916)

Rutherford, Mark (Hale White, William), 'Our London Letter', *Norfolk News*, 4 May 1872

Rutton, W. L., 'Samuel Plimsoll, Cheriton Church and the Vicinity', *Home Counties Magazine*, vol. 13, 1911

Rylands, Peter, *Correspondence and Speeches of Mr Peter Rylands MP. With a sketch of his career by his son Louis Gordon Rylands* (A. Heywood & Son, Manchester, 1890)

Scrutton, Thomas, 'Are Twelve Millions Wasted?', *Nineteenth Century*, April 1889

Shaftesbury, Earl of (Cooper, Anthony Ashley), *Speech of the Earl of Shaftesbury at the Annual Meeting of the Church Pastoral Aid Society, at St James's Hall on Thursday May 8 1873* (W. H. Dalton, 1873)

Sharrah, William and Day, John William, *Tales of the Sea: being an account of the great storm in Bridlington Bay etc 10th February 1871* (Hull, 1876)

Simpson, A. W. B., *Cannibalism and the Common Law* ([1984] Penguin, London, 1986)

Sims, George R., *Among My Autographs* (Chatto & Windus, London, 1904)

Smith, Paul, *Disraeli: A Brief Life* ([1996] Cambridge University Press, Cambridge, 1999)

Smyth, Admiral W. H., *The Sailor's Word-Book, An Alphabetical Digest of Nautical Terms* (Blackie, London, 1867)

Society for Improving the Condition of the Merchant Seaman, *Report of the Committee . . . with suggestions for amending the Merchant Shipping Act* (London, 1867)

Stenton, Michael, *Who's Who of British Members of Parliament*, vol. 1 (Harvester Press, Hassocks, 1976)

— and Lees, Stephen, *Who's Who of British Members of Parliament*, vol. 2 (Harvester Press, Hassocks, 1978)

Stephens, F. G., 'Gosforth House, Tynemouth', 'The Private Collections of England', no. III, *Athenaeum*, no. 2395, 20 September 1873

Sweet, Matthew, *Inventing the Victorians* (Faber & Faber, London, 2001)

Terry, Ellen, *Memoirs* (Gollancz, London, 1933)

'A Thirty Years' Student', 'The Load Line for All Ships and Where Are its Difficulties' with 'quality of material, form of construction, abilities of commander, cause of loass, grain cargoes, collisions etc to which is added The Unseaworthy Ships Act 1875' (Simpkin Marshall & Co., London, 1875)

Thompson, Alfred and Lewis, Leopold, eds., *The Mask: A Humorous and Fantastic Review of the Month*, vol. 1, February 1868

Thompson, George Carslake, *Public Opinion and Lord Beaconsfield* (Macmillan, London, 1886)

Thompson, Sydney T., 'The Great Gale 1871 and the Funerals of the Drowned Men', transcript of lecture, 1996

Thorne, James, *Handbook to the Environs of London* (John Murray, London, 1876)

Thornton, R(onald) H(obhouse), *British Shipping* (Cambridge University Press, Cambridge, 1939)

Timbs, John, *Curiosities of London: Exhibiting the most rare and remarkable objects of interest in the metropolis, with nearly sixty years personal recollections* (London, 1867)

Tomlin, Edward, 'The Wreck of the London: In Memory of G. V. Brooke' (London, 1868)

Toynbee, Capt. Henry, 'The Social Condition of Seamen: A Paper read at the Royal United Service Institution' (London, 1866)

— 'On Mercantile Marine Legislation: A Paper Read before the Society of Arts' (London, 1867)

Tupper, Edward, *Seamen's Torch: The Life Story of Captain Edward Tupper, National Union of Seamen* (Hutchinson, London, 1938)

Turner, E. S., 'Plimsoll Rules the Waves', in *Roads to Ruin: The Shocking History of Social Reform* (Michael Joseph, London, 1950)

Turner, John M., *Twentieth Century Circus People: A Dictionary of British Circus Biography*, vol. 4, *1901–1950*

Victoria, Queen of England, *Letter from Queen Victoria to Disraeli 25 July 1875*, Bodleian Library, Hughenden Papers 79/1 fos. 1–52 B/XIX/B319/37

— *Letters of Queen Victoria, second series 1870–1878: A Selection from Her Majesty's Correspondence and Journal*, ed. George Earle Buckle (John Murray, London, 1926)

Villiers, Alan, ed., *Pioneers of the Seven Seas* (Routledge, Kegan, Paul, London, 1956)

'A Visitor', *The Great Exhibition: A Poetical Rhapsody* (Sheffield, 1851)

Wade, Gabriel (Plimsoll, Samuel Richard Cobden), *Three Ways* (Chapman & Hall, London, 1929)

Wallace, Frederick William, *Under Sail in the Last of the Clippers* (Brown, Son and Ferguson, Glasgow, 1936)

Webb, Sidney and Webb, Beatrice, eds., *The History of Trade Unionism* (Longmans Green and Co., London, 1920)

Whitaker, H. E., *Men of the Storm: The Story of Bridlington's Lifeboats* (Bridlington, 1947)

White's Directory of Sheffield (1852)

Wilcox, Timothy, 'The Aesthete Expunged, The Career and Collection of T. Eustace Smith MP', *Journal of the History of Collections*, vol. 5, no. 1 (Oxford University Press, Oxford, 1993)

Williams, Dorothy M., *Shaftesbury: The Story of His Life and Work as the Emancipator of Industrial England (1801–1885)* (London, 1925)

Wilson, A. N., *The Victorians* (Hutchinson, London, 2002)

Wilson, Joseph Havelock, *My Stormy Voyage Through Life* (National Sailors' and Firemen's Union, London, 1925)

Wilson, Mike, 'The Great Gale of 1871', *Bridlington's Historic Heritage No. 2* (Bridlington, 2002)

— *Full Fathom Five* (Biscuit Publishing, 2005)

Wilson, R., *The Life and Times of Queen Victoria*, vol. II (Cassell, London, 1900)

Wollaston, Rev. H. N., 'Death's Warning Voice: Loss of the SS London, a Sermon preached at Trinity Church, East Melbourne on Sunday evening 25 March 1866' (Melbourne, 1866)

Wotton, Hampden, 'On receiving from Edward Bates Esq MP in recognition of a copy of verses composed on his donations to the Plymouth charities, "The Handy-Volume Shakespeare", complete in thirteen volumes, beautifully bound in purple morocco' (Plymouth, 1875)

'The Wreck of the Northfleet', song on *Ballads of Britain and Ireland, Storm and Shipwreck* (Folktrax 512), performed by Harry Upton, Balcombe, Sussex, 1963

Wreck of the 'London' (with illustrations) (Sampson, Low, Son and Marston, London, 1866) [BL 10026 ccc 33]

Zetland, the Marquis of, ed., *The Letters of Disraeli to Lady Bradford and Lady Chesterfield*, vol. 1, *1873–5* (Ernest Benn Ltd, 1929)

ACKNOWLEDGEMENTS

Thanks are due to the following people, who are not to be blamed for the questions I didn't ask them:

Nouf Al-Rawaf, University of Warwick Library; Katherine Baird, London College of Fashion; Malcolm Barr-Hamilton, Borough Archivist, Tower Hamlets; Mary Baumann, US Senate Historical Office; Harry Benford, University of Michigan; staff of the Bishopsgate Institute Library; Nicky Barut and colleagues, Sheffield Town Hall; Linda Bland, Cumbria Local Studies librarian; Simon Blundell, Archivist, The Reform Club; Kevin Bolton, Manchester Archives and Local Studies, Central Library; Geoffrey Boland, Local Studies Library, Kingston upon Hull; David Bowcock, Assistant County Archivist, Carlisle; Jane Bradley, Bristol Reference Library; David Bristow, the Cliffe Bonfire Committee; staff of the British Library in the Humanities, Rare Books, Manuscripts, Social Sciences, and Patents reading rooms of St Pancras and in the Newspaper Library at Colindale; Alison Brown, Archives Officer, Bristol Record Office; Barbara Cavanagh, Motley Books; Alasdair Clarke, shipping agent; Nigel Counsell, Cardiff Coins and Medals; Anne Cowne, Information Officer, Lloyd's Register; John Culme, of footlightnotes.tripod.com; Aline De Bievre, shipping journalist; Clyde Dissington, The Magic Attic, Swadlincote, Derbyshire; Jan Dumbell, Newcastle Local Studies Centre; Joan Ferry, Woodson Research Center, Fondren Library, Rice University, Houston, Texas; Inter-library loans staff of Finsbury Park Library; Alison Forrester, House of Commons Information Office; James Gregory, University of Southampton; Michael Hansell of Leeds Indexers; Dr Marjory Harper, University of Aberdeen; Laura Hitchcock of EMPICS; Amanda Hodgson, Nottingham Local Studies Library; Jacky Hodgson, Head of Special Collections, University of Sheffield Library; Eric Hollerton, Local Studies Librarian, North Shields Central Library; the Honourable Company of Master Mariners; Oliver House and staff of the Bodleian Library, Oxford; Roger Ivens, Oldham Archives; Ian Jack;

386 THE PLIMSOLL SENSATION

Elizabeth Jones QC; Steve Kentfield, East London Postcard Company; Helen Kent and Michael Kitchen of the London Transport Museum; Andy King, Curator of Industrial & Maritime History, Bristol Industrial Museum; Andrew Kirk, London Theatre Museum; Susanna Lamb, Madame Tussaud's; staff of the Leeds Library; staff of Leeds City Library; the London Metropolitan Archive; Nigel Lutt, Archivist, Bedfordshire County Council; Jennifer Lynch, House of Lords Record Office (The Parliamentary Archives); Councillor Michael Meadowcroft, Leeds; Colin Michell, sailor; Helen Orme, Kent archives; George Patterson, University of Durham; Chris Pond, parliamentary historian; staff of the Public Records Centre, Islington; staff of the Public Record Office, Kew; Christina Raddon, building surveyor for the Bristol bust; Sir William Reardon Smith; Marianne Reynolds, Cincinnati Library; Mark Schumacher, University of North Carolina at Greensboro; Deborah Scriven, Local Studies Librarian, Wakefield; Nick Serpell, Richard Quirk and the Friends of Highgate Cemetery; Anne Sharp, Local Studies Librarian, South Tyneside Central Library; Caroline Shaw of the Rothschild Archive, great-granddaughter of Samuel Plimsoll; Catherine Shaw, great-granddaughter of Samuel Plimsoll; Sally Shaw, formerly of Manchester City Council, granddaughter of Samuel Plimsoll; Celia Sisam, formerly of St Hilda's College, Oxford; Matthew Skidmore, Hellen Pethers and staff of the Caird Library, The National Maritime Museum; Margaret Sherry Rich and Anna Lee Pauls, Princeton University Library; Charles H. Smith, Western Kentucky University, Bowling Green; Julie Spragg and staff of Islington Central Library; Steven Spencer, Brynmor Jones Library, University of Hull; Sarah Stocks, Bridlington Library; Sarah Taylor, Bristol Record Office; Richard Temple and James King, Modern Records Centre, University of Warwick Library; Annette Templar, Kidderminster Library; Sydney T. Thompson; Ann Toseland, Cambridge University Library; Martin C. Tupper, Islington Local History Centre, Finsbury Library; John M. Turner, circus historian; Capt. Hannu Vartiainen of the Rauma Maritime Museum, Finland; the Reverend John and Mrs Linda Wardle, Priory Church, Bridlington; Mike Weaver, Working Class Movement Library, Salford; Mike and Diane Wilson, Bridlington local historians; Colin Wight, British Library website; Mark Wollaeger, Vanderbilt University, Tennessee; Richard Woodhead, marine architect; and Mark Young, Derby Local Studies Library.

Thanks, too, for practical help, to: Alex Gallacher of 0800 Computer Services; to Nicola Baird, Katy Bevan, David A. Black, Cortina Butler, John Clark, Fiona Crawford, Melinda Derbyshire, Eugene Ludlow, Kate O'Rourke, Gareth Rees, Kiva Shea, Anne Simpson, and Gail and Alastair Smith.

To all at Little, Brown, now or until recently, particularly: Kirsteen Astor, Peter Cotton, Ian Crane, Richard Dawes, Stephen Guise, Ursula Mackenzie, Philip Parr, Alan Samson, Linda Silverman, Tim Whiting and David Young.

To John Saddler of the Saddler Literary Agency, the best of agents.

Especial thanks, with love, to John and Gabriela Jones, to Rachel and David Clark, to Nicholas Clee for so many things, including making this book possible, and to Rebecca and Laura Clee for their patience and tolerance, without which it would have been impossible.

And to Langdon Hammer of Yale University who started it all by remarking on the pub sign.

INDEX